Fixed Income Relative Value Analysis

Second Edition

Founded in 1807, John Wiley & Sons is the oldest independent publishing company in the United States. With offices in North America, Europe, Australia, and Asia, Wiley is globally committed to developing and marketing print and electronic products and services for our customers' professional and personal knowledge and understanding.

The Wiley Finance series contains books written specifically for finance and investment professionals as well as sophisticated individual investors and their financial advisors. Book topics range from portfolio management to e-commerce, risk management, financial engineering, valuation, and financial instrument analysis, as well as much more.

For a list of available titles, visit our Web site at www.WileyFinance.com.

Fixed Income Relative Value Analysis

A Practitioner's Guide to the Theory, Tools, and Trades

DOUG HUGGINS
CHRISTIAN SCHALLER

Second Edition

WILEY

Registered Office(s)

John Wiley & Sons, Inc., 111 River Street, Hoboken, NJ 07030, USA

John Wiley & Sons Ltd, The Atrium, Southern Gate, Chichester, West Sussex, PO19 8SQ, UK

Editorial Office

The Atrium, Southern Gate, Chichester, West Sussex, PO19 8SQ, UK

For details of our global editorial offices, customer services, and more information about Wiley products visit us at www.wiley.com.

Library of Congress Cataloging-in-Publication Data is Available:

ISBN 9781394189083 (Hardback)
ISBN 9781394189090 (ePDF)
ISBN 9781394189106 (ePub)

Cover Design: Wiley
Cover Image: Courtesy of Doug Huggins and Christian Schaller

Set in 10/12pt STIX Two Text by Straive, Chennai

SKY10071666_040424

Contents

Preface to the Second Edition

Some important changes have occurred in the fixed income markets since we published the first edition of *Fixed Income Relative Value Analysis* in 2013, many of these due to the eventual policy response to the great financial crisis of 2008–2009: new reference rates, increasing default risk of governments, more regulation and capital constraints.

NEW REFERENCE RATES

Probably the most important effect of the great financial crisis from the viewpoint of relative value analysts and hence of this book was the transition away from LIBOR to other reference rates. After central banks largely disintermediated the interbank lending markets[1] that had been the lifeblood of the money markets, it was only natural that banks would prefer to borrow from and lend to a central bank rather than another commercial bank. But as a result of this change, the liquidity in the interbank market declined considerably, casting suspicion on interbank lending reference rates, such as LIBOR. The final straw for the LIBOR market was the rate rigging scandal that encompassed a number of large banks, starting in 2008. In response to these issues, central banks in a number of jurisdictions pushed market participants away from LIBOR and toward reference rates of their own design, such as SOFR in the US. In fact, the move to SOFR was the impetus for our recent book, *SOFR Futures and Options* (Huggins and Schaller, 2022).

Since SOFR differs from LIBOR in a number of important ways, the SOFR swaps market differs from the LIBOR swaps market in a number of important respects. For example, LIBOR references unsecured transactions, whereas SOFR references secured transactions. This change alone has a material effect on valuations, particularly on the relative valuations between swaps and bonds.

---

[1]Central banks not only have disintermediated the money markets in some jurisdictions, they have also disintermediated some of the bond markets. For example, the buying of JGBs by the official sector in that market has reduced the liquidity of the world's largest bond market at times to a trickle.

On one hand, the multitude of reference rates (Chapter 11 provides an overview) for swaps has complicated the already complex relationships between asset, basis, and credit default swaps further. On the other hand, the transition from LIBOR to SOFR has eliminated the unsecured–secured basis in the asset swap spreads of government bonds, which has had several welcome effects:

- Asset swap spreads versus SOFR can be modified to become suitable rich/cheap indicators for all bonds worldwide (Chapter 17). We have therefore reviewed the strong statement of the first edition that asset swap spreads should never be used to assess the RV between bonds. While it is still true for swap spreads versus LIBOR and OIS, par asset swap spreads versus SOFR can be modified to become a reasonable alternative to fitted curves.
- Asset swap spreads versus SOFR can rather easily be linked with the credit risk of the sovereign issuer. Hence, the first hurdle facing an arbitrage equality between swap spreads and CDS, which occupied many pages of the first edition due to the correlation between credit risk and the unsecured–secured basis, now has a straightforward solution (Chapter 16).

A less welcome consequence of the transition to SOFR are the structural breaks in time series, for example, for cross-currency basis swaps between EURIBOR and USD LIBOR, which switched to USD SOFR. This is a general problem for analysts requiring long-term time series as input variables for their models. For the most basic of those time series, interest rates, we propose the solution of using constant maturity par yields from a fitted curve on government bonds (Chapter 8) rather than swap rates. And it is also a specific problem for this book, written shortly after the transition and hence with too little data for swaps with new reference rates to present meaningful case studies. We have therefore decided to keep many of the case studies of the first edition, which cover the subprime and euro crises and thus remain of interest, though this means that we need to carry some "historical ballast" and speak from time to time of (basis) swaps with USD LIBOR as the reference rate. Apart from these case studies, we have aimed for a complete update to the current reference rate situation.

INCREASING DEFAULT RISK OF GOVERNMENTS

The implementation of zero or even negative policy rates posed a challenge to analysts – as does its unwinding, which occurs at the same time as budget deficits and bond issuance soared, in part as a consequence of the fiscal response to the COVID-19 pandemic. An immediate implication for modeling government bonds is that the formerly common simplifying assumption that certain government bonds were default-free is less justifiable these days. As a result, incorporating credit considerations into the analysis of government bonds has become increasingly important. We have responded to this development by adding a term for credit difference to the term for funding difference in our swap spread model. While the sovereign CDS was already treated extensively in the first edition, it remained an external addition to the relationship between bonds and swaps, into which it has now been integrated (Chapter 12).

On the other hand, moves in rates and volatility even to unprecedented levels are the sorts of changes for which most good relative value models are well-suited or can be adapted. We provide a study of the impact of zero-interest rate policy on PCA eigenvectors in Chapter 3 and offer some remarks about Shadow Rate Models in Chapter 6. If those were the only changes occurring in the fixed income markets, the need for a second edition of *Fixed Income Relative Value Analysis* would be less clear.

But the move from LIBOR to overnight reference rates, non-negligible default risk of government bonds, and tighter regulation are the sorts of changes that require us to review and partly modify our approaches. The basic economics underlying our models are the same. They are still predicated on the principles that arbitrage opportunities are unsustainable and that instruments with similar risks should be expected to generate similar returns (Chapter 1). But the application of these principles via models needs to change as the structure of the market changes. And that's the primary motivation behind this second edition of the book.

REGULATION AND CAPITAL CONSTRAINTS

The Basel III process has culminated in quite a number of additional regulations designed to improve the safety and soundness of the world's banks, especially the largest institutions that tend to dominate the fixed income markets. One effect of these regulations is that bank balance sheets face many more constraints now than they did a decade ago. And the effect of these constraints is that the relevant cost for a bank contemplating a new position is no longer the marginal cost of funds in the market, such as interest rates paid on retail or commercial deposits. Rather, it's the *shadow cost* of the least onerous constraint currently binding the bank's balance sheet. For example, if a bank needs to shed an asset currently generating a return on capital of 7% in order to make room for another asset, then 7% is the relevant hurdle for the new asset, even if retail deposits cost the bank much less.

The presence of so many binding constraints on bank balance sheets has a number of important implications for the fixed income markets, two of which are discussed in Chapter 18. First, relative value analysts must incorporate these shadow costs into their analysis as and when these constraints are binding on the balance sheets of the firms for which they work. Second, analysts must incorporate the fact that traders at other firms will often face the same sorts of shadow costs and that these generally won't be observable in the market. In the old days, it wasn't difficult to produce a reasonable estimate of the marginal costs that other market participants faced when analyzing certain trades. These days, we typically have very little understanding of the shadow costs faced by traders at the largest banks.

As a result, it has become more difficult for relative value analysts to produce useful forecasts about the eventual richening or cheapening of various instruments. Given that the problem of unobservable input variables exists independently of the sophistication of the model, the analytic ideal to explain and predict all pricing relationships via no-arbitrage models needs to be reviewed. While these relationships continue to provide important insights, their influence on market prices on a given day depends on the unobservable shadow cost of arbitrage capital of the marginal market participant.

Chapter 18 highlights one of the more notable instances of this phenomenon: the repo spike of September 2019. As Jamie Dimon later stated publicly, JP Morgan wasn't in a position to satisfy the demand for cash against collateral that day, due to binding regulatory constraints on its balance sheet. He also noted that this was a change for the bank and that the bank had provided additional funds in similar situations prior to these additional regulations. We presume other banks faced similar constraints on their balance sheets at the same time. Repo rates are fundamental to a large number of relative value trades, and all of these are affected in some way when repo rates spike as high as they did that day. Relative value analysts have no choice but to grapple with these shadow costs and their effects on pricing in the fixed income markets, despite the fact that it can be a difficult task.

COMPUTATIONAL ACCESS TO COMPLEX MODELS

Beside these policy-related changes, over the last decade, even more computational capabilities have become available to the average market participant. Much of these have been directed at machine learning and artificial intelligence, including efforts to find attractive opportunities in fixed income markets. As far as we are aware, the widespread benefits of these approaches are still uncertain. We have heard reports of some firms generating attractive returns with these approaches and have been pleased with a few of our own ventures in this area. But, in general, we're still unclear whether the benefits of mass adoption of these approaches in the fixed income markets will produce the results for which so many analysts are working.

On the other hand, we have also used the enhanced computational capabilities available these days to make use of statistical models that may have been too slow or cumbersome for the average analyst in the past. One of these is the multivariate Ornstein–Uhlenbeck (MVOU) process – a generalization of the univariate Ornstein–Uhlenbeck process discussed in the first edition of this book and appearing again in Chapter 2 of this edition. The MVOU process has some distinct benefits when applied to financial markets, but it also comes with some distinct costs. In particular, it involves numerical optimizations over a larger number of parameters, which can take some time. But as computational speeds improve, the times required to perform these optimizations decrease, particularly when making use of the shortcuts we discuss in Chapter 4 for initializing the optimization algorithm with a guess that is likely to be in the vicinity of the optimized parameter estimates.

With change comes opportunity. But to benefit from opportunity, we need to respond effectively to change. This second edition of *Fixed Income Relative Value Analysis* represents our response to the changes that have occurred in the markets in recent years. We hope that readers are able to use the ideas in this edition to profit from the opportunities afforded by these changes.

CHAPTER 1

Relative Value

THE CONCEPT OF RELATIVE VALUE

Relative value is a quantitative analytical approach toward financial markets based on two fundamental notions of modern financial economics.

> **Proposition 1:** If two securities have identical payoffs in every future state of the world, then they should have identical prices today.

Violation of this principle would result in the existence of an arbitrage opportunity, which is inconsistent with equilibrium in financial markets.

This proposition seems relatively straightforward now, but this wasn't always the case. In fact, Kenneth Arrow and Gérard Debreu won Nobel prizes in economics in 1972 and 1983 in part for their work establishing this result. And Myron Scholes and Robert Merton later won Nobel prizes in economics in 1997 for applying this proposition to the valuation of options. In particular, along with Fischer Black, they identified a self-financing portfolio that could dynamically replicate the payoff of an option, and they were able to determine the value of this underlying option by valuing this replicating portfolio.

Most of the financial models discussed in this book are based on the application of this proposition in various contexts.

> **Proposition 2:** If two securities present investors with identical risks, they should offer identical expected returns.

This result may appear intuitive, but it's somewhat more difficult to establish than the first result. Of particular interest for our purposes is that the result can be established via the *Arbitrage Pricing Theory*, which assumes the existence of unobservable, linear factors that drive returns.

In this case, it's possible to combine securities into portfolios that expose investors to any one of the risk factors without involving exposure to any of the other risk factors. In the limit, as the number of securities in the portfolio increases, the security-specific risks can be diversified away. And in this case, any security-specific risk that offered a non-zero expected return would present investors with an arbitrage opportunity, at least in the limit, as the remaining risk factors could be immunized by creating an appropriate portfolio of tradable securities.

For our purposes, this is a powerful result, as it allows us to analyze historical data for the existence of linear factors and to construct portfolios that expose us either to these specific factors or to security-specific risks, at our discretion. In fact, *principal component analysis* (PCA) can be applied directly in this framework, and we'll rely heavily on PCA as one of the two main statistical models we discuss in this book.

THE SOURCES OF RELATIVE VALUE OPPORTUNITIES

From these two propositions, it's clear that the absence of arbitrage is the assumption that drives many of the models we use as relative value analysts. This should come as no surprise, since one of the main roles of a relative value analyst is to search for arbitrage opportunities.

But for some people, this state of affairs presents a bit of a paradox. *If our modeling assumptions are correct about the absence of free lunches, why do analysts and traders search so hard for them?*

This apparent paradox can be resolved with two observations. The first is the recognition that arbitrage opportunities are rare precisely because hard-working analysts invest considerable effort trying to find them. If these opportunities could never be found, or if they never generated any profits for those who found them, analysts would stop searching for them. But in this case, opportunities would reappear, and analysts would renew their search for them as reports of their existence circulated.

The second observation that helps resolve this paradox is that even seemingly riskless arbitrage opportunities carry some risk when pursued in practice. For example, one of the simpler arbitrages in fixed income markets is the relation between bond prices, repo rates, and bond futures prices. If a bond futures contract is too rich, a trader can sell the futures contract, buy the bond, and borrow the purchase price of the bond in the repo market, with the bond being used as collateral for the loan. At the expiration of the contract, the bond will be returned to the trader by his repo counterparty, and the trader can deliver the bond into the futures contract. In theory, this would allow the trader to make a riskless arbitrage profit. But, in practice, there are risks to this strategy.

For example, the repo counterparty may fail to deliver the bonds to the trader promptly at the end of the repo transaction, in which case the trader may have difficulty delivering the bonds into the futures contract. Failure to deliver carries significant penalties in some cases, and the risk of incurring these penalties needs to be incorporated into the evaluation of this seemingly riskless arbitrage opportunity.

These perspectives help us reconcile the existence of arbitrage opportunities in practice with the theoretical assumptions behind the valuation models we use. But they don't explain the sources of these arbitrage or relative value opportunities, and we'll discuss a few of the more important sources here.

Demand for Immediacy

In many cases, relative value opportunities will appear when some trader experiences an unusually urgent need to transact, particularly in large size. Such a trader will transact his initial business at a price that reflects typical liquidity in the market. But if the trader then needs to transact additional trades in the same security, he may have to entice other market participants to provide the necessary liquidity by agreeing to transact at a more attractive price. For example, he may have to agree to sell at a lower price or to buy at a higher price than would be typical for that security. In so doing, this trader is signaling a demand for immediacy in trading, and he's offering a premium to other traders who can satisfy this demand.

The relative value trader searches for opportunities in which he can be paid attractive premiums for satisfying these demands for immediacy. He uses his capital to satisfy these demands, warehousing the securities until he can liquidate them at more typical prices, being careful to hedge the risks of the transactions in a cost-effective and prudent manner.

Because these markets are so competitive, the premiums paid for immediacy are often small relative to the sizes of the positions. As a result, the typical relative value fund will be run with leverage that is higher than the leverage of, say, a global macro fund. Consequently, it's important to pay attention to small details and to hedge risks carefully.

Misspecified Models

It sometimes happens that market participants overlook relevant issues when modeling security prices, and the use of misspecified models can result in attractive relative value opportunities for those who spot these errors early.

For example, until the mid-1990s, most analysts failed to incorporate the convexity bias when assessing the relative valuations of Eurodollar futures contracts and forward rate agreements. As market participants came to realize the importance of this adjustment, the relative valuations of these two instruments changed over time, resulting in attractive profits for those who had identified this issue relatively early.

In recent years, as credit concerns have increased for many governments, it has become increasingly important to reflect sovereign credit risk as an explicit factor in swap spread valuation models, and we discuss this issue in considerable detail in this book.

Regulatory Arbitrage

The fixed income markets are populated by market participants of many types across many different regulatory jurisdictions, and the regulatory differences between them can produce relative value opportunities for some.

For example, when thinking about the relative valuations of unsecured short-term loans and loans secured by government bonds in the repo market, traders at European banks will consider the fact that the unsecured loan will attract a greater regulatory charge under the Basel accords. On the other hand, traders working for money market funds in the US won't be subject to the Basel accords and are likely to focus instead on the relative credit risks of the two short-term deposits. The difference in regulatory treatment may result in relative valuations that leave the European bank indifferent between the two alternatives but that present a relative value opportunity for the US money market fund.

THE INSIGHTS FROM RELATIVE VALUE ANALYSIS

In some sense, relative value analysis can be defined as the process of gaining insights into the relationships between different market instruments and the external forces driving their pricing. These insights facilitate arbitrage trading, but they also allow us more generally to develop an understanding of the market mechanisms that drive valuations and of the ways seemingly different markets are interconnected.

As a consequence, relative value analysis, which originated in arbitrage trading, has a much broader scope of applications. It can reveal the origins of certain market relations, the reasons a security is priced a certain way, and the relative value of this pricing in relation to the prices of other securities. And in the event that a security is found to be misvalued, relative value analysis suggests ways in which the mispricing can be exploited through specific trading positions. In brief, relative value analysis is a prism through which we view the machinery driving market pricing amidst a multitude of changing market prices.

As an example, consider the divergence of swap spreads for German Bunds and US Treasuries during the financial crisis, which might appear inextricable without considering the effects of cross-currency basis swaps (CCBS), intra-currency basis swaps (ICBS), and credit default swaps (CDS).

In this case, CCBS spreads widened as a result of the difficulties that European banks experienced in raising USD liabilities against their USD assets. On the other hand, arbitrage between Bunds, swapped into USD, and Treasuries prevented an excessive cheapening of Bunds versus USD LIBOR. As a consequence, Bunds richened significantly against EURIBOR (see Chapter 16 for more details).

However, given the relationship between European banks and sovereigns, the difficulties of European banks were also reflected in a widening of European sovereign CDS levels. Hence, Bunds richened versus EURIBOR at the same time as German CDS levels increased.

An analyst who fails to consider these interconnected valuation relations may find the combination of richening Bunds and increasing German CDS opaque and puzzling. But a well-equipped relative value analyst can disentangle these valuation relations explicitly to identify the factors that are driving valuations in these markets. And armed with this knowledge, the analyst can apply these insights to other instruments, potentially uncovering additional relative value opportunities.

THE APPLICATIONS OF RELATIVE VALUE ANALYSIS

Relative value analysis has a number of applications.

Trading

One of the most important applications of relative value analysis is relative value trading, in which various securities are bought and others sold with the goal of enhancing the risk-adjusted expected return of a trading book.

Identifying relatively rich and relatively cheap securities is an important skill for a relative value trader, but additional skills are required to be successful as a relative value trader. For example, rich securities can and often do become richer, while cheap securities can and often do become cheaper. A successful relative value trader needs to be able to identify some of the reasons that securities are rich or cheap in order to form realistic expectations about the likelihood of future richening or cheapening. We discuss this and other important skills throughout this book.

Hedging and Immunization

Relative value analysis is also an important consideration when hedging or otherwise immunizing positions against various risks. For example, consider a flow trader who is sold a position in ten-year (10Y) French government bonds by a customer. This trader faces a number of alternatives for hedging this risk.

He could try to sell the French bond to another client or to an interdealer broker. He could sell another French bond with a similar maturity. He could sell Bund futures contracts or German Bunds with similar maturities. He could pay fixed in an interest rate swap. He could buy payer swaptions or sell receiver swaptions with various strikes. He could sell liquid supranational or agency bonds issued by entities such as the European Investment Bank. Depending on his expectations, he might even sell bonds denominated in other currencies, such as US Treasuries or UK Gilts. Or he might choose to implement a combination of these hedging strategies.

In devising a hedging strategy, a skilled trader will consider the relative valuations of the various securities that can be used as hedging instruments. If he expects Bunds to cheapen relative to the alternatives, he may choose to sell German Bunds as a hedge. And if he believes Bund futures are likely to cheapen relative to cash Bunds, he may choose to implement this hedge via futures contracts rather than in the cash market.

By considering the relative value implications of these hedging alternatives, a skilled flow trader can enhance the risk-adjusted expected return of his book. In this way, the value of the book reflects not only the franchise value of the customer flow but also the relative value opportunities in the market and the analytical skills of the trader managing the book.

Given the increasing competitiveness of running a fixed income flow business, firms that incorporate relative value analysis as part of their business can expect to increase their marginal revenues, allowing them to generate higher profits and/or to offer liquidity to customers at more competitive rates.

Security Selection

In many respects, a long-only investment manager faces many of the same issues as the flow trader in the previous example. Just as a flow trader can expect to enhance the risk-adjusted performance of his book by incorporating relative value analysis into his hedging choices, a long-only investment manager can expect to enhance the risk-adjusted performance of his portfolio by incorporating relative value analysis into his security selection process.

For example, an investment manager who wants to increase his exposure to the 10Y sector of the EUR debt market could buy government bonds issued by France, Germany, Italy, Spain, the Netherlands, or any of the other EMU member states. Or he could buy Bund futures or receive fixed in a EURIBOR or ESTR interest rate swap. Or he might buy a US Treasury in conjunction with a cross-currency basis swap, thereby synthetically creating a US government bond denominated in euros.

An investment manager who incorporates relative value analysis as part of his investment process is likely to increase his alpha and therefore over time to outperform an otherwise similar manager with the same beta who doesn't incorporate relative value analysis.

THE CRAFT OF RELATIVE VALUE ANALYSIS

Relative value analysis is neither a science nor an art. Rather, it's a craft, with elements of both science and art. For a practitioner to complete the journey from apprentice to master craftsman, he needs to learn to use the tools of the trade, and in this book we introduce these tools along with their foundations in the mathematical science of statistics and in the social science of financial economics.

We also do our best to explain the practical benefits and potential pitfalls of applying these tools in practice. In the development of an apprentice, there is no substitute for repeated use of the tools of the trade in the presence of a master craftsman. So we make every effort in this book to convey the benefit of our experience over many years of applying these tools.

Since financial and statistical models are the tools of the trade for a relative value analyst, it's important that the analyst chooses these tools carefully, with an eye toward usefulness, analytical scope, and parsimony.

Usefulness

In our view, models are neither right nor wrong. Pure mathematicians may be impressed by truth and beauty, but the craftsman is concerned with usefulness. To us, various models have varying degrees of usefulness, depending on the context in which they're applied.

As Milton Friedman reminds us in his 1966 essay "The Methodology of Positive Economics," models are appropriately judged by their implications. The usefulness of a particular model is not a function of the realism of its assumptions but rather of the quality of its predictions.

For relative value analysts, models are useful if they allow us to identify relative misvaluations between and among securities, and if they improve the quality of the predictions we make about the future richening and cheapening of these securities.

For example, we agree with critics who note that the Black–Scholes model is *wrong*, in the sense that it makes predictions about option prices that are in some ways systematically inconsistent with the prices of options as repeatedly observed in various markets. However, we've found the Black–Scholes model to be useful in many contexts, as have a large number of analysts and traders. It's important to be familiar with its problems and pitfalls, and like most tools it can do damage if used improperly. But we recommend it as a tool of the trade that is quite useful in a number of contexts.

Analytical Scope (Applicability)

For our purposes, it's also useful for a model to have a broad scope, with applicability to a wide range of situations. For example, principal component analysis (PCA) has proven to be useful in a large number of applications, including interest rates, swap spreads, implied volatilities, and the prices of equities, grains, metals, energy, and other commodities. As with any powerful model, there is a cost to implementing PCA, but the applicability of the model once it has been built means that the benefits of the implementation tend to be well worth the costs.

Other statistical models with broad applicability are those that characterize the mean-reverting properties of various financial variables. Over considerable periods of time, persistent mean reversion has been observed in quite a large number of financial variables, including interest rates, curve slopes, butterfly spreads, term premiums, and implied volatilities. And in the commodity markets, mean reversion has been found in quite a number of spreads, such as those between gold and silver, corn and wheat, crack spreads in the energy complexes, and crush spreads in the soybean complex.

The ubiquity of mean-reverting behavior in financial markets implies that mean reversion models have a tremendous applicability. As a result, we consider them some of the more useful tools of a well-equipped relative value analyst, and we discuss them in some detail in this book.

Parsimony

From our perspective, it's also useful for a model to be parsimonious. As Einstein articulated in his 1933 lecture "On the Method of Theoretical Physics," "It can scarcely be denied that the supreme goal of all theory is to make irreducible basic elements as simple and as few as possible without having to surrender the adequate representation of a single datum of experience."

In our context, it's important to note the relative nature of the word "adequate." In most circumstances, there is an inevitable tradeoff between the parsimony of a model and its ability to represent experience. The goal of people developing models is to improve this tradeoff in various contexts. The goal of people using models is to select those models that offer the best tradeoff between costs and benefits in specific applications. And it's in that sense that we characterize the models in this book as being useful in the context of relative value analysis.

SUMMARY OF CONTENTS

Relative value analysis models can be divided into two categories: statistical and financial. Statistical models require no specific knowledge about the instrument that is being modeled and are hence universally applicable. For example, a mean reversion model only needs to know the time series, not whether the time series represents yields, swap spreads, or volatilities, nor what drives that time series.

Financial models, on the other hand, give insight into the specific driving forces and relationships of a particular instrument (and are therefore different for each instrument). For example, the specific knowledge that swap spreads versus LIBOR include the unsecured–secured basis can explain its statistical behavior.

While we present the models in two separate categories, comprehensive relative value analysis combines both. The successful relative value trader described above might first use statistical models to identify which instruments are rich and cheap relative to each other, and then apply financial models in order to gain insights into the reasons for that richness and cheapness, on which basis he can assess the likelihood for the richness and cheapness to correct. If he sees a sufficient probability for the spread position to be an attractive trade, he can then use statistical models again to calculate, among others, the appropriate hedge ratios and the expected holding horizon.

Statistical Models

The two types of statistical models presented here are designed to capture two of the most useful statistical properties frequently observed in the fixed income markets: the tendency for many spreads to revert toward their longer-run means over time and the tendency for many variables to increase and decrease together. The first chapters model these properties separately, while the last chapter models the two properties simultaneously.

Mean Reversion

Many financial spreads exhibit a persistent tendency to revert toward their means, providing a potential source of return predictability. In this chapter, we discuss stochastic processes that are useful in modeling this mean reversion, and we present ways in which data can be used to estimate the parameters of these processes. Once the parameters have been estimated, we can calculate the half-life of a process and make probabilistic statements about the value of the spread at various points in the future.

We also present the concept of a first passage time and show ways to calculate probabilities for first passage times. Once we have these first passage time densities, we can provide probabilistic answers to some of the more perplexing questions that are typical on a trading desk. *Over what time period should I expect this trade to perform? What sort of return target is reasonable over the next month? How likely am I to hit a stop-loss if placed at this level?* First passage time densities can provide probabilistic answers to these questions, and we discuss practical ways in which they can be implemented in a trading environment.

Principal Component Analysis

Many large data sets in finance appear to be driven by a smaller number of factors, and the ability to reduce the dimensionality of these data sets by projecting them onto these factors is a very useful method for analyzing and identifying relative value opportunities. In this chapter we discuss PCA in some detail. We address not only the mathematics of the approach but also the practicalities involved in applying PCA in real-world applications, including trading the underlying factors and hedging the factor risk when trading specific securities.

Multivariate Mean Reversion

Chapter 2 discusses ways to model univariate series that exhibit mean reversion and Chapter 3 ways to model multivariate series that exhibit correlation. In this chapter, we discuss the multivariate Ornstein–Uhlenbeck process as a way to model multivariate series that exhibit both mean reversion and correlation. This combined perspective is capable of capturing a richer set of behaviors than even the combination of the two separate approaches, such as the nonmonotonic behavior in the path of expected values over time.

Financial Models

The financial models in this section are relative value models in that they value one security in relation to one or more other securities. To some extent, the chapters build on one another, with the material for one chapter serving as a starting point for the material in another chapter. And the links between asset, basis, and credit default swaps result in strong interdependencies between the chapters treating them, which therefore together form a "swap block" of chapters.

Some Comments on Yield, Duration, and Convexity

A working knowledge of bond and interest rate mathematics is a prerequisite for this book. But we believe some of the basic bond math taught to practitioners is simply wrong, or at the very least misleading. For example, the *basis point value* of a bond is fundamentally a different concept from the *value of a basis point* for a swap, yet many practitioners are unclear about this difference. As another example, the Macaulay duration of a bond is often referred to as the weighted average time to maturity of a bond, but this is only true when all the zero-coupon bonds that constitute the coupon-paying bond have the same yield, a condition that is almost never observed in practice. We also discuss the frequent misuse of bond convexity and suggest a more practical interpretation of the concept.

Some Comments on Yield Curve Modeling

While yield curve models take center stage in many academic papers, the practical focus of this book downgrades their role to supporting concrete analytic tasks. But even here, they are ubiquitous. This chapter therefore reflects on the implicit model assumptions. It also offers some thoughts about mixed jump-diffusion processes and shadow rate models.

Bond Futures Contracts

A simple no-arbitrage relation applies to the relative values of a cash bond, the repo rate for the bond, and the forward price of the bond. But government bond futures contracts typically contain embedded delivery options, which complicate the analysis. We present a multi-factor model for valuing the embedded delivery option, which can be implemented in a spreadsheet using basic stochastic simulation.

Fitted Bond Curves

Fitting curves to the prices of government bonds observed in the market provides two main results: (1) times series of constant maturity par (or zero) bond yields as input variables for a PCA, for example; and (2) a fair value for every individual bond, i.e. a common yardstick to measure its richness or cheapness relative to other bonds. We discuss different functional forms and add external explanatory variables to the curve fitting process, allowing adjustment for impacts from benchmark status or repo specialness on bond prices.

An Analytic Process for Government Bond Markets

Before starting the "swap block" of chapters, we take stock of the statistical and financial models presented so far and illustrate how they could be combined into a comprehensive analytical process for government bond markets.

Overview of the Following Chapters: Asset Swaps, Basis Swaps, Credit Default Swaps, and Their Mutual Influences

All global asset swaps, basis swaps, and credit default swaps are linked, resulting in interesting and complex relationships. A consequence for the presentation in this book is, therefore, that the individual pricing of the different types of swaps takes place in the framework of mutual dependencies. This framework is sketched at the beginning of the swap block of chapters in order to equip the reader with a map through the multitude of relationships between the instruments described in following chapters. Once the journey through the swap block of chapters is completed, these mutual influences can be analyzed quantitatively to a certain extent.

Reference Rates

The key conceptual approach to price swap spreads is to consider them as a basis swap between the repo rate of the bond and the reference rate of the swap, the types of which have increased following the (partial) transition away from LIBOR. This chapter classifies the different reference rates, provides a model for the spreads between them and for their spread to the repo rate. The basis between unsecured and secured reference rates is identified as a major driving force of these spreads.

Asset Swaps

With this foundation it is straightforward to calculate the impact of different funding rates (repo for the bond, LIBOR, OIS or SOFR for the swap) on asset swap spreads. Since an asset swap not only exchanges funding rates but also credit exposure, the impact of different credit risk needs to be added to the swap spread model. The CDS provides a market price for the credit risk of bonds and thus is an obvious candidate to be included among the input variables for the swap spread model.

Credit Default Swaps

However, the price of sovereign CDS usually expresses the credit risk together with the value of the delivery option and of the fact that in case of default the compensation is paid in USD. The foremost task of this chapter is therefore to extract the pure credit information from the CDS market in order to be able to use it as input in the swap spread formula. Unfortunately, the scarcity of observations of previous relevant government defaults results in a significant estimation error. We then discuss also other applications of CDS in RV analysis and trading.

Intra-Currency Basis Swaps

ICBS exchange two different reference rates in the same currency. Hence, they can be valued by applying the model for spreads between reference rates.

Cross-Currency Basis Swaps

CCBS exchange reference rates in different currencies. Since by convention one leg is always USD SOFR and there is no secured reference rate in other currencies, they also involve an exchange between different types of reference rates. By combining ICBS and CCBS, any reference rate in any currency can be swapped into any other. These basis swaps therefore fulfill the function of building blocks and of linking all global swap markets.

Combinations and Mutual Influences of Asset, Basis, and Credit Default Swaps

By combining asset and basis swaps, every bond can be expressed as a spread versus USD SOFR, which is therefore a universal yardstick for comparing all global bonds and the basis for asset allocation and funding decisions. Likewise, the CDS also measures every bond as a spread versus USD SOFR. Using the insights into the delivery option and USD-redemption from the CDS chapter, we present arbitrage relationships between both.

The existence of a universal yardstick and of arbitrage relationships results in strong interdependencies between all asset, basis, and credit default swap markets worldwide. Their analysis is therefore a complex task which should take all these mutual influences into account. We present case studies to illustrate how the links work in practice.

Global Bond RV Via Fitted Curves and Via SOFR Asset Swap Spreads

We show that the deficiencies of swap spreads as rich/cheap indicator for bonds are a consequence of the difference between the swap and bond yield curves, which are manageable in case of SOFR swap spreads only. Hence, to compare bonds in USD, the universal yardstick "SOFR swap spreads" provides a suitable alternative to fitted curves. When comparing bonds in another currency, however, fitting a curve through the basis swapped bonds remains the only reasonable option.

Other Factors Affecting Swap Spreads

At the end of the swap block of chapters we consider those driving factors not captured in its conceptual foundation, such as the impact of increasing leverage constraints and shadow costs. Since some of these variables are unobservable, the goal of modeling and predicting the relationships between bonds and swaps allows only partial and approximative solutions.

Options

We address the analysis and trading of options in a relative value context by discussing three broad categories of option trades. In the first, the trader simply buys or sells an option with a view that the underlying will finish in-the-money or out-of-the-money, with no dynamic trading. In the second, the trader attempts to capitalize on the difference between the implied volatility of the option and the actual volatility that the trader anticipates for the underlying instrument, by trading the option against a dynamic position in the underlying. In the third, the trader positions for a change in the implied volatility of the option, irrespective of the actual volatility of the underlying instrument.

Relative Value in a Broader Perspective

We conclude our sometimes rather technical description of relative value analysis by taking a broader perspective on its macroeconomic functions. At a time when professionals in the financial services industry increasingly need to justify their role in society, we present a few thoughts about the benefits of arbitrage for society.

Throughout the book, we offer pieces of general advice – words of wisdom that we've gleaned over time. We've been mentored by some of the best in the business over the years, with particular thanks to our managers and colleagues in Anshu Jain's Global Relative Value Group at Deutsche Morgan Grenfell, and especially to David Knott, Pam Moulton, and Henry Ritchotte. They were good enough to impart their wisdom to us, and we're happy to pass along this treasure trove of useful advice, hopefully with a few additional pearls of insight and experience that we've been able to add over the years.[1]

Please visit the website accompanying this book to gain access to additional material, www.wiley.com/go/fixedincome

---

[1]When reviewing the first edition of this book, Christian Carrillo, Martin Hohensee, Antti Ilmanen, and Kaare Simonsen provided valuable feedback, enhancing our product. Many participants of our training courses have contributed to the improvements of the second edition.

Statistical Models

CHAPTER 2

Mean Reversion

WHAT IS MEAN REVERSION AND HOW DOES IT HELP US?

Mean reversion is one of the most fundamental concepts underpinning relative value analysis. But while mean reversion is widely understood at an intuitive level, surprisingly few analysts are familiar with the specific tools available for characterizing mean-reverting processes.

In this chapter, we discuss some of the key characteristics of mean-reverting processes and the mean reversion tools that can be used to identify attractive trading opportunities. In particular, we address:

- model selection;
- model estimation;
- calculating conditional expectations and probabilities;
- calculating ex ante risk-adjusted returns, particularly Sharpe ratios;
- calculating first passage times, also known as stopping times.

For each concept, we start with a verbal and intuitive description of the concept, followed by a mathematical definition of the concept, and finish with an example application of the concept to market data.

A variable is said to exhibit mean reversion if it shows a tendency to return to its long-term average over time. Mathematicians will object that this definition is simply an exercise in replacing the words "exhibit," "mean," and "reversion" with the synonyms "shows," "long-term average," and "return". To address such objections, we'll provide a more mathematical definition shortly. But first we'll attempt to establish some further intuition about mean-reverting processes. To some extent, Justice Stewart's famous maxim on pornography, "I know it when I see it," applies to mean reversion. With that in mind, let's take a look at some processes that exhibit mean reversion and a few that don't.

Figure 2.1 and Figure 2.2 show two simulated time series. Both have an initial value of zero, and both have identical volatilities. But one is constructed to be a simple random walk, with zero drift, while the other is constructed to have a tendency to return toward its long-run mean, constructed to be zero

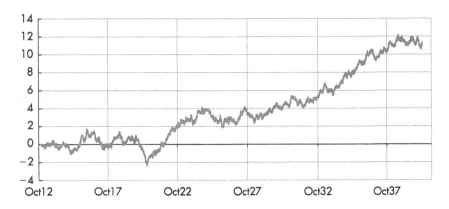

FIGURE 2.1 Simulated random walk.
Source: Authors.

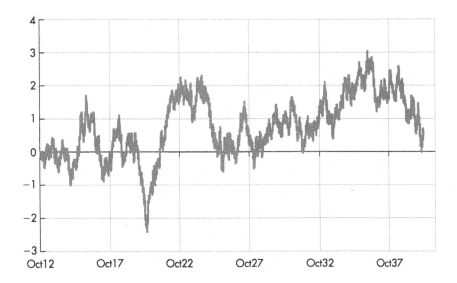

FIGURE 2.2 Simulated mean-reverting process.
Source: Authors.

in this example. In fact, the two series were constructed with identical normal random variates. In the case of the random walk, the mean of each observation was the value of the previous observation, so that the process was a martingale. In the case of the mean-reverting process, the mean of each observation was set to reflect the tendency for the process to return to the mean. At this point, we'd hope most readers would identify Figure 2.2 as the one with the mean-reverting variable. If we observe both figures closely, we can see that the mean-reverting process is in some sense a transformation of the random walk in Figure 2.1.

The speed with which a variable tends to revert toward its mean can vary. For example, Figure 2.3 and Figure 2.4 show time series that were simulated using the same random normal variates that generated the mean-reverting variable in Figure 2.2 but with an important difference. The variable in

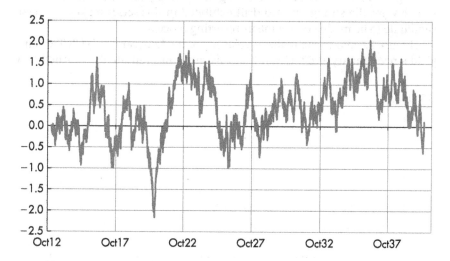

FIGURE 2.3 Simulated mean-reverting process: faster mean reversion.
Source: Authors.

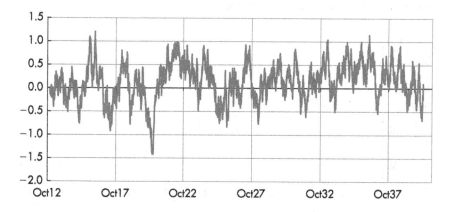

FIGURE 2.4 Simulated mean-reverting process: even faster mean reversion.
Source: Authors.

Figure 2.3 was constructed to have a faster speed of mean reversion than the variable in Figure 2.2, while the variable in Figure 2.4 was constructed to have a still faster speed of mean reversion.

While it's well and good to consider variables simulated via known equations by a computer, traders and analysts have to make judgments about real-world data, which are almost always messier in some respects than simulated data. So it's also useful to consider a few real-world examples.

Figure 2.5 shows the spot price of gold in US dollars since January 1975. In our view, the strong upward drift exhibited in this series makes it a poor candidate to be modeled by a mean-reverting process.

Figure 2.6 shows the realized volatility of the ten-year (10Y) US Treasury yield since January 1962. Given that this series has repeatedly returned to a

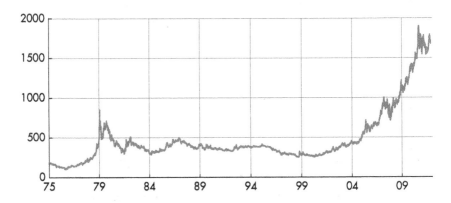

FIGURE 2.5 Spot price of gold in US dollars since January 1975.
Source: data – Bloomberg, chart – Authors.

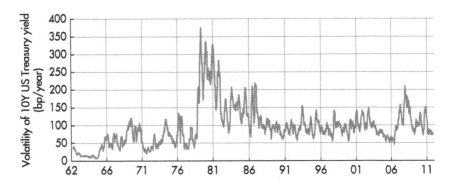

FIGURE 2.6 Realized volatility of 10Y US Treasury bond yield (bp/year).
Source: data – Bloomberg, chart – Authors.

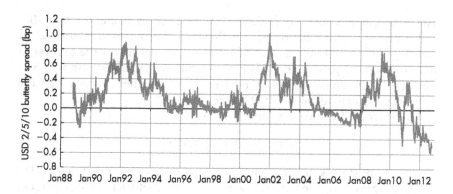

FIGURE 2.7 2/5/10 butterfly spread along USD swap curve since 1988.
Source: data – Bloomberg, chart – Authors.

long-run mean in the past, it appears to be a relatively good candidate for modeling with a mean-reverting process.

As another example, Figure 2.7 shows the 2Y/5Y/10Y butterfly spread along the USD swap curve since 1988. Given the number of times during the sample that this spread returns to its long-run mean, we consider it another good candidate for modeling with a mean-reverting process.

Mathematical Definitions

Having provided verbal and graphical intuition regarding mean reversion, it's time to attempt to provide a few useful mathematical definitions.

Stochastic Differential Equation

First, we'll provide a brief definition of a *stochastic differential equation* (SDE). In practice, this term is fairly simple to define, as most of the definition is contained within the name. In other words, it's an equation that character-izes the random behavior of a variable over an infinitesimal period of time. As a result, it gives us the data-generating mechanism for the variable. For example, the equation would allow us to simulate the variable over time using a computer.

For example, $dx_t = k(\mu - x_t)dt + \sigma dW_t$ is the SDE for an Ornstein–Uhlenbeck (OU) process, the continuous-time limit of a first-order autoregres-sive process. The OU process is a popular SDE for modeling mean-reverting variables, as it has moments and densities that can be expressed analytically. In this equation, dx_t is the change in the value of the random variable x at time t, over the infinitesimal interval dt. The speed of mean reversion is given by the parameter k and the long-run mean of the variable is given by μ.

The instantaneous volatility of the variable is given by σ, and the term dW_t is the change in the value of W_t over the instantaneous time interval dt. In fact, W_t is ultimately the source of randomness that drives the process in this equation. In particular, W_t is a pure random walk, often referred to as Gaussian white noise. W_t is also referred to as a Wiener process, after the American mathematician Norbert Wiener.

In general, SDEs take the form

$$dx_t = f(x_t)dt + g(x_t)dW_t$$

The term $f(x_t)$ is the drift coefficient of the equation, and it defines the mean of the process. The term $g(x_t)$ is the diffusion coefficient of the equation, and it defines the volatility of the process.

Linking mathematics with intuition, one can think of this SDE as separating the driving forces of a trade into a non-stochastic part (there is no randomness in the drift term $f(x_t)dt$) and into a stochastic part (the diffusion coefficient $g(x_t)dW_t$). Depending on the choice of the functional form for the drift coefficient, it may contain other non-stochastic elements besides the mean reversion as well. Hence, the drift coefficient can be interpreted as containing the non-stochastic, therefore predictable, driving forces of a trade, i.e. as a quantification of its return predictability. In contrast, the diffusion coefficient can be associated with the stochastic, unpredictable risk in a trade. Together, the SDE can be thought of as separating and connecting return and risk. As a consequence, expressing a trade via such an SDE is a suitable way to calculate its relative performance and risk characteristics, such as a Sharpe ratio. We will illustrate this calculation with an example below.

Analysts familiar with regressions may find the perspective on mean reversion depicted in Figure 2.8 intuitive. Using the data of the example shown in Figure 2.18 and their discrete steps, in this case, trading days, each point represents the move from a given day to the next, i.e. $x_{t+1} - x_t$, as a function of the (negative) distance from the mean on that given day, i.e. $\mu - x_t$. The resulting cloud of points shows the daily moves on the y-axis as depending on the (negative) distance from the mean on the x-axis. One can now fit a linear regression line through these observations. The slope of this linear regression line is linked to the speed of linear mean reversion, i.e. the parameter k of an OU process. In fact, the slope of the regression line (0.055) is very close to the speed of mean reversion (0.056) of an OU process fitted to the same data. And adding other non-stochastic elements besides the mean reversion to the drift term would correspond to moving to a multiple regression.

Conditional Density

Next, we'll define the *conditional density* of a process, also referred to as a *transition density*. In particular, the conditional density gives us the probability

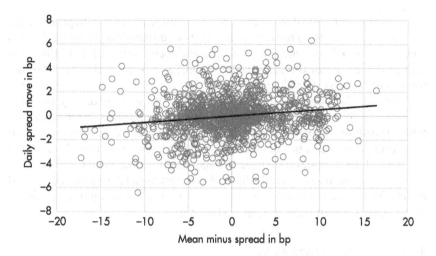

FIGURE 2.8 Daily moves of the swaption volatility difference EUR 5Y5Y – GBP 5Y5Y as a function of the (negative) distance to the mean.
Source: Authors.

density for the future value of a random variable conditional on knowing some other information about the variable. In the case of a time series process, the conditioning information is usually some earlier value of the variable. For example, in the case of the OU process, the transition density of $x_{t+\tau}$ for $\tau > 0$ is a normal density with mean given by $\mu + (x_t - \mu)e^{-k\tau}$ and with a variance given by $\frac{\sigma^2[1-e^{-2k\tau}]}{2k}$.

Unconditional Density

The unconditional density of a process is the probability density for the future value of a random variable without being able to condition the density on any additional information. You could think of the unconditional density as the histogram that would result from simulating the process over an infinitely long period. More precisely, it's the limit of the conditional density $p(x_{t+\tau})$ as τ goes to infinity. So in the case of the OU process, the unconditional density is a normal density with mean given by μ and with variance given by $\frac{\sigma^2}{2k}$.

Stationary Densities and Mean-Reverting Processes

In some cases, a variable will have a conditional density, but it won't have an unconditional density. In other words, the limit of the conditional density $p(x_t)$ won't converge to a limiting density.

A simple example of this would be a random walk with drift, given by the SDE $dx_t = \rho dt + \sigma dW_t$. The transition density or unconditional density for this process is normal with mean $x_t + \rho \tau$ and variance given by $\sigma^2 \tau$. In this case, neither the mean nor the variance has a limit as $\tau \to \infty$, and the limit of the conditional density doesn't exist.

Even in the case of a random walk with no drift, given by the SDE $dx_t = \sigma dW_t$, there is no unconditional density. In this case, the mean for all future transition densities is simply the current value of the variable x_t, but since there is no limit to the variance of the process, there is no limit to the conditional density, and the unconditional density doesn't exist.

However, in many cases, the limit of the conditional density will exist, and the random variable is said to be mean reverting. We also say that stationary density exists and that the process is stationary.

Return Predictability and Alpha

Having provided some intuition and some mathematical definitions of mean-reverting processes, it's helpful to take a step back and consider the usefulness of mean-reverting models for investors and traders.

Return predictability is a necessary, though not sufficient, condition for generating alpha, defined here as an atypically high, risk-adjusted return. If we identify a financial variable that exhibits return predictability, then either the risks of that variable are predictable or the risk-adjusted returns are predictable.

Mean reversion is a form of return predictability. If a financial variable exhibits mean reversion, then we can use that information to improve our predictions for the future value of the variable. In our view, more often than not, mean reversion in a financial variable is an indication that risk-adjusted returns of the variable are predictable. Of course, in some cases, some or all of the mean reversion in a variable will be the result of risks that exhibit mean reversion rather than the result of mean reversion in the risk-adjusted returns. But, in our view, the more typical result is that the risk-adjusted returns are predictable. In this case, mean reversion can be used to generate alpha for traders and investors.

DIAGNOSTICS FOR MODEL SELECTION

The key for modeling any mean reversion in the variable x is to select a functional form for the drift coefficient, $f(x)$, that is useful in depicting the tendency of x to decline toward its long-run mean when it's above the mean and to increase toward its long-run mean when it's below the mean. So at a minimum, we need a function $f(x)$ that satisfies three conditions:

- The value of $f(x)$ is negative when x is above the long-run mean.
- The value of $f(x)$ is positive when x is below the long-run mean.
- The value of $f(x)$ is zero when x is equal to the long-run mean.

Of course, one simple function that satisfies these properties is a line, in which $f(x)$ could be parameterized as $f(x) = k(\mu - x)$. In this case, μ is the long-run mean of the process and k is the strength with which the variable x is "pulled" toward the long-run mean. An equivalent parameterization of $f(x)$ is $f(x) = a + bx$, in which case, $a = k\mu$, and $b = k$.

As it happens, the simplicity of this linear parameterization simplifies the estimation of parameters from historical data, as the likelihood function will often have a closed-form representation in this case, depending on the specification of the diffusion coefficient, $g(x)$. The linear specification for $f(x)$ also simplifies the calculation of transition densities and first passage time densities for x.

But of course a line is not the only function that could be used to represent the mean-reverting tendencies of x, and we may be willing to sacrifice some simplicity in exchange for a functional form for the drift coefficient that is more useful in capturing the actual mean-reverting tendencies exhibited in the data.

For example, a more flexible functional form that has been used in a variety of applications is $f(x) = a + bx + cx^2 + dx^3$, a third-order polynomial in x. In particular, this nonlinear specification allows for the variable x to exhibit increasingly strong mean reversion as it moves further away from the long-run mean. A similar function form that has been used successfully in a variety of applications is $f(x) = \frac{a}{x} + bx + cx^2 + dx^3$, as the $\frac{1}{x}$ term allows for the drift coefficient to become increasingly strong as x approaches zero, allowing zero to act as a reflecting barrier for the process. Examples of these three functional forms appear in Figure 2.9.

In this case, we want to restrict the value of d to be non-positive, to avoid the drift coefficient going to infinity as x increases, in which case x would be an explosive process rather than a stationary, mean-reverting process. For a similar reason, we'd like to restrict the value of a to be non-negative.

Strictly speaking, the drift coefficient, $f(x)$ also needs to satisfy other, rather technical, mathematical conditions in order to ensure that this SDE has a solution. In practice, we tend to assume that these conditions are satisfied (perhaps more often than we should), as the processes typically studied in financial applications tend to be well behaved.

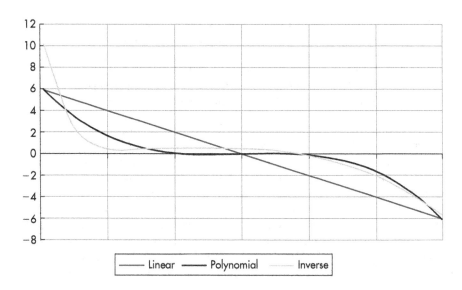

FIGURE 2.9   Examples of drift coefficients.
Source: Authors.

At this point, we should stress that the drift coefficient, $f(x)$, can assume an unlimited variety of functional forms, including nonparametric forms, and the particular form used in practical applications must be specified by the analyst.

If the analyst is open to sacrificing some analytical tractability in an attempt to more usefully model certain aspects of the process, he would benefit from some diagnostic guidance as to the functional forms for $f(x)$ that are likely to be most useful.

To our knowledge, the most useful diagnostic is one suggested by Richard Stanton in a Stanford research paper in the mid-1990s. The basic idea behind this diagnostic tool is to create a nonparametric, empirical approximation of the drift coefficient using historical data. An illustration of this is provided in Figure 2.10.

Each point in the graph represents the estimated strength of mean reversion when the variable assumes values in the neighborhood of that point. Perhaps the most expedient way to explain this concept is to start by listing the steps involved in creating the graph.

1. Group the observations into "buckets," with the number of buckets determined by the analyst.
2. For each bucket, calculate the average subsequent change of each observation in the bucket.

3. For each bucket, plot a point with a horizontal coordinate equal to the midpoint of the observations in the bucket and with a vertical coordinate equal to the average subsequent change of the observations in the bucket.

For example, let's imagine that we have 1,000 observations in our data series and that we want to group these into 20 buckets of equal width, with equally spaced midpoints. We can separate the range (high–low) into 20 segments of equal length and then place each of our 1,000 observations into one of these 20 buckets. Some buckets may have many observations, while some buckets may have relatively few observations. As a general rule, if a bucket has very few observations, it would be wise to decrease the number of buckets, which should increase the number of observations in most buckets, in an attempt to reduce the estimation error of the average change within that bucket.

Once each observation has been placed into a bucket, calculate the subsequent change of each observation in the bucket. For example, if the 400th data point in the series has been placed into the sixth bucket, the subsequent change associated with the 400th observation would be the 401st observation less the 400th observation, even if the 401st observation is itself within a different bucket.

In other words, we're calculating the average change of observations whose starting values are within the same bucket, and then we repeat the calculation for each of the remaining buckets.

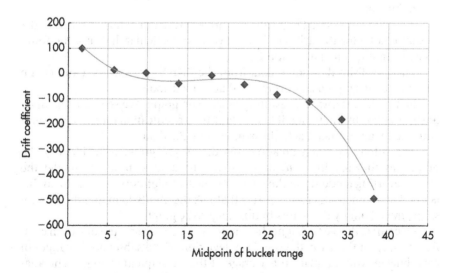

FIGURE 2.10   Diagnostic tool for drift coefficient.
Source: Authors.

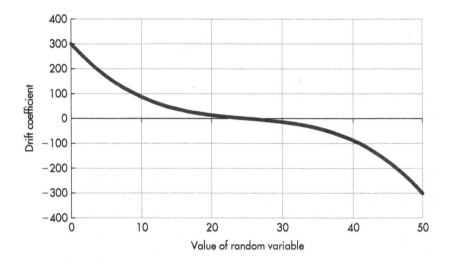

FIGURE 2.11   Target drift coefficient.
Source: Authors.

In this example, once we're done with the calculations in each of these 20 buckets, we'll have 20 points to plot on our diagnostic graph. The horizontal coordinate of each point will be the midpoint of the bucket, and the vertical coordinate of each point will be the average change of the observations in that bucket.

As an illustration, let's specify a nonlinear functional form for $f(x)$ and a constant value for the drift coefficient, $g(x)$. In particular, let's use the functional form illustrated in Figure 2.11.

Then let's simulate some data from the SDE we've specified and create our diagnostic graph using the method described above.

Figure 2.12 shows the resulting diagnostic graph. We see that this diagnostic graph is useful in that it helps identify a specification for $f(x)$ consistent with the mean reversion actually exhibited by the data.

The intention when creating this diagnostic graph is to identify the properties that are likely to be useful to the analyst trying to model the mean-reverting tendency in the data. The most straightforward way to do this is to select a functional form for $f(x)$ that has the ability to match the general shape traced out by the points in this diagnostic graph.

Of course, the same diagnostic graph can be created for the diffusion coefficient, $g(x)$. In this case, the standard deviation of the subsequent changes in each bucket would replace the average of the subsequent changes. The analyst then can specify a functional representation for $g(x)$ that most usefully captures the key properties of the diffusion coefficient, $g(x)$, as a function of x.

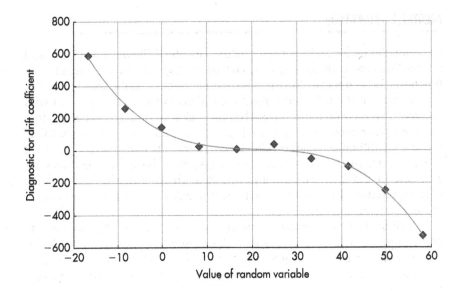

FIGURE 2.12 Diagnostic graph for drift coefficient.
Source: Authors.

As with the drift coefficient, $f(x)$, there are some technical conditions that must be satisfied for $g(x)$ in order to ensure that the SDE has a solution. In practice, we simply tend to make sure that $g(x)$ has some commonsense restrictions. For example, we'd like to restrict $g(x)$ to assuming only positive values, as a negative value for the diffusion coefficient would be equivalent to allowing time to run backward for our process.

In practice, a diagnostic graph for the diffusion coefficient often reveals relatively high levels of volatility at high distances from the mean (see Figure 2.21 for a real-world example). This corresponds to the fact that when the entry level into a trade is statistically attractive (far away from its mean), often also its volatility is higher than on average, and can be explained by the observation, that particularly good entry opportunities tend to occur in times of market turmoil ("buy when there is blood on the streets"). But this also means that the assumption of a constant volatility (i.e. independent of the distance from the mean), as in an OU process, can lead to underestimating the risk of a trade and to an overestimation of its Sharpe ratio. Using a diagnostic graph reveals whether the assumption of constant volatility is appropriate or needs to be corrected in order to reflect higher volatility and hence lower expected Sharpe ratios for a trade put on at extreme distance from its mean.

MODEL ESTIMATION

Once functional forms have been specified for the drift coefficient, $f(x)$, and for the diffusion coefficient, $g(x)$, the analyst must specify precise values for the functions $f(x)$ and $g(x)$ within the class of functions having the specified forms. For example, if the drift and diffusion coefficients have been specified with parametric representations, the analyst must choose specific, numeric values for these parameters. If nonparametric representations have been specified, the analyst still must assign specific values to the functions $f(x)$ and $g(x)$ over the relevant domain. For example, one could define the drift and diffusion for each bucket and run a Monte Carlo simulation by determining for each step of the simulation, in which bucket it lies, and using the values for this bucket to calculate the next step.

Most analysts will choose to specify numeric values for $f(x)$ and $g(x)$ to "most closely match" a set of historical data. For example, we can specify $f(x)$ and $g(x)$ so that the resulting SDE is the one from which the data are most likely to have been generated. This is the principle behind maximum likelihood estimation.

However, some analysts may prefer a different approach to specifying the drift and diffusion coefficients. For example, some analysts may want to specify $f(x)$ and $g(x)$ so that the moments of the resulting transition densities most closely match the empirical moments of the historical data. For example, some analysts will specify drift and diffusion coefficients so that their SDE has a conditional mean and a conditional variance that match the conditional means and variances of their historical data. More generally, we could match the theoretical and empirical expected values for a variety of functions of the data. Indeed, this is the general approach behind the method of moments. In some cases, using the method of moments will produce results that are precisely identical to the results obtained via maximum likelihood, though in general this need not be the case.

In some cases, an analyst may prefer to specify part or all of the SDE so that the theoretical moments of the process match some other data. For example, when the variable we're modeling is the price of a security that serves as the underlying instrument for one or more derivative securities, the analyst may wish to specify the SDE so that the theoretical volatility of the process following the SDE is the same as the volatility implied by the prices of the derivative securities.

The important point to note is that different criteria can be used when specifying precise, numeric values for the drift coefficient, $f(x)$, and the diffusion coefficient, $g(x)$. The particular criteria used in any given application should be chosen in accordance with the goal of the analysis.

In some cases, an analyst may wish to conduct the analysis twice using different criteria in each instance, to see whether the results of the analysis are robust to the choice of criteria. For example, if the ex ante Sharpe ratios of a trade are very different depending on whether the SDE is specified via maximum likelihood estimation or by matching the implied volatilities in the options markets, this difference is likely to be useful information for the analyst.

If an analyst elects to specify $f(x)$ and $g(x)$ via estimation using historical data, he needs to keep in mind that some estimation approaches can be problematic, conceptually and practically. For example, for some functional specifications of $f(x)$ and $g(x)$ (e.g. $f(x)$ is a line and $g(x)$ is a constant), the transition densities that comprise the likelihood function will have closed-form expressions. But for general choices of $f(x)$ and $g(x)$, there will be no closed-form representations of the likelihood function. In theory, the analyst could proceed in this case by calculating the likelihood function using numerical methods, such as simulations or by solving the partial differential equations for each transition density numerically, using finite difference grids. In practice, such methods are so numerically cumbersome as to be intractable (or at least impractical).

This problem also affects the method of moments in cases for which there are no closed-form representations of the moments of the process. When no closed-form expressions exist for the likelihood function, analysts sometimes approximate the likelihood functions. When the likelihood function is approximated, we refer to the approach as pseudo-maximum likelihood estimation (PMLE) or quasi-maximum likelihood estimation (QMLE).

In the case of PMLE, the approximations are based on the fact that the transition densities for the process are increasingly well approximated by normal densities when the time period between observations decreases. In other words, for small time intervals, the transition densities appear "locally normal."

One problem with PMLE is that the estimators obtained by maximizing the pseudo likelihood function are generally not consistent, meaning the estimate can't be guaranteed to converge to the true parameter value as more data become available. In addition, we typically don't know the distribution of the estimator, even asymptotically, complicating the process of making inferences and testing hypotheses from the data.

At times, the lack of consistency and asymptotic normality will be an acceptable price to pay in order to work with an estimation procedure that is tractable in practice. In particular, this will be the case when the drift and diffusion are relatively "smooth" and particularly when the time between successive observations is small. Note that both of these conditions increase the extent to which the transition densities appear "locally normal."

In our experience working with a large variety of financial variables over many years, the results obtained by using PMLE with daily data are virtually indistinguishable from the results one gets from using the exact likelihood function. In other words, the cost of using PMLE rather than exact MLE tends to be small. Given that PMLE is much more tractable than most other methods in these cases, we recommend without any hesitation using PMLE when dealing with daily data.

While the scope of this book doesn't include the basics of maximum likelihood estimation (which we assume most analysts know), we can provide a sketch of the process.

Typically, a multivariate, nonlinear, numerical optimizer will choose parameter values so as to maximize the likelihood function, which is a function of both the historical data and the parameter values. The likelihood function is the product of the transition densities governing all the observations (i.e. the density of each observation conditional on the preceding observation). Clearly, each transition density is a function of two adjacent observations and of the historical data. From a purely computational perspective, working with the sum of functions often is easier than working with the product of functions. (For example, a product of many functions all of which are less than one may result in a value that is small relative to the precision of the machine performing the calculations.)

As it happens, the logarithm of a function achieves its maximum at the same point as the original function. And since the log of a product of functions is equivalent to the sum of the logarithms of the individual functions, this log likelihood function typically is very straightforward to calculate. As a result, it's often easier to maximize the logarithm of the likelihood function.

Once the log of the likelihood function has been specified, the analyst finds the set of parameter values that maximizes the value of this function, subject, possibly, to any constraints imposed by the analyst.

There are a variety of numerical algorithms for performing this nonlinear, numerical (possibly constrained) optimization. We won't discuss different algorithms in this book, except to note that gradient methods of one sort or another are almost always preferred by experienced analysts, as they tend to find local optima fairly quickly.

It's useful to note that these optima may be local rather than global, so it's good practice to start the optimization algorithm from a variety of starting points, to see whether the optimum obtained is robust to the choice of starting point. In our experience, most likelihood functions appear to be fairly well behaved, in the sense that we observe robust convergence to the global optimum. But this isn't always the case, and it's usually worth testing this proposition informally, to enhance our confidence in the results.

Once the drift and diffusion functions have been estimated, it's typically useful to plot the estimates, for a couple of reasons. First, plotting the coefficients can sometimes reveal nonsensical results, such as a diffusion coefficient that is negative over a portion of its range. Second, our intuition about the behavior of a financial variable will be a function of the overall drift and diffusion functions rather than a particular parameter that appears in the drift or diffusion coefficient. Unless you're a savant, you're likely to gain intuition via graphical consideration of the coefficients that you wouldn't obtain by simple inspection of the parameter values.

In the theory of estimation, hypothesis testing is often an important topic. However, it's beyond the scope of this book. For our purposes, we'll simply mention that it's useful to have a sense for precision of our estimates of the drift and diffusion coefficients. As is often the case, a larger amount of data allows us to estimate the coefficients with greater precision than we can with a smaller amount of data. When it's important to gain some qualitative sense for the precision of our estimate, simulation often can be a useful exercise, for two reasons. First, in many cases, the asymptotic distributions of the estimators aren't known. And, second, even when we know the asymptotic distribution of an estimator, we don't know whether our particular data set is large enough for the asymptotic results to be relevant.

To simulate the distributions of the drift and diffusion coefficients, under the hypothesis that these coefficients have known values, we can simulate the process so as to generate a simulated sample equal in size to our actual sample. Then we can estimate the drift and diffusion coefficients using the simulated sample as our historical observations. If we repeat this procedure, say, 10,000 times, we'll obtain 10,000 individual estimates of the drift and diffusion coefficients, which we could use to quantify the estimation error of our estimators or for the purpose of making inferences and/or testing hypotheses, under the hypotheses that the data were generated from the SDE used to generate our simulated data.

As it happens, this approach to quantifying estimator error, making inferences, and/or testing hypotheses tends to produce better results than relying upon the asymptotic results in cases where they're known, since in this case we don't rely on the assumption that our data are of sufficient length for the results to approach an asymptotic limit.

CALCULATING CONDITIONAL EXPECTATIONS AND PROBABILITY DENSITIES

In the previous section, on estimation, we discussed the notion that transition densities tend to appear locally normal as the time between successive observations decreases, even for rather general diffusion processes. And we used this result to motivate our discussion of PMLE as an approach toward estimation of the drift coefficient, $f(x)$, and the diffusion coefficient, $g(x)$. But when we're assessing the merits of a trade over a horizon of more than, say, one week, we can rely less on the local normality of our transition densities. In these cases, we need to be able to calculate transition densities and their properties using other approaches.

As we mentioned previously, it is possible to solve for transition densities by solving the underlying partial differential equations that they must satisfy. One approach to doing this is to use finite difference grids. While this approach is straightforward at a conceptual level, it tends to be cumbersome in practice.

A more useful approach is to compute the transition densities and their moments numerically via stochastic simulations. The basic idea is simple. For any SDE, we simply simulate paths between the desired starting time and starting point until the desired ending time. By simulating more paths, we can compute these densities and their moments with as much accuracy as we'd like.

If we'd like to know the mean of a transition density, we can simulate sample paths and calculate the sample average of the terminal values. If we'd like to know the standard deviation of a transition density, we can simulate sample paths and calculate the sample standard deviation of the terminal values.

Similarly, if we'd like to consider the transition density in its entirety, we can simulate sample paths and produce a histogram of the resulting terminal values. An example of this is given in Figure 2.13.

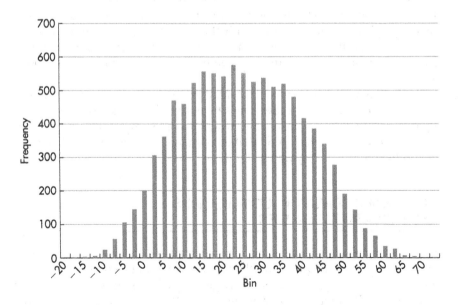

FIGURE 2.13   Histogram of simulated values.
Source: Authors.

One way to increase the smoothness of the depicted transition density is to simulate an increasing number of sample paths. However, another way is to impose some smoothness conditions on the results directly. For example, we can produce a smooth, continuous, and differentiable function representing a transition density nonparametrically by applying a kernel density to the data.

For example, one form of kernel density is the Gaussian kernel density, which uses the Gaussian function (i.e. a normal density) as its kernel. The functional form of the Gaussian kernel density, Q, is given by:

$$Q(x; h) = \sum_{i=1}^{N} K_i(x; h)$$

$$K_i(x; h) = \frac{1}{h\sqrt{2\pi}} e^{\frac{-(x-y_i)^2}{2h^2}}$$

where x is the argument of the kernel density, Q; K is our Gaussian kernel; N is the number of data points, y_i, used to estimate the nonparametric density; and h is the bandwidth parameter, which determines the smoothness of the Gaussian kernel density.

An analogy to a histogram might be helpful. Recall that a histogram sums the number of observations that fall into a particular bin or bucket. If an observation falls into a bucket, it increases the frequency of that bucket by one, and it doesn't change the frequency of any other buckets.

In contrast, when evaluating the kernel density for any particular argument, every data point makes some contribution to the value of the kernel density evaluated at that argument. If a data point is close to the argument, it makes a relatively large contribution, and if the data point is far from the argument, it makes a relatively small contribution.

The relative sizes of the contributions of each data point are determined in part by the bandwidth parameter, h, which acts like the standard deviation of the Gaussian kernel. When h is small, the standard deviation of each Gaussian kernel is small. In that case, data points that are close to the argument make particularly large contributions to the Gaussian kernel, and data points that are far from the argument make particularly small contributions to the Gaussian kernel, since the standard deviation causes the Gaussian density to be especially peaked around its mean. When h is small, the standard deviation of the Gaussian kernel is large, and there is relatively less difference between the contribution to the kernel density made by data points that are close to the argument and those that are far from the argument. In this sense, the bandwidth parameter, h, plays a key role in determining the tradeoff between the smoothness and the granularity in the Gaussian kernel density.

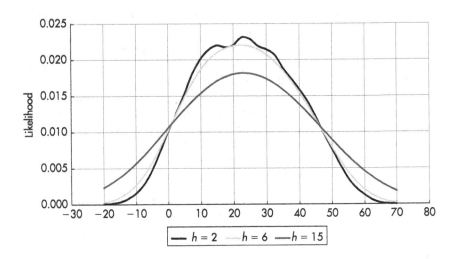

FIGURE 2.14 Nonparametric kernel densities with different bandwidths.
Source: Authors.

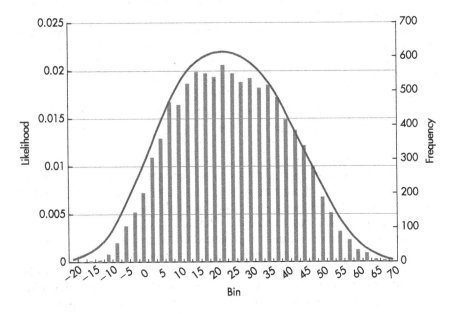

FIGURE 2.15 Nonparametric kernel density and histogram.
Source: Authors.

The bandwidth parameter, h, is specified by the analyst. There are a number of optimal criteria that have been developed for this bandwidth parameter under various assumptions. But in our experience, it's fine simply to use the "eyeball metric" in which the choice is made to produce a nonparametric density that appears most useful from simple visual inspection. To illustrate, Figure 2.14 shows nonparametric densities corresponding to the simulated data of Figure 2.13 for three different choices for the bandwidth parameter: $h = 2$, $h = 6$, and $h = 15$.

In our view, $h = 2$ produces a density that is insufficiently smooth, while $h = 15$ produces a kernel density that may have been smoothed too much.

Figure 2.15 shows the kernel density corresponding to bandwidth parameter $h = 6$, along with the histogram from Figure 2.13.

In our view, this choice for the bandwidth parameter produces the nonparametric density with the most useful tradeoff between smoothness and granularity.

CALCULATING CONDITIONAL, EX ANTE RISK-ADJUSTED RETURNS

Sharpe Ratio as One Measure of Risk-Adjusted Return

Traders and investors tend to use a wide variety of measures to quantify risk, including value at risk, probability of threshold loss, and expected maximum drawdown. Each of these has merit, and we recommend viewing risk from multiple perspectives whenever possible. So we encourage using all these measures, and others, to gain an understanding of risks.

But for the purpose of this chapter, we'll focus our discussion of risk on a single measure: standard deviation. In choosing this risk measure, we don't mean to imply that standard deviation is somehow superior to other measures of risk. But it is relatively simple to calculate, and most people have at least a rudimentary intuition about standard deviations, whereas this isn't always the case when dealing with other risk measures.

One of the fundamental results of financial economics is that investors face tradeoffs between the risks to which they expose their portfolios and the returns that they reasonably can expect to earn. As a result, in any ex ante evaluation of a trade or portfolio, or in any ex post performance attribution exercise, one should consider risks and returns simultaneously.

There are a variety of ways in which analysts can compare risks and returns. The one we focus on in this chapter is to calculate risk-adjusted returns, that is we adjust returns for the risks incurred in the pursuit of those returns.

There are a number of sophisticated ways in which analysts could try to adjust returns to reflect risks, many of which rely on multi-factor pricing models. Again, we encourage analysts to avail themselves of these models and to perform these risk-adjustment exercises whenever possible.

But for the purpose of this chapter, we'll focus on one of the simplest approaches possible: we'll simply calculate the return per unit of risk, where risk is taken to be the standard deviation. In other words, we'll divide the return by the risk.

In this chapter, we refer to this measure as the Sharpe ratio. Strictly speaking, the Sharpe ratio is the ratio of excess return to standard deviation, where excess return is defined as the difference between the return of the asset and the risk-free rate over the same period. In this chapter, we take liberties by referring to the ratio of return to risk with the term Sharpe ratio. In most of our analysis, trades already are financed at a rate equal to (or very close to) the risk-free rate. So the returns we experience already are net of the risk-free rate. So we actually are dealing with Sharpe ratios, properly defined. However, we appreciate that this won't be the case for everyone, and we encourage people to be sure to use excess returns rather than unadjusted returns when calculating Sharpe ratios.

Once we have specified an SDE to model the mean reversion of a trade, and once we have calibrated the parameters of the model (most likely, but not necessarily, estimating these via historical data), we can calculate the conditional expected value and the conditional standard deviation of the return distribution.

In the case of simple models, such as the OU process, the transition densities are normal, and the expected values and the standard deviations of the transition densities can be calculated analytically via closed-form expressions.

In the case of more complex models, we face a number of choices, as mentioned above, including numerical solutions to partial differential equations or series approximations to the actual densities.

In our experience, these methods are relatively difficult to implement in practice, and we prefer simply to calculate these conditional moments via simulation. Once the conditional expected value and the conditional standard deviation of the return have been calculated, the conditional Sharpe ratio can be calculated simply by dividing the conditional expected return by the conditional standard deviation.

Conditional Sharpe ratios can be calculated for each individual trade in a portfolio, but we remind readers that the relevant consideration is the effect that inclusion of a trade has on the conditional risk-adjusted return of the entire portfolio. In other words, when evaluating the attractiveness of a trade, the important consideration is not the risk-adjusted return of the trade on a stand-alone basis but rather the extent to which adding a position can improve the risk-adjusted return of the overall portfolio.[1]

We have described above how the general SDE can be interpreted as separating and connecting the predictable return (e.g. from mean reversion) and unpredictable risk of a trade. Using the Excel sheet accompanying this chapter, we will now illustrate how the representation of a trade via such an SDE can be used to estimate its Sharpe ratio. Modeling the trade via an OU process, the sheet "Calc" shows in column L the expected future path of the trade, reflecting the return predictability from mean reversion. Hence, the expected (excess) return after n weeks can be calculated by subtracting the expected value after n weeks (shown in the n-th row below cell L2) from the entry level (shown in cell L2). The modeled evolution of the variance is given in column O. The Sharpe ratio at a specific time in the future, say, 4 weeks after entry, can be calculated by dividing L2 minus L6 by the square root of O6, resulting in a 4-week Sharpe ratio of 0.76 (annualized 2.73, by multiplying with the square root of 52/4).

One can also obtain a path of the expected annualized Sharpe ratio for holding the trade over different horizons. When trades are modeled with an OU process, the expected annualized Sharpe ratio decreases with the holding horizon. This reflects the fact that the contribution from mean reversion is higher, the further the trade is away from its mean; as it approaches its mean, the return predictability from further mean reversion decreases relative to the risk from randomness, which the OU process assumes to be constant.[2] Consequently, at least when modeling trades with OU, it will usually appear advisable to use short holding horizons and tight targets (e.g. half the distance to the mean rather than the mean itself), as described below.

First Passage Times

Consider a swap spread trading currently at 40 basis points (bp). Let's imagine that we start a stopwatch with the spread at 40 bp, and then we stop the

---

[1]In most relative value analysis of fixed income markets, we tend to model swap rates and bond yields rather than swap net present values and bond prices. As these tend to be interest-bearing instruments, one needs to consider not only the change in the interest rate over time but also the fact that these instruments pay interest, may involve financing, and experience "pull-to-par" effects over time – a collection of features often referenced under the broad rubric of "carry." Spread trades with positive carry are particularly attractive in that they provide an additional positive bias to a trade, and these considerations should be included when calculating ex ante Sharpe ratios as well.

[2]By contrast, if volatility also decreases as the trade approaches its mean, it is conceivable that the expected Sharpe ratio will increase with the holding period.

stopwatch when the spread first reaches a level of 50 bp. The first passage time from 40 bp to 50 bp is the amount of time recorded by the stopwatch when it reaches this 50 bp level. In this case, it's the amount of time it takes for the spread to hit 50 bp, given that it's currently trading at 40 bp. For this reason, the first passage time is also referred to as the *hitting time*, and we'll use these two terms interchangeably.

The first thing to note about the first passage time is that it is specified by two values: a starting value and an ending value. In our example, the starting value was 40 bp, and the ending value was 50 bp. But we could have just as easily specified that the ending value would be 35 bp, or 20 bp. But of course, if we had specified a different stopping value, we would be considering a different hitting time.

The second thing to note about these first passage times is that they're random variables. We don't know the amount of time that will pass before our swap spread hits 50 bp. It could take 10 minutes, or it could take 10 weeks. It could even take 10 months or 10 years.

As random variables, we can calculate moments and other expectations of functions of hitting times. In other words, we can calculate means, standard deviations, skewness, kurtosis, densities, distributions, etc. for first passage times.

As an illustration, imagine that the SDE followed by the swap spread in our example was $dx = k(\mu - x)dt + v\,dw$, with $k = 0.30$, $\mu = 20$ and $v = 20$. In this case, we can generate, say, 10,000 simulated paths, all starting at 40 bp and then calculate the first passage times to a level of 50 bp along these sample paths. We'll have a simulated sample of 10,000 hitting times, which we can use to make a histogram, generate a nonparametric density, calculate an average hitting time, etc. In particular, Figure 2.16 illustrates a histogram and a nonparametric density resulting from this exercise.

The hitting times have a number of practical applications, in that they allow us to answer a number of very useful questions. For example, consider a few useful questions in the context of trading:

- What is the likelihood of stopping out of a trade during the next two weeks if I set my stop at 55 bp?
- At what level should I set my stop if I want the probability of hitting my stop within the next month to be 20%?
- What is the likelihood of hitting my profit target during the next two months if I set it at 35 bp?
- How much time should I expect to pass before this spread next reaches its long-term mean?
- What is a 70% symmetric confidence interval for the amount of time that will pass before this spread next reaches its long-run mean?

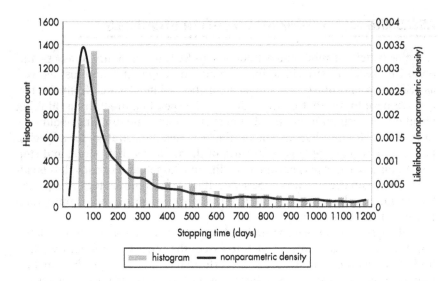

FIGURE 2.16 Nonparametric kernel density and histogram.
Source: Authors.

Note that these last two questions can't be answered simply by considering the transition densities for the process used to model the spread. For example, let's consider a case in which we have used a linear specification for the drift coefficient in the SDE used to model our variable. In that case, the expected value of our variable as a function of time will be exponential, approaching the long-run mean asymptotically but never actually reaching the long-run mean.

In this case, we might ask a different question that gives a false impression of being similar, namely, "How far into the future is the expected value of my variable equal to the long-run mean?" In this case, the answer is that there is no point in the future at which the expected value of the process is equal to the long-run mean, as the expected value approaches the long-run mean asymptotically. In this case, therefore, we might erroneously conclude that expected first passage time to the long-run mean is infinite.

We can see intuitively that this is the wrong answer simply by thinking of a simulation exercise. If we start the process at the current value of our variable and simulate it over a long period, it's very likely that the process will cross back and forth over the long-run mean quite a few times.

The key for anyone who finds the relation between these two questions paradoxical is to appreciate that they're two different questions. One question refers to the path of expected values as a function of time, whereas the other question refers to the expected values of the times taken to travel a certain distance along a sample path.

ASSESSING AND OPTIMIZING EXECUTION STRATEGIES

A major benefit of modeling a trade via an SDE is the ability to assess and optimize execution strategies, for example, the target and stop loss as well as scaling in and out of a trade as a function of its distance from the target. We have found that many traders, while spending much time thinking about *which* position to put on, do not spend much time thinking about *how* to execute it. Rather than aiming for the best execution strategy for a specific position, they may apply general rules-of-thumb to set their target and stop loss. Using an SDE to play around with different targets and stop loss levels can then provide an eye-opening experience: it is not uncommon for the expected Sharpe ratio of the same trade to double simply by using a more appropriate target and stop loss level.

Likewise, if an investor is subject to constraints such as maximum drawdown levels, he can apply an SDE to assess the impact of different ways to fulfill his constraints on the expected performance. For example, he may find that meeting the constraint only by setting a stop loss would result in a too low expected Sharpe ratio, but that adding a scaling strategy increases the anticipated performance to an acceptable level.

While the optimal execution strategy depends on the individual trade, the SDE used to model it and the goals and constraints of the trader, we can share a few general experiences:

- Since the contribution from mean reversion increases with the distance from the mean, trades lose their attractiveness as they approach their mean. Hence, it is usually not advisable to hold a trade until it hits its mean. Setting the target at half the way to the mean or (depending on the alternative trades available) even tighter levels therefore results in higher expected Sharpe ratios.
- Rather than setting the stop loss at a fixed level, it could follow the evolution of the 2-sigma bands of the SDE, for instance (see the chart in the sheet accompanying this chapter).
- Scaling in and out of a position as it moves away and toward its mean is an execution strategy which embodies the idea of mean reversion: The further away from the mean, the higher the expected Sharpe ratio, *hence* the higher the size should be. In line with this, using scaling strategies usually results in at times significantly higher expected Sharpe ratios. However, scaling conceptually conflicts with stop loss: as the trade moves away from its mean and target, the size is increased, until it hits its stop loss, where the size is suddenly set to zero. Hence, while scaling is a suitable execution strategy to increase the return of mean reverting positions, its applicability depends on the individual constraints of the investor.

A PRACTICAL EXAMPLE INCORPORATING ALL THE IDEAS

The Difference between EUR and GBP 5Y5Y Swaption Volatilities

As an example, let's consider the difference between implied volatilities, expressed in bp/year, between 5Y (five-year) options on 5Y swaps denominated in EUR and GBP from 25-May-05 until 4-Jul-12.

The two series are shown in Figure 2.17.

The main point to note from Figure 2.17 is the strong correlation between the two series over time. In particular, the correlation over the period shown in the graph was 0.87.

Figure 2.18 shows the EUR 5Y5Y swaption volatility less the GBP 5Y5Y swaption volatility over the same period.

There are two points worth noting in Figure 2.18.

- The difference between the EUR and GBP swaption volatilities does appear to have been mean reverting over the period.
- The difference appears to be more volatile during the second portion of the data sample than it does during the first portion.

To illustrate this aspect of the data more clearly, Figure 2.19 shows the daily changes in the series displayed in Figure 2.18.

Figure 2.19 supports our intuition from Figure 2.18 that the volatility of the difference has increased during our sample. There are approaches for dealing with changes in parameter values over time, but these are beyond the scope of this book. For our purposes, we'll simply note this feature of the data and keep it in mind as we draw inferences from our analysis.

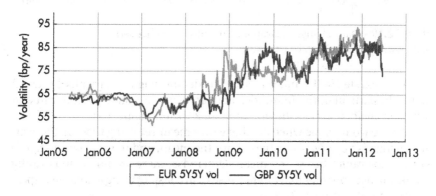

FIGURE 2.17   EUR and GBP 5Y5Y implied swaption volatilities.
Source: data – Bloomberg, chart – Authors.

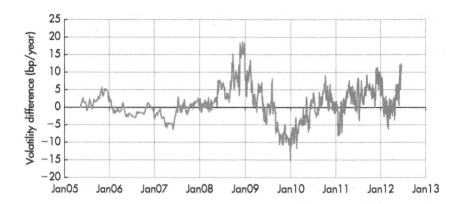

FIGURE 2.18 Swaption volatility difference: EUR 5Y5Y – GBP 5Y5Y.
Source: data – Bloomberg, chart – Authors.

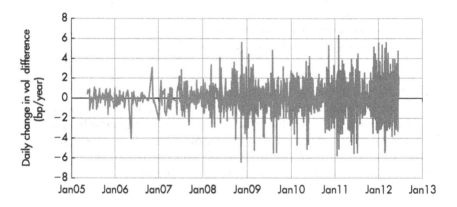

FIGURE 2.19 Daily change in swaption volatility difference series.
Source: data – Bloomberg, chart – Authors.

The next step in the analysis is to consider the diagnostic graphs discussed above. In particular, the first-order nonparametric estimates of the drift and diffusion coefficients are shown in Figure 2.20 and Figure 2.21.

As one would hope when dealing with a mean-reverting process, the average change is negative for values above the mean, and the average change is positive for values below the mean. Otherwise, there are no obvious strong nonlinearities apparent that might cause us to consider using a nonlinear specification for the drift coefficient.

In this case, we may wish to investigate further the benefits of a nonlinear specification for the diffusion coefficient, given that a bucket at either end of

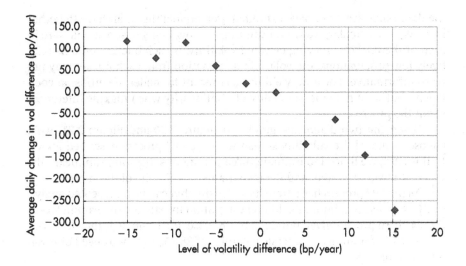

FIGURE 2.20 First-order nonparametric estimate of drift coefficient.
Source: Authors.

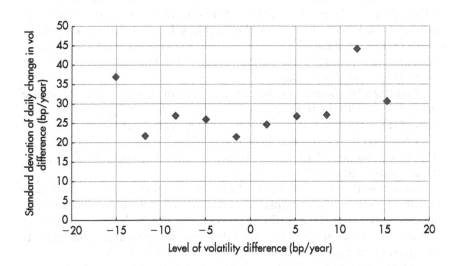

FIGURE 2.21 First-order nonparametric estimate of diffusion coefficient.
Source: Authors.

the data range seems to have exhibited greater volatility than have the other buckets. In particular, we would want to see how many observations were in each of the buckets showing elevated volatility. If each bucket contains relatively few observations, the volatility information from each bucket may not be so informative. For now, we'll use a constant to model the diffusion coefficient, but we'll note the possibility of nonlinearity when making inferences about the process.

Given the two diagnostic graphs in Figure 2.20 and Figure 2.21, we'll choose to model the volatility spread with the OU process described above. In this case, we'll need to estimate three parameters: the long-run mean, the speed of mean reversion, and the instantaneous volatility of the spread.

As the OU process has a transition density that can be represented analytically, we'll use maximum likelihood estimation to estimate the parameters of the specified process given our data. In this case, the estimate is for a long-run mean of 1.0, for an instantaneous volatility of 28.25, and for a speed of mean reversion of 16.5.

As seen from the equation above giving the conditional mean of the OU process, the expected value of the process decays exponentially, approaching the long-run mean asymptotically.

In this case, it's also useful to express the speed of mean reversion in terms of the half-life of the process, the amount of time by which the expected value of the process is halfway between the current value and the long-run mean. In our example, the half-life of the process is 15.4 calendar days, meaning we can expect the spread to close half the remaining distance toward its long-run mean every 15.4 calendar days.

Figure 2.22 shows the unconditional density (or stationary density) for the process along with the transition densities for a variety of time horizons. The current value of the spread, 12.35, is denoted by a gray vertical line.

From Figure 2.22, we see the way in which the transition densities shift their means and standard deviations over time as they approach their limit, the unconditional density for the process.

Note also that the probability of the spread being greater in the future than it is now decreases over time. For example, the probability on a one-week horizon is 18%, but the probability on a one-month horizon is only 4%. At a horizon of three months, the probability that the spread is greater than its current value of 12.35 is less than 1%, according to this model.

Another way to quantify the behavior of this volatility spread is to calculate the risk-adjusted return over various horizons. We do this by dividing the expected value of the change over the horizon by the standard deviation of the change over the same horizon. As this measure resembles the well-known Sharpe ratio, we'll refer to it by this name in the remainder of this chapter.

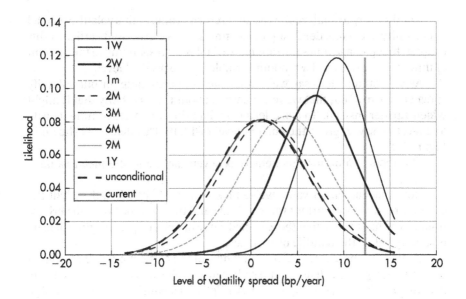

FIGURE 2.22 Unconditional and conditional densities for the volatility spread. *Source:* Authors.

The Sharpe ratio on a one-week horizon is already 0.91, and this increases to 1.78 on a one-month horizon. By three months, the ratio has increased to 2.26.

However, to compare Sharpe ratios for different horizons, we should normalize all the calculations to the same time interval, since the expected values of random variables are additive, while the standard deviations increase at the rate $\sqrt{N}$, where N is the number of times the opportunity is taken. (In other words, to compare an investment with a one-year horizon to an investment with a one-month horizon, we need to consider repeating the one-month opportunity for 12 successive occasions.)

In this case, the annualized Sharpe ratio for the one-week investment horizon is 6.56, while the annualized Sharpe ratio for a one-month investment horizon is 6.12. The annualized Sharpe ratio on a three-month horizon is 4.5.

The fact that the annualized Sharpe ratios decline over time tells us that the best risk-adjusted opportunity is at short horizons. In other words, most of the performance in the trade is expected to come in the early days. The implication is that if we had repeated opportunities to commit to trades with similar risk-adjusted return profiles, it would be better for us to hold these positions for short periods of time and then reallocate our capital to other short-term opportunities.

Another way to analyze the risk and return profile of this volatility spread opportunity is to consider first passage times. As we discussed earlier in this chapter, first passage times are random variables corresponding to the amount of time that elapses until a random variable hits a specified level.

As an example, let's say we're interested in positioning for our volatility spread to narrow, but that we're concerned about the possibility that it might widen further instead. To start, let's calculate the first passage time density to a level of, say, 7, given the current level of 12.35. This density is shown in Figure 2.23.

The modal value for this density is seven days, and the mean value is 14.9 days.

Note that the target value we've picked, 7, is slightly less than half the distance between the current value of 12.35 and the mean of 1.046. So perhaps it should be no surprise that the expected value of our first passage time density is slightly below the half-life of 15.4 days.

In general, there is no need for the half-life to correspond to the mean of the first passage time density, in part because each first passage time density is defined by a different target. For example, let's consider the first passage time density corresponding to the mean of the process, in this case, 1.046. This density is shown in Figure 2.24.

In this case, the modal value is 26 days, and the average value is 38.25 days. In comparison, the expected value of the volatility spread in the

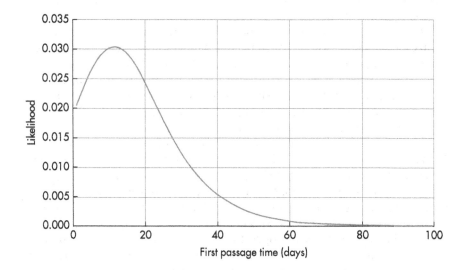

FIGURE 2.23 First passage time density of volatility spread from 12.35 to 7. *Source:* Authors.

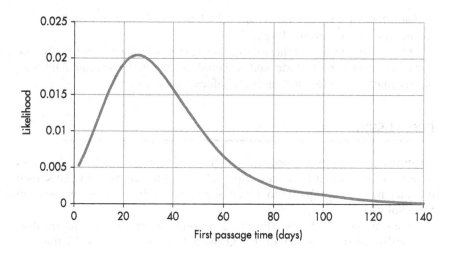

FIGURE 2.24   First passage time density of volatility spread from 12.35 to 1.046.
Source: Authors.

future, according to our model, is *never* precisely equal to its mean, since the expected value approaches the mean asymptotically from its current value. Of course, saying that an infinite amount of time must pass before the expected value equals the long-run mean isn't the same as saying that we expect an infinite amount of time to pass before the volatility spread next reaches its long-run mean.

First passage time densities are useful for a variety of reasons. For example, we can use them to make probabilistic statements about profit targets or stop levels. As an example, let's say we're interested in setting a target of 7, with the current level at 12.35. The first passage time density for this scenario is shown in Figure 2.24. We saw earlier that the average hitting time was 14.9 days, but we can make additional probabilistic statements using this density. For example, the probability of hitting our target of 7 within five days is 13.1%, and the probability of hitting the target within 10 days is 45.1%. For 15 days, the probability is 66.5%. From these statements, we also can calculate that the probability of hitting the target between five and 10 days is 32.0%.

As another example, let's say we're considering placing a stop at 16.35, four volatility points above the current level of 12.35. By calculating the first passage time density to 16.35, we can calculate that the probability of hitting our stop within 10 days is 5.2%. The probability of hitting this stop within 20 days is 8.8%. For 30 days, the probability of hitting this stop is 9.5%. It's 10.5% for 40 days, and 11.1% for 50 days. If we're uncomfortable with those probabilities for any reason, we can calculate a new set of probabilities that correspond to another stop level.

Of course, in some of these cases, our stop would have been hit after we had taken profits on the trade, and we could use simulations to calculate multiple scenarios, such as "hitting 16.35 before hitting 8.35."

CONCLUSION

Mean-reverting processes provide a rich set of tools for modeling financial time series exhibiting mean-reverting behavior. But care needs to be shown in choosing the appropriate tool for the job and in drawing inferences from the results.

For example, the decision to employ a nonlinear specification for the drift and/or the diffusion coefficient should be made carefully. In general, the non-linear specification allows the model to capture a richer set of dynamics in the process, but it also allows a great opportunity to capture spurious aspects of the data that may result from nothing more than sampling error.

There are no clear rules for making these sorts of determinations, and our best advice is for the analyst to benefit from experience. We've attempted to provide the benefit of our experience in this chapter and throughout the book. But in the end, multiple repeated applications of the approach discussed in this chapter are likely to be of greatest use to the relative value analyst over time.

CHAPTER 3

Principal Component Analysis

INTRODUCTION: GOAL AND METHOD

The market presents itself to the observer through a surface of incommensurably many data and movements. The links between those data and movements, for example, the tendency of two-year (2Y) and 10Y interest rates to rise and fall together, point toward a more or less systematic mechanism hidden in the core of the market. Our goal is to see through the surface of the market and into its structural core.

To do so, we face the problem of finding the right (degree of) formal assumptions about the structure of a market. As an extreme position, if we made no formal assumptions at all, we would remain stuck to the surface of incommensurable market data, unable to understand anything about their structural core. So, in order to reach our goal we will need to use structural terms (i.e. mathematical formalism) and hence to impose some assumptions on the market. However, we shall use those assumptions which have turned out to fit the structure of the real market well and otherwise keep them as minimal as possible, thereby leaving enough space for the market to express its own mechanisms in our form.

Principal component analysis (PCA) has only one (main) assumption: that the market is driven by a set of uncorrelated linear factors. This is not only a relatively weak assumption (allowing the market to fill in the remaining structural information, in particular about the shape and strength of each factor) but also a very useful one both for relative value (RV) analysis and hedging. It satisfies the condition of arbitrage pricing theory (see Chapter 1) and allows us to construct portfolios that are exposed to or hedged against any factor, just as specified by the investor. For the purpose of RV analysis,[1] PCA therefore appears to be a useful tool.

The main goal of this chapter is the empirical illustration of the way PCA leads us through the surface of the market into its core, where we can see its inner driving forces, gaining meaningful and deep insights into

---

[1]Other purposes may require other tools.

market mechanisms. After developing the mathematics, we shall spend a large part of this chapter exploring the application of PCA to actual market mechanisms, thereby illustrating the way the structure of real markets reveals itself through PCA.

On one hand, the relationship between the market and mathematical form can involve problematic assumptions. On the other hand, however, it also connects the real world to its mathematical representation. PCA is therefore a link between the economy and mathematics, generating economically relevant statistics. In the example of 2Y and 10Y rates from above, a PCA could identify one factor behind moves of both rates in the same direction, and another, uncorrelated factor behind moves of both rates in opposite directions. Interpreting the identities of those factors (perhaps linked to economic data, like inflation) gives a deep understanding of the driving forces of the yield curve. In the next step, an investor who has a view on those factors (e.g. inflation) could construct through PCA the best trading position and hedge it against factors on which he has no view.

With PCA linking statistics to fundamentals, it also links the first to the second part of the book. While the focus in the preceding section was on statistics, it now shifts to statistics linked to economic insights. Correspondingly, the present goal is not an optimization of Sharpe ratios but to gain insights into the fundamental mechanisms. This will complement statistical optimality with the confidence of understanding the real economic driving forces behind a trade.

AN INTUITIVE APPROACH TO PCA

An assumption-free start to market analysis could be to simply plot data observations in a scatter chart. Figure 3.1 shows an example for 2Y versus 10Y Bund yields (from 1996 to mid-2012). Then, one can try to distinguish structural relationships. In the current example, there seems to be a strong relationship driving both yields up and down together, which has been in force more or less over the whole time period. Moreover, that relationship seems to be rather linear and can thus be approximated quite well by a straight line. In addition, there seems to be a second mechanism driving both yields in opposite directions. Compared to the first relationship, however, it appears to be weaker than the first one over the whole time period and with an impact that varies significantly over time, being quite strong when 2Y yields were around 4% and less so in other sectors. Furthermore, it is not clear whether this relationship can be reasonably assumed to be linear as well.[2]

---

[2]One could also remark a systemic divergence from the line for very low yield levels. The discussion following Figure 3.24 will reveal the background of that deviation.

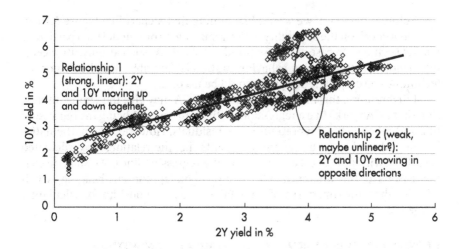

FIGURE 3.1 Structure of point cloud of 2Y and 10Y Bund yields.
Sources: data – Bloomberg; chart – Authors.

Data period: 1 Jan 1996 to 4 Jun 2012, weekly data.

Broadly speaking, PCA assumes the relationships to be linear and uncorrelated[3] and provides a *quantification* of the intuitive approach from above, telling us in mathematical form:

- *which* (linear) relationships exist in a given set of market data (i.e. what the *shape* of market mechanisms looks like). In the current example, this would correspond to quantifying the impact of the relationship 1 and 2 (short and long Bund yields moving up and down together or in opposite directions) on 2Y and 10Y yields.
- *how strong* the relationships are relative to each other, that is how much of market action (yield curve variation) is explained by a particular mechanism.

In mathematical terms, the shape of market mechanisms corresponds to the eigenvectors and their relative strength to the (scaled) eigenvalues of a PCA.

---

[3]The absence of correlation is a result of the linear algebra behind a PCA. It is also a very convenient feature for the usual purposes of relative value analysis, as it allows decomposing a market into uncorrelated factors, which is the basis for analyzing them individually. However, it is also conceivable to construct a factor model with correlated factors. For example, in order to obtain a particular analytical goal it might be useful to model a market as a function of two macroeconomic variables, even if they are correlated.

Before moving on, we would like to note that a chart like Figure 3.1 can serve as a check on the suitability of the assumptions of a model for a particular market segment. In case of the assumptions of a PCA (such as linearity) seeming to violate actual market behavior, caution is advisable, and the diagnostic techniques discussed in Chapter 2 could be used.

Furthermore, this intuitive approach to PCA may give the wrong impression that PCA works like a regression, with relationship 1 being the regression line and relationship 2 representing the residuals. However, the mathematics is different, and so (usually) are the results (i.e. the relationships calculated via a PCA will in most cases differ from the regression line). We shall discuss the reasons for the difference in the section about appropriate hedging, which will also show the superiority of using PCA-based relationships for calculating hedge ratios.

FACTOR MODELS: GENERAL STRUCTURE AND DEFINITIONS

We shall now repeat the discussion from above in formal terms, thereby constructing PCA. The goal of understanding the few key mechanisms behind all market moves can be mathematically addressed by extracting the most relevant information from a given set of market data. Expressing this a bit more formally, it means reducing the dimensionality, with the remaining dimensions containing most of the information. Thus, the result of this exercise will reveal the number, strength, and shape of the market mechanisms.

We observe a number n of market data (e.g. yields) y_i^t ($i = 1, \ldots, n$) at time t. The general form of a k-factor linear model is given by:

$$\begin{pmatrix} y_1^t \\ \vdots \\ y_n^t \end{pmatrix} = \sum_{i=1}^{k} \alpha_i^t \cdot \begin{pmatrix} f_{i1} \\ \vdots \\ f_{in} \end{pmatrix} + \begin{pmatrix} \varepsilon_1^t \\ \vdots \\ \varepsilon_n^t \end{pmatrix}$$

where α_i^t (a number which changes over time) is called the i-th factor (at time t), $\begin{pmatrix} f_{i1} \\ \vdots \\ f_{in} \end{pmatrix}$ (a vector which does not change over time) is called the i-th factor loading and $\begin{pmatrix} \varepsilon_1^t \\ \vdots \\ \varepsilon_n^t \end{pmatrix}$ (a vector which changes over time) is called the k-factor-residual (at time t), that is the portion unexplained by the factors.

The factor loadings, which do not change over time, can be considered as containing the market mechanisms, while the factors show how much of a specific market mechanism is active at a certain point in time. As an intuitive comparison, consider a sound mixer: the (invariable) individual sounds correspond to the factor loadings, while their (variable) strengths at a certain point in time (as adjusted by the volume regulator on the mixer board) correspond to the factors. The other way around, we can decompose the overall sound we hear into its individual components by looking at the regulators and labels on the mixer. Likewise, we are able to decompose the overall market action we observe into its individual driving forces by looking at the factors and factor loadings of a PCA.

Example: Imagine we decide to model the yield curve from 1 to 10 years

$(n = 10)$ by $\begin{pmatrix} y_1^t \\ \vdots \\ y_{10}^t \end{pmatrix} = \alpha_1^t \cdot \begin{pmatrix} 1 \\ \vdots \\ 1 \end{pmatrix}$ (a one-factor model). This particular factor

loading allows only parallel shifts. This is an example for a very strong assumption from our side, which limits our perceptive ability to observing parallel shifts only. The reality of the market would protest against our imposed form by exhibiting large residuals.

So far, we have only assumed that market mechanisms are linear factors. The question is how much more we should assume. The answer to that question classifies factor models into two categories.

In the first category, the analyst determines the factor loadings himself. The Nelson–Siegel (NS) model is a prominent example of this approach,

assuming *a priori* that the first factor loading is the vector $\begin{pmatrix} 1 \\ \vdots \\ 1 \end{pmatrix}$ and the second

a vector whose entries follow the discount factor curve. Thus, it expands the simple one-factor model from our example above (parallel shifts) with a second factor accounting for curve steepening and flattening.

The advantage of that approach is that by choosing the factor loadings appropriately, one can ensure that the model exhibits the desired properties (e.g. is arbitrage-free). This is probably the main reason academic market analysis often prefers factor models falling into the first category.

The disadvantage is that the model results may reflect the assumptions of the analyst rather than the true market mechanisms. In the case of the NS model, for example, curve steepening and flattening moves that do not follow the shape of the assumed discount factor curve cannot be explained and will appear as residuals. Hence, the steepening mechanism of the real market will be ignored in the factor loadings (overwritten by an arbitrary *a priori* assumption) and pushed into the residuals unexplained by the factors of the model.

In the second category, the factor loadings are extracted from the market: rather than making his own *a priori* assumptions about the factor loadings (i.e. market mechanisms), the analyst lets the market reveal its own dynamics and *then a posteriori interprets* the factor loadings. For our goal of seeing into the core of the actual market (rather than imposing our hypotheses on it), the second category is thus the right place to look.

PCA is the main representative of the second category: it forces the market to reveal its mechanisms under the form of uncorrelated linear factors but usually leaves enough freedom for the market to reveal its real dynamics within that formal framework. For example, the steepening mechanism (net of direction) of the market will show up in the second factor loading just as it is, revealing the actual market dynamics rather than overwriting them with *a priori* assumptions of the analyst. Consequently, market mechanisms will be visible in the factor loadings rather than pushed into the residuals.

PCA: MATHEMATICS

Since PCA is a tool from linear algebra, we first need to represent the market in the form of a matrix. The straightforward approach is therefore to express the structural information contained in the market under consideration in the form of a covariance matrix.[4]

Technical Points

- Market data should be of sufficient length to allow the parameters of the model to be estimated with sufficient accuracy.
- Depending on the goal of the analysis, either level or change data can be used as inputs.
- It is important to use the *covariance* rather than the *correlation* matrix since the difference in volatility (sensitivity) is a key element of the analysis and must not be netted out by using correlations.

Now that we have the market information in the form of a covariance *matrix*, we can extract information by applying the powerful tools of linear algebra, transforming the covariance matrix into the orthonormal basis of its eigenvectors.

---

[4]Obviously, we lose some statistical information in this step, in particular above the second order. However, in practice, this is seldom of relevance for the goals of relative value analysis.

Definition: If $Ax = \lambda x\,(x \neq 0)$, for a matrix A, then the vector x is called an eigenvector of A and the number λ is the associated eigenvalue of A.

Hence, an eigenvector does not change its direction, only its length, when the matrix is applied to it. For example, if A represents the rotation of a globe by 90 degrees, then the rotation axis through the two poles is an eigenvector with an associated eigenvalue of one. Another example: if one holds a ball with both hands and squeezes it, the line connecting both hands contains eigenvectors, whose associated eigenvalue is less than one.

Theorem: For every positive semi-definite covariance matrix[5] Cov, it is true that

$$Cov = B^{-1} \begin{pmatrix} \lambda_1 & 0 & 0 \\ 0 & \ddots & 0 \\ 0 & 0 & \lambda_n \end{pmatrix} B,$$

where λ_i are the eigenvalues of Cov and the columns of B consist of the eigenvectors of Cov.

Intuitive interpretation: The matrix B acts like a transformation of the coordinate system and allows us to consider the covariance matrix from the perspective of the orthonormal basis given by its eigenvectors. Since these eigenvectors are orthogonal, they decompose the covariance matrix into uncorrelated relationships. Moreover, the eigenvector associated with the greatest absolute eigenvalue points to the direction of the highest variation, that is, it represents the most important structural relationship in the market.

Example: $Cov = \begin{pmatrix} 7 & 3 \\ 3 & 2 \end{pmatrix}$ has the eigenvalues 8.4 and 0.6 with eigenvectors (e.g.) $\begin{pmatrix} 0.91 \\ 0.42 \end{pmatrix}$ and $\begin{pmatrix} -0.42 \\ 0.91 \end{pmatrix}$. Figure 3.2 shows the image of the unit circle under Cov and illustrates that most variation occurs along the direction of the first eigenvector.

---

[5]In fact, this theorem is true for every matrix that is symmetric and positive semi-definite.

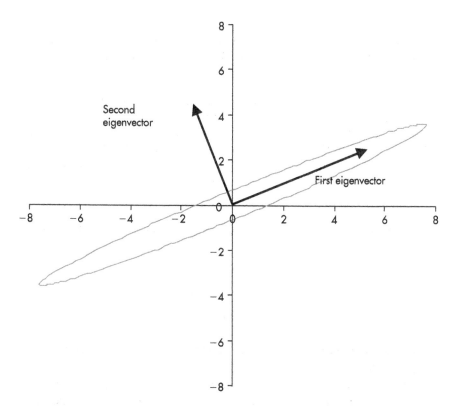

FIGURE 3.2 *Cov* and examples for its two eigenvectors.
Source: Authors.

Technical Point: Numerical Issues Involved in Eigenvalue Calculation

Eigenvalue calculation is famous for its numerical challenges. The main problem is to distinguish between two different eigenvalues and two slightly different numerical representations of the same eigenvalue. Since some of the eigenvalues tend to get very small when their number increases, this distinguishing becomes quite difficult for large covariance matrices and requires numerical representations with many digits and very high accuracy.

When an in-house PCA tool is required, the following hints could be useful:

- Scale the covariance matrix appropriately.
- Use a combination of numerical methods. In particular, since the largest eigenvalue is of crucial importance for the application of PCA to markets, confirm it through the Lanczos algorithm.

- Use as starting points for a Newton algorithm on the characteristic polynomial of the covariance matrix after a Householder transformation the following set of numbers: $a + 2 \cdot b \cdot \cos\left(i \cdot \frac{\pi}{n+1}\right)$ for $i = 1, \ldots, n$, with $a = \frac{1}{n}\sum_{i=1}^{n} a_i$, $b = \frac{1}{n-1}\sum_{i=2}^{n} b_i$ and with

$$\begin{pmatrix} a_1 & b_2 & 0 & 0 \\ b_2 & a_2 & \ddots & 0 \\ 0 & \ddots & \ddots & b_n \\ 0 & 0 & b_n & a_n \end{pmatrix}$$

being the Householder transformation of the covariance matrix.
- Additionally, run a systematic search for eigenvalues, whereby the largest eigenvalue found via the Lanczos algorithm determines the width of steps and range of starting points for the Newton algorithm.
- Run checks, whether the computed eigenvectors are really eigenvectors (i.e. fulfill $Ax = \lambda x$) and orthogonal to each other.

The PCA sheet on the website accompanying this book implements these tricks. However, also due to numerical restrictions of Excel, it reaches its limitations rather soon and should not be expected to work for larger covariance matrices.

PCA AS A FACTOR MODEL

PCA becomes a factor model by using the eigenvectors e_{ij} of the covariance matrix as factor loadings, that is by defining $f_{ij} := e_{ij}$, with the factor model being thus:

$$\begin{pmatrix} y_1^t \\ \vdots \\ y_n^t \end{pmatrix} = \sum_{i=1}^{n} \alpha_i^t \cdot \begin{pmatrix} e_{i1} \\ \vdots \\ e_{in} \end{pmatrix}$$

where $\begin{pmatrix} e_{i1} \\ \vdots \\ e_{in} \end{pmatrix}$ is the i-th eigenvector.

We sort the eigenvalues (and associated eigenvectors) by the percentage of total variation explained, that is

$$|\lambda_1| \geq |\lambda_2| \geq \cdots \geq |\lambda_n|$$

Hence, the first factor explains most of the market variation, the second explains most of the market variation not explained by the first factor, and so on. Correspondingly, the first factor loading, that is the first eigenvector, reveals the structure of the most important market mechanism, the second eigenvector the structure of the second most important, and so on. The importance of a market mechanism, that is the strength of its impact on the overall market variation, is quantified by the eigenvalues.

Technical Point

If x is an eigenvector of Cov, then for every $a \neq 0$, ax is also an eigenvector of Cov. Thus, for every eigenvalue, there exist infinitely many eigenvectors, pointing in the same direction (or, if $a < 0$, in the opposite direction), but of different length. Any one of those can be chosen as a factor loading, and there is no reason to prefer one over the other.

In the end, one needs to arbitrarily decide the length of a particular eigenvector. For example, eigenvectors often are scaled to have unit length. However, there still exist two eigenvectors, x and y, with length one, with $x = -y$. Again, there is no criterion to decide for one or the other and one has to arbitrarily choose one. However, it is therefore important for the analyst to conduct the analysis and interpret the results with the particular choices of eigenvectors in mind. For example, if rates are an increasing function of factor 1 when x is chosen as the eigenvector, then rates will be a decreasing function of factor 1 when $y = -x$ is chosen as the eigenvector. Many analysts have fallen into this trap, which can be avoided only by constantly remembering the eigenvectors. As in this example, factors are only meaningful when analyzed in conjunction with the factor loadings.

INSIGHT INTO MARKET MECHANISMS THROUGH INTERPRETATION OF THE EIGENVECTORS

So far, we have developed the mathematical framework for PCA. For the rest of the chapter, we will see how PCA reveals the inner structural relationships of the market and how it can be applied to trading.

For the following example, we use weekly data from 4 Jan 2010 to 3 Oct 2011 for generic Bund yields (yield level, not change) for two, five, seven and 10 years. The input data and the PCA can be seen in the PCA sheet accompanying this book. In the first step, the covariance matrix is calculated and depicted in Figure 3.3. While this is not a necessary step in the analytical process based

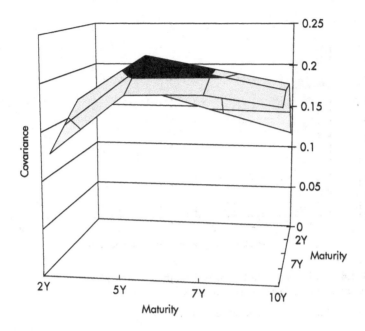

FIGURE 3.3 Covariance across the Bund yield curve.
Sources: data – Bloomberg; chart – Authors.

Data period: 4 Jan 2010 to 3 Oct 2011, weekly data.

on PCA, displaying and examining the covariance matrix (i.e. the input into a PCA) can already give an intuition about the market mechanisms (i.e. the output of a PCA). In Figure 3.3, we can observe an area of maximal covariance in the medium part of the yield curve.

Then, the information about the market (as represented in the covariance matrix) is extracted through a PCA. As with any factor model, the eigenvectors of the covariance matrix represent the structural relations and mechanisms between the data series, while the eigenvalues show the relative significance of these factors in explaining the behavior of the data.

A typical situation for the relative strength of the factors, as quantified by the relative size of their eigenvalues, is depicted in Figure 3.4. As can be seen in Figure 3.4 in the case of the Bund yield curve, the first factor explains more than 90% of the yield curve variation; and the first three factors together, almost everything. This means that basically the whole information the Bund market provides can be reduced to, captured, and expressed in three numbers (the first three factors), with the factor loadings translating the information between the full Bund market and the three factors (numbers) back and forth.

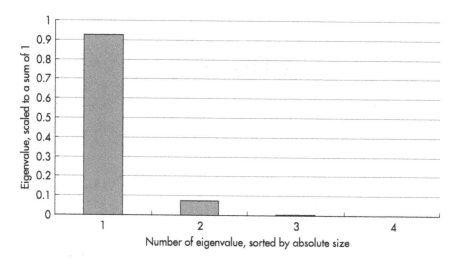

FIGURE 3.4   Scaled eigenvalues of a PCA on the Bund yield curve.
Sources: data – Bloomberg; chart – Authors.

Data period: 4 Jan 2010 to 3 Oct 2011, weekly data.

The next step to extract information about market mechanisms from a PCA is to examine the shape of the eigenvectors. The interpretation of the structural information contained in the eigenvectors can be done by applying the following scheme: if the i-th factor (α_i) increases by one, what happens to the rate curve? The answer to this question translates the market mechanisms from the mathematical language of eigenvectors of the covariance matrix into everyday terms.

In the following, we provide this interpretation for the first three eigenvectors of a PCA on the Bund curve, which are depicted in Figure 3.5. In this example, we find that a unit increase in the first factor corresponds to an increase in every point along the yield curve, since every entry in the first eigenvector has the same sign. Hence, we can interpret the first factor as representing the directional dynamics of the yield curve.

Moreover, the *shape* of the first eigenvector in Figure 3.5 represents the *shape* of directional moves: if α_1 increases by one, all yields increase, but medium yields (five-year, or 5Y) increase more than both short (2Y) and long (10Y) yields. This can be translated into everyday terms by saying that the pivotal point of directional moves of the yield curve is the 5Y area. We note that the output (eigenvector) of a PCA corresponds to the input (covariance matrix), with the shape of the first eigenvector reflecting the maximal covariance in the medium part of the yield curve we observed in Figure 3.3.

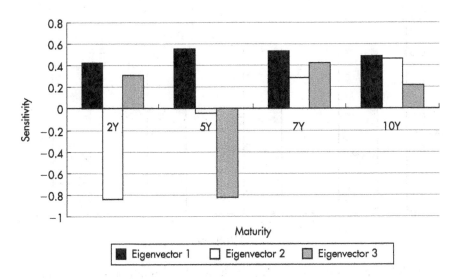

FIGURE 3.5 First three eigenvectors of a PCA on the Bund curve.
Sources: data – Bloomberg; chart – Authors.

Data period: 4 Jan 2010 to 3 Oct 2011, weekly data.

Now, let's compare this with the first eigenvector of a PCA on the Bund curve with data from 1993 to 1997, which is depicted in Figure 3.6. While for 5Y, 7Y, and 10Y the sensitivity is almost identical to the current situation, back in the 1990s, the sensitivity of 2Y yields was as high as that of 5Y yields (i.e. the market exhibited a bull-steepening/bear-flattening pattern). This is typical for a market with an active central bank driving the yield curve up and down, which corresponds to a higher sensitivity of shorter yields to directional moves, hence a higher entry in the first eigenvector. Thus, the decreasing activity of the central bank from the 1990s until 2011 (partly a function of rates approaching zero) is reflected by the decreasing sensitivity of 2Y yields to the first factor. Note how the mathematics (entry in eigenvector) corresponds to real economic mechanisms. Even if we did not know anything about central bank history, one look at the PCA results would reveal both the structural shift in market mechanisms (pivotal point of directional moves shifting from the short end to the medium curve sector) and its likely source. Also note the stability displayed by the eigenvector over 20 years (apart from the short end), which we shall analyze in more detail later in this chapter.

Furthermore, note the difference to the approach of a factor model in the first category, like the NS model: rather than *assuming a priori* that direction is the strongest market dynamic, the market reveals that this is the case for this

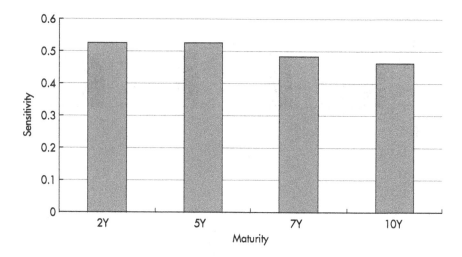

FIGURE 3.6   First eigenvector of a PCA on the Bund curve with data from 1993 to 1997.
Sources: data – Bloomberg; chart – Authors.

Data period: 1 Jan 1993 to 31 Dec 1997, weekly data.

particular market segment. And contrary to the *a priori* assumption of parallel shifts in the NS model, it shows that the real directional market mechanism follows a 2Y-5Y bear-steepening/5Y-10Y bear-flattening shape.

Also, together with the information about the eigenvalues shown in Figure 3.4, we have found (rather than assumed) that directional market mechanisms have indeed the strongest impact on the yield curve and can quantify their strength relative to other factors. Moreover, we could compare the strength of directional mechanisms in different markets and how it evolves over time by following the evolution of the scaled first eigenvalue. Interestingly, we found that the development of markets is characterized by a decreasing scaled first eigenvalue. In undeveloped markets, almost 100% of the action is explained by one single variable (direction), while increasing sophistication results in other mechanisms gaining strength. For example, while around the year 2000 the Indian domestic bond market had a scaled first eigenvalue of virtually one, it has now decreased to levels more in line with Western government bond markets, reflecting its increasing development. The Indian MIFOR–MIBOR basis swap market, on the other hand, has always been similar to the Bund market depicted in Figure 3.4. This could be interpreted as evidence that the basis swap market has induced the development of the domestic Indian bond market. In a sense, the scaled first eigenvalue is a universal (reverse) indicator of the sophistication of a market, allowing comparisons over space and time.

Moving on with the interpretation to the second eigenvector, if α_2 increases by one, short yields decrease and long yields increase. Thus, the second factor represents the slope element of the curve that is not explained by the first factor (i.e. by directional impacts on the slope). This is due to the entries in the second eigenvector crossing the x-axis once. Again, the shape of the second eigenvector reveals and quantifies the shape of steepening moves.

And if α_3 increases by one, short yields increase, medium yields decrease, and long yields increase, which we interpret as the curvature dynamics of the curve (not explained by the first and second factors). This corresponds to the entries in the third eigenvector crossing the x-axis twice.

These results are typical, with the i-th eigenvector crossing the x-axis $i - 1$ times.[6] However, it is not always the case, as in a particular market steepening moves could explain more of the overall yield curve variation than directional moves. Sometimes, no reasonable interpretation is possible at all, which could indicate that modeling this particular market through PCA is not useful. An advantage of PCA versus factor models falling into the first category is that it reveals these issues as they are, including cautioning against its own use when appropriate.

APPLYING EIGENVECTOR INTERPRETATION IN DIFFERENT MARKETS

Statistical models like PCA require no specific knowledge about the instrument that is being modeled and hence are universally applicable. PCA only needs to know the time series, not whether the time series represents yields, swap spreads, or volatilities, or what drives that time series. Thus, the range of its possible applications is far larger than the yield curve example we have been using so far. In fact, interpretation of eigenvectors may become less predictable and straightforward, hence more interesting and revealing, when PCA is applied to other markets. Here, we illustrate the use of PCA in a number of different contexts, starting with volatility data as input variables.

The two-dimensional surface of at-the-money-forward (ATMF) volatilities (or, if skew is considered as well, the three-dimensional volatility cube) must first be transformed into a one-dimensional vector. After the PCA is conducted, the outcome in vector form can be displayed again in a two-dimensional format. The complete results are discussed in detail in Chapter 19, from which we pick the chart of the second eigenvector as a typical result in Figure 3.7.

Usually, the first factor represents the overall level of volatility, the second factor differentiates across expiry, and the third one across underlying swap

---

[6]One can back up this statement theoretically by linking PCA to a Fourier analysis.

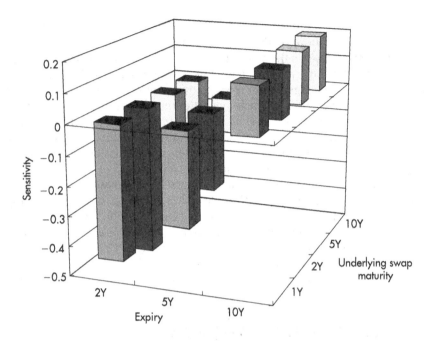

FIGURE 3.7 Second eigenvector of a PCA of the vega sector of the JPY implied volatility surface.
Sources: data – Bloomberg; chart – Authors.

Data period: 5 Jan 2009 to 19 Sep 2011, weekly data.

maturity of the options. However, the second and third factors sometimes change place (i.e. the differentiation across underlying maturity explains more of the overall variation of the volatility surface than the differentiation across expiry). Thus, PCA decomposes the volatility surface into its two dimensions (expiry and underlying swap maturity), with the first factor affecting both dimensions and the second and third factors reflecting the dimension-specific information.

When the number of instruments in the data set increases, as in the case of volatility analysis, the ability of PCA to reduce the dimensionality of the data becomes increasingly important. One can use that ability to detect relationships in large data sets. One tool supporting this process is cluster analysis, which depicts each instrument as a function of its sensitivity to various factors (typically the first and second, as in Figure 3.8[7]). If the first and second

---

[7]Note that the input data for Figure 3.8 consist of the whole volatility surface, while for Figure 3.7 only options with an expiry of at least 2Y are used. The reason for this is explained in Chapter 19. As there are two different PCAs behind the two charts, the sensitivities to factor 2 displayed in Figure 3.7 and Figure 3.8 are also different.

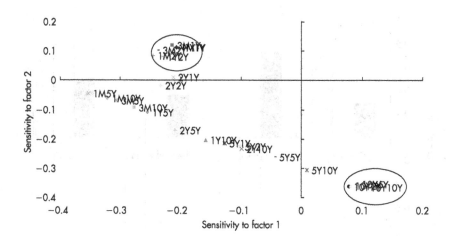

FIGURE 3.8   Example for a cluster analysis of the whole JPY volatility surface.
Sources: data – Bloomberg; chart – Authors.

Data period: 5 Jan 2009 to 19 Sep 2011, weekly data.

eigenvalues are large relative to the others, then the behavior of an instrument will be largely determined by its sensitivity to the first and second factors. Thus, if two instruments have similar sensitivities to the first and second factors (i.e. they are close to each other in Figure 3.8), they can be expected to behave similarly (i.e. to form a "cluster"). In the example in Figure 3.8, we can observe two clusters: one containing all options with both short expiries and short underlying swap maturities and the other containing all options with both long expiries and long underlying swap maturities. We therefore conclude that volatilities at both ends of the diagonal of the volatility surface usually move closely together, while further away from those two corners of the volatility surface, options behave more individually. The same sort of analysis can be applied to other combinations and numbers of factors as well, for example, by forming three-dimensional clusters of the first three sensitivities.

In Chapter 13, we shall use PCA to gain insights into the structure of various credit default swap (CDS) markets. Picking one result as an example, Figure 3.9 shows the first three eigenvectors of a PCA with the 5Y CDS quotes of sovereign issuers in the core Eurozone as input. The first eigenvector (in which all entries are positive) represents the overall level of Eurozone CDS quotes, with the sensitivities measuring the impact a general widening of Eurozone CDS quotes has on individual countries: it affects France more than Austria, Austria more than the Netherlands, and the Netherlands more

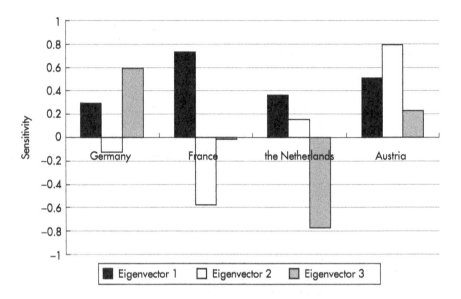

FIGURE 3.9   First three eigenvectors of a PCA on 5Y CDS for core Eurozone sovereign issuers.
Sources: data – Bloomberg; chart – Authors.

Data period: 6 May 2009 to 26 Sep 2012, weekly data.

than Germany. The second eigenvector groups together Germany and France (negative sensitivities) versus the Netherlands and Austria (positive sensitivities). Thus, if factor 2 increases, the CDS of the small core countries widen relative to the CDS of the big core countries. Therefore, factor 2 can be interpreted as differentiating between the big and small countries in the core Eurozone. This means that the size of the bond market is the second-most-important determining factor of core Eurozone countries' CDS levels (after the overall CDS level as measured by factor 1).

For an example from the commodity market we have run a PCA on weekly data for the front month contract on the three soy-related series (soybeans, soybean meal, and soybean oil) from 2000 onward. The scaled eigenvalues shown in Figure 3.10 indicate that almost everything is explained by factor 1, with factor 2 having only 0.2% of explanatory power and factor 3 virtually nothing. This indicates that differentiation across the three soy products is limited relative to the variability of the overall price changes in the three commodities.

Figure 3.11 displays the eigenvectors. Note that the difference in sensitivities to the first factor is a function of the difference in the size of the

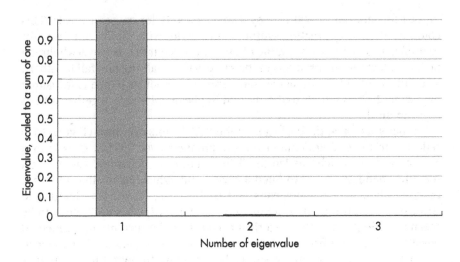

FIGURE 3.10   Scaled eigenvalues of a PCA on the soy market.
Sources: data – Bloomberg; chart – Authors.

Data period: 3 Jan 2000 to 6 Aug 2012, weekly data.

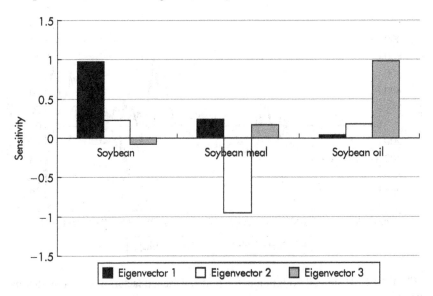

FIGURE 3.11   Eigenvectors of a PCA on the soy market.
Sources: data – Bloomberg; chart – Authors.

Data period: 3 Jan 2000 to 6 Aug 2012, weekly data.

input numbers (e.g. 1,600 for soybeans versus 51 for soybean meal). This could be avoided by creating synthetic time series with similar numbers, for example, all starting with a value of one. It turns out that the overwhelming factor 1 affects all soy products in the same way (i.e. all rise and fall together). The (little) differentiation between different soy products which is measured by factor 2 shows that soybeans and soybean oil move together versus soybean meal.

Finally, a look at the evolution of the PCA factors over time (Figure 3.12) reflects the increasing demand for soy products over the last decade in a rise of factor 1, which has led to all three products richening. Factor 2, on the other hand, has not exhibited a clear trend, which means that the price differentiation between soybeans and soybean oil, on the one hand, and soybean meal, on the other, tends to be temporary (i.e. factor 2 tends to be mean reverting). From this historical perspective, the current unprecedented deviation of factor 2 from its mean could be seen as a good trading opportunity. Factor 2 being too low (historically) translates through the sensitivities to eigenvector 2 in soybean meal being too expensive versus soybeans and soybean oil. Hence, a low factor 2 reflects the relative richness of soybean meal versus other soy products.

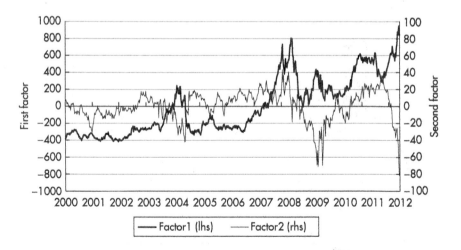

FIGURE 3.12   Historical evolution of the first and second factors of a PCA on the soy market.

Sources: data – Bloomberg; chart – Authors.

Data period: 3 Jan 2000 to 6 Aug 2012, weekly data.

Up until this point, the analysis has been purely statistical, revealing the driving forces of historical and current pricing. This provides a good basis for a trading decision, which needs to incorporate elements besides statistical properties as well. For example, is the current deviation of factor 2 an outlier that can be expected to revert to mean as quickly as it did in the past? Or is there a potential for the current drought to cause a permanent regime shift in the soy markets? While this assessment is beyond the reach of statistics, PCA both enables us to detect and formulate these trading decisions and indicates that any cause for a permanent regime shift would need to be extraordinarily strong – stronger than anything that has happened over the past decade. Thus, PCA shows that arguing for a regime change (i.e. for no reversion of factor 2 to the longstanding mean) would require very good reasons.

An investor believing in the current drought not to be such an extraordinary regime-changing event and thus in factor 2 continuing its decade-long behavior and returning to its mean may therefore want to consider selling soybean meal versus either soybeans or soybean oil. Which of the two is better? And precisely how much should be bought for one short soybean meal futures contract? The answer to these questions is again within the realm of statistics. Given the much stronger impact of factor 1 on the soy market, there is actually a high risk that a position that intends to exploit the current mismatch in factor 2 could end up being driven mainly by factor 1 and not 2 (i.e. overall direction of soy, not the spreads between different soy products), if hedge ratios are not calculated properly. Subsequently, we shall develop PCA into tools that answer these questions.

These examples could serve to give an impression of the analytical strength of PCA, thereby empirically proving our claim that PCA is a very useful tool for the relative value craftsman to dig out and clarify the key market mechanisms hidden below a muddy surface of incommensurable market actions.

So far, we have used PCA to gain insights into the structural core of markets. From now on, we shall focus on applying these insights to find, analyze, and construct trading ideas. This will take place in the framework of PCA and thus show the way PCA supports the translation of its insights into practical trading positions.

DECOMPOSING MARKETS INTO UNCORRELATED FACTORS

As the eigenvectors are orthogonal, the factors are uncorrelated by construction. Hence, one can decompose a complex market into individual, uncorrelated, and simple relationships. This ability is the key to a variety of analyses.

Technical Points

- Factors are uncorrelated, not necessarily independent. This issue has led to the development of independent component analysis recently, though we have not seen a convincing application to market analysis yet.
- While factors are uncorrelated over the whole sample period, there can occur significant measured correlation within subperiods. Thus, the rolling correlation of factors should be investigated before relying on the model. This is a key point, which we shall discuss in detail toward the end of this chapter.

The decomposition into uncorrelated factors isolates a particular relationship from others. This makes it possible to analyze and trade individual market mechanisms, such as yield curve steepness, without being influenced by other effects, such as direction.[8] The most important application of this ability is the exclusion of directional effects (typically associated with the factor with the greatest explanatory power). If relative value trades are defined as offering return opportunities that are uncorrelated to market direction, then the ability of PCA to produce and analyze time series uncorrelated with market direction is a key aspect of the analysis.[9] In other words, if the first factor represents the market direction (beta), then alpha (P&L uncorrelated to the market direction) can be found in the other factors.

Using the example of the Bund yield curve from Figure 3.5, the second factor has been interpreted as explaining the steepness not explained by the first, directional factor (i.e. representing the *non-directional steepness*). Note that also the first factor has a steepness component (i.e. direction impacts steepness). If yields increase, the 5Y-10Y yield curve tends to flatten. The second factor is uncorrelated to direction *and to directional impacts on the steepness* and therefore shows the steepness of the curve *net* of directional impacts.

To repeat this key point: given the current yield level, the curve should have a certain steepness, given by the first eigenvector. The second factor shows the steepness of the curve that remains after taking into account the

---

[8]This requires the assumption that the future curve dynamic will be the same as the current curve dynamic expressed in PCA eigenvectors. Toward the end of this chapter we shall investigate the validity of this assumption.

[9]Likewise, one could use the same techniques to analyze and execute trading positions, which are uncorrelated to, for example, non-directional steepness (represented here by the second factor). However, in practice, most of the time the main concern will be to prevent the all-pervasive directional effects from influencing relative value positions, in other words to create alpha.

steepness already explained by the direction. There were many instances in which the 5Y-10Y yield curve has been steep but in which the steepness was due entirely to the low yield level, while on a non-directional basis the curve was actually too flat. In this case, one could argue for a non-directional steepening trade hedged against directional impacts, despite the steepness of the 5Y-10Y curve.

This example illustrates the importance of factor decomposition for RV analysis:

- Given the all-pervasive directional effects (e.g. on curve steepness, curvature, swap spreads, volatility) the indispensable prerequisite for any RV analysis is a measure for steepness or curvature *unaffected* by directional effects. The second and third factors provide that measure and thus the *starting point* for any RV analysis.
- As the first eigenvector shows the way yield levels affect slope, we can hedge against these effects, thereby formulating RV trades with no directional exposure.
- PCA is thus a direct way to gain access to true RV trades and thereby to much more trading, sales, and research opportunities than straight directional positions. Simply put, by using a three-factor model, one obtains three uncorrelated time series and thus three times as many possibilities for trades.

EMBEDDING PCA IN TRADE IDEAS

So far, we have discovered two important features of PCA: its ability to decompose a market into uncorrelated factors and the possibility of interpreting these factors economically (via examining the shape of the eigenvectors).[10] Together, PCA decomposes a market into uncorrelated factors with an economic meaning.

The process of taking a view on the market therefore can be achieved by taking a view on each of the factors. Hence, for each factor, the analyst can decide independently whether to take a view on that factor. His decision should reflect:

- statistical criteria like mean reversion
- fundamental and structural criteria
- flow and other concerns.

---

[10]While the shape of the eigenvector always allows an economic interpretation of the factors such as "yield curve steepness," it may not always be possible to link each of the factors with an obvious and specific macroeconomic variable such as "inflation." In fact, the latter relationship will be the subject of a heuristic regression below.

A key benefit of PCA is that it links all those criteria (separately for each of the separate factors). PCA factors are not only mean reverting but often also have a meaningful economic interpretation. Hence, they do not only fulfill the desired statistical properties but also reveal (in fundamental terms) *why* they have those properties. For example, knowing that the first factor is linked to GDP growth explains its mean reversion by the business cycles and its slow speed of mean reversion by the length of those cycles.

Hence, PCA decomposes the market into uncorrelated mean-reverting factors, which often carry an economic meaning. In other words, PCA allows us to combine statistical analysis with economic analysis so as to associate statistical features of a trade with particular fundamental considerations. For example, the second factor may be negatively correlated to the EUR exchange rate. In this case, a statistically attractive steepening trade looks even more appealing to an investor if he expects the EUR to weaken for fundamental reasons.

While statistical analysis is by construction backward-looking, linking it to fundamental variables enables traders to incorporate forward-looking (economic) expectations. This ability to incorporate potential future risks in the analysis is a key benefit of linking statistics to external driving forces. In the example above, a steepening trade may well look statistically attractive, but this could all be due to EUR strength. Thus, a further EUR strengthening, which may be caused by political decisions independent of any statistical properties, is a risk to the trade. The link of statistics through a PCA to these external driving forces can identify these risks. An analyst knowing that the statistically attractive steepness is due to EUR strength will refrain from the trade if he sees a significant risk for further EUR appreciation. As in this example, outside information about macroeconomic events can help with both explaining some observed statistical properties and incorporating forward-looking information into the analysis.

The general form of this analysis is to investigate the following link, (e.g. via a regression):

Factor ~ External explaining variable(s)

While by construction this type of analysis is outside of the statistical reach of PCA, PCA both *enables* this analysis by generating the dependent variable and *facilitates* the search for relevant external explaining variables by revealing the meaning of its factors. One could investigate the link to external variables by heuristic methods, for example, by trying all available financial time series in a regression table against all factors. Note that some financial time series could be trending and therefore not suitable for a regression.[11] The interpretation of

---

[11] Over the time period used for Table 3.1, the independent variables – including the S&P500, EUR, and Oil – did not exhibit a significant trend and are therefore included. Of course, this could be different over other time periods.

TABLE 3.1   Correlations of the First Three Factors of a PCA on the Bund Yield Curve versus Candidates for External Explaining Variables

	Factor 1	Factor 2	Factor 3
Factor 1 of a PCA on USD swaps	0.73	0.62	−0.10
Factor 2 of a PCA on USD swaps	0.89	0.40	−0.02
Factor 3 of a PCA on USD swaps	−0.21	−0.59	0.31
5Y Bund vol (6M rolling)	−0.52	−0.65	0.03
S&P500	0.60	−0.55	0.11
VIX	−0.72	0.01	−0.16
EUR FX rate	0.44	−0.63	−0.23
Oil	0.58	−0.63	0.08

the eigenvectors can facilitate the search for the "right" explanatory variables. As these relationships evolve, we recommend monitoring them over time, for example, via rolling correlations. For the example of a PCA on the Bund yield curve, the correlations versus some candidates for external driving forces[12] are summarized in Table 3.1.

It can be seen that both factor 1 and factor 2 are significantly influenced by a number of macroeconomic variables. We note in particular the strong link to the US yield curve (as represented by the factors of a PCA) with the surprising fact that factor 1 of the Bund PCA is most correlated to factor 2 of the USD PCA and factor 2 of the Bund PCA to factor 1 of the USD PCA. This could be the starting point for a further investigation, which may reveal interesting differences in the driving forces of global bond markets and their interconnections. Furthermore, the link between factor 2 and currencies as well as commodities jumps out at you, indicating that further analysis may well yield valuable results. Factor 3, on the other hand, seems to be rather uncorrelated to external driving forces. This could indicate that factor 3 is a relatively "pure" relative value factor (i.e. with little correlation to macroeconomic events). This is a typical result, that is, while the lower factors often exhibit a high correlation to macroeconomic variables (reflecting the high impact of economic events on markets), higher factors are usually less correlated. As a rule of thumb, the higher the factor, the more weight statistical analysis carries, while the examination of potential external economic risks and the incorporation of forward-looking analysis described above become less important.

---

[12]Additionally, economic variables like inflation or GDP (growth) could be included. However, given the low frequency of these data (e.g. quarterly), it is statistically meaningful only for time series spanning several years, not in the current example, which has less than two years of data.

As an alternative to the regression of PCA factors versus explaining variables, which is done outside of the PCA itself, one could also include the candidates for explaining variables in the PCA, for example, by running a PCA on input data consisting of time series for Bund yields and USD swap rates simultaneously.

Furthermore, PCA may reveal how flows affect the pricing. For example, how much does the k-factor residual for 5Y rates move when a new 5Y bond is issued? Is this a stable pattern? Is the spike linearly dependent on the issuance size? This allows traders to incorporate more technical issues into the framework of a PCA.

Let's see how the ability of PCA to decompose the Bund yield curve into economically meaningful uncorrelated and statistically mean-reverting factors could support finding trade ideas in practice. Figure 3.13 shows the evolution of the first three factors of the Bund yield curve over time.

Using mean reversion models, we can assess for all factors the distance from their long-run means and the speed with which they are likely to return to these means. In our current example, we may conclude that factor 1 has insufficient speed of mean reversion and thus we take no view. Similarly, factor 2 is relatively close to its mean, so we take no view. Factor 3, however, seems to be considerably away from its mean and to have a high speed of mean reversion. Hence, we decide to investigate further for trade ideas based on factor 3 (i.e. butterflies hedged against factors 1 and 2).

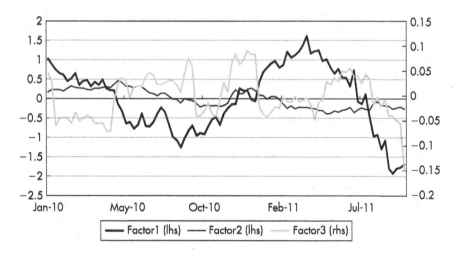

FIGURE 3.13 History of the first three factors of a PCA on the Bund yield curve. *Sources:* data – Bloomberg; chart – Authors.

Data period: 4 Jan 2010 to 3 Oct 2011, weekly data.

The statistical side of that investigation is done by a formal mean reversion model, which can calculate the expected return and risk attributes of various trades for specific time horizons.

Factor 3 has little exposure to economic variables and can thus be treated as a "pure" relative value play on mean reversion, with little risk of its statistical properties being thrown off track by macroeconomic events. In this case, the regression Table 3.1 can serve as justification for restricting the analysis to statistics.

If we took a view on factor 1, on the other hand, we would need to consider the link of the time series of factor 1 and its statistical properties to its external driving forces. Since we found factor 1 to be positively correlated to USD rates and negatively to volatility, among others, the spike in the VIX on 3 Oct 2011 could help us understand the current statistical deviation from the mean. And if we thought that volatility was going to decrease again soon (e.g. because we expected the ECB to calm fears about the euro crisis), we would have both a statistical (mean reversion) and a fundamental reason to bet on an increase in factor 1. Conversely, the mean reversion of factor 1 (as given by statistics) certainly supports our fundamental expectation for volatility to decrease again (i.e. for the current point to be an outlier, i.e. a good entry opportunity). Additionally, one could run a regression between the VIX and factor 1 and decide via the current residual whether the fundamental expectation of decreasing volatility would be better expressed by a short option or a short Bund position.

As in this example, PCA guides the analyst through the process of taking informed views (or the informed absence of a view) on each of the uncorrelated factors: it reveals the statistical properties and economic meaning of each factor behind a position and gives thereby a good basis for a reasonable and substantiated decision, separately for each factor, whether or not to take a view on it.

Once the analyst has decided on which factors he wants to take a view, PCA does both jobs that are needed to execute that view via the most suitable position:

- PCA provides the hedge ratios to immunize against exposure to factors to which he does not want to be exposed.
- The $(n - 1)$-factor residuals indicate those individual instruments that provide the best execution for his view on factor n. This can also be used to apply PCA for general asset selection purposes.

In the following, we will develop these features of PCA, before we integrate them back into the process of finding and analyzing trades.

APPROPRIATE HEDGING

PCA not only breaks down the driving forces of a trade (like a 5Y-10Y steepening position) into uncorrelated factors but also quantifies their impact and thereby allows us to hedge against specific factors. In order to create a 5Y-10Y steepening position which is not affected by the first factor (i.e. by direction and by directional impacts on the slope), we can simply see how changes in the first factor impact 5Y and 10Y yields and choose the hedge ratios in such a way that both net out. This leaves a position, which is hedged against changes in the first factor, that is, a steepening trade which is only affected by the non-directional steepness (and higher factors like curvature), not by directional impacts on the curve and thus a source of P&L uncorrelated to market direction (alpha).

In the PCA framework, hedge ratios are calculated in order to immunize a portfolio against changes in factors. In order to execute the non-directional 5Y-10Y steepening position of the example above, we need to hedge against changes in the directional factor α_1, and the ratio of notionals for 5Y and 10Y is thus:

$$\frac{n_5}{n_{10}} = \frac{BPV_{10}}{BPV_5} \cdot \frac{e_{110}}{e_{15}}.$$

In the formula above, the ratio $\frac{e_{110}}{e_{15}}$ represents the quotient of 10Y and 5Y sensitivities to changes in the first factor. This may sound similar to the "beta-adjustment" of basis point value (BPV) hedge ratios by the slope of the regression line of a regression between the two instruments involved. However, as a regression minimizes the *conditional* expected value of deviations, it is conceptually quite different from a PCA. This is reflected in the practical problem that, unless the correlation is 1 or −1, the hedge ratio determined by beta adjustment changes when the dependent and independent variable in the regression are exchanged. PCA works without conditional expected values and is hence free from this problem.

Hedge ratios against more factors are best calculated via matrix inversion. For example, the hedge ratio for a 2Y-5Y-10Y butterfly which is neutral to changes in the first and second factor can be calculated for a given notional n_5 for 5Y by:

$$\begin{pmatrix} n_2 \\ n_{10} \end{pmatrix} = \begin{pmatrix} BPV_2 \cdot e_{12} & BPV_{10} \cdot e_{110} \\ BPV_2 \cdot e_{22} & BPV_{10} \cdot e_{210} \end{pmatrix}^{-1} \cdot \begin{pmatrix} -n_5 \cdot BPV_5 \cdot e_{15} \\ -n_5 \cdot BPV_5 \cdot e_{25} \end{pmatrix}$$

We argue that hedge ratios should be based on PCA rather than on BPV neutrality. BPV neutrality corresponds to assuming arbitrarily that all entries in the first eigenvector are the same (which is in fact our very crude example for a factor model of the first category at the beginning of this chapter). The market tells us that they are not. In other words, directional shifts do affect different points on the yield curve in different ways. If the 5Y Bund yield increases by one basis point (bp), the 10Y yield is expected to increase by 0.87 bp. True neutrality with respect to the level of yields needs to take these impacts of the direction on the curve shape into account by using hedge ratios based on PCA eigenvectors. By contrast, BPV neutrality results in positions with directional exposure.

To illustrate our point, we have regressed a BPV-neutral weighted 2Y-5Y-7Y butterfly and a PCA-neutral weighted 2Y-5Y-7Y butterfly on the Bund curve against the first factor (representing directionality), the second factor (representing non-directional steepness), and the third factor (representing curvature net of the impacts of the first and second factors on curvature, i.e. net of the impacts of direction and of non-directional steepness on curvature[13]). The results are depicted in Figure 3.14. It turns out that the BPV-neutral butterfly is not only directional but also provides little exposure to the third factor. Hence, by choosing BPV-neutral weights for a 2Y-5Y-7Y butterfly, the investor ends up with a fuzzy exposure to direction, non-directional steepness, and just a bit of net curvature. Given the strength of directional impacts, virtually all of his performance will be driven by the market direction, thus transacting Bund futures would have resulted in almost the same exposure (with fewer costs and a cleaner understanding of the risk profile). Presumably, he wanted to be exposed to factor 3 rather than a fuzzy combination of risks; however, by BPV-neutral weighting, he lost almost all net curvature exposure and ended up with a risk profile he probably did not even know of (because PCA is needed for the decomposition into factors) and is now heavily dependent on the market direction against which he thinks he is "hedged." Note that this example is still benign in the sense that at least the correlation of the BPV-neutral butterfly to the third factor is positive. However, this does not need to be the case and there are instances where BPV-neutral steepeners are actually non-directional *flatteners*. Thus, BPV-neutral "hedging" may give any exposure, by chance the right one, a completely different one (like in the butterfly example above, which is mainly dependent on factor 1 rather than 3), or even an exposure which is opposite to the intended one. Only PCA allows the decomposition of the exposure into its components – and hence also the calculation of the "right" hedge ratio (i.e. the one leaving only the desired exposure).

---

[13]These verbal monstrosities are the translation of mathematical factor decomposition into everyday terms.

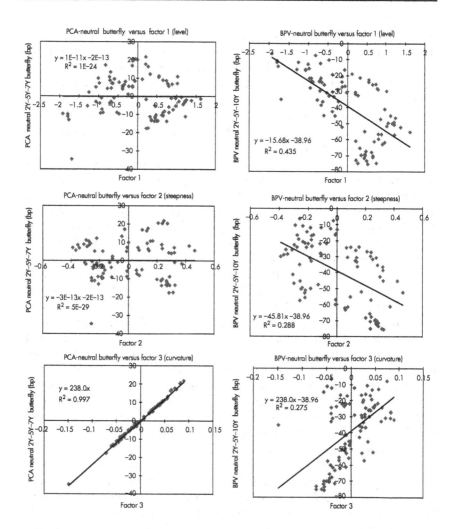

FIGURE 3.14 Driving forces of a BPV-neutral and a PCA-neutral 2Y-5Y-7Y butterfly on the Bund curve.

Sources: data – Bloomberg; chart – Authors.

Data period: 4 Jan 2010 to 3 Oct 2011, weekly data.

This is depicted in Figure 3.14 in the regression charts of the PCA-neutral butterfly, which is fully exposed to the net curvature (factor 3). Further, this is the only factor to which the PCA-neutral butterfly is exposed.[14] Hence, only the PCA hedge produces a position with a clean and clear exposure to precisely those factors, to which an exposure is intended.

Note the difference of goals in PCA-neutral hedging and hedge ratios, which are calculated in order to maximize Sharpe ratios. While hedge ratios determined by maximizing Sharpe ratios (or another desired feature) obviously have the best statistical properties, PCA-neutral positions give a clear picture, to which factors a trade is exposed. And since these factors often have a meaningful economic interpretation, the investor can assess and adjust his risk profile in economic terms. For example, he knows that the PCA-neutral butterfly is hedged against directional impacts on the yield curve. One cannot say that statistically optimized hedge ratios or PCA-neutral hedge ratios are "better", they just achieve different goals by construction: statistical optimality of a position or a position with a clear exposure to economically interpretable variables. In a manner of speaking, the investor choosing PCA-neutral hedge ratios rather than those optimizing Sharpe ratios gives up some statistical benefits in order to gain the confidence of knowing the exposure of his trade in economic terms, for example, the confidence of knowing that it is immune from directional impacts.

ANALYZING THE EXPOSURE OF TRADING POSITIONS AND INVESTMENT PORTFOLIOS

Just as in the example of Figure 3.14, any position can be regressed against the uncorrelated factors of a PCA. Thereby, its driving forces reveal themselves. This gives a clear picture of what really impacts the P&L of complex trades. For those investors using BPV-neutral hedging, the result can be quite surprising, as in the example above. Fortunately, if the actual exposure turns out to be different from the desired one, applying the appropriate PCA hedge ratios solves the problem.

For example, if a market maker has just transacted a BPV-neutral 2Y-5Y-7Y butterfly with an investor, he could run the regressions from above,

---

[14]In fact, it is also exposed to factors 4 and higher, but they have much less impact on the overall yield curve variation (and butterfly trade performance) than factor 3 does. The crucial point is to hedge against all factors of lower order than the one to which exposure is wanted.

find that he is now exposed 44% to factor 1, 29% to factor 2, and 28% to factor 3, see how this nets out with other positions in his portfolio and initiate the appropriate hedging (against those factors to which he does not want to be exposed).

Moreover, basing analysis on orthogonal eigenvectors "orthogonalizes" the mind of analysts. It helps us provide a clean and clear analysis. Which trade is exposed to which factors? Do I like that exposure or not? If not, how can I hedge against it? Do I recommend a butterfly due to its directionality or due to its curvature exposure? This breakdown of any trade into its uncorrelated driving forces prevents the all-too-common mix-up of arguments, for example, an analyst arguing via curvature for a butterfly while it has, in fact, a purely directional exposure.

Market Reconstruction and Forecasting

Reversing the decomposition of a complex market into its uncorrelated components, factor models in general allow an approximate reconstruction of the larger market from a limited number of factors.

And among all factor models, PCA does the best job in that it provides the closest possible reconstruction to reality, given limited information. This is the basis for a variety of applications, a couple of which we briefly highlight now.

Often, market participants are interested in knowing how a certain event would impact the overall market. For example, how would the yield curve be expected to react if CPI were to increase by 1%? Or what would it mean for the yield curve, if 2Y Bund yields increased by 25 bp? In mathematical terms, this corresponds to reconstructing the whole set of information (yield curve) from one single piece of information (short rates go up by 25 bp). The first eigenvector contains just this transformation, as it translates the movement of one point on the yield curve into the move of the whole curve. Using the sensitivities of Figure 3.5, an increase of 2Y yields by 25 bp would be associated with 5Y yields rising by 33 bp, 7Y by 24 bp, and 10Y by 23 bp on average. These numbers are given by multiplying 25 bp with the ratio of sensitivities to the first factor, just as in the calculation of PCA hedge ratios. Since by construction, the first factor contains maximum information, the PCA reconstruction minimizes the residuals (i.e. provides the best possible picture of the overall market, given the informational constraints).

If the reaction of the yield curve to external driving forces should be estimated, the change of an external variable can in a first step be translated via a regression into changes of factors and then the yield curve can be reconstructed from those factors. For example, a change in the EUR FX rate affects all three factors of a PCA on the Bund curve (see regression Table 3.1). Thus, the impact of a one-point change in the EUR FX rate on the whole Bund yield curve can be assessed by calculating its impact on the first three factors (via a regression) and then reconstructing the whole yield curve from those factors.

A similar method can be used to hedge and price trading books. Imagine that since the last close, Schatz, Bobl, and Bund futures have moved by 2, 3, and 2 bp respectively. Now, a client asks a trader to buy an illiquid 7Y Bund, in which no market action has occurred since the last close, from him. The best hedge the trader can achieve in that situation is to reconstruct the yield curve (or only the 7Y point) from the information about the 2Y, 5Y, and 10Y points via the first three factors of a PCA and hedge his position in an illiquid 7Y Bund via a combination of Schatz, Bobl, and Bund futures. The hedge ratios are calculated as described above in order to achieve neutrality against the first three factors. Again, given the constraints (just three liquid instruments), this is the best hedge possible (i.e. it has smallest residual to the actual moves of the 7Y Bund).

A Yield Curve Model Based on PCA

PCA is a deterministic linear algebra tool that simply transforms the basis of the covariance matrix without introducing any stochastic process. Correspondingly, if there are n input variables, PCA will return n factors ($k = n$), and the PCA model outlined above has no residual.

One can now *artificially* introduce a residual by redefining factors as residuals. With

$$\begin{pmatrix} \varepsilon_1^t \\ \vdots \\ \varepsilon_n^t \end{pmatrix} := \sum_{i=k+1}^{n} \alpha_i^t \cdot \begin{pmatrix} e_{i1} \\ \vdots \\ e_{in} \end{pmatrix},$$

the PCA model

$$\begin{pmatrix} y_1^t \\ \vdots \\ y_n^t \end{pmatrix} = \sum_{i=1}^{n} \alpha_i^t \cdot \begin{pmatrix} e_{i1} \\ \vdots \\ e_{in} \end{pmatrix}$$

becomes

$$\begin{pmatrix} y_1^t \\ \vdots \\ y_n^t \end{pmatrix} = \sum_{i=1}^{k} \alpha_i^t \cdot \begin{pmatrix} e_{i1} \\ \vdots \\ e_{in} \end{pmatrix} + \begin{pmatrix} \varepsilon_1^t \\ \vdots \\ \varepsilon_n^t \end{pmatrix}$$

and now *looks like* a k-factor stochastic yield curve model.

This specific approach has two important consequences. First, the analyst can decide the number of factors to use for a PCA-based model. There is no argument that forces him to limit the factor decomposition to two, three, or seven factors. Hence, he can choose the number of factors freely in his model. He will typically base his choice on the goal of the analysis and the structure of the eigenvalues. In particular, external knowledge about market mechanisms can be introduced via the selection of the number of factors. If, for example, in the process of eigenvector interpretation it turns out that the yield curve is driven by the first three factors, then the analyst can conduct a three-factor decomposition and justifiably treat the remaining factors as stochastic residuals.

Second, and key for the following, the residuals will continue to exhibit a factor structure when the number of factors used in the model is lower than the number of factors exhibited by the data. In the example above, the two-factor residuals will consist of both the third factor and the three-factor residuals (which, in this example, are assumed to have no clear factor structure and are therefore indiscriminately treated as noise). In general, if the eigenvalues are decreasing quickly, it will hold true that

$$
\begin{pmatrix} \varepsilon_1^t \\ \vdots \\ \varepsilon_n^t \end{pmatrix} \approx \alpha_{k+1}^t \cdot \begin{pmatrix} e_{k+11} \\ \vdots \\ e_{k+1n} \end{pmatrix},
$$

that is:

k-factor residual $\approx (k + 1)$-th factor $\times$ $(k + 1)$-th factor loading.

In particular, the shape of k-factor residuals will correspond to the shape of the (k+1)-th factor loading and the size of k-factor residuals to the size of the (k+1)-th factor. Thus, k-factor residuals are high if and only if factor $(k+1)$ is high (in absolute terms). And as high residuals indicate candidates for trading opportunities, the analyst only needs to follow a few factors in order to keep track of all potential trades. This obviously greatly simplifies the task of screening the market for trade ideas.

PCA AS A TOOL FOR SCREENING THE MARKET FOR TRADE IDEAS

This factor structure means in practice that by following a few uncorrelated factors the analyst can monitor all relevant market developments in an easy and orderly manner. Outliers in the factors can be directly translated into candidates for trade ideas. By contrast, the set of all BPV-neutral butterflies, which may at first glance appear to offer more independent trading possibilities (through different combinations, like 1-2-3, 1-2-5, 2-5-7), do not contain *more* information than the three factors (and their residuals) but just represent the same information in different and meaningless *mixtures*. For example, a 1-3-5 butterfly may mix 70% of factor 1, 25% of factor 2, and 5% of factor 3. A 2-7-10 butterfly may mix 80% of factor 1, 10% of factor 2, and 10% of factor 3. All these mixtures are endless repetitions of the same information, which can be identified and expressed cleanly, clearly, and easily through a few uncorrelated PCA factors.

Therefore, the yield curve model based on PCA can be used to screen the market for statistically attractive trading opportunities.

Applying this theory to the example of the Bund yield curve, we see with one glance on Figure 3.13 that factor 2 is close to its mean and hence it makes no sense to look for non-directional steepness positions.[15] Factor 3, on the other hand, seems to be significantly away from its mean (and, unlike factor 1, exhibits a sufficient speed of mean reversion). Thus, we would focus our attention on butterfly positions (neutral against factors 1 and 2).

Note again that almost all the relevant information needed to assess the statistical features and attractiveness of yield curve trades is contained in the single Figure 3.13. A screenshot like this can therefore greatly simplify the efforts of an analyst and direct them toward the most promising targets. This is a direct exploitation of the mathematics of a PCA, which reduce almost all the information contained in the Bund curve to three numbers (factors). Correspondingly, the single Figure 3.13 contains all information about the historical evolution of the Bund market, in an orderly and clear way. This is the basis that enables in practical terms an easy and systematical screening of the whole Bund market for trades, missing none and counting no one twice. After getting used to it, one does not like to follow a market in a different form than a factor decomposition like Figure 3.13.

PCA as a Tool for Asset Selection

Having identified butterflies as candidates for curve trades, we can select the best maturities (from a statistical point of view) by looking at their two-factor residuals (i.e. the sum of the third factor times the third factor loadings and the three-factor residuals). In case of the eigenvalues decreasing quickly, this will almost equal the *shape* of the third factor loadings, and indeed the shape seen in Figure 3.15 is very similar to that of the third-factor loadings depicted in

---

[15]This discussion is obviously restricted to statistical reasons for a trade. Of course, there can be other reasons, like fundamental views or anticipated flows, for or against a trade.

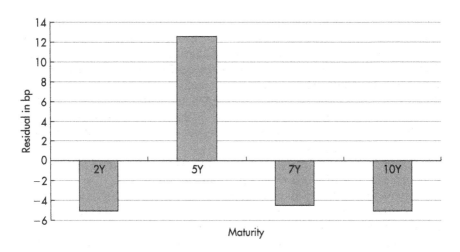

FIGURE 3.15 Two-factor residuals.
Sources: data – Bloomberg; chart – Authors.

Data period: 4 Jan 2010 to 3 Oct 2011, weekly data; current residuals as of 3 Oct 2011.

Figure 3.5 (mirrored by the x-axis since the third factor is currently negative). Consequently, a 2Y-5Y-10Y butterfly maximizes the potential profit from the current deviation of factor 3 from its mean.

Moreover, the third factor mainly determines the *size* of the two-factor residuals (i.e. the potential profit from mean reversion). Given that factor 3 is currently quite exceptionally far away from its mean (Figure 3.13), the residuals (Figure 3.15) are large by historical standards and hence the 2Y-5Y-10Y butterfly looks attractive also from a historical point of view. Note how favorably such a PCA-based top-down analysis compares to the bottom-up approach of screening all possible butterfly combinations.[16]

When analyzing swap curves, the selection of the best maturities can of course also be done by displaying a residual chart like Figure 3.15 for the swap rates of each maturity. Additionally or alternatively, one can use the consecutive one-year forward swap rates (i.e. the 1Y, 1Y forward 1Y, 2Y forward 1Y, 3Y forward 1Y, etc. swap rate) as input in a PCA. This is like running the analysis on the consecutive building blocks of the yield curve rather than on the

---

[16]Actually, PCA was first applied in engineering with the aim of finding the common behavior of a production series and to detect outliers, quite similar to our application in finance, where common behavior = market mechanisms and outliers = candidates for trading opportunities.

combinations of those building blocks into usual swap rates. Since there is less information overlap between the consecutive one-year forward swap rates than between usual swap rates (the 29Y and 30Y swap rates contain the same consecutive 29 one-year forward swap rates and differ just in the last one), usually the correlation between the consecutive one-year forward swap rates is lower, which may result in better statistical properties of the PCA. Furthermore, the output of that PCA will be a residual chart showing richness and cheapness *of the individual building blocks* of the yield curve. For the example of a factor 3 trade on the consecutive one-year forward swap rate curve, the picture of two-factor residuals could look like the one shown in Figure 3.16.

Then, the areas of richness and cheapness can be combined. In the example of Figure 3.16, the resulting butterfly trade would be pay 3Y (the combination of 1Y, 1Y forward 1Y, and 2Y forward 1Y), receive 3Y forward 4Y (the combination of 3Y forward 1Y, 4Y forward 1Y, 5Y forward 1Y, and 6Y forward 1Y), pay 7Y forward 3Y (the combination of 7Y forward 1Y, 8Y forward 1Y, and 9Y forward 1Y). Note that this approach allows a much sharper selection of rich and cheap areas than the usual swap rates. For example, the cheap 5Y swap rate contains the rich 2Y swap rate, while the 3Y forward 4Y rate does not. Thus, combining the building blocks of the rich and cheap rate curve areas together offers the maximal exploitation of the residuals. On the other hand, transaction costs are usually higher for awkward forward rate combinations than for plain vanilla swap rates.

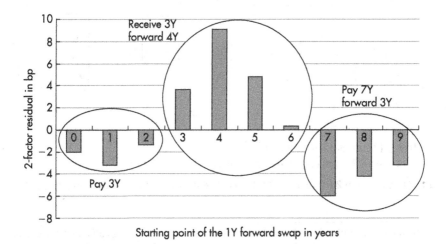

Starting point of the 1Y forward swap in years

FIGURE 3.16 Two-factor residuals of a PCA on consecutive one-year forward EUR swap rates.
Sources: data – Bloomberg, authors; chart – Authors.

There is hence a tradeoff between the higher residuals and the higher transaction costs for trades on the consecutive forward rate curve. Altogether, using consecutive forward rates is particularly advisable in case the statistical properties of the PCA need to be improved and in case the profit from asset selection (residuals) is high.

In general terms, once an investor has defined the desired factor exposure of his portfolio, the PCA residuals to these factors will show the best way to get this exposure. And since the residuals are uncorrelated to the factors, this asset selection method offers a source of profit which is uncorrelated to the factors (i.e. to whether the view on factors turns out to be right or wrong).

For example, imagine an investor is bullish on Bunds in general and thus decides to buy a Bund[17] (i.e. to get exposure to factor 1). He can then look at the chart shown in Figure 3.17 of one-factor residuals (i.e. the difference between actual Bund yields and where they typically should be, given the overall yield level). (Note again how closely the shape of one-factor residuals follows the

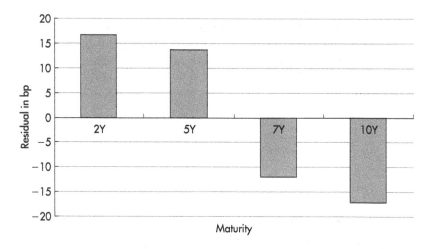

FIGURE 3.17　One-factor residuals.
Sources: data – Bloomberg; chart – Authors.

Data period: 4 Jan 2010 to 3 Oct 2011, weekly data; current residuals as of 3 Oct 2011.

---

[17]Of course, he could also receive swaps instead, or buy futures, or calls on futures, etc. We shall discuss asset selection among different classes of instruments in the following chapters.

shape of the second eigenvector.) A residual of 17 bp for 2Y means that a 2Y Bund trades 17 bp too cheaply relative to the overall yield level (factor 1). These 17 bp are a source of profit uncorrelated to the direction (i.e. alpha), enhance the return in case of the bet on direction turning out to be right, and serve as a cushion in case of the bullish view turning out to be wrong.

Of course, it is also possible to trade only the residuals, without exposure to the factors. In the case of a three-factor model, this corresponds in our framework to taking no view on any of the three factors, hence hedging against all of them (by using a combination of four instruments, what is sometimes called a *condor*), leaving exposure only to the residuals. As we have seen already, the influence of economic variables is typically concentrated on the lower factors; hedging against all factors and just exploiting the residuals (i.e. the combination of all higher "factors") usually leads to "pure" relative value trading with a focus on statistical properties.[18]

EXAMPLE OF A PCA-BASED TRADE IDEA

Let us now put together the elements developed above to illustrate the flow of analysis that could lead to a PCA-based trade recommendation. For the sake of simplicity, we present it in the form of a step-by-step guide (Box 3.1), but note that this cooking recipe is only a rough template that may need to be adjusted to different situations. Also, a reader wishing to get started with PCA would do well to set up an IT environment that was able to reproduce the charts used here. To facilitate this task, we have put the Excel sheet that produced these screenshots on the website accompanying the book, while referring to the disclaimer and warnings contained in it.

As the example is taken from government bond markets, the PCA is applied in combination with the fitted curve model described in Chapter 8, both as origin of the input data (constant maturity time series) into the PCA and for selecting the specific bonds in the maturity segments identified by PCA. Moreover, mean reversion models from Chapter 2 are used. While the focus of this step-by-step guide is on the contributions of PCA, Chapter 9 will embed it into a more complete analytic process for government bond markets.

---

[18]Any correlation a high factor (e.g. factor 7) might have to an external economic variable is likely to disappear in the combination of the high factors (e.g. factors 4–10) to a residual.

Box 3.1
Constructing Trade Ideas with PCA: A Step-by-Step Guide

Step 1: Decide on the relevant input data for the PCA, depending on the goals of the analysis: time horizon, type and number of variables, change or level data. Usually, at least one year of data is advisable. In our example, we use weekly level data for 2Y, 5Y, 7Y, and 10Y Bund yields from 4 Jan 2010 to 3 Oct 2011. In order to avoid rolldown effects and distortions from benchmark premia etc., constant maturity time series from a fitted curve model as described in Chapter 8 are the preferred choice for input data.

For heuristic purposes (i.e. to find the best instruments), use a large number of variables (e.g. all yields from 1 to 30 years); if the instruments of the trade are already known, restrict the input to these. Actually, one can run the PCA twice, first with a large set of variables (like from 1 to 30 years), and after the best instruments have been found for a second time (e.g. just with 2Y, 5Y, and 7Y for a butterfly trade), in particular to calculate the hedge ratios.

Step 2: Run the PCA. Check numerical stability and the results: are the calculated eigenvectors really eigenvectors and orthogonal to each other?

Step 3: Display the eigenvalues (Figure 3.4) and assess the factor structure of the market analyzed. In particular, does factorization makes sense at all (i.e. do the eigenvalues exhibit a clear factor structure)? A strong decrease of eigenvalues (i.e. $|\lambda_1| >> |\lambda_2| >> \cdots >> |\lambda_n|$) together with a high correlation within the data, corresponds to a clear factor structure and allows a meaningful reduction in the dimensionality of the data, of information into factors.

On the other hand, if correlation within the data is small, meaningful information reduction will be impossible. For example, if $Cov = \begin{pmatrix} 1 & 0 & 0 \\ 0 & \ddots & 0 \\ 0 & 0 & 1 \end{pmatrix}$, then every point on the yield curve will have its own factor.

Step 4: Display the (relevant) eigenvectors (Figure 3.5) and interpret them.

Step 5: Display the time series of the (relevant) factors (Figure 3.13). This is a crucial result that serves as the basis for a number of subsequent actions, for example:

- Assess the statistical qualities of each factor; in particular, is it close to its mean or far away?
- Check the correlation between factors over subperiods. We discuss this issue in detail later.

- Use the time series of a factor as input into an Ornstein–Uhlenbeck (OU) process, for example, to assess its speed of mean reversion.
- Use that time series as explaining variable in regressions, as in Figure 3.14, in order to check the exposure of a certain position. In particular, after a trade idea has been formulated, run those regressions in order to confirm that it really has the desired exposure (especially that an RV trade is really non-directional).
- Use that time series as dependent variable in regressions versus external (candidates for) explaining variables. This is the link of the statistical analysis to the fundamental and structural analysis, which allows complementing backward-looking statistics with forward-looking expectations about macroeconomic events and potential risks. For the current example, we have provided that analysis in Table 3.1.

Step 6: Based on statistical, fundamental/structural and flow/other considerations, decide on which factor you want to take a view. In the example above and restricting ourselves to statistical reasons only, we might conclude that factor 1 has too little speed of mean reversion, thus take no view. Factor 2 is close to its mean, thus we take no view. Factor 3, however, seems to be significantly away from its mean and to have a high speed of mean reversion. Hence, we decide to investigate further for trade ideas based on factor 3 (i.e. butterflies hedged against factors 1 and 2).

Step 7: In order to select the best points on the yield curve to express that view, display the relevant residual chart, in our example, the two-factor residual chart (Figure 3.15). Decide on the maturities.[19] In our example, we may want to choose sell 2Y, buy 5Y, sell 7Y (10Y has a little more negative residual than 7Y, but we might decide that the additional 0.5 bp residual is not worth the risk of going out three years further on the yield curve).

Step 8: Calculate the hedge ratios. In our example, we achieve factor 1 and 2 neutrality (i.e. the exposure to the time series of Figure 3.18) by selling 80m 2Y, buying 100m 5Y, and selling 58m 7Y Bunds. This has been calculated by a matrix inversion as discussed above. The numbers worked out as follows: with a BPV for 2Y of 1.98, for 5Y of 4.86, and for 7Y of 6.62 and sensitivities of 0.42, 0.55, and 0.53 to the first and of −0.84, −0.04, and 0.29 to the second factor of 2Y, 5Y, and 7Y (these numbers are the entries of the eigenvectors, which can be taken from the sheet on the website),

---

[19]Again, other considerations than statistics play a major role, too, in particular, flow information and carry/roll-down concerns.

the matrix $\begin{pmatrix} BPV_2 \cdot e_{12} & BPV_7 \cdot e_{17} \\ BPV_2 \cdot e_{22} & BPV_7 \cdot e_{27} \end{pmatrix}$ is $\begin{pmatrix} 0.84 & 3.51 \\ -1.66 & 1.91 \end{pmatrix}$ and its inverse thus $\begin{pmatrix} 0.26 & -0.47 \\ 0.22 & 0.11 \end{pmatrix}$. Multiplying to that matrix the vector $\begin{pmatrix} -n_5 \cdot BPV_5 \cdot e_{15} \\ -n_5 \cdot BPV_5 \cdot e_{25} \end{pmatrix}$ (with n_5 to be assumed to be one), that is $\begin{pmatrix} -2.69 \\ 0.22 \end{pmatrix}$ gives the vector of weights for 2Y and 7Y: $\begin{pmatrix} -0.80 \\ -0.58 \end{pmatrix}$. Then, the relative weights can be scaled to the desired trade size, in the example above by multiplying with 100m.

Step 9: Calculate and display the time series of the butterfly using these hedge ratios (Figure 3.18). This represents the actual performance of the trade (if executed with constant maturity time series) in the past and the future performance will depend on that series. Now, run the regressions from Figure 3.14 in order to check that the individual selection of maturities offers the desired factor exposure.[20]

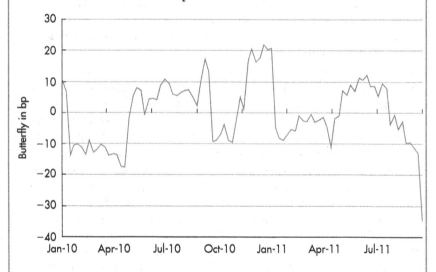

FIGURE 3.18 PCA-neutral 2Y-5Y-7Y butterfly.
Sources: data – Bloomberg; chart – Authors.

Data period: 4 Jan 2010 to 3 Oct 2011, weekly data.

---

[20] It could happen, for example, that the sensitivities to factor 3 of all the specific instruments selected are zero and that therefore the performance of the specific butterfly is uncorrelated to factor 3 and rather a function of factor 4.

Step 10: Run the OU model for the time series of Figure 3.18 in order to assess the expected performance of the trade. As outlined in Chapter 2, calculate:

- the expected profit. In our example: 32 bp;[21]
- the expected downside risk. In the OU framework, the stop loss could be set at the two-sigma level (Figure 3.19), resulting in a stop loss level that moves over time. In our example this approach would result in a stop loss level at −42 bp (loss of 7 bp) after one week.

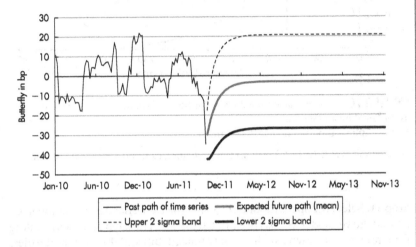

FIGURE 3.19 PCA-neutral 2Y-5Y-7Y Bund butterfly and its future path as modeled by an OU process.
Sources: data – Bloomberg; chart – Authors.

Data period: 4 Jan 2010 to 3 Oct 2011, weekly data as input; forecast period as output from OU model.

- The first passage time density and the expected time until mean reversion (Figure 3.20). In our example, the trade returns to its (estimated) mean (yields 32 bp profit) on average over 84 calendar days.

---

[21] This chart has been generated by applying the general tool on the website, which estimates the mean. In the current case, the estimated mean of −3 bp is slightly different from the actual mean, which is 0 for any factor or residual time series from a PCA. If the actual mean is known, as in the current case, the estimation of the mean from the general tool on the website could be overwritten. Then, the expected profit would be 3 bp higher.

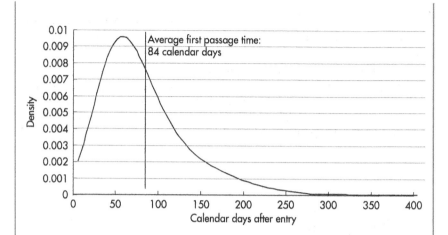

FIGURE 3.20 First passage time density for the PCA-neutral 2Y-5Y-7Y butterfly as modeled by an OU process.
Sources: data – Bloomberg; chart – Authors.

Data period: 4 Jan 2010 to 3 Oct 2011, weekly data as input for the OU model.

Step 11: Select the specific bonds by using the rich/cheap information from a fitted curve model as discussed in Chapter 8. This step results in dealing from now on with two usually closely related, but still different butterflies: One with the constant maturity time series used so far, the other one with the actual bonds traded. Due to the problem of rolldown, PCA (eigenvector) and mean reversion calculations should be based on the former, as above; but the hedge ratio and hence the carry should reflect the BPV of the actual bonds traded.

Step 12: Re-calculate the hedge ratios. As the BPV for the specific bonds can be different from the BPV of the constant maturity time series, the hedge ratio calculation described above should be repeated with the BPV of the specific bonds.[22] Based on the expected holding horizon

---

[22]Ideally, one would also want to re-run the PCA with the specific bonds selected, but faces the issue of rolldown. Hence, the best compromise practically possible seems to be using the BPV of the specific bonds and the eigenvectors of the PCA on constant maturity time series.

(84 calendar days) of the OU process and the hedge ratios, calculate the carry. Note that in the absence of BPV neutrality carry cannot naturally be expressed in bp terms anymore. Therefore, calculate the carry in money terms (i.e. euros and cents), based on the PCA-neutral hedge ratios. In a PCA framework, it is natural to express carry in money terms; should expression in bp terms be required, it must be stated, to *which* maturity the bps refer (as PCA does away with the false assumption of parallel curve shifts). In our example, the 84 calendar day carry is EUR 70,000 positive,[23] thus rather negligible compared to the profit potential from mean reversion. If the carry had been significantly negative, calculating additionally the carry until the 90% quartile of Figure 3.20 could have helped assessing whether the trade was still attractive in case it took unusually long to revert back to its mean.[24]

And how did the trade in Box 3.1 perform in reality? Figure 3.21 compares the actual evolution with the forecast of the OU model. It may be no surprise to the reader that we have picked an example that worked well. In the following we will discuss instances where PCA might not work that smoothly, categorizing the problems of PCA into:

- Correlation between factors during subperiods. This mainly affects short-term trades, like the RV position just described.
- Instability of the eigenvectors. This mainly affects long-term trades, such as curve positions motivated by cyclical macro-economic considerations.

---

[23] As this is for illustration purposes only, we have used general collateral (GC) rates for the carry calculation.

[24] Imagine a trade with a 10 bp profit potential and a three-month negative carry also of 10 bp. If the OU model shows an expected holding horizon of just two weeks (over which the negative carry is, say, 2 bp), the negative carry might be acceptable. The confidence in this position could increase further if the OU process suggests a 90% chance of the 10 bp profit to materialize over one month. Alternatively, one could calculate the probability of the mean reversion taking longer than three months (i.e. the likelihood that the negative carry would exceed the profit from mean reversion).

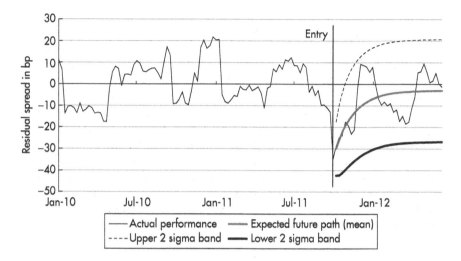

FIGURE 3.21 Performance of Bund butterfly after entry compared to OU model forecast.

Sources: data – Bloomberg; chart – Authors.

Data period: 4 Jan 2010 to 11 Jun 2012, weekly data.

PROBLEMS AND PITFALLS OF PCA 1: CORRELATION BETWEEN FACTORS DURING SUBPERIODS

By construction, factors are uncorrelated over the whole sample period used as input data into a PCA, which allows one to construct a position hedged against certain factors. However, there could occur correlation between factors during subperiods. In such a case, the hedge could break down during that subperiod. For example, a trade on factor 2 hedged against factor 1 would be exposed to factor 1 during a time period, in which ephemeral correlation between factor 1 and factor 2 occurred. In this case, the performance of what was intended to be a non-directional steepening position would be driven (ephemerally) by direction.

To see how the theoretical problem of correlation between factors during subperiods can affect trades, let's consider the example of a 2Y-10Y PCA-neutral steepening trade on the Bund curve. In October 2010 and October 2011, the time series shown in Figure 3.22 may well have looked too good to resist from entering the trade.

However, before hitting the target (reverting back to mean), a steepening position entered in October 2011 broke through the OU stop loss and subsequently underperformed further. The reason for this misbehavior can be seen in the graph in Figure 3.23, which regresses the residual spread (PCA-neutral steepening trade) against the first factor, just as in Figure 3.14.

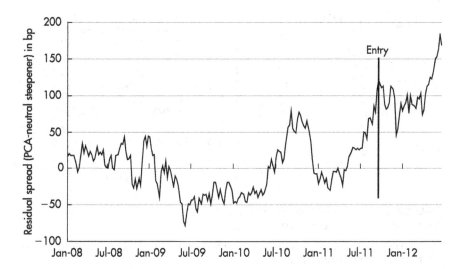

FIGURE 3.22 PCA-neutral 2Y-10Y Bund steepening position.
Sources: data – Bloomberg; chart – Authors.

Data period: 7 Jan 2008 to 11 Jun 2012, weekly data.

It turns out that, while overall the correlation is zero, there has been a high correlation to the first factor on the left-hand side of the chart in Figure 3.23. Further investigation reveals that in the six months before entry the trade (a factor 2 position) followed factor 1 very closely. Thus, the reason for the underperformance of the PCA-neutral Bund steepening trade was that it was in fact a directional trade, and, since the direction happened to work against it, its less-strong factor 2 exposure could not save it from losing.[25] Compare this situation with the regressions depicted in Figure 3.14, where we have argued against BPV-neutral weighting due to its factor 1 exposure: in times of ephemeral correlation between the factors, a PCA-neutral trade shares the fate and criticism of BPV-neutral trades.

The good news is that in many cases correlation between factors during subperiods can be spotted before entering into a trade. To do so, it is crucial to run the regressions (step 5 of the flow above). Often, a potential problem with factor correlation announces itself, as in the current example. Thus, if there has been a high correlation between the factors in the time period before (as in Figure 3.23), caution is advisable. By contrast, the 2Y-5Y-7Y butterfly

---

[25] Also in October 2010, there was a high correlation to factor 1, but this time the direction worked in favor of the steepening trade. Thus, in 2010, the trade made money, but for the wrong reason: not because it was a factor 2 position hedged against factor 1 as intended but because we were lucky that the direction worked in our favor.

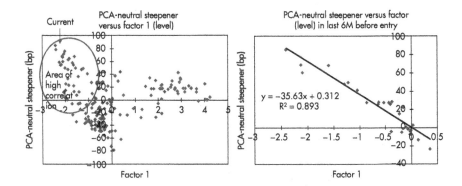

FIGURE 3.23 PCA-neutral steepener versus factor 1.
Sources: data – Bloomberg; chart – Authors.

Data period: 7 Jan 2008 to 22 Aug 2011, weekly data (left chart), 28 Feb 2011 to 22 Aug 2011, weekly data (right chart).

entered on 3 Oct 2011 did not exhibit a significant correlation of factors before entry: the entry level is the isolated point in the lower left corner of Figure 3.14. Unlike the cloud of points along a regression line in Figure 3.23, in the case of the butterfly from Figure 3.14, there is no correlation problem visible – and this was one reason why one trade worked (Figure 3.21) and the other did not (Figure 3.22).

In recent times, the reason for correlation of factors between subperiods is often the shift in the credit assessment of sovereign issuers. Imagine that a PCA is calculated on data before credit risk became an issue in Western government bond markets. From the point in time onwards when it did become an issue, it will impact factor 1 (the yield level tends to increase when credit risk increases) *and* factor 2 (since the longer the maturity, the more it will be affected by increasing credit risk,[26] thus an increase in credit risk tends to lead to a higher non-directional steepness of the yield curve). Consequently, the emergence of credit concerns has often resulted in significant correlation between factors 1 and 2. We shall address this issue in detail in Chapter 13 and show how running a PCA on CDS-adjusted yield curves (bond yield minus CDS) can solve the problem.

---

[26] As can be seen from Moody's transition matrix, for example, this statement is true for good credits, such as Western government bonds at the start of the recent crisis. When the credit becomes bad, however, the dynamics can change and increasing credit risk can then affect shorter maturities more. See Chapter 13 for more details.

In our experience, ephemeral correlation between factors is the main pitfall of PCA. Conversely, consistently checking for factor correlation, for example, through the method described above, reduces the risk of PCA leading to unsatisfactory trades significantly. When we started using PCA systematically as a tool to find and construct trades in global bond markets about 25 years ago, we did not pay enough attention to the correlation problem and produced a ratio of profitable to overall PCA-based trade ideas of 82%.[27] After figuring out that many of the 18% of losing trades were due to the correlation issue, we avoided this trap better and could increase the success ratio to just over 90%, with the number of trades obviously going down. In general, experience is required to strike the right balance between having too many trades and being overly cautious. In the current case, striking this balance requires experience to judge the level of correlation between factors in the subperiod that is acceptable before entering a trade. As a rough guide, Figure 3.14 (isolated current point out of cloud of points with no correlation) and Figure 3.23 (correlated cloud of points leading to current point) provide an illustration of unsuspicious and suspicious situations.

PROBLEMS AND PITFALLS OF PCA 2: INSTABILITY OF EIGENVECTORS OVER TIME

If eigenvectors change after entering into a trade with PCA hedge ratios, the trade will become exposed to unintended factor risk. Imagine again that we have entered into a trade on factor 2 and hedged against factor 1. If the first eigenvector for the time period during which we hold the trade turns out to be different from the first eigenvector calculated on the sample period before the trade (and thus used for determining the hedge ratios for factor 1 neutrality), then we will be hedged against the "wrong" first eigenvector and exposed to the first factor. Thus, a change of the first eigenvector results in the hedge breaking down and in directional exposure. While the cause can be different, the problem is the same as in the case of correlation between factors occurring after entering into a PCA-neutral position: it loses its neutrality and becomes exposed to factors it was not intended to. This section addresses the potential

---

[27]We generated these trade ideas by screening mainly Western government bond markets through an approach similar to the step-by-step guide from above, including macroeconomic analysis (as in Table 3.1) when necessary. A trade was counted as profitable when it reverted back to its mean before hitting the stop loss. Since we pursued an analytical goal, we disregarded issues arising in a trading context, such as bid–ask spreads and capital charges.

issue of unstable eigenvectors and offers practical solutions, whose suitability depends on the specific circumstances.

First of all, sometimes a perceived instability of eigenvectors is the result of a too-short sample period for the PCA calculation. This can be easily avoided by choosing a longer time period (step 1) (in case of yield curve analysis usually at least one year).

Moreover, it is important to distinguish changes in factors from changes in factor loadings: changes in factors occur all the time and are no problem for the PCA model and hedges based on it. For example, yields could fluctuate between 1% and 10% (i.e. α_1 exhibits a high volatility), while the eigenvectors remain stable. If the central bank is driving yields both up and down, then the first eigenvector should maintain its downward sloping shape (depicted in Figure 3.6). However, if the central bank cuts rates to zero and then announces that it will maintain a zero policy rate for a number of years, the sensitivity of short rates to directional moves can be expected to decrease versus the sensitivity of long rates. This corresponds to a change in the first factor loading.

Over the last couple of years, many central banks have established a zero-interest-rate-policy (ZIRP) or a similar approach for a significant period of time. This provides an opportunity to study the impact of the shifts between normal central bank policy (with high volatility at the short end) and ZIRP (with low volatility at the short end) on the PCA eigenvectors.

Figures 3.24 and 3.25 depict the evolution of the first eigenvector over time for the US Treasury yield curve, the former using consecutive five-year intervals since 1978, the latter consecutive one-year intervals since 2015. A few observations are worth highlighting:

- In the majority of time periods, the shape of the first eigenvector is downward sloping, i.e. the shorter the rate the higher its sensitivity to changes in the overall yield level. This corresponds to periods with normal central bank policy, when a high degree of uncertainty about the future policy path is reflected in a high volatility of short maturities.
- When the Fed removes the uncertainty about its future policy path, intending to amplify the support of economic recovery, this "unusual" policy is reflected in an "unusual" shape of the first eigenvector, provided that it persists for a sufficiently long period. Correspondingly, the exceptional monetary policy following the financial crisis and lasting for several years has caused exceptionally low levels of rate sensitivity at the short end of the UST yield curve.

Like its cause, i.e. exceptional central bank policy, eigenvector instability is mainly an issue for long-term trades. A curve trade held over several years or even decades would have been affected by the changes depicted in Figures 3.24 and 3.25. As the speed of mean reversion tends to increase with the number of the factor (see above), this problem is less relevant for RV trades on higher factors. For example, the trade on factor 3 used as example in the step-by-step guide has an average first passage time of 84 calendar days (Figure 3.20), over which time a major Fed policy change is unlikely. In fact, in our experience as RV analysts looking for short-term trading positions, eigenvector instability has seldom had an influence on the performance – unlike the correlation during subperiods described above. By contrast, using PCA for expressing long-term positions on macro-economic cycles via factor 1 does not only suffer from a relatively low expected Sharpe ratio due to the slow speed of mean reversion, but also requires stability of the first eigenvector over the economic cycle. But as the cycle can lead to unusual central bank policy,[28] the required stability cannot be taken for granted.

Figure 3.25 suggests that since 2022 the first eigenvector is back to its "normal" shape before ZIRP started. The major exception to this observation is

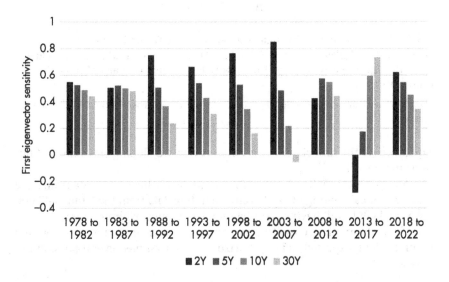

FIGURE 3.24   Evolution of the first eigenvector for US Treasuries since 1978.
Sources: data – Market Yield on U.S. Treasury Securities at Constant Maturity, Quoted on an Investment Basis, retrieved from FRED, Federal Reserve Bank of St. Louis; chart – Authors.

Data period: 1 Jan 1978 to 31 Dec 2022, weekly data, broken down into five-year sections.

---

[28] Recall that policy rates simply going up or down is not a problem; the instability arises when the way in which policy rates increase or decrease changes, for example, when the central bank newly establishes ZIRP.

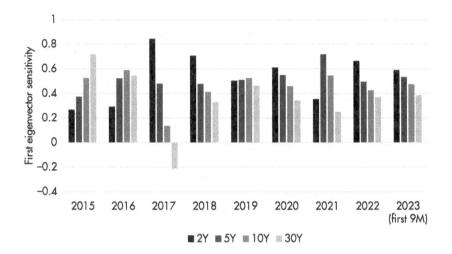

FIGURE 3.25 Evolution of the first eigenvector for US Treasuries since 2015.
Sources: data – Market Yield on U.S. Treasury Securities at Constant Maturity, Quoted on an Investment Basis, retrieved from FRED, Federal Reserve Bank of St. Louis; chart – Authors.

Data period: 1 Jan 2015 to 30 Sep 2023, weekly data, broken down into one-year sections.

Japan, where the first eigenvector remains upward-sloping since the BoJ has implemented ZIRP.[29]

As a practical matter, for the US it seems advisable to use data from 2022 onwards for calculating PCA, thereby excluding data from the "unusual" policy period while still having a sufficiently large range of observations.

If instability of eigenvectors is a concern, particularly for trades with a relatively long expected holding horizon, an analyst has several possibilities to react:

- As a start, it may be generally a good idea to test the impact of different shapes of the eigenvectors (e.g. from ZIRP) on the performance of the trade. If the performance is sufficient in all reasonable scenarios, the concern about stability can be alleviated.

---

[29]Also the introduction and most recent relaxation of "yield curve control," that is, a cap on 10Y JGB rates, has been visible in the shape of the eigenvectors. An isolated discontinuation of yield curve control could be expected to cause the first eigenvector to become steeper, while discussion about an end to the ZIRP would move Japan closer to the "typical" shape already visible in the other major markets.

■ One can try and intentionally position for the short end of the eigenvector to change: we know that a change in the eigenvector will result in the PCA hedge breaking down. But if we can forecast how the eigenvector is going to change, we can position ourselves in such a way that we will end up being overhedged in a falling and underhedged in a rising market (i.e. turn the problem of changing eigenvectors into a profitable trading strategy that has similarities with delta hedging a long option position). For example, if the BoJ ends the zero interest rate policy, an increase in rates (factor 1) should be linked to the short end becoming more volatile (sensitivities in first eigenvector increasing at the short relative to the long end). A curve-flattening position dynamically hedged against (the changing) factor 1 should therefore in fact be overhedged in declining and underhedged in increasing markets.[30]

■ Another method to mitigate the problems of eigenvector instability is to use other input variables, which are less influenced by shifts in monetary policy. For example, the shadow rate may well keep the "usual" volatility characteristics even if central banks switch to "unusual" ZIRP. Also using bond yield minus CDS could be an alternative. We'll revisit this topic in the relevant Chapters 6 and 13.

■ And, of course, if the risk of eigenvector instability is deemed too high for a particular trade to be mitigated by any of these methods, one can simply do without the benefits of PCA.

PCA as a Tool to Construct New Types of Trades

Finally, we provide an example of how PCA could be used in the currency market, thereby underlining its universal applicability. At the same time, we shall illustrate how creatively a PCA can be applied, using the step-by-step guide from above as stepping stones to a trade idea, which only PCA enables but in which PCA is just one of several parts.

When running a PCA on JPY, GBP, SEK, CHF, AUD, and SGD (versus USD), it is useful to adjust the series for the difference in absolute values in order for the charts to be legible (otherwise, e.g.100 JPY per USD versus 0.6 GBP per USD would show up as huge difference in sensitivities to the eigenvectors). Thus, we have run the PCA on synthetic currencies, starting all at a value of 1 on 4 Jan 1999. The PCA then uses weekly data of these synthetic series from 4 Jan 1999 until 25 July 2011 and can be seen on the Excel sheet on the website accompanying this book.

---

[30]This strategy was first published in the ABN AMRO Research note from 17 Nov 2006 "Exploiting the regime shift with PCA weighted flatteners" and is mentioned here with kind permission from RBS.

Figure 3.26 depicts the scaled eigenvalues. It turns out that the relative explanatory strength of the first and second factor in the FX market is similar to the bond market, while the eigenvalues above 3 decrease slower than in the case of bonds.

In Figure 3.27, the eigenvectors are displayed. As in the case of a PCA on bonds, the first eigenvector has only positive entries (i.e. a change in factor 1 affects all currencies similarly). However, the sensitivities may seem puzzling: if factor 1 increases, SEK, CHF, and AUD increase a lot, while JPY, GBP, and SGD less so. Since few FX traders think of grouping currencies in such a manner, this puzzle may represent an interesting, PCA-induced insight, but requires further examination, which will be provided below by looking simultaneously at the time series of factor 1.

Likewise, factors 2 and 3 cause differentiation among currencies (e.g. if factor 2 rises, JPY, CHF, and SGD increase, while GBP, SEK and AUD decrease). This grouping may sound more familiar, as it puts "low risk" and "high risk" currencies together.

Since the interpretation of eigenvectors (i.e. market mechanisms) is less straightforward than in the case of Bunds, we need to consider additionally the time series of the factors and their link to external variables in order to be able to complete the interpretation of the PCA results. The evolution of the factors is shown in Figure 3.28.

This graphical representation may well evoke the visual memory of the analyst. For example, he may find that the evolution of factor 1 is almost a

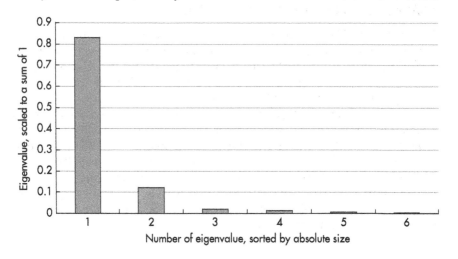

FIGURE 3.26   Scaled eigenvalues of a PCA on currencies.
Sources: data – ECB; chart – Authors.

Data period: 4 Jan 1999 to 25 Jul 2011, weekly data.

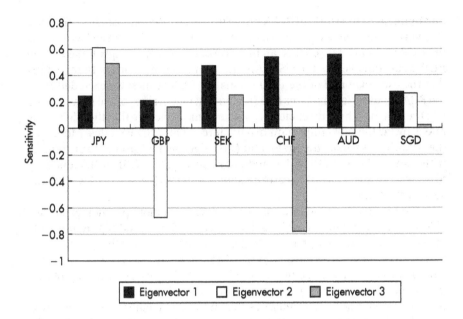

FIGURE 3.27   Eigenvectors of a PCA on currencies.
Sources: data – ECB; chart – Authors.

Data period: 4 Jan 1999 to 25 Jul 2011, weekly data.

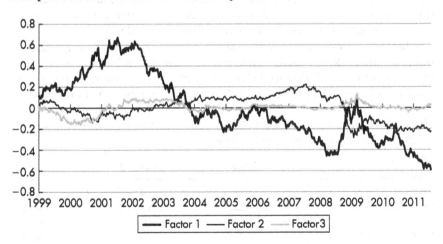

FIGURE 3.28   Factors of a PCA on currencies.
Sources: data – ECB; chart – Authors.

Data period: 4 Jan 1999 to 25 Jul 2011, weekly data.

mirror image of the USD–EUR FX rate. This visual discovery can be confirmed (e.g. via a regression, which returns a correlation of −0.94 between factor 1 and the EUR exchange rate). Thus, an increase of factor 1 is strongly linked to the EUR weakening versus the USD. An interesting consequence of that result is that the exchange rate of the USD versus the EUR (which we excluded from the PCA input series) explains 83% (scaled first eigenvalue) of the moves of the USD versus the other currencies. Hence, one may conclude that the USD–EUR rate is by far the most important driving force of all USD FX rates. Moreover, the sensitivities versus the first factor (first eigenvector) group the currencies with a strong (SEK, CHF, AUD) and not so strong (JPY, GBP, SGD) tendency to weaken versus the USD in case of factor 1 going up (i.e. the EUR weakening against the USD).

The time series of factor 2 corresponds well to a more psychological variable such as "risk on/risk off." And as expected, factor 2 falling significantly in 2009 (and staying low) has resulted in those currencies with a positive sensitivity to factor 2 ("safe havens") (JPY, CHF, SGD) to outperform those with a negative sensitivity to factor 2 ("risky") (GBP, SEK, AUD). This is probably the picture most traders have in mind when they think about the FX market. Note, however, that a PCA relegates this market mechanism to number two, revealing that it only explains 12% of the FX market action – and reveals the more important structure given by eigenvector 1.

In cases of puzzling eigenvectors, it is often useful to calculate a table of heuristic regressions, with the factors as dependent variables and with various candidates serving as independent or explanatory variables. We have tried a couple of those regressions and present the results in Table 3.2.[31]

Table 3.2 confirms our optical interpretation of factor 1 being closely linked to the EUR and factor 2 being a "risk on/risk off" factor, which has therefore some correlation to the direction of USD interest rates (as represented in the first factor of a PCA on USD swaps) and the VIX. Furthermore,

TABLE 3.2 Correlations of the First Three Factors of a PCA on Currencies versus Candidates for External Explaining Variables

	Factor 1	Factor 2	Factor 3
EUR	−0.94	−0.01	0.13
S&P500	−0.20	0.27	−0.66
VIX	0.15	−0.46	0.28
US swap PCA factor 1	0.64	0.55	−0.49
US swap PCA factor 2	0.42	−0.10	0.16
US swap PCA factor 3	−0.13	−0.04	−0.41
Oil	−0.86	−0.12	−0.07

---

[31] For some series, the time period for the regression is slightly different.

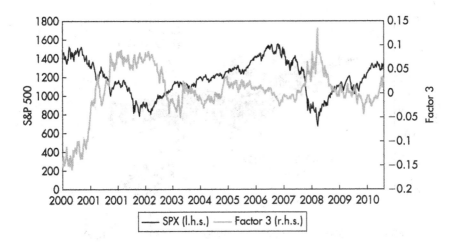

FIGURE 3.29 Factor 3 of a PCA on currencies versus the S&P500 index.
Sources: data – ECB, Bloomberg; chart – Authors.

Data period: 3 Jan 2000 to 25 Jul 2011, weekly data.

Table 3.2 reveals that the third factor is linked to the S&P500 index – and, indeed, taking another look at the time series of factor 3 in the chart above confirms that it is a close mirror image to the stock market. This relationship is depicted in Figure 3.29 in more detail.

These new insights, which a PCA provides into the FX market, could be used to model currencies by a three-factor model, with the factors linked to external variables like EUR, risk adversity (e.g. VIX), and stock prices.

In the following, however, we would like to show how the insights of a PCA into market mechanisms can be used to construct new trading positions, which would not be possible or understandable outside of the PCA framework.

While there is a reasonable correlation between factor 3 and the S&P500, currently (25 July 2011), the residual of a regression is rather high. Figure 3.30 illustrates that the current point is quite far away from the regression line. Note that if we use shorter time horizons for the regression, we still witness a significant residual. This means that the relationship between factor 3 and stock prices, which has been relatively stable over the past 12 years, is currently disturbed. Thus, if we believe that the long-term relationship will hold in future (and we see no reason not to do so), we may want to bet on the residual disappearing.[32] Hence, we investigate for a trade of factor 3 of a PCA on currencies versus the S&P500 index.

Since we cannot trade factor 3 directly, we need to find a portfolio of three currencies, hedged against factors 1 and 2 and highly correlated to factor 3. Given the relatively high strength of factor 4 in particular, not every two-factor

---

[32]Ideally, we would like to see an even higher correlation, though.

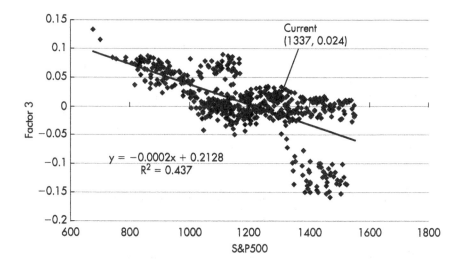

FIGURE 3.30 Regression of factor 3 of the PCA on currencies versus the S&P500 index.
Sources: data – ECB, Bloomberg; chart – Authors.

Data period: 3 Jan 2000 to 25 Jul 2011, weekly data.

neutral combination of currencies can be expected to work, as it could be mainly a function of factor 4 rather than factor 3. In addition, we would like to improve our return by choosing a combination of currencies with a high two-factor residual. These residuals are shown in Figure 3.31, and thus both a JPY–CHF–SEK and a JPY–SGD–SEK PCA-neutral combination of currencies (similar to a butterfly on the yield curve) seem attractive. However, only the first one has a strong correlation to the third factor, so we choose this one.

Now, we can formulate our trading strategy, which is to trade a two-factor PCA-neutral portfolio of JPY, CHF, and SEK versus the S&P500 index. The hedge ratio between the portfolio of currencies and the S&P500 index is given by the slope of the regression line, while the weightings of the currencies in the portfolio are determined by the conditions of neutrality versus factors 1 and 2 of the PCA on currencies. The result is the exposure to the residual of a regression between the portfolio of currencies and the S&P500 index, whose time series is shown in Figure 3.32.

Of course, we can now run a mean reversion model on that series and judge whether the statistical properties, like speed of mean reversion, seem sufficiently good to enter the trade. Figure 3.33 depicts the actual performance of the trade versus the forecast of the OU model. Since the actual performance followed the lower 2-sigma band of the OU simulation closely, one can say that an investor entering the trade was quite lucky to be able to realize the

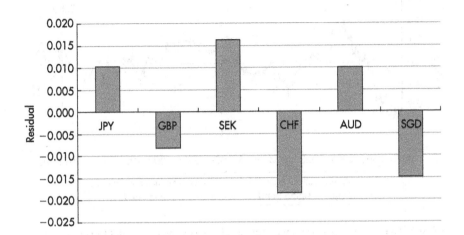

FIGURE 3.31   Two-factor residuals of a PCA on currencies.
Sources: data – ECB; chart – Authors.

Data period: 4 Jan 1999 to 25 Jul 2011, weekly data; current residuals as of 25 Jul 2011.

FIGURE 3.32   Residual of a regression between a PCA-neutral portfolio of currencies
and the S&P500 index.
Sources: data – ECB, Bloomberg; chart – Authors.

Data period: 3 Jan 2000 to 25 Jul 2011, weekly data.

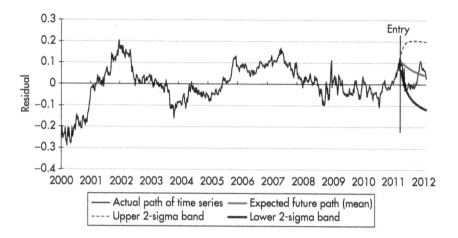

FIGURE 3.33   Actual performance of the trade versus the OU model forecast. *Sources:* data – ECB, Bloomberg; chart – Authors.

Data period: 3 Jan 2000 to 25 Jul 2011, weekly data as input in OU model; forecast period as output of OU model versus weekly market data from 1 Aug 2011 to 4 Jun 2012.

profit potential from the time series returning to its mean (i.e. the residual of the regression disappearing) soon.

This example demonstrates how PCA both yields new insights into a variety of markets and is the basis for new trading opportunities. By producing time series (like factor 3) that are not directly observable in the market but can be traded nevertheless (in this example through a two-factor neutral portfolio), PCA opens the door to a multitude of new and creative analyses and trading opportunities. The advantages of these new positions, besides their analytical challenges and illuminating results, are that they offer:

- a good chance to find a source of profit which is uncorrelated to more common positions;
- trading ideas that are unlikely to be analyzed by many people and therefore likely to be profitable. While lots of analytical effort is invested in 2Y-5Y-10Y butterflies on the yield curve, probably no one ever thought of the trade developed above. Hence, PCA is also a tool to find value off the beaten track, as it allows constructing new trade ideas individually.

Our goal is not to promote trading stock indices versus portfolios of currencies but to encourage using PCA as a compass to venture into unknown territory, where golden fruits may be growing on the trees.

CHAPTER **4**

Multivariate Mean Reversion

INTRODUCTION

In the previous two chapters, we discussed ways to model univariate series that exhibit mean reversion and ways to model multivariate series that exhibit correlation. In this chapter, we discuss ways to model multivariate series that exhibit both mean reversion and correlation. More specifically, we discuss the *multivariate Ornstein–Uhlenbeck* (MVOU) *process*.

The MVOU process is capable of capturing a richer set of behaviors than are the univariate Ornstein–Uhlenbeck (OU) process and principal components analysis (PCA), even when the OU process and PCA are used together. For example, as we'll see below, the MVOU process is capable of modeling nonmonotonic behavior in the path of expected values over time, whereas this behavior is not a feature of the OU process or of PCA.

Another important characteristic of the MVOU process is that it can model horizon-dependent correlation, i.e. correlation that depends on the elapsed time between observations. As we'll see, it's not unusual for market data to exhibit horizon-dependent correlations, a characteristic that neither the univariate OU process nor PCA can model, even when used together.

The cost of this additional capability is that the MVOU process is more complicated than either the OU process or PCA, and it's more difficult to implement in practice. However, this additional difficulty is manageable. For example, all the calculations displayed in this chapter were performed in an Excel spreadsheet, including the multivariate optimization. And in our experience, the additional capabilities of the MVOU model are often well worth the additional effort.

In this chapter, we'll first discuss the mathematics and intuition behind the MVOU process. Then we'll consider some practical examples featuring two applications of the MVOU process to fixed income markets.

Mathematics

The mathematics of the MVOU process are similar in many respects to those of the OU process. But there are some important differences due to the

111

multivariate nature of the MVOU process. In addition, some of the quantities that must be calculated to implement the MVOU process can be a bit tricky, and we'll discuss these in separate text boxes.[1]

Stochastic Differential Equation

For a set of m variables given by the vector, X_t, the stochastic differential equation (SDE) for the MVOU process can be written:

$$dX_t = -\Theta(X_t - \mu)dt + SdB_t$$

where

$-\Theta$ is an $m \times m$ matrix, which we'll refer to as the *transition matrix*

μ is an m-element vector containing the means of the m variables

dt denotes an instantaneous change in time

S is an $m \times m$ matrix, which we'll refer to as the *scatter matrix*

dB_t is the instantaneous change in an m-element vector of independent Brownian motions.

It's instructive to consider this equation in scalar notation as well as in matrix notation. In, particular, let's consider an example with three variables, index by $i = 1, 2, 3$, such that X_{it} and B_{it} represent the i-th elements of X_t and B_t. Denote the elements of Θ and S by θ_{ij} and S_{ij} for $i, j = 1, 2, 3$. To simplify the expressions, and without loss of generality, we'll assume that the long-run means for each of the three variables are equal to zero – i.e. $\mu = 0$. Then, in scalar notation, we have

$$dX_{1t} = (-\theta_{11}X_{1t} - \theta_{12}X_{2t} - \theta_{13}X_{3t})dt + S_{11}dB_{1t} + S_{12}dB_{2t} + S_{13}dB_{3t}$$
$$dX_{2t} = (-\theta_{21}X_{1t} - \theta_{22}X_{2t} - \theta_{23}X_{3t})dt + S_{21}dB_{1t} + S_{22}dB_{2t} + S_{23}dB_{3t}$$
$$dX_{3t} = (-\theta_{31}X_{1t} - \theta_{32}X_{2t} - \theta_{33}X_{3t})dt + S_{31}dB_{1t} + S_{32}dB_{2t} + S_{33}dB_{3t}$$

If θ_{11} is positive and $\theta_{12} = \theta_{13} = 0$, then X_{1t} follows a simple univariate Ornstein–Uhlenbeck process.[2] But let's assume that θ_{12} is positive. Then X_{1t} will have a tendency to decline when X_{2t} is high, and X_{1t} will have a tendency

---

[1] In the first section of this chapter, we follow the excellent presentation provided in Meucci (2010).
[2] Since all the B_{it} terms are normal, their weighted sum is normal, and the univariate SDE for X_{1t} can be written in the form of a univariate OU process.

to increase when X_{2t} is low. In this case, X_{1t} will exhibit a tendency to move away from X_{2t}. We sometimes talk about X_{1t} being repulsed by X_{2t}. On the other hand, if θ_{12} is negative, then X_{1t} will have a tendency to increase when X_{2t} is high, and X_{1t} will have a tendency to decrease when X_{2t} is low. In this case, we sometimes refer to X_{1t} being attracted by X_{2t}.

If the value of θ_{21} is zero, then this effect is asymmetric, with X_{1t} 'paying attention to' X_{2t} but with X_{2t} 'ignoring' X_{1t}. But if θ_{21} is negative, then X_{2t} will be attracted to X_{1t}.

Any combination is conceivable in this case. One variable could be attracted to a second, while the second is repulsed by the first. Or the second variable could ignore the first. Typically, we'd expect any attraction between two variables to be mutual, but that need not be the case.

The elements of the scatter matrix S, S_{ij}, impart correlation between the elements of X_t. But they're not the only way that the elements of X_t could be correlated. Even if all the off-diagonal elements of S were equal to zero, the elements of X_t could be correlated by virtue of the off-diagonal elements of Θ. In other words, even if the elements of X_t aren't subject to similar shocks imparted by the Brownian motions, they will exhibit correlation if they are attracted or repulsed by one another.

It's particularly interesting that off-diagonal elements of Θ impart horizon-dependent correlations between the elements of X_t. In other words, the correlation between X_{1t} and X_{2t} could be negative over a horizon of one day, zero over a horizon of one month, and positive over a horizon of six months. We'll see that this capability of the MVOU model is useful in capturing horizon-dependent correlations observed in actual market data.

The Differential Equation Within the MVOU Process

For intuition, let's consider the drift coefficient, $-\Theta(X_t - \mu)$, and the diffusion coefficient, S, in turn.

Without the diffusion coefficient, we have the differential equation, $dX_t = -\Theta(X_t - \mu)dt$, with the solution $X_v = \mu + e^{-\Theta(v-t)}(X_t - \mu)$, for $v > t$. In the event the mean vector, μ, were simply the 0 vector, this equation reduces to $X_v = e^{-\Theta(v-t)}X_t$.

Note that $e^{-\Theta(v-t)}$ is a matrix. In fact, for some fixed amount of time, $\tau = v - t$, we can define a matrix, $A = e^{-\Theta\tau}$. Then we could approximate the value of $X_{t+i\tau}$ by repeated application of the matrix, A. That is, $X_{t+i\tau} = A^i X_t$, for $i = 1, 2, 3 \ldots$

All the elements of X_t will shrink toward zero over time (again, assuming $\mu = 0$), provided the absolute values of the eigenvalues of A are all less than one. Given that $A = e^{-\Theta\tau}$, this eigenvalue condition for A will be satisfied when all the eigenvalues of Θ are positive.

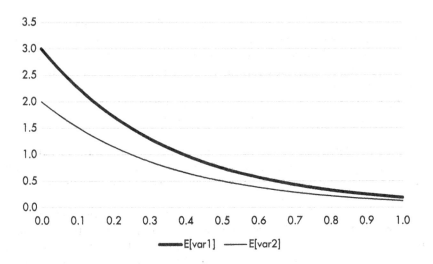

FIGURE 4.1   Expected values over time.
Source: Authors.

Let's consider this in a bivariate example. In particular, let's specify a transition matrix

$$\Theta = \begin{bmatrix} ln(2)/0.25 & 0 \\ 0 & ln(2)/0.25 \end{bmatrix}$$

so that each variable has a half-life of three months (0.25 years).[3] Let's also assume that the starting values for the two variables are 3 and 2. Then the path of expected values given by the transition matrix, Θ, is shown in Figure 4.1.

The expected spread between the two variables (var1 – var2) is shown over time in Figure 4.2.

Because both variables have identical half-lives, the spread also follows a univariate Ornstein–Uhlenbeck process with a half-life of three months.

Now let's see what happens if we specify a half-life of one month for the second variable while leaving the half-life of the first variable at three months. In other words, we specify the transition matrix

$$\Theta = \begin{bmatrix} ln(2)/0.25 & 0 \\ 0 & ln(2) * 12 \end{bmatrix}$$

Figure 4.3 shows the path of the two expected values over time.

---

[3] As a reminder, the half-life is given by $ln(2)/\theta$.

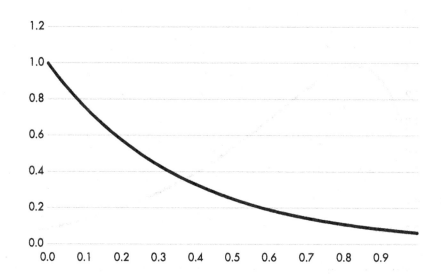

FIGURE 4.2 Expected spread over time.
Source: Authors.

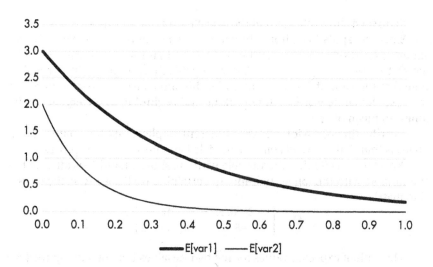

FIGURE 4.3 Expected values over time, given different half-lives.
Source: Authors.

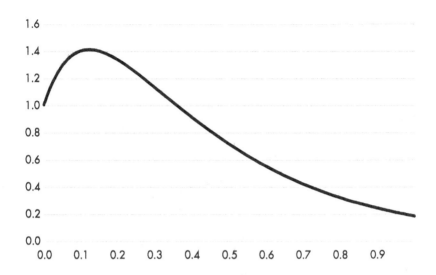

FIGURE 4.4   Expected spread over time, given different half-lives.
Source: Authors.

Figure 4.4 shows the path of the expected spread over time.

Since the spread is a linear function of two stationary variables, it's also stationary. However, it's clear from Figure 4.4 that the spread can't be written in the form of a univariate Ornstein–Uhlenbeck process. In particular, note that the path of expected values for this spread isn't even monotonic. It increases for some weeks before peaking and beginning a convergence to its long-run mean of zero.

Clearly, this behavior has very different implications for relative value analysis than if the spread could be modeled as a univariate OU process.

Now let's specify that the variable with the shorter half-life is attracted to the variable with the longer half-life. In particular, we'll specify as the transition matrix

$$\Theta = \begin{bmatrix} ln(2)/0.25 & 0 \\ -8 & ln(2) * 12 \end{bmatrix}$$

The path of expected values for the two variables is shown in Figure 4.5.

The path of expected values for the spread is shown in Figure 4.6.

Note that the path of expected values for the spread crosses the long-run mean of zero and then converges to this long-run mean from below. Intuitively, one might conclude that the spread has 'overcorrected' or 'overshot' its long-run mean. But while it's probably accurate to say that the spread is expected to overshoot its long-run mean, it's not useful to think of this as an

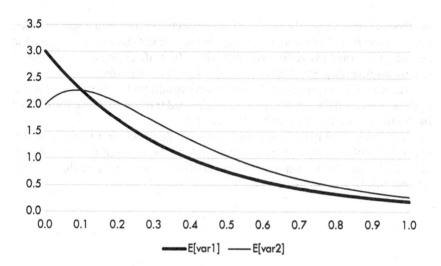

FIGURE 4.5 Expected values over time, given different half-lives and a one-way attraction
Source: Authors.

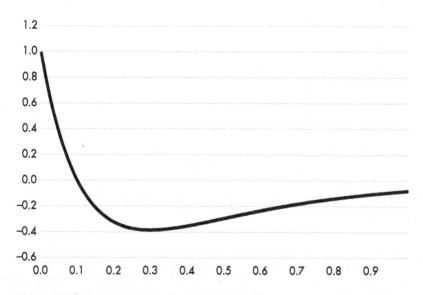

FIGURE 4.6 Expected spread over time, given different half-lives and a one-way attraction.
Source: Authors.

overcorrection. Rather, this is simply the expected behavior of a spread based on relatively straightforward dynamics for the two variables that comprise the spread – i.e. a mean-reverting variable with a half-life of one month attracted to a mean-reverting variable with a half-life of three months.[4]

Another way to represent the dynamics introduced by the drift coefficient in the stochastic differential equation is to consider the vector field introduced by the transition matrix, shown as Figure 4.7.

The horizontal axis corresponds to the value of the first variable in this example, while the vertical axis corresponds to the value of the second variable, such that the values of the two variables at any point in time can be represented by a point on this graph.

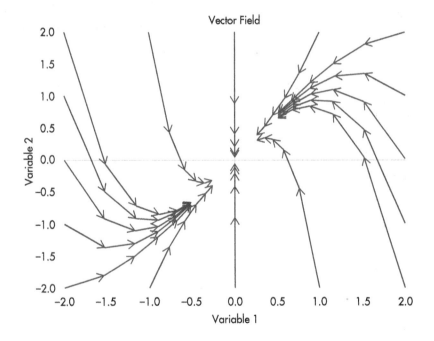

FIGURE 4.7   Vector field corresponding to the transition matrix.
Source: Authors.

---

[4]Apparent "overshooting" of the sort shown in Figure 4.6 is sometimes attributed to momentum exhibited by a series. While we do believe there are times when genuine momentum is present in a data set, this example illustrates that 'overshooting' can be exhibited by linear systems even in the absence of momentum.

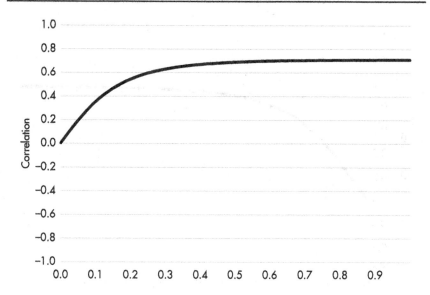

FIGURE 4.8   Correlation as a function of horizon.
Source: Authors.

In the absence of any stochastic effects introduced by the Brownian motions, the two variables would follow the arrows that illustrate the vector field in Figure 4.7. The curvature apparent in this vector field representation is due to the fact that the second variable is attracted by the first.

Also interesting in this example is the correlation between the two variables as a function of horizon, shown in Figure 4.8.

The correlation between the two variables over a horizon of one day is nearly zero, as we've specified that the two variables are not affected by common shocks, and one day isn't much time for the attraction of one variable to the other to affect the correlation. But on a horizon of one month, the correlation has increased to 0.30, and on a horizon of three months, the correlation has increased to 0.6, owing to the cumulative effect of the second variable being attracted to the first variable over time.

Next, let's leave the transition matrix the same as in the last example, but let's change the scatter matrix so that the two variables react in different directions to changes in the two Brownian motions. In other words, let's specify the scatter matrix

$$S = \begin{bmatrix} 1 & -0.2 \\ -0.2 & 1 \end{bmatrix}$$

Our intuition is that the correlation should be negative over short horizons, owing to the fact that the two variables react in opposite directions to

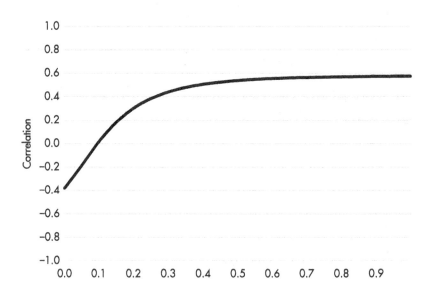

FIGURE 4.9 Correlation as a function of horizon with opposite reactions to changes in Brownian motions.
Source: Authors.

changes in the two Brownian motions. But we should also expect this negative correlation to lessen over time, as the effect of the second variable being attracted to the first has a chance to affect the correlation. Figure 4.9 shows this correlation as a function of the horizon.

In this case, the correlation not only lessens over time; it changes sign. The correlation is -0.4 over a one-day horizon but is 0.4 on a three-month horizon.

Horizon-dependent correlations would have significant implications for portfolio construction in general and for relative value trading in particular, if we observed them in practice. And, as it happens, we do observe them in practice – fairly regularly, in fact. As a result, we suggest relative value analysts calculate correlations over multiple horizons (e.g. one day, one week, two weeks, three weeks, one month, two months, three months). If we observe horizon-dependent correlations in our data, we probably should model the data with a process that admits horizon-dependent correlations. And given its flexibility, the MVOU is a strong candidate in such cases.

Conditional Density

The conditional density of the MVOU process is multivariate normal with mean vector equal to

$$E[X_t] = \mu + e^{-\Theta(t-s)}(X_s - \mu), \text{ for } t > s,$$

and covariance matrix

$$vec(\mathbf{\Sigma}_t) = (\mathbf{\Theta} \oplus \mathbf{\Theta})^{-1}(\mathbf{I}_{m^2} - e^{-(\mathbf{\Theta} \oplus \mathbf{\Theta})(t-s)})vec(\mathbf{\Sigma})$$

where $\mathbf{\Sigma} = \mathbf{SS}'$ and $\mathbf{I}_{m^2}$ is the $m^2 \times m^2$ identity matrix.

The text box contains some tips for calculating these quantities.

Calculating the Conditional Covariance Matrix

THE *vec*() FUNCTION

The *vec*() function simply flattens an array. For example,

$$vec \begin{bmatrix} a & c \\ b & d \end{bmatrix} = [a\ b\ c\ d].$$

We'll use the notation, *inversevec*[], to refer to the inverse of this flattening.

$$inversevec[a\ b\ c\ d] = \begin{bmatrix} a & c \\ b & d \end{bmatrix}.$$

THE KRONECKER PRODUCT

$\otimes$ denotes the Kronecker product. If $\mathbf{A}$ is an $m \times n$ matrix and $\mathbf{B}$ is a $p \times q$ matrix, then $\mathbf{A} \otimes \mathbf{B}$ is an $mp \times nq$ matrix of the form

$$\begin{bmatrix} a_{11}\mathbf{B} & \cdots & a_{1n}\mathbf{B} \\ \vdots & \ddots & \vdots \\ a_{m1}\mathbf{B} & \cdots & a_{mn}\mathbf{B} \end{bmatrix}.$$

THE KRONECKER SUM

$\oplus$ denotes the Kronecker sum. If $\mathbf{A}$ is an $m \times m$ matrix and $\mathbf{B}$ is an $n \times n$ matrix, then

$$\mathbf{A} \oplus \mathbf{B} = \mathbf{A} \otimes \mathbf{I}_n + \mathbf{B} \otimes \mathbf{I}_m$$

THE MATRIX EXPONENTIAL

There are a few ways to calculate the exponential of a matrix. It's worth stressing that simply calculating the exponential of each element in the matrix is **not** one of these ways.

(continued)

(continued)

In our experience, one of the most robust ways to calculate a matrix exponential is to do the following:

1. Decompose a matrix into its eigenvectors and eigenvalues.
2. Replace each eigenvalue with its exponential.
3. Reformulate the matrix as a product of its eigenvectors and the exponentiated eigenvalues.

For example, we can express the $m \times m$ matrix, A, as $Q\Lambda Q^{-1}$, where Q is an $m \times m$ matrix in which each column is an eigenvector of A, and Λ is an $m \times m$ diagonal matrix, in which each element of the main diagonal is an eigenvalue of A. Define the matrix, Ω, to be the diagonal matrix containing the exponentials of the eigenvalues in Λ. In other words, with

$$\Lambda = \begin{bmatrix} \lambda_1 & \cdots & 0 \\ \vdots & \ddots & \vdots \\ 0 & \cdots & \lambda_m \end{bmatrix}, \text{ we have}$$

$$\Omega = \begin{bmatrix} e^{\lambda_1} & \cdots & 0 \\ \vdots & \ddots & \vdots \\ 0 & \cdots & e^{\lambda_m} \end{bmatrix}$$

Then $e^A = Q\Omega Q^{-1}$

Unconditional Density

The unconditional density of the MVOU process is also multivariate normal, with a mean vector equal to the limit of the conditional mean vector as $t - s \to \infty$

$$\lim_{t-s \to \infty} [\mu + e^{-\Theta(t-s)}(X_s - \mu)] = \mu$$

And with a covariance matrix equal to the limit as $t - s \to \infty$ of the conditional covariance matrix

$$\lim_{t-s \to \infty} [(\Theta \oplus \Theta)^{-1}(I_{m^2} - e^{-(\Theta \oplus \Theta)(t-s)})vec(\Sigma)] = (\Theta \oplus \Theta)^{-1}vec(\Sigma)$$

So that the unconditional covariance matrix is

$$inversevec[(\Theta \oplus \Theta)^{-1}vec(\Sigma)]$$

Likelihood Function and Log Likelihood Function

As usual, the likelihood function is the product of the conditional densities, and the log likelihood function is the sum of the natural logarithms of the conditional densities.

Some analysts make use of the first observation in a data set by adding to the likelihood and log likelihood functions the unconditional density applied to the first observation.

EXAMPLES

BTP Butterfly

One of our favorite applications of the MVOU model was the butterfly spread involving three BTPs: 1.65% of Mar-32, 2.25% Sep-36, and 5% Sep-40, discussed in Huggins (Jan 2019) and shown in Figure 4.10 from January 2017 through January 2019.

BPV-neutral butterfly spreads can have a tendency to be directional. In fact, we get some indication of this already from Figure 4.10, which shows that the yield of the Mar-32 issue increased by a greater amount than did the yields of the other issues in the sell-off of May of 2018. Figure 4.11 illustrates the apparent strength of the directionality by showing the average of the three

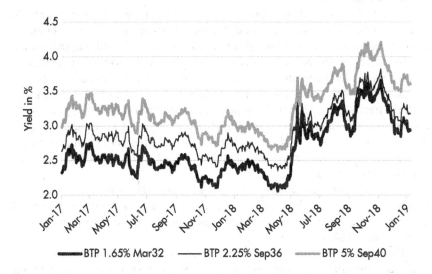

FIGURE 4.10 Yields of BTP 1.65% Mar-32, BTP 2.25% Sep-36, and BTP 5% Sep-40. *Source:* Huggins (Jan 2019).

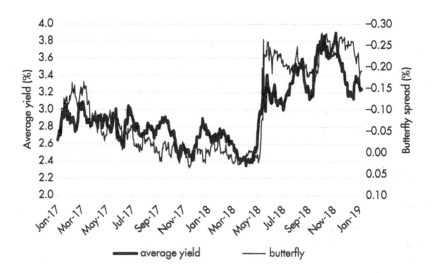

FIGURE 4.11 Butterfly spread and average yield.
Source: Huggins (Jan 2019).

bond yields along with the butterfly spread. We show the butterfly spread on an inverted axis to highlight the strong negative correlation between the spread and the yield level.

In fact, if we estimate the correlation coefficient between the average yield and the butterfly spread, without differencing either variable, we obtain an estimate of −0.88, further highlighting the strong directionality of this trade.

But many analysts prefer to compute instead the correlation coefficient of the *changes* in the variables. And as it happens, the estimated correlation coefficient between the daily change in the average yield and the daily change in the butterfly spread is 0.06. This positive correlation estimate appears quite counterintuitive, given the two series shown in Figure 4.11. In an attempt to reconcile our intuition with the calculated correlation coefficient, we might try using weekly data rather than daily data. And, in fact, this does give us a negative result of −0.27.

That number still seems a little low, given the two series shown in Figure 4.11, so we might recalculate the correlation coefficient using a data frequency of two weeks. And as it happens, the estimate is even more negative, at −0.57.

The good news is that our estimated correlation coefficient accords better with our intuition as we increase the time between successive observations. But the bad news is that it seems as if we're massaging the data quite a bit to get a number we like. By moving from a daily frequency to a frequency of two weeks, we've thrown out 90% of the data in our sample. As a general rule, if we have to throw out 90% of a data sample for our model to make sense, it's probably a good idea to reconsider our model.

So let's see how the MVOU model performs in this situation.

Initializing the Optimization Routine When Performing Maximum Likelihood

The three-variable system, modeled in the case of our BTP butterfly, isn't particularly large, but it does have 21 parameters we need to estimate: three long-run means, nine elements of the transition matrix, and nine elements of the scatter matrix.

With this number of parameters, it's useful to initialize the optimization algorithm at a point in the parameter space that is likely to be near (in some sense) the solution. One way to do this is to match empirical moments of the data.

For the three long-run means, the simple averages are usually very good starting points. Particularly when an analyst has an ample amount of data, these simple averages are usually quite close to the values for the long-run means that correspond to the optimized value of the likelihood function.

For the elements of the transition matrix, we suggest choosing elements of Θ so that the elements of $e^{-\Theta\tau}$ (for τ equal to one day) match as closely as possible the elements of the transpose of the linear regression coefficient matrix, $(\dot{X}'\dot{X})^{-1}\dot{X}'X$, where X is the $n \times m$ matrix containing n observations of the m variables, and $\dot{X}$ is the data matrix lagged by one day. In particular, we tend to choose the elements of Θ to minimize the sum of squared differences between the elements of $e^{-\Theta\tau}$ and the elements of $X'\dot{X}(\dot{X}'\dot{X})^{-1}$.

For the elements of the scatter matrix, we suggest choosing elements of S so that the elements of the one-day conditional covariance matrix in the model match as closely as possible the elements of the empirical covariance matrix using one-day changes in each data series. As with the transition matrix, we tend to choose these elements to minimize the sum of squared differences between these two matrices.

Figure 4.12 shows the estimated correlation coefficient as a function of the horizon.

As we discussed, the estimated correlation coefficient is clearly dependent on the horizon. No doubt the graph would look a little better if the estimate

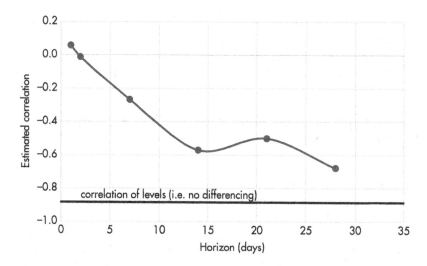

FIGURE 4.12 Correlation as a function of horizon.
Source: Authors.

of the correlation coefficient over the three-week horizon was between the estimate for the two-week horizon and the four-week horizon. But we only have 35 non-overlapping observations for the three-week horizon, so we need to make allowances for some degree of estimation error in these estimates. But in our view, the pattern is nearly a textbook example of horizon-dependent correlation that is well modeled by the MVOU process.

Figure 4.13 shows the empirical correlation coefficients shown above along with the fitted correlation coefficients produced by the MVOU model once calibrated to the data.

In our view, the fitted MVOU process does a pretty good job of modeling the horizon-dependent correlations between the butterfly spread and the average yield, capturing the positive correlation over short horizons and approaching the level correlation (i.e. the correlation of the data without differencing) asymptotically, coming fairly close to the estimated correlation coefficients for other horizons at the same time.

This calibration tells a story in which the three yields are highly correlated, even over a horizon of one day. But on any given day, the yield of one bond may move more or less than the yields of the other two bonds, in a manner that causes the butterfly spread to be essentially uncorrelated with the yield level *on that day*. But these somewhat random, idiosyncratic one-day changes to the butterfly spread tend to 'correct' over time owing to the attractions of the yields to one another.

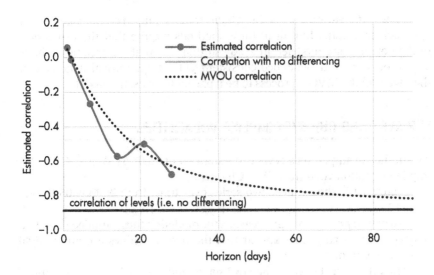

FIGURE 4.13 Correlation coefficient: estimated from data and fitted by MVOU model.
Source: Authors.

So with all this in mind, how are we to answer the question regarding the directionality of the butterfly spread? Is selling the Sep-36 issue against the Mar-32 and Sep-40 issues just a proxy for being long the BTP market? The answer is that it depends on the horizon. Over short horizons, there is essentially no directionality in the butterfly spread. But over longer horizons, the butterfly exhibits considerable directionality.

A trader might take the view that the horizon over which he expects the trade to perform is greater than one month, so that the relevant correlation to use is a negative number in the vicinity of, say, -0.70. But if he were to rely on that negative correlation when constructing a portfolio of trades, he's likely to find that his portfolio exhibits greater volatility over shorter horizons than he expected, owing to the fact that, over short horizons, his butterfly spread wasn't exhibiting much directionality at all.

This is also a problem for risk managers, who typically don't incorporate horizon-dependent variances and covariances into their analysis. It's also likely to pose a problem for anyone calculating risk-adjusted returns for the portfolio, as the calculated ex post correlation between the butterfly spread and the direction of the market, and therefore the volatility of the portfolio, will depend on the data interval over which observations are taken. For example, a reported Sharpe ratio might look materially different using daily data than using monthly data.

There are various ways in which traders and risk managers might approach this issue. But all of these methods require that the instruments in the portfolio are modeled in a way so that the model correlations show a degree of horizon-dependence consistent with the empirical data. And for that, we find the MVOU process to be a particularly useful model.

EUR 5Y5Y AND GBP 5Y5Y IMPLIED VOLATILITIES

As another example, let's revisit the analysis of EUR 5Y5Y and GBP 5Y5Y implied swaption volatilities from Chapter 2.

Figure 4.14[5] shows these two series over time, from 25-May-05 through 3-Jul-12.

We have *a priori* economic reasons for modeling these implied vols as stationary series. And it does appear that the two volatilities are pretty highly correlated with one another.

The difference between the GBP series and the EUR series over time is shown in Figure 4.15.

From this graph, it certainly appears that the spread is mean-reverting. Of course, the difference between two stationary series is also stationary, so this observation shouldn't come as a surprise. The more interesting issue is the extent to which the positive correlation evidenced in Figure 4.14 is the result of any attraction that might exist between the variables, of the sort inherent in the MVOU model.

FIGURE 4.14   EUR and GBP 5Y5Y implied swaption volatilities.
Source: data – Bloomberg, chart – Authors.

---

[5]Figures 4.14 and 4.15 are identical to Figures 2.17 and 2.18 and are repeated here for convenience.

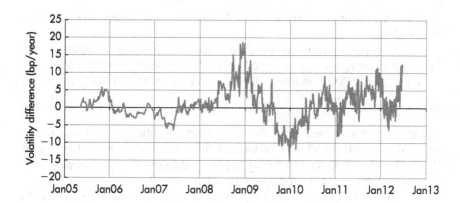

FIGURE 4.15 Swaption volatility difference: EUR 5Y5Y – GBP 5Y5Y.
Source: data – Bloomberg, chart – Authors.

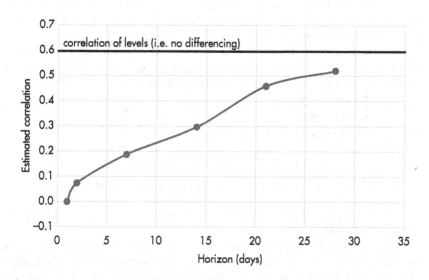

FIGURE 4.16 Estimated correlation coefficient as a function of horizon.
Source: Authors.

Figure 4.16 shows the estimated correlation coefficient between the two series as a function of horizon (i.e. the time between successive, non-overlapping data used in the calculation).

Consistent with the discussion above, the estimated correlation coefficient is close to zero on a horizon of one day and becomes increasingly positive as the horizon increases. By a horizon of 28 days, the estimated correlation is 0.52, not far from the correlation of 0.60 calculated using the original, undifferenced data.

At this point, particularly given horizon-dependent correlation, the MVOU process appears to be a good choice for modeling these two series.

Fitting an MVOU model to this data produces an estimated transition matrix of $\Theta = \begin{bmatrix} 8.93 & -8.06 \\ -7.42 & 8.66 \end{bmatrix}$. The first element in the top row shows the strength of mean reversion in the EUR series. A figure of 8.93 would correspond to a half-life of only 28 days, if there were no other influences on the EUR series. The corresponding figure for the GBP series is shown as the second element in the second row of this matrix.

The second element of the first row shows the extent to which the EUR series appears to be attracted to the GBP series. Recall that a negative number means that the EUR series is attracted to the GBP series. (A positive number would suggest that the EUR series is repelled by the GBP series.)

The first element of the second row of this matrix shows the extent to which the GBP series is attracted to the EUR series. Again, this estimate suggests that the GBP series is attracted to the EUR series.

We can gain some further intuition about these dynamics by multiplying the transition matrix by some time horizon, such as one day, and then calculating the exponential of the resulting matrix. In this case, the result is $e^{-\Theta(t-s)} = \begin{bmatrix} 0.976 & 0.020 \\ 0.022 & 0.977 \end{bmatrix}$. We can gain some further intuition by writing the two equations that this matrix represents.

$$E[EUR_t] = \mu_{EUR} + 0.976(EUR_s - \mu_{EUR}) + 0.020(GBP_s - \mu_{GBP})$$

$$E[GBP_t] = \mu_{GBP} + 0.022(EUR_s - \mu_{EUR}) + 0.977(GBP_s - \mu_{GBP})$$

for $t - s =$ one day, where μ_{EUR} and μ_{GBP} are the long-run means of the EUR and GBP implied vols.

In words, the EUR series is expected to close 2.4% of the gap between its current value and its long-run mean but is also expected to move a bit higher when the GBP series is elevated relative to its long-run mean. The figures for the GBP series are quite similar.

The estimated scatter matrix is $\begin{bmatrix} 21.48 & -0.043 \\ 0.106 & 18.45 \end{bmatrix}$. If we convert that to a covariance matrix over a horizon of one day, we get $\begin{bmatrix} 1.23 & 0.026 \\ 0.026 & 0.910 \end{bmatrix}$. The corresponding standard deviation for the EUR series is 1.11 bp/year, while the standard deviation for the GBP series is 0.95 bp/year. The correlation coefficient obtained from this matrix is 0.025.

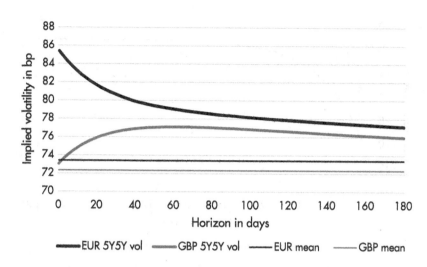

FIGURE 4.17 Expected values as a function of time.
Source: Authors.

These figures are consistent with the estimated standard deviations and correlation coefficient obtained using daily observations, particularly given that a fair number of the 'daily' observations in our sample are separated by more than one day, owing to the existence of weekends and holidays.

The paths of the expected values for each series are shown in Figure 4.17.

Note that both series start above their long-run means. But while the EUR series initially is expected to decline toward its mean, consistent with our intuition regarding mean-reverting series, the GBP series is expected to *increase* toward the EUR series initially before beginning a decline.

The attraction that seems to exist between the two variables is responsible for the fact that two variables that appear to be uncorrelated over very short horizons can appear highly correlated over longer horizons. The effect of the attraction cumulates over time, with the result that the correlation over longer horizons is quite a bit greater than the correlation over very short horizons.

With all this in mind, was the univariate OU process used in Chapter 2 a bad choice? It depends. Figure 4.18 shows the path of expected values for the spread using the MVOU model and using the OU model. The two appear virtually indistinguishable.

Figure 4.19 shows the path of the conditional standard deviation of the spread, as calculated by the two models.

The two models appear to produce nearly identical results. As it happens, this is consistent with a basic result that a linear combination of variables that follow a MVOU process can be modeled as a univariate OU process if

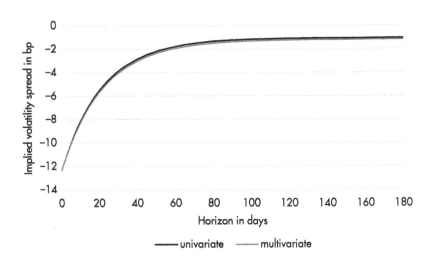

FIGURE 4.18 Expected spread as a function of time.
Source: Authors.

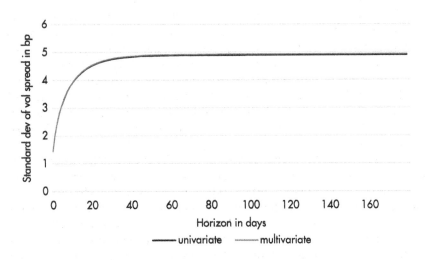

FIGURE 4.19 Standard deviation of the spread as a function of time.
Source: Authors.

and only if the linear combination is orthogonal to one of the eigenvectors of the transition matrix. The eigenvectors of the transition matrix discussed above appear as the columns of the matrix $\begin{bmatrix} -0.728 & -0.716 \\ -0.686 & -0.699 \end{bmatrix}$, and the second of these is essentially orthogonal to the weight vector used to construct this simple spread, [−1 1]. So this happens to be a case in which our spread can be modeled with a univariate process.

Given these results, is the MVOU model superfluous in this case? Not at all. It provided insights about the correlation structure of the data as a function of the horizon that the univariate model can't provide. And it showed that the expected path of the GBP implied volatility series is nonmonotonic, likely to increase initially before decreasing later – again, something the univariate model is unable to address.

CONCLUSIONS AND IMPLICATIONS

Are the additional benefits of the MVOU model worth the additional costs required to implement the model relative to the univariate OU model and principal components analysis?

In our view, the cost–benefit analysis will favor the MVOU in some cases but not in all cases. For example, if it's useful to know whether one or more of the variables is likely to exhibit a nonmonotonic path of expected values, the MVOU process is probably worth the additional effort. Similarly, if a quick check of the correlation structure of the available data suggests horizon-dependent correlation, we would suggest using the MVOU model.

On the other hand, if the empirical data doesn't exhibit horizon-dependence, it may be more straightforward to use PCA to model the data. And if the weights used to construct a spread (or portfolio) are orthogonal to one of the eigenvectors of the transition matrix, then the linear combination can be modeled with a univariate OU process anyway, though – as we saw in one of our examples – it might still be useful to know the specific paths of expected values in any event.

MVOU models can be implemented in packaged software so that the computational costs are hidden from the analyst. However, there are other costs to implementing the MVOU process that are worth considering. For example, the MVOU process is the continuous-time limit of a first-order vector autoregressive (VAR) process. In general, econometricians approach vector autoregressions with a bit of skepticism, as the greater number of parameters affords the analyst more of an opportunity to overfit the data. In fact, one of our former professors, Arnold Zellner, used to joke that VAR stood for "very awful regressions" precisely for this reason.

A cottage industry has arisen to help analysts avoid the pitfalls of over-fitting, and we encourage analysts using MVOU models to familiarize them-selves with some of these methods. In our own experience, we've found it useful to impose *a priori* constraints on some of the parameters, in order to reduce the effective degrees of freedom that otherwise might lead us to over-fit data. For example, when modeling multiple points on a yield curve, we sometimes impose the constraint that only adjacent points on the curve can influence one another. This assumption alone will reduce the number of free parameters in the transition matrix from m^2 to $3m - 2$.

Another *a priori* restriction we sometimes impose is that any influence between variables is symmetric. In other words, the influence exerted by one variable on another is identical to the influence that the second variable exerts on the first. When this constraint is justified by the economics of the situation, it will reduce the number of free parameters in the transition matrix to $\frac{m^2+m}{2}$.

Of course, there are risks in imposing *a priori* constraints, even when they're motivated by sound economic logic. But we're persuaded that there are times when, as per Judea Pearl's maxim: *"you are smarter than your data."* That's true when imposing constraints on parameters within a specific model like the MVOU model. And it's also true when choosing among models. Over time, we've become more comfortable using our experience to choose among the three statistical models discussed in this book. And we expect the same will be true of other analysts as they gain practical experience implementing these models.

Financial Models

CHAPTER 5

Some Comments on Yield, Duration, and Convexity

INTRODUCTION

This book is intended for somewhat experienced fixed income analysts, traders, and portfolio managers, so we assume the reader has more than a passing familiarity with the concepts of yield, duration, and convexity. However, we do come across some confusion concerning these concepts from time to time, so we'll offer a few thoughts in this chapter, designed to help clarify potential misunderstandings.

SOME BRIEF COMMENTS ON THE YIELD OF A COUPON-PAYING BOND

A bond that pays a coupon is simply a portfolio of zero-coupon bonds, and the price of the coupon bond is the sum of the prices of the zero-coupon bonds.

However, the yield of a coupon bond generally can't be expressed as a linear combination of the yields of the constituent zero-coupon bonds. Nevertheless, many investors would like to be able to talk about the yield or the rate of return of a coupon bond. To that end, the yield of a coupon bond is typically defined as the discount rate that when applied to all cash flows produces a net present value equal to the invoice price of the bond. In other words, it's the value of y that satisfies

$$P = \sum_{i=1}^{K} \frac{X_i}{\left(1 + \frac{y}{c}\right)^{cT_i}}$$

where P is the price of the bond; K is the number of cash flows, X_i is the size of cash flow i, c = the compounding frequency, and T_i is the time until the i-th cash flow is due to be received.

In the limit, as the compounding frequency increases, we have

$$P = \sum_{i=1}^{K} X_i e^{-yT_i}$$

At this point, it's worth mentioning a few issues with the concept of yield for a zero-coupon bond.

- For a zero-coupon bond, the yield has the straightforward interpretation as the rate of return. For a coupon bond, this interpretation is not straightforward. For example, the yield is the rate of return of the coupon bond under the assumption that all cash flows are reinvested until maturity at a rate of return equal to the yield of the coupon bond. But why would we assume that the bond coupons could be reinvested at the bond yield? It would seem more realistic to assume that the bond coupons are reinvested at the forward rates corresponding to each coupon. For example, for a coupon bond maturing in 10 years, we might assume that the coupon paid at the end of the fifth year could be reinvested for another five years at the current five-year (5Y) rate five years forward. The useful point to note here is that the yield is unlikely to be the rate of return of the bond, even if the bond is held to maturity.
- In general, the yield of a coupon bond is not equal to the yields of any of the constituent zero-coupon bonds. In fact, the yield of a coupon bond isn't even a weighted average of the yields of the constituent zero-coupon bonds.

Strictly speaking, the yield of a coupon bond is simply a nonlinear transformation of price and time that makes it easier for investors to compare the relative values of bonds. But while there's nothing wrong with applying a nonlinear transformation to prices to make investing easier, investors too often apply the concept of the bond yield in ways that are misleading and can lead to incorrect or otherwise unjustified inferences.

For example, consider two coupon-paying bonds, with the same maturity date and the same issuer, and assume that one has a greater coupon than the other. Assume also that each of the two bonds is priced exactly in line with the yield curve, in the sense that there are no reconstitution arbitrage opportunities available.

If the yield curve is upward-sloping, it's very likely that the bond with the greater coupon will have a lesser yield than the other bond. And if the yield curve is downward-sloping, it's very likely that the bond with the greater coupon will have a greater yield than the other bond. In this case, it would be inappropriate to use the unadjusted yield spread between the two bonds as an indication of the relative value between the two bonds. Yet we see these sorts of comparisons being made by analysts and traders more often than we'd like.

A BRIEF COMMENT ON DURATION

Macaulay Duration

In 1938, Frederick Macaulay published an article in which he discussed the weighted average time to maturity of a stream of payments. Since then, Macaulay's duration has been taught to almost every bond analyst and trader.

In particular, the standard formula for the Macaulay duration of a coupon-paying bond is:

$$D_M = \sum_{i=1}^{K} T_i \frac{\frac{X_i}{\left(1+\frac{y}{c}\right)^{cT_i}}}{P}$$

which gives the weighted average time to maturity of a coupon-paying bond, assuming the present values of the cash flows are obtained by discounting each cash flow using the yield to maturity of the coupon-paying bond. For a zero-coupon bond, the Macaulay duration is simply the maturity of the bond.

However, there is no reason to discount each cash flow at the same yield, unless somehow the individual prices of the constituent zero-coupon bonds are unknown. As long as we know the prices of the individual zero-coupon bonds, we could calculate the weighted time to maturity of the bond directly.

Fisher–Weil Duration

In 1971, Lawrence Fisher and Roman Weil, of the University of Chicago, published an article in which they discuss another measure of duration, similar to Macaulay duration but with the price of each cash flow corresponding to the actual term structure of interest rates. In other words, the present value of each cash flow corresponded to the actual prices of the zero-coupon bonds that constitute the coupon-paying bond. In this respect, the Fisher–Weil duration is a more accurate reflection of the weighted average maturity of the bond.

The standard formula for the Fisher–Weil duration is similar to the formula for the Macaulay duration but with the yield of each cash flow used in place of the yield for the entire bond.

$$D_{FW} = \sum_{i=1}^{K} T_i \frac{\frac{X_i}{\left(1+\frac{y_i}{c}\right)^{cT_i}}}{P}$$

The Fisher–Weil concept of duration provides a more accurate measure of the weighted time to maturity of a coupon-paying bond, yet the formula for the

Macaulay duration is still used far more frequently in our experience, perhaps given the view that it's easier to implement, given it requires only a single yield.

In our view, the additional steps required to calculate the Fisher–Weil measure of duration are worth the effort, and we suggest using this measure in place of the Macaulay measure.

A COMMON MISAPPLICATION OF CONVEXITY

As the price of a bond is a convex function of its yield, its price will change more in the event its yield decreases by 25 bp than if its yield increases by 25 basis points (bp). For example, the German Bund with a coupon of 3.25%, maturing on 4 Jul 2032, had a price of EUR 122.713 and a yield of 2.197%. At a yield of 1.947, its price would be higher by EUR 6.36, and at a yield of 2.447%, its price would be lower by EUR 5.96. If there were an equal chance of either scenario today, the expected return of the bond would be +0.2% (non-annualized), despite the fact that the yield distribution in this case was presumed to be symmetric.

This is the case not only in this example but in general, due to *Jensen's inequality*, which states that the expected value of a convex function of a random variable is greater than or equal to the function evaluated at the expected value of the random variable.

The impact of Jensen's inequality is an increasing function of the volatility of the random variable. For example, if there were an equal chance that the yield of our bond would increase or decrease by 50 bp rather than by 25 bp, the expected return would be +0.7%. If the potential yield change were 75 bp, the expected return would be +1.5%, and if the potential yield change were 100 bp, the expected return would be +2.6%.

Since the favorable impact of convexity appears to be an increasing function of volatility, many analysts compare this convexity effect to an option, which also has a convex return structure. Just as the fair price of an option increases with the volatility of the underlying asset, so too should the fair value of this convexity effect increase with the volatility of the bond's yield.

But, as we'll soon see, there's a problem with this argument.

All else being equal, the convexity of a bond price as a function of its yield is an increasing function of the time to maturity of the bond. That is, longer-dated bonds have greater convexities than shorter-dated bonds, all else being equal.

For instance, a 30-year (30Y) zero-coupon bond with a yield of 2.25% and with an equal chance of experiencing a 100 bp yield increase or decrease would have an expected return of +4.5%. If the same bond matured in 50 years, the expected return would be 12.8%. If the bond matured in 100 years, the expected return would be a remarkable 54.3%.

To illustrate our point, let's consider hypothetical bonds with even greater times to maturity. For example, if the bond had a 200Y maturity, the expected return in our example would be 276.2%. If the bond had a maturity of 500 years, the expected return would be 7,320%. And if there were such a thing as a millennial bond (i.e. a zero-coupon bond that matured in 1,000 years), its expected return would be more than one million percent. One million dollars invested in this bond would be associated with an *expected* value of more than 22 billion dollars. It's clear that there is something seriously problematic in this example.

In our example, we held constant the probabilities of our two yield scenarios, and we observed the effect on the expected return when the maturity of the bond was increased. As an alternative, let's hold constant the expected return on the bond and observe the effect on the probability of a yield decrease as the maturity of the bond is increased.

A 30Y zero-coupon bond with a yield of 2.25% would have an expected return of 4.53% (non-annualized) if there were a 50% chance of a 100 bp yield increase and a 50% chance of a 100 bp yield decrease. If the bond had a maturity of 50 years, then to keep the expected return equal to 4.53%, the probability of a yield decrease would have to decline to 42% (with the probability of a 100 bp increase at 58%). If the maturity of our zero-coupon bond were 75Y, the probability of the lower yield would decline to 35%. With a 100Y bond, the probability of a 100 bp yield decrease would be only 29%.

Continuing toward the limit, the probability in the case of a 200Y bond is 12.5%; the probability in the case of a 500Y bond is seven-tenths of 1%, and the probability in the case of our hypothetical millennial bond is only 0.0000485.

These examples highlight an important point made in the 1990s by Philip Dybvig, Jonathan Ingersoll, and Stephen Ross, who showed that *in the limit* the long zero-coupon rate could never fall.[1]

Of course, bonds with the sorts of maturities used in these examples simply don't trade in the real world. But by considering the traditional convexity argument in the limit, we've come upon an interpretation of convexity that makes far more economic sense than the traditional interpretation does.

The traditional interpretation is that convexity transforms symmetric yield distributions into asymmetric return distributions, which increase the value of highly convex bonds. *Our interpretation is that convexity transforms symmetric return distributions into asymmetric yield distributions.* And this interpretation makes far more economic sense, in our view.

---

[1] Philip H. Dybvig, Jonathan E. Ingersoll, Jr., and Stephen A. Ross (1996) Long forward and zero-coupon rates can never fall. *Journal of Business* **69**(1), 1–25.

Note that this result helps explain the typical shape of the first eigenvector obtained when conducting principal component analysis (PCA) of yield curves. Long rates tend not to be as volatile as short rates are, which means that short rates are more sensitive to changes in the first principal component in the context of a PCA. This result is intuitive once we realize that the asymptotic rate can never decrease, since a rate that can never decrease must not spend much time increasing either.

Note too that this convexity result is consistent with the mean reversion of short rates. If there's a sense in which long rates are (potentially complicated) averages of the overnight rate, then mean reversion in the short rate will lead to long rates being less volatile than short rates as a simple statistical result. In the limit, the average of a mean-reverting short rate is the unconditional mean of the short rate process.

CHAPTER **6**

Some Comments on Yield Curve Models

INTRODUCTION

While yield curve models take center stage in many academic papers, the practical focus of this book downgrades their role to supporting concrete analytic tasks. But even here, they are ubiquitous: the OU process described in Chapter 2 corresponds to a Vasicek model, and the functional forms used in Chapter 8 can be considered as model assumptions.

A natural question is therefore whether the different models applied to different analytic tasks can be integrated into a single one. Using different models may well capture the individual features of different markets but runs the risk of inconsistent pricing, of engaging yourself in model arbitrage. Using a single model requires consistent assumptions about market mechanisms but runs the risk of observing these universal assumptions rather than specific market mechanisms. While a comprehensive treatment of modeling is outside the scope of this book, this chapter does offer a few general thoughts.

When yields approached or even breached what was previously considered to be their boundary, the assumptions and applicability of many models were questioned. At the same time, the demand for models dealing with boundaries increased, for instance, to predict the effect on the yield curve of a lowering of the ECB's condition for bonds to be included in an asset purchase program from −25 bp to −50 bp. We have applied Shadow Rate (SR) models to answer these questions and share our experiences.

REMARKS ABOUT MIXED JUMP-DIFFUSION MODELS

The benefits of using one single model for pricing all instruments relevant for the analysis are obvious: consistent model assumptions about the market behavior are the basis for consistent pricing and aggregating all market information allows both the extraction of the typical mechanisms and the assessment of all individual instruments against these mechanisms.

In principle, the more markets and segments a model covers, the further these benefits extend. Using an example from the money markets, one could assume a jump process (with the jumps occurring at the FOMC meeting dates) and calibrate it to the 1M and 3M SOFR future contracts. This aggregates the information contained in the SOFR future market into "the market consensus" about the evolution of SOFR rates (given by the jump process) and thereby provides a benchmark against which every individual contract can be priced.[1] Now, one could do the same separately with FF future contracts – which will usually result in a different jump process and thus in the question, which of the two is the 'correct' representation of the market consensus? The better alternative to modeling the FF futures separately seems therefore to integrate them into the model for SOFR futures, i.e. to expand the input variables used for calibration of the jump process to include both SOFR and FF futures. This ensures consistency of the model assumptions (in this case, about the Fed policy rate) by sticking with one jump process only and allows assessing the richness and cheapness of both SOFR and FF futures versus one single and uniform benchmark. Hence, one can compare SOFR futures not only against other SOFR futures, but also against FF contracts and expand the RV trades based on this curve model. Moreover, in addition to aggregating the information from future markets into a consensus about the evolution of the policy rate, the uniform approach also gives a measure for the implied evolution of the overall secured (SOFR) – unsecured (FF) spread, with which the rich/cheap measure can be adjusted.[2] Chapter 17 will apply the same idea to bond markets.

Following this consideration, it is tempting to conclude that the broader the application of the model and the more input variables used for calibration, the better it will be. However, if the goal of the analysis is limited to specific instruments, it is usually advisable to limit the input to these as well, thereby avoiding influences from variables irrelevant to the analysis. For example, if a trader can only transact in SOFR futures, he may want to intentionally exclude the information contained in FF contracts from his model.

Assuming the goal is a model that covers both the short and the long end of the yield curve and can be used as a basis to price derivatives as well, one can list its required features:

- Monetary policy has a major influence on the whole yield curve. At the short end, this influence occurs mostly at known dates (the scheduled policy meetings), which can be appropriately modeled by a jump process. However, in order to capture the volatility between scheduled

---

[1] Huggins and Schaller (2022), Figures 6.2, 6.3, and 6.4. The adjustment of SOFR futures for non-linearities is also discussed in this chapter.
[2] Huggins and Schaller (2022), p. 63 and Figure 2.19.

meetings – specifically also from unscheduled meetings[3] – and to describe the yield curve behavior in the absence of known meeting dates (maybe from about 2Y onwards), the jump process needs to be complemented with other terms, such as diffusion and drift.

- Likewise, if derivatives are also part of the instruments analyzed, including a diffusion term is essential. For example, a purely deterministic process would return a value of zero for all out-of-the-money short-term interest rate options that expire before the next policy meeting takes place.
- Given the variety of reference rates (see Chapter 11), if instruments based on different reference rates are analyzed, if can be useful to include a variable (ideally time-dependent) for their spread in the model. In the example above, this would be the secured (SOFR)-unsecured (FF) spread. This allows extracting information about secured-unsecured yield spreads *at the same time* as information about the yield curve and hence to incorporate it into rich/cheap assessments.

These requirements lead to using mixed jump-diffusion (and drift) models. While a number of standard jump-diffusion models have been extensively discussed and partly offer the advantage of closed-form solutions, in our experience, the incorporation of real-market features quickly leaves the academically cultivated territory. For example, one may want to include an additional variable for the secured-unsecured basis as just mentioned or assume correlations between certain variables with the goal of reflecting actual market mechanisms more closely. The price for deviating from standard models is to be forced to use numerical simulations. Fortunately, due to the advances in IT, the price has decreased to a level where it seems well worth paying it in most circumstances.

The choice of both the (functional form of the) model and of the market instruments used to calibrate it typically has a major influence on the results of the analysis. Huggins and Schaller (2022, specifically Table 2.2) illustrate the effects for the example of pricing SOFR futures via models with and without diffusion, etc. Hence, the benefits of applying universal models need to be balanced with the risk of ending up observing the model assumptions rather than the actual market. Using one single model for all markets offers the advantage of consistent assumptions and pricing as well as a single benchmark for RV assessments – but runs the risk of imposing these assumptions too uniformly. This is one reason why this book aims for rather modest modeling and a clear view on specific market mechanisms. (See the introduction to Chapter 3.)

---

[3]Unscheduled meetings are a major problem for models using a jump process, because they tend to happen in exceptional circumstances and take unforeseen decisions.

REMARKS ABOUT SHADOW RATE MODELS

A straightforward approach to deal with the problem of boundaries (such as 0% or the buying limit of ECB) in a Vasicek framework consists in modeling a so-called Shadow Rate (SR) via a standard Vasicek process and to define the actual rate observed in the market as the maximum of the SR and a certain defined lower limit (which can change with the maturity, if required). The idea is to assume 'standard' behavior of the SR and to explain the actual market rates as being determined only by those instances in which the SR exceeds the boundary. This idea can be easily implemented in a simulation: the actual market rate is modeled as the average over all simulated paths of the maxima of the boundary and the SR of each specific path.

SR models therefore allow us to determine the impact that a change in the boundary is expected to have on the shape of the yield curve. Simply change the boundary, re-run the simulation, and compare the results. This was valuable information for analysts trying to predict the consequences of the ECB deciding to adjust the yield limit of the bonds included in its asset purchase programs. For instance, if a lowering of the boundary from −25 bp to −50 bp was discussed, the expected effect of the 2Y-10Y yield curve slope could be obtained from an SR model.

Unfortunately, SR models are often not well-behaved optimization problems, with two almost identical optima being achieved by significantly different parameters. For example, almost the same fit of an SR model to the actual yield curve could be caused by a much higher standard deviation together with a much lower mean and/or higher speed of mean reversion. When calculating a history of SR model parameters, frequent jumps (between the parameters leading to almost identical optima) may therefore occur. One (imperfect) way to address this issue is to fix the parameters step by step. For example, if a history of the starting point for the SR is desired, one could start by optimizing over all parameters (except the level of the boundary) of the SR model: starting point, variance, mean, speed of mean reversion. Once the history has been created, one could then take the average of the parameters for mean and mean reversion and re-run the SR model by only changing the starting point and variance. Then, one can also fix the average of the variance and obtain the desired history of the starting point of the SR in a third and final optimization of this parameter only. Figure 6.1 depicts the result of this exercise, i.e. the evolution of the EUR O/N SR as implied by the EUR yield curve from 1Y to 10Y. The significantly negative levels (less than −15%) of the SR reflect the extreme situation during 2014: only such a low level of the SR was consistent with the exceptional shape of the observed EUR yield curve.

Figure 6.1 also illustrates the fact that the SR maintains its volatility (which Vasicek assumes to be uncorrelated to the yield level) even in times

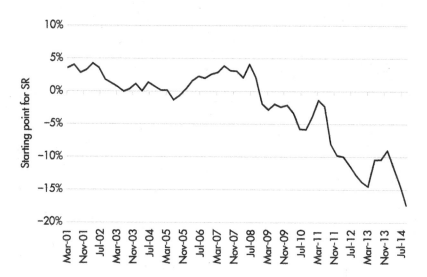

FIGURE 6.1 Evolution of the O/N Shadow Rate implied by the EUR yield curve. *Source:* Authors.

when the observed yield volatility is very low, as was the case during the period of zero/negative-interest-rate policy. Hence, using a yield curve of Shadow Rates could be one way to address the problem of unstable eigenvectors highlighted in Chapter 3: whereas central banks announcing their intention to keep rates at low levels (e.g. 0%) for a long time remove uncertainty from the short end of the curve and thus affect the shape of the first eigenvector, the eigenvectors calculated on a curve of SR are quite immune. However, the desirable stability of eigenvectors calculated on SR is obtained by relying on the Vasicek assumption of no correlation between volatility and yield level, which often may not reflect the actual market behavior the PCA intends to capture. Moreover, as SR are not traded, profiting from the insights gained by a PCA on SR is not as straightforward as in the case of running a PCA on tradeable instruments.

CHAPTER 7

Bond Futures Contracts

FUTURES PRICE AND DELIVERY OPTION

The key difference between a bond forward and a bond futures contract is the existence of a *set* of deliverable bonds, called the *deliverable basket*. In particular, the person with a short position in a bond futures contract (i.e. the short) has a choice of bonds he can deliver. Since the bonds in the deliverable basket have different coupons and maturity dates, the exchanges introduce the concept of a *conversion factor* (CF), which is applied to the price of each bond when determining the invoice price that the short receives when delivering a particular bond into a particular futures contract. In order to make all deliverable bonds comparable, a CF is defined for each, which roughly corresponds to one-hundredth of the price of the deliverable bond at a certain yield level (often 6%). This yield level is called the *notional coupon* of the bond futures contract.

Technical Points Regarding the Conversion Factor

- The CF is a constant for each individual deliverable bond.
- The CF of a bond will depend on the expiration date of the futures contract. For example, if a bond is deliverable into both the March and the June contracts, it will have a different CF for each expiration month.
- In general terms, the CF of a bond is one-hundredth of the price the bond would have at expiration of the futures contract if the bond yield was equal to the notional coupon for that contract.
- The notional coupon of the futures contract is defined at the time the contract is first listed by the exchange. Like the CF, once the notional coupon for a particular expiration month is defined, it does not change.

(continued)

(continued)

- However, exchanges can and do sometimes switch to a new notional coupon when listing a new futures contract, particularly when the yields of the bonds in the deliverable basket are far from the notional coupon used most recently.
- Changes to the notional coupon can have a material effect on the value of the delivery option and the value of the futures contract, as discussed below.
- Note that the calculation of the CF as specified in the contract documentation may not correspond exactly to one-hundredth of the bond price at the yield of the notional coupon. The exchanges publish formulae that analysts can use to predict the CF before a contract is listed, but the analyst should be careful to confirm the CF for each contract when it is listed, as the CF published at the time of listing is determinative, irrespective of any formulae the exchange may have published to assist analysts.

The Delivery Process

At delivery, the person with the short position in the bond futures contract can choose to deliver any bond in the deliverable basket and will receive a payment of the futures price, F, multiplied by the CF for the bond he has chosen, in exchange for delivery of the bond. Thus, if the yield at delivery equals the notional coupon of the bond futures contract, and if the CFs represent exactly one-hundredth of the prices of the bonds at that yield level, then the futures contract should trade at 100, and the prices of all deliverable bonds should be equal to the compensation received for their delivery into the futures contract. In that case, the short would be indifferent about the bond he chooses to deliver. In general, however, there are differences with regards to the payoffs at delivery between the deliverable bonds. Assuming the short buys a deliverable bond right at delivery at price P, and delivers it immediately into the futures contract, his P&L will be $F \times CF - P$. If there are n deliverable bonds in the basket with prices $P_1, \ldots, P_n$ and conversion factors $CF_1, \ldots, CF_n$, he can compare the payoffs for buying and delivering each of them with a table like this:

$$\text{Bond 1}: F \times CF_1 - P_1$$

$$\ldots$$

$$\text{Bond n}: F \times CF_n - P_n$$

The deliverable bond with the best payoff (i.e. the largest number in the table above) is called the *cheapest-to-deliver* (CTD), and the short will usually

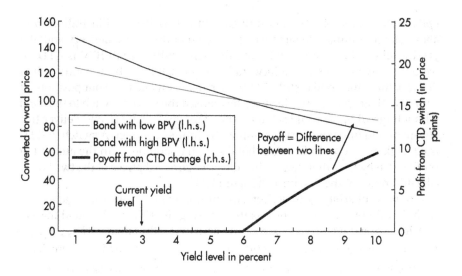

FIGURE 7.1 CTD situation as a function of the yield level.
Source: Authors.

deliver that bond. If the yields of all deliverable bonds at delivery were equal to the notional coupon of the bond futures contract, and if the CF of each bond was exactly equal to one-hundredth of the price of the bond at that yield level, then all deliverable bonds would be equally CTD.[1] At higher yield levels, only the bonds with largest basis point values (BPVs) in the basket tend to be CTD, while at lower yield levels only the bonds with the smallest BPV in the basket tend to be CTD. The reason for this behavior is illustrated in Figure 7.1. When the general level of yields is high, the converted prices (*P/CF*) of large BPV bonds tend to be low relative to the converted prices of bonds with a smaller BPV. If the two bonds of Figure 7.1 were the only ones that were deliverable, the one with the lower converted price would be CTD at a given yield level. Thus, the CTD would switch between the bond with a small BPV to the bond with a large BPV at the notional coupon (6% in this example). This switching point is also called the *inflection point*.

CTD Switches and the Delivery Option

Since the short has the right to choose the bond he delivers, he can profit from changes in the CTD. The monetary value of that right is called the *delivery*

---

[1]In this scenario, a difference in coupons would result in some bonds being rich relative to others, given the coupon effect, perhaps even allowing reconstitution arbitrage (via the strip market).

option (DO) value of the bond futures contract. Using the illustration from above as an example, imagine we are three months before delivery and at a yield level of 3%. At that yield level, the bond with a small BPV is CTD, so we could buy that bond on a forward basis and sell the futures contract. If at delivery the same bond is still CTD, we can deliver it and close our positions at zero cost. If, however, a rise in yields has caused the CTD to switch to the bond with a large BPV, we could sell our bond, buy the new CTD, and deliver this cheaper bond into our short position in the futures contract. A switch in CTD is equivalent to a profit from our bond switch operation, with the amount of profit given by the difference of the converted forward prices of the two bonds (the difference of the two lines in Figure 7.1).

To prevent arbitrage at delivery, the futures contract must settle at a price such that there is no profit or loss from buying the CTD in the bond market and delivering it into the contract. Thus, at delivery, the equation $F \times CF_{\text{CTD}} - P_{\text{CTD}} = 0$ holds and implies a fair futures price of $\frac{P_{\text{CTD}}}{CF_{\text{CTD}}}$. Likewise, before delivery, the fair futures price is a function of the converted forward price of the CTD. But as the CTD can still change, it needs to be adjusted for the DO value, and the fair futures price is given as $\frac{FwdP_{\text{CTD}}}{CF_{\text{CTD}}} - DO$.

Net and Gross Bond Basis

That arbitrage relationship at delivery is the key for basis trades between deliverable bonds and the future, with the following conventions:

$$\text{Gross basis} = P - F \times CF$$

$$\text{Net basis} = FwdP - F \times CF$$

Note that the fair value of the CTD net basis is equal to $DO \times CF_{\text{CTD}}$. Thus, if there is no DO, in particular at the delivery date, then the fair value of the CTD net basis is 0. And as the DO is never negative, the fair value of any net basis is always greater than or equal to zero.[2]

From these equations, it is clear that the DO is key to pricing and trading bond futures contracts. All other aspects of the contract can be hedged in the markets. For example, the forward price of a deliverable bond is a direct function of the bond and of the repo market. (The CF is a pre-defined constant.) Thus, the model used to calculate the fair value of the DO will determine the

---

[2]At times, specific situations like penalties for failing to deliver might result in a negative net basis being observed in the market.

fair value of the futures contract and therefore whether basis trades are attractive. In addition, the better the DO is understood, the better the futures contract can be applied for hedging purposes, and the more informed the appropriate time for rolling over front into back month contracts can be decided.

Imagine that the net basis of the CTD quotes in the market at 5 cents and that the CF of the CTD is 1. If the model used to evaluate the DO returns a fair DO price of 2 cents, selling the CTD net basis (i.e. selling the CTD in the forward market and buying the futures contract) appears attractive. If another model returns a fair DO price of 10 cents, however, buying the CTD net basis looks profitable. This illustrates the crucial importance of the model used to price the DO for correctly evaluating the fair value of the futures contract and for ensuring that one is on the right side of basis trades.

As the futures price observed in the market in some sense should reflect the average pricing model used by market participants, having a better model enables us to exploit the shortcoming of the average model. The CTD net basis in the market is a function of the DO models of the other market participants, which we can compare with the results of our DO model. If we have a superior DO model and the market price is not in line with its results, we can translate the superiority of our model directly into profitable trading strategies by entering into CTD net basis positions. For example, if the DO model used by market participants gives a fair value of the DO of 5 cents, and if the CF of the CTD is 1, then the CTD net basis should trade at 5 cents. If our better model gives us a fair value for the DO of 10 cents, then we can translate the theoretical advantage of our model into trading profit by buying the CTD net basis in a market that underestimates its value.

We shall therefore describe two different DO models. The first one is the one-factor DO model commonly used in the market, while the second one is a superior multi-factor DO model we developed while working at ABN Amro. The model arbitrage mentioned in the previous paragraph will therefore consist in assessing the market price for the DO (CTD net basis/CF), calculated by one-factor models, through the lens of a multi-factor model.

ONE-FACTOR DELIVERY OPTION MODELS[3]

Figure 7.1 can serve as the basis for a straightforward DO model. Since the payoff profile from a CTD switch is a function of the yield level, the value of the DO can be estimated by using an option pricing model.

---

[3]To our knowledge, that model was first described in *The Treasury Bond Basis* by Galen Burghardt, Terry Belton, Morton Lane, and John Pappa, published by McGraw-Hill in 1989.

- The payoff profile of the DO is almost that of a put or call.[4] In the example of Figure 7.1, buying the CTD net basis is like buying a fraction of puts on the future. Note that this relationship in principle allows trading the CTD net basis versus options on the bond futures contract. Usually, however, the CTD switch situation is more complex than in Figure 7.1, which makes that arbitrage rarely practicable, as discussed below.
- The strike price of the DO is determined by the CTD inflection point. Note that the DO is always an OTM (out-of-the-money) option, as the CTD needs to change (i.e. something needs to happen) for the DO to produce profit. This means that the DO has only time value and is the reason that the DO value is equal to zero at the delivery date.
- The market consensus about yield level volatility until delivery is reflected in the option prices quoted in the market (e.g. from the options on bond futures).

With this information, the DO can be calculated through an option model like Black–Scholes, using the payoff profile from Figure 7.1 and the expected volatility of the market until delivery (e.g. as reflected in the bond futures option quotes) as inputs. Qualitatively, the DO value will be large, if:

- The CTD switching point is close to the current yield level. This corresponds to the strike price of an OTM option being close to the current market price. In this case, not a lot needs to happen for the CTD to change and there is a high likelihood of a CTD switch occurring before delivery.
- The delivery date is far away. In this case, there is considerable time for a CTD switch to occur and thus there is a high likelihood of a CTD switch occurring before delivery.
- The volatility is high. In this case, there is a high likelihood of a CTD switch occurring before delivery.
- The difference between the converted BPV of the old CTD and that of the new CTD (after a switch takes place) is large. In this case, a given amount of change in yield level causes a high profit from switching out of the old into the new CTD. In Figure 7.1, a large difference between the converted BPVs corresponds to a large difference in the slope of the converted forward price lines and hence to a larger payoff in the case of a CTD switch. Therefore, the profit from a CTD switch tends to be an increasing function of the difference between the converted forward BPVs.

---

[4]Due to convexity effects, the relationship of the payoff to the yield level is not exactly linear.

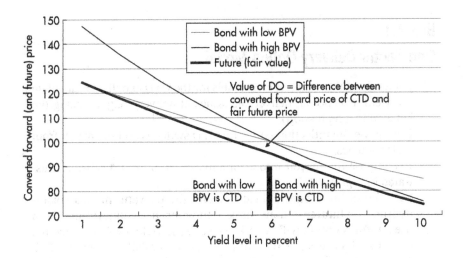

FIGURE 7.2 Fair futures price as a function of the yield level.
Source: Authors.

The first feature of our list means that for a given bond futures contract at a given date, the DO value is largest when the price of the futures contract is at the CTD inflection point. In other words, the impact on the fair futures price is a decreasing function of the distance between the yield of the current CTD and the inflection point. This result is illustrated in Figure 7.2.

Given the use of futures contracts for hedging bonds, an important application of this model is the calculation of the correct BPV for the futures contract. Simply assuming that the BPV of the futures contract is equal to the converted forward BPV of the CTD, $\frac{FwdBPV_{CTD}}{CF_{CTD}}$, ignores the impact of the DO on the futures price and might only be an acceptable approximation, particularly when the yield of the CTD is far from the inflection point. In addition, that number changes in a discontinuous fashion at the inflection point, which is a major problem for bond hedges using futures contracts. It is therefore necessary to use the slope of the 'Future (fair value)' line in Figure 7.2 as the BPV for the futures contract in hedging operations. That number is called the option-adjusted BPV (OABPV) and can be obtained by calculating the fair value of the future (i.e. $\frac{FwdP_{CTD}}{CF_{CTD}} - DO$) at two slightly different yield levels, thereby taking the impact of the change of the yield level on the DO into account.

Since changes in the absolute yield level may impact different deliverable bonds to a different extent, one should adjust the calculation for this effect, for example, by using the betas of a regression of the yield level of a deliverable bond versus the yield level of the CTD. The DO calculation then looks like the one shown in Box 7.1.

Box 7.1
One-Factor Delivery Option Model

- For a reasonable range of yield levels for the CTD at delivery, calculate the yield levels of all deliverable issues at delivery (e.g. by using the betas from a regression).
- Determine the inflection points for CTD switches and the payoff from CTD switches.
- Decompose that payoff into a combination of puts and calls, as illustrated in Figure 7.1.
- For each of these puts and calls, obtain the relevant implied volatility from the futures options market. In order to account for the skew, use a futures option with a strike close to the yield level, at which the CTD switch occurs (i.e. the 'strike' of the put or call from Figure 7.1). Thus, each of the puts and calls are priced with an individual implied volatility.
- For each of these puts and calls, calculate the value. This could be done by using the implied volatility and 'strike''' levels as input into the Black–Scholes formula.
- The DO is the sum of the option prices obtained in the previous step.
- Alternatively, the payoff function (Figure 7.1) could be numerically integrated over the probability density for the CTD yield, which again can be obtained from the futures options market. This alternative is preferable in case of the payoff function exhibiting a significant convexity. On the other hand, as it is easier to account for the skew through individual puts and calls rather than through an adjustment of the probability density for the CTD yield, this alternative is not advisable in the presence of a large skew.

THE NEED FOR MULTI-FACTOR DELIVERY OPTION MODELS

By construction, the DO model described above is a one-factor model. It can only assess the impact of changes in the absolute yield level on the DO; it cannot consider CTD switches that occur due to reasons other than a change in the overall yield level. Thus, those CTD switches that happen without a change in absolute yield level are outside of the scope of that model, which may therefore underestimate the value of the DO. In other words, as the model only assesses the DO coming from changes in the absolute yield level, it is conceptually ignorant of DO value coming from other sources, for example, from a bond becoming CTD due to only its individual repo rate decreasing.

In general, the DO value arises from the volatilities of the differences between the prices of deliverable bonds, which thereby determine the likelihood of and profit from CTD switches. The prices of the deliverable bonds, and hence the differences in prices, can be modeled indirectly by modeling the yields of the deliverable bonds.

In the one-factor model discussed above, all changes in the yield spreads between deliverable bonds were the result of the different yield betas associated with each bond. When our main yield factor increased, the yields of bonds with large betas would increase by more than would the yields of bonds with smaller betas. So while the one-factor model is capable of producing varying yield spreads, the entirety of the variation in yield spreads is the result of an increase or decrease in the general level of yields.

But while the results of our PCA chapter indicate that roughly 95% of the variation in yields generally can be attributed to a single factor (see Figure 3.4), it is *not* the case that the vast majority of the variation in yield *spreads* can be attributed to a single factor. In fact, the proportion of yield *spread* variation that can be attributed to changes in the overall level of yields depends on the situation.

- If the market yield level is close to the notional coupon of the bond futures contract, CTD switches between the short end and the long end of the basket can occur. These switches are usually caused by a change in the overall yield level and therefore captured by a one-factor model. Correspondingly, they show up in Figure 7.1 and Figure 7.2, which depict the perspective of one-factor models.

  As explained above, these CTD switches between the short and long end of the basket result in a large DO value due to the big difference in converted BPVs. Thus, when the market yield level is close to the notional coupon of the bond futures contract, one-factor models can be expected to capture the most important source of the DO value.
- The further the market yield level is away from the notional coupon of the bond futures contract, the less likely those CTD switches between the long and short end of the basket become. As a consequence, the DO value calculated by a one-factor model decreases and converges to zero. In the example of Figure 7.1, at a yield level of 3%, it is extremely unlikely to reach the 6% needed for a CTD switch caused by changes in the overall yield level in the few months until delivery, and thus the model based on Figure 7.1 will return a negligible DO value.

- Thus, the relative importance for yield spread volatility of factors other than the overall yield level is an increasing function of the distance between the CTD yield and the notional coupon of the bond futures contract. Consequently, there is a tendency for one-factor DO models to understate the value of the DO when the yield of the CTD is far from the notional coupon.

As a result, when yields dropped globally toward levels far below the notional coupons, the one-factor DO models working well at a 6% yield level became less useful. Since most market participants did not adjust their models to reflect the new source of DO value, the net bases quoted in the market nowadays systematically underestimate the real value of the DO (i.e. tend to be too low).

As an illustration, we consider the source of yield spread volatility between deliverables in a low-yield environment for the case of JGB futures, for which this situation first was relevant. While the deliverable basket extends from seven to 10.5 years, the low yield level in Japan means that the bond with the shortest maturity is always clearly CTD and that there is practically no chance for a bond with a longer maturity to become CTD, as seen in Figure 7.1. However, there are often two or even three bonds with the same shortest maturity and only a minimal difference in coupon, thus with almost the same BPV. These two or three bonds can all easily become CTD, thus there can be CTD switches between the two or three candidates with the same maturity. In fact, because the CTD candidates are so similar, CTD switches between them are quite common. Seen through the perspective of a one-factor model, a change in the overall yield level impacts all CTD candidates in almost the same manner, given the almost identical BPV and sensitivity. Thus, even if a CTD switch occurs, the profit is negligible, as argued above. In other words, while the similarity of CTD candidates may make CTD switches between them likely, the similarity of converted BPVs also means that the impact of a change in the overall yield level on the yield spread volatility between them is only marginal. Hence, applying a one-factor model to the basket of JGB futures returns a DO value close to zero.

In reality, however, the yield spread volatility between CTD candidates can be quite large, in part because the delivery situation can magnify the natural yield spread volatility. Imagine that many investors have a short CTD net basis position on their books. If the CTD switches to another candidate, which initially may be just a little bit cheaper, they need to be concerned about being delivered the new CTD into their long futures position. Thus, in order to hedge their risk, they need to sell the new and buy back the old CTD, an operation that may magnify an initially small yield spread between the two CTD candidates and may cause more investors to close their positions, leading to a reinforcing cycle. Note that this potentially significant yield spread volatility between deliverables is not caused and not even accompanied by any change in the overall yield level. Hence, by construction it cannot contribute toward the DO value in the context of a one-factor model, even though a long net basis position could yield significant profit in this scenario.[5]

When yields are far below the notional coupon, the yield spread volatility between deliverables is therefore not a function of the 95% of overall yield volatility explained by the overall yield level (and captured by one-factor models) but rather of the 5% of overall yield volatility not explained by the overall yield level (and not captured by one-factor models). Hence, at current yield levels, it is the 5% of overall yield volatility explained by greater factors (2, 3, ...), which matters for the yield spread volatility between deliverables. Consequently, a DO model claiming applicability in any yield environment needs to take more factors into account. DO modeling therefore needs to respond to the drop in yield levels far below the notional coupon by moving from one-factor to multi-factor models.

A FLEXIBLE MULTI-FACTOR DELIVERY OPTION MODEL[6]

Since it is impossible to determine ex ante *which* factor will be responsible for yield spread volatility between deliverables, we advise using *all* factors. That is, we replace the one-factor model by a model that has as many factors as there are bonds in the deliverable basket. The full information needed to assess the yield spread volatility between deliverables and thus the value of the DO can be represented for a deliverable basket with n bonds with the yields y_1, ... , y_n by the variables

- y_1: the absolute yield level of the first deliverable bond. The designation 'first' is arbitrary. For example, the bond with the shortest maturity in the basket could be considered the first bond, as could the CTD.
- $y_2 - y_1$, ... , $y_n - y_1$ (i.e. the yield spread between every other bond and the first one).

---

[5]This is also the reason why an arbitrage between the net basis and futures options is only practicable when CTD switches between the short and long end of the basket are the main driving force of the net basis.

[6]That model was developed by us as employees of ABN Amro and first published in the ABN Amro research note "Exploiting the ignored delivery option in JGB contracts" from 21 February 2002. It is reproduced here with kind permission from RBS.

Note that this set of variables is just a different way of modeling all yields $y_1, \ldots, y_n$. The reason for this particular representation will become clear later on. While we can make reasonable assumptions about how yield spread variables behave in a delivery situation, expressing that impact of a futures contract on the relationships between deliverable bonds in the form of correlations between $y_1, \ldots, y_n$ would be a major and unnecessary challenge.

We allow for correlation between all of the variables (i.e. both between the absolute yield level and yield spread variables[7] and between different yield spread variables). Furthermore, we assume all variables are normally distributed. Note that this is the only assumption of the model and in our view not a very strong or particularly restrictive assumption. If a particular market was found to behave differently, the following simulation could be adjusted accordingly. (For example, one could replace the normal distribution with a lognormal distribution.) We can now obtain an estimate for the DO through the steps shown in Box 7.2.

Box 7.2
Multi-Factor Delivery Option Model

- Define the yield volatility of the first deliverable bond.
- Define the yield spread volatility for the variables $y_2 - y_1, \ldots, y_n - y_1$.
- Define the correlations between all of the variables $y_1, y_2 - y_1, \ldots, y_n - y_1$. We shall discuss ways to set these input parameters below.
- Run a Monte Carlo simulation with normally distributed random variables each with zero mean and with standard deviations and correlations defined as above, simulating the evolution of the yield (spreads) of all deliverable bonds until the delivery date.
- Translate the results of each simulation into a table of yields $y_1, \ldots, y_n$ at delivery and calculate the corresponding converted prices. In order to adjust for the difference between forward and spot prices, add the difference between the current converted forward price and the average of the future converted prices at delivery generated by the simulation to each of the simulation results. In this way, the mean of the simulated prices on the delivery date for each bond will equal the forward price for each bond.

---

[7]The yield beta of a one-factor model would show up via the covariance matrix in the multifactor model.

- For each of the mean-adjusted simulation results, identify the bond that is CTD and the extent of any profit from a CTD switch.
- Calculate an estimate for the DO value as the average of the profit from CTD switches over all simulations, taking the CFs into account.
- Calculate for each deliverable bond an estimate for the probability of being CTD at delivery date by dividing the number of simulations in which it finishes as CTD by the number of all simulations.

Based on these results, one can repeat the calculation of the fair value of the future and related numbers from above with a better estimation for the value of the DO. In particular:

- Calculate the fair futures price as $\frac{FwdP_{\text{CTD}}}{CF_{\text{CTD}}} - DO$.
- Repeating the exercise for the back month contract, calculate the fair futures roll (calendar spread).
- Calculate the OABPV (with reference to the first bond) by repeating the Monte Carlo simulation on a set of yields y_i as starting points, which reflects the typical impact of a 1 bp increase in y_1 on the yields of all deliverables. Then, the OABPV is the difference between the fair futures price and the fair futures price of the simulation starting with the shifted yields. As required, this calculation takes the impact of a different yield level on the DO into account.

  One way to obtain the set of yields y_i, which reflects the typical impact of a 1 bp increase in y_1 on the yields of all deliverables, is to perform a PCA on the covariance matrix given by the input parameters. Then, the sensitivities to the first factor show how a 1 bp increase of y_1 is expected to influence the yields of the other deliverables. This is an application of the curve reconstruction technique through PCA outlined in Chapter 3.

A good graphical representation of both the input parameters into that Monte Carlo simulation and its output can be obtained by using the change in the yield spread variables until delivery as coordinates and plotting the resulting CTD of each simulation as a specific mark (such as points for the first bond, crosses for the second, etc.) into that coordinate system. An example for such a chart is given in Figure 7.3, which provides immediate intuition of the scenarios under which each bond is likely to be CTD.

The shape of the scatterplot in Figure 7.3 is determined by the two yield spread volatilities and by the correlation between the two yield spreads.

The CTD probability for each bond corresponds to the relative frequency of the symbols in the scatterplot depicted in Figure 7.3. Also, by assessing the

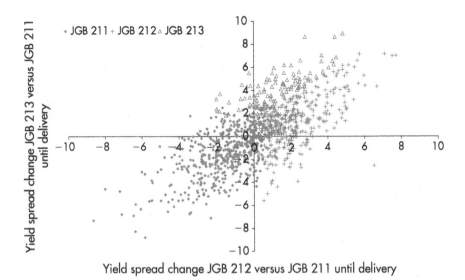

FIGURE 7.3   Results of a Monte Carlo simulation of the CTD situation at delivery date as a function of the yield spread changes between CTD candidates until delivery. *Source:* ABN Amro (reproduced here with permission from RBS).

positions of the symbols, one can get an understanding of the way a shift in yield spreads influences the CTD situation or, conversely, which yield spread move would need to happen in order for a particular bond to become CTD.

Choosing Input Parameters for the Multi-Factor DO Model

After outlining the model, we now discuss ways to choose its input parameters. The yield volatility, which is the only parameter involved in one-factor models, can be set equal to the implied volatility of options on bond futures. With regards to defining the parameters for yield spread volatilities, we face a basic problem in that historical yield spread volatility is of limited value.

Outside of the context of a deliverable basket, there is usually little reason for very similar bonds to exhibit significant yield spread volatilities. For example, why should an investor's preference for JGB 212 1.5% maturing on 22 June 2009 and JGB 213 1.4%, also maturing on 22 June 2009, suddenly change? In fact, these very similar issues are not considered as *individual* bonds but rather as almost identical representations of the same issue. Therefore, before becoming relevant for delivery into a futures contract, the yield spread volatility between deliverables is typically small.

But this situation changes when the bonds enter into competition for CTD status. JGB 212 might be CTD, but JGB 213 is not, which has a major impact on the treatment of both issues in the repo market and in basis trades. We have given an example earlier of the way a CTD switch can impact the yield spread between the two deliverable bonds involved. Hence, bonds gain an individuality, an individual treatment in the bond and repo markets, through the context of a deliverable basket. And consequently, the CTD situation is a major (most of the time the only) reason for a significant yield spread volatility between otherwise very similar bonds. Figure 7.4 shows the way the yield spread volatilities between CTD candidates increase as the delivery date approaches. On average, the yield spread volatility more than doubles in the year prior to delivery, reflecting the strong impact of a delivery situation on *individual* bonds versus their peers. In the case of a squeeze situation, the increase of yield spread volatility can be far above that in typical circumstances.

The calculation of the DO value through a multi-factor model requires an input parameter for the yield spread volatilities before delivery (i.e. before the actual impact of the specific delivery situation on the yield spread volatilities can be known). In addition, that input parameter has a significant importance for the resulting DO value, which (in case of a large distance between the

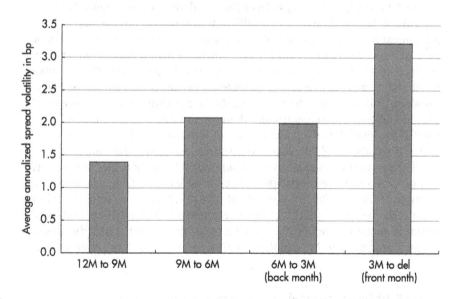

FIGURE 7.4 Evolution of the yield spread volatility between CTD candidates as they approach delivery in the example of JGB futures contracts.
Source: ABN Amro (reproduced here with permission from RBS).

actual yield level and the notional coupon) often depends almost exclusively on that input variable. Actually, drawing the estimated DO value as a function of the yield spread volatility used in the Monte Carlo simulation often reveals an almost linear relationship, with the line crossing through the origin of the coordinate system.

A possible solution to this problem could be first to calculate the historical yield spread volatility between the deliverable issues before they became part of the deliverable basket and then to adjust that yield spread volatility by the factor of its average increase into delivery, as shown in Figure 7.4. This main or average scenario could further be complemented by alternative scenarios, for example, reflecting the expected increase of yield spread volatility in case of a CTD squeeze. As a general remark, it is advisable to run the DO model described above several times for a set of different input parameters in order to gain an insight into the value of the DO and thus the expected performance of related trades (such as net basis positions) under various scenarios.

As an alternative[8] to using constant values for the yield spread volatilities throughout the simulation, for example, by adjusting the historical yield spread volatilities by a factor derived from Figure 7.4, one can also reflect the expected increase in yield spread volatility as delivery increases directly in the simulation. In this case, the evolution of yield spread volatility shown in Figure 7.4 is applied to every path of the simulation behind Figure 7.3.

All the correlations in this multi-factor model usually remain stable in the context of a delivery, unlike the yield spread volatilities themselves. Moreover, in many cases, the resulting DO value is not significantly affected by a small change in the correlation parameters. For the purpose of the DO model, it is therefore usually fine to use the historically observed correlations as input variables. Still, as the impact of changes to the correlation parameters could be exceptionally strong in a particular delivery situation, we recommend checking the results of the DO model also for alternative correlation scenarios, just as described above for alternative yield spread volatility parameters.

The reward for these efforts is the ability to detect DOs that are undervalued in a market whose participants stick mostly to one-factor models. In the example of the JGB futures contract of Figure 7.3, the one factor model outlined at the beginning of this chapter returned a DO of less than 1 sen, while the multi-factor DO model[9] suggests it is in fact worth 7 sen. Thus, the methodological progress can be exploited by finding and buying valuable DOs at a

---

[8] Rubin Rajendram has pointed out this alternative to us.
[9] Using the same yield volatility as the one-factor model and historical yield spread volatilities and correlations, with the yield spread volatilities adjusted by the factor from Figure 7.4.

bargain price. As long as the majority of market participants continue using one-factor models, the profit from buying undervalued DOs (e.g. through long CTD net basis positions) must come from actual CTD switches. The downside in case there is no CTD switch is very limited if the DO can be bought almost for free, as in the JGB futures example above. In addition, however, the increasing application of multifactor models should result in a general trend, correcting the current undervaluation of DOs toward an overall increase in net bases.

In summary, a better estimation for the DO value allows a better estimation for the fair value of the futures contract, which enhances:

- basis trading
- hedging of bonds with the future (using the OABPV)
- rolling over from the front in the back month contract.

CHAPTER **8**

Fitted Bond Curves

INTRODUCTION

Which of an issuer's bonds are rich, and which are cheap? And how do we know? To answer these questions, we first need to better define the terms rich and cheap in this context.

Not surprisingly given that our subject matter is relative value, we'll define these words in relative terms rather than in absolute terms. In particular, we say that a bond is rich if its price is greater than we'd expect conditional on the available information, including but not limited to the prices of the issuer's other bonds. Other information might include whether the bond is special in the repo market, whether the bond is deliverable into a futures contract, and the liquidity of the bond as proxied by the bid–ask spread.

FRAMEWORK OF ANALYSIS

Whenever we're dealing with expectations conditional on a set of information, we're in the realm of regression analysis. In particular, at any point in time, we'll specify the price of each bond in our data set as the dependent variable and the relevant conditioning information as the independent variables, as in the cross-sectional regression given by:

$$P_i = A(\Theta_i; \alpha) + B(\Psi_i; \gamma) + \varepsilon_i$$

where P_i is the price of the i-th bond in our data set, $i = 1, \ldots, N$; $A(\Theta_i; \alpha)$ is a function of the parameter vector α, and of Θ_i, an array of dimension $2 \times M_i$ that represents the dates and sizes of the M_i cash flows that constitute bond i; $B(\Psi_i; \gamma)$ is a function of the $k \times 1$ parameter vector, γ, and of the $k \times 1$ vector Ψ_i, which contains the independent variables other than the cash flow dates and amounts on which we condition our expectations of the bond prices; and ε_i is a random error term, unique to each bond in our data set.

167

In this equation, we suppress any notation to indicate that this regression applies at any and all times. For example, without loss of generality, we could subscript all the variables and parameters in the equation with a time index.

The ε_i terms, for all $i = 1, \ldots, N$ are the terms that represent the richness and cheapness of the bonds in our data set, with positive values indicating the bond in question as rich.

Because $A(\Theta_i; \alpha)$ is a function involving the cash flows of the coupon bond, and because the value of a coupon bond is a linear function of the values of the individual cash flows, $A(\Theta_i; \alpha)$ generally will have a form given by:

$$A(\Theta_i; \alpha) = \sum_{l=1}^{M_i} C_{il} \phi(\tau_{il})$$

where C_{il} is the size of the i-th cash flow for bond i, and $\phi(\tau_{il})$ is the discount factor associated with the i-th cash flow for the i-th bond, to be received at time τ_{il}.

With this in mind, we see that the key to taking a view as to the richness or cheapness of specific bonds among a collection of bonds is to ascertain an appropriate discount function $\phi(\tau)$ that is presumed to apply generally to the collection of bonds at any particular point in time.

As with standard regressions, we can proceed once we've made some distributional assumptions on the error terms. In particular, we'll assume that the error terms in the equation for P_i are independent of one another and that they're normally distributed, each with a mean equal to zero. For now, we'll also assume that all the error terms have variances that are identical to each other. In this case, the maximum likelihood estimators for α and γ are identical to the estimators obtained via ordinary least squares (OLS). If we have reason to believe that the error terms are in some sense heteroscedastic, we can use weighted least squares (WLS) in place of OLS.

To make the regression operational, we need to specify two more aspects of our regression. First, we need to decide on a functional form for the discount factor function $\phi(\tau)$. Second, we need to specify the independent variables on which we believe the bond prices are conditioned.

SPECIFYING A FUNCTION FOR DISCOUNT FACTORS

We use the term *discount factor* to refer to the price of a zero-coupon bond as a percentage of its face value. In the context of our exercise, we assume that at any point in time there exists one and only one discount factor corresponding to every future date on which a zero-coupon bond could mature. An absence of arbitrage ensures the uniqueness of each discount factor and that all discount factors are non-negative.

In the past, it was common to make the additional assumption that all discount factors were no greater than one, in order to preclude negative interest rates. The argument was that investors could choose to keep their money under a proverbial mattress rather than on deposit earning a negative interest rate. But the spate of negative interest rates in recent history suggests there aren't enough mattresses under which to keep funds safe from negative interest rates. In more economic terms, banks clearly provide services for which depositors are willing to pay in the form of below-market interest rates, even if that means accepting negative nominal interest rates.

When choosing a functional form for $\phi(\tau)$, two conditions seem natural.

Criterion 1: We'd like a discount function that approaches zero in the limit as time increases. That is, $\lim_{\tau \to \infty} \phi(\tau) = 0$, where ϕ is the discount function and τ is the time until the relevant cash flow is received.

Criterion 2: To prevent arbitrage, we also require $\lim_{\tau \to 0} \phi(\tau) = 1$. Otherwise, an investor would be able to purchase (or sell) a zero-coupon bond an instant before maturity and earn a riskless profit well in excess of the riskless rate.

In our experience, exponential functions are useful for this purpose, and they clearly satisfy criteria 1 (C1) and 2 (C2).

For example, if we specify yields in terms of continuously compounded rates, we could use the general specification

$$\phi(\tau) = e^{-h(\tau)}$$

where $h(\tau)$ is a continuous function of τ.

As long as $h(\tau)$ is bounded, $\phi(\tau)$ will satisfy C1 and C2 above. Actually, boundedness is too strong a condition in this case. For example, if $h(\tau)$ is a polynomial in τ, it will also satisfy C1 as all polynomials increase at a slower rate than the exponential function. Nevertheless, the concept of an unbounded yield curve presents difficulties with economic interpretation if not necessarily with the mathematics. It's also nice, if not necessary, for $h(\tau)$ to have a limit as $\tau \to \infty$. (Note that polynomials do not satisfy this criterion.)

Depending on the functional form used for $h(\tau)$, there can be a number of advantages in specifying a functional form for the yield curve rather than for the discount factor function directly. In addition to the ease with which conditions C1 and C2 can be satisfied, specifying a functional form for the zero-coupon yield curve tends to offer greater intuition to the analyst during the curve-fitting exercise. For example, if a particular attempt to fit the curve is producing modeled yields that are systemically too high for bonds maturing between seven and 10 years, it's typically easier to ascertain the desired changes to make when specifying a yield curve than it is when specifying a discount factor function that may contain upward of 10 constituent functions, all specified in terms of zero-coupon bond prices.

Ultimately, however, the choice is a function of the quality of the fit and of the ease with which the analyst is able to implement the model.

WEIGHTS

Thus far, we've maintained the assumption that the error terms have identical distributions, with zero means and with variances equal to one another. If there are reasons to believe that the variances of the error terms are not equal, we can modify our approach to accommodate WLS. In other words, we can choose parameters to minimize:

$$\sum_{i=1}^{N} \frac{\varepsilon_i^2}{U_i}$$

where U_i is the weight assumed to be proportional to the variance of ε_i.

In our experience, there are a few criteria that could help guide the choice of weights in this context:

- **Basis point values:** Some analysts take the view that bonds with large basis point values have prices that are measured with less precision and therefore with greater error than bonds with smaller basis point values. In particular, if the variances of the error terms for the fitted yields were assumed to be equal, then the variances of the fitted prices would be roughly proportional to the basis point values of the bonds.
- **Deliverability:** As discussed in Chapter 7 on future delivery options, bonds that are deliverable into a futures contract may experience greater price volatility than similar bonds that are not deliverable.
- **Repo specialness:** Bonds that are experiencing episodic specialness in the repo market have a tendency to have greater spot price volatility than other bonds.

Ultimately, the heteroscedasticity of the error terms is an empirical matter. We suggest analysts use judgment in deciding what forms of heteroscedasticity are likely to be present in the markets they're analyzing.

SETTING UP THE OPTIMIZATION

Reflecting the ideas outlined above in a numerical optimization, the key is to minimize an error term by changing the parameters controlling the discount factor curve *at the same time and in the same optimization* as the regression coefficients versus external explanatory variables, such as issuance size. Hence, the general approach is to minimize an expression like the following by changing the parameters determining the discount factor curve *df* and the regression coefficients $\gamma(k)$:

$$\sum_{b \in Bonds} \left| \sum_{l \in CF(b)} CF(i) \times df(t_i) + \sum_{k \in External} \gamma(k) \times k(b) - Dirtyprice(b) \right|^{1 \text{ or } 2 \text{ or} \ldots}$$

where:

- $CF(i)$ is the i-th cash flow of the bond b at time t_i
- df is the discount factor curve
- $\gamma(k)$ is the regression coefficient versus external variable k (such as issuance size).

In case of exponential splines being used as functional form for the discount factor curve, i.e. $df(t) = \sum_{j=1}^{n} \beta_j \times e^{-jt\alpha}$, the parameters β_j and α are subject to the optimization – *at the same time* as the $\gamma(k)$.

Hence, the *output* of the optimization will be a fitted curve *df* (in the case of exponential splines given by the parameters β_j and α) and the regression coefficients $\gamma(k)$ versus external driving forces.

When setting up the optimization, the analyst faces a number of important decisions regarding the *input*:

- the choice of the sets "Bonds" and "External"
- the choice of the functional form for *df*, and in case of exponential splines of their number n
- the choice of the final exponent (of the absolute spread between fitted and actual dirty price). While quadratic error terms seem to be considered as standard, in our experience, this often results in outliers gaining too much influence on the result of the optimization; we therefore recommend trying the exponent 1 instead of 2 as well.

These choices fall to the discretion of the analyst and require careful adjustment to the markets analyzed and analytic goals.

Example: Fitting the German Bund Curve

The Setting: German Bunds, Using Size, Age, and Deliverability as Additional Conditioning Variables

The best way to illustrate these concepts is to work through a specific example. In this case, we use the closing prices of coupon-paying German Bunds, OBLs, and Schatze on 7 Dec 2012. As additional independent variables, we'll include:

- **Time since issuance:** New issues may be in greater demand than older issues.
- **Issue size:** To achieve benchmark status, a bond needs to be issued in sufficient size.
- **Deliverability:** Bonds that are deliverable into futures contracts, in particular the cheapest-to-deliver (CTD), may be priced differently from other bonds.

Note that theoretical arguments can be made for the coefficients on these three variables to be positive or negative. For example, benchmark issues may be easier to sell short, making them less expensive than otherwise comparable issues. Likewise, if a CTD issue is easier to sell short, its price might be less than it would be otherwise. So ultimately, the signs of the coefficients will be determined by the data.

Our list of explanatory variables isn't meant to be exhaustive. There are reasons to include repo specialness as a variable. It's also useful to consider whether recent CTDs might maintain residual richness or cheapness for a period and whether likely future CTDs might contain some anticipatory richness or cheapness. For illustrative purposes, however, we'll focus on the explanatory variables listed above.

Figure 8.1 shows the term structure of yields for coupon-paying German Bunds as of the close of trading on Friday, 7 December 2012. We exclude bonds with times to maturity of less than one year, as we find money markets are best modeled separately.[1]

---

[1]Money market instruments, including bonds with less than a year to maturity, require a greater degree of analytical precision than longer-dated bonds, for a number of reasons. For example, money market instruments are particularly sensitive to central bank policy, and at times we observe sharp discontinuities between instruments maturing before particular central bank meeting dates and those maturing after.

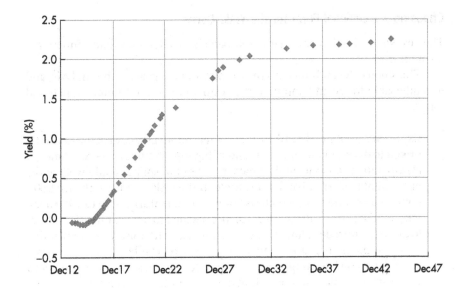

FIGURE 8.1 Bund yields as of 7 Dec 2012.
Source: Data – Bloomberg; Chart – Authors.

TABLE 8.1 Deliverable Issues into March 2013 Futures Contracts

Schatz	Bobl	Bond	Buxl
BKO 0% 12-Dec-14	DBR 4% 4-Jan-18	DBR 2% 4-Jan-22	DBR 4.75% 4-Jul-40
DBR 3.75% 4-Jan-15	OBL 0.5% 13-Oct-17	DBR 1.75% 4-Jul-22	DBR 4.25% 4-Jul-39
OBL 2.5% 27-Feb-15	DBR 4.25% 4-Jul-18	DBR 1.5% 4-Sep-22	DBR 3.25% 4-Jul-42
OBL 2.25% 10-Feb-15			DBR 2.5% 4-Jul-44

Table 8.1 shows the issues that are deliverable into the Schatz, Bobl, Bund, and Buxl futures contracts expiring in March 2013.

We define our deliverability variable in such a way that the deliverability variable is not simply one if a bond is deliverable and zero otherwise. Rather, this variable is set equal to the price value of a basis point for the bond if the bond is deliverable, and it's set to zero otherwise. As a result, the coefficients for these variables have the interpretation of being the number of basis points by which an issue tends to be rich when it is the deliverable issue into one of the futures contracts.

Choosing a Functional Form for the Yield Curve

The next step in implementing this approach is specifying a suitable functional form for $h(\tau)$.

This choice depends on both the market and the goals of the analysis, and it is advisable to try and compare the results of several different functional forms.

- Exponential splines described above offer the advantage of being naturally linked to discount factor curves and of having a limit for $\tau \to \infty$. Hence, if *extrapolations* are part of the goals, exponential splines could well be the only suitable alternative. For example, if the task is to price the first 50Y bond of a government, which has only issued maturities up to 30Y so far, polynomials are no alternative. Having decided to use exponential splines leads to the next decision on how many to use, with the answer depending again on the market and analysis goals. For typical bond markets, seven could be a good starting point, with too few splines causing a too sticky curve and too many splines following each outlier too closely.
- Cubic splines consist of a series of cubic polynomials between carefully chosen knot points (e.g. 0Y, 1Y, 2Y, etc.), constructed so as to ensure continuity in the function, first and second derivative. They are more suitable to reflect changes in the first derivative of the yield curve. For example, if the market assumptions about monetary policy result in interest rates rising between 0Y and 1Y, falling between 1Y and 2Y before rising again, cubic splines are in a better position to capture this behavior than exponential splines. Having decided to use cubic splines leads to the next decision on how many and which knot points to use. Since changes in the first derivative of the yield curve are more common at the front end influenced by monetary policy expectations, it is typically advisable to increase the distance between knot points with maturity.
- If cubic splines provide unsatisfactory results, the analyst can specify different functional forms between the knot points and obtain maximum smoothness, defined here as the integral of the square of the second derivative of the function.

For this example, we choose cubic splines and place the knots between each cubic spline at maturities (in years) of: 0, 0.5, 1.0, 1.5, 2, 5, 7, 10, 12, 15, 20, 30, and 35.

The details of this calculation are explained in the box and the resulting regression residuals are shown in Figure 8.2.

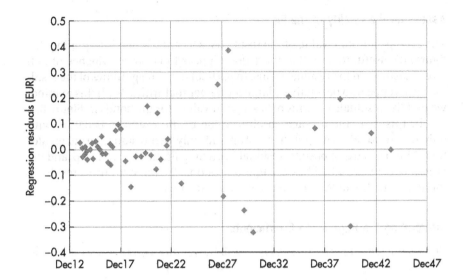

FIGURE 8.2 Bund regression residuals expressed in EUR.
Source: Authors.

Technical Points for Calculating Cubic Splines

While determining the parameters of each cubic polynomial is a straight-forward linear algebra problem (solve for the parameters to fulfill the continuity in the function, first and second derivatives), this calculation needs to be repeated in every step of the optimization outlined above. Hence, it is important to use a numerically quick set-up, e.g. the following routine:

Given the knot points (x_i, y_i) define h_i as the distance $x_i - x_{i-1}$ between consecutive maturities and the tridiagonal nxn-matrix A by placing 2 in the main diagonal, $\frac{h_i}{h_i + h_{i+1}}$ to the left and $1 - \frac{h_i}{h_i + h_{i+1}}$ to the right (in the first and last row, all entries are 0 except for 2 in the main diagonal).

Note that the matrix A is independent of the values y_i, which change during the optimization. Hence, the inverted matrix A^{-1} only needs to be calculated once and can be used for all steps of the optimization, improving the speed significantly.

With $d_i := \left(\frac{y_{i+1} - y_i}{h_{i+1}} - \frac{y_i - y_{i-1}}{h_i} \right) \frac{6}{h_i + h_{i+1}}$ (and $d_1 := d_n := 0$) and $M := A^{-1}d$,

the spline value at time to maturity $t \in [x_i, x_{i+1}]$ is given by $\frac{M_i(x_{i+1} - t)^3}{6h_{i+1}} +$

$\frac{M_{i+1}(t - x_i)^3}{6h_{i+1}} + \left(y_{i+1} - \frac{M_{i+1}h_{i+1}^2}{6} \right) \frac{t - x_i}{h_{i+1}} + \left(y_i - \frac{M_i h_{i+1}^2}{6} \right) \frac{x_{i+1} - t}{h_{i+1}}$

Assessing the Quality of the Fit

The average absolute value of the residuals is 9 cents. When interpreting this figure, it's useful to note that there does appear to be some evidence of heteroscedasticity in the residual terms. In particular, the magnitudes of the residual terms appear to be relatively large for longer maturities. With this in mind, we plot the residuals in terms of basis point values for the bonds in Figure 8.3.

In this case, the average absolute value of the residuals is 0.9 bp, with only one residual term less than −2 bp and only two residual terms greater than 2 bp. The largest positive residual has a magnitude of only 2.3 bp, and the largest negative residual has a magnitude of only 2.2 bp. With these results in mind, the quality of the fit appears to be satisfactory.[2]

Interpreting the Regression Coefficients

The coefficients for the size, age, and deliverability variables are shown in Table 8.2.

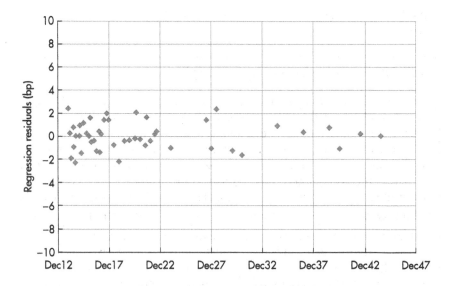

FIGURE 8.3 Bund regression residuals expressed in basis points.
Source: Authors.

---

[2]Given that the residuals appear somewhat heteroscedastic when expressed in terms of price and less so when expressed in terms of basis points suggests further analysis may be warranted to assess the merits of WLS in this case.

TABLE 8.2 Bund Regression Coefficients

Independent variable	Coefficient estimate
Amount outstanding (EUR bn)	EUR 0.025
Issue age (years)	0.027 years
Schatz deliverable? (bp)	3.6 bp
Bobl deliverable? (bp)	2.8 bp
Bund deliverable? (bp)	2.1 bp
Buxl deliverable? (bp)	2.4 bp

The coefficient for the amount outstanding suggests that larger issues tend to be more expensive, which would be consistent with the existence of a benchmark effect in this market. In particular, an additional EUR 1 bn outstanding corresponds to an additional 2.5 cents in the value of the bond.

The coefficient for the age of the bond suggests that bonds tend to cheapen with age. This also is consistent with a benchmark effect, and it's perhaps consistent with a repo effect as well. In particular, in the German market, bonds tend to cheapen at a rate of 2.7 cents per year, all else being equal.

The results are broadly similar for the deliverability variables. In particular, issues that are deliverable into the Schatz, Bobl, Bund, and Buxl contracts tend to have yields that are lower by 2 to 4 bp than other bonds. The fact that the premium for the Schatz contract is the largest perhaps shouldn't be surprising, since the basis point values are so small for the bonds that are deliverable in the Schatz contract.

Statistical Analysis of Rich/Cheap Figures

In our experience, the rich/cheap indicators for individual bonds generally tend to revert around a mean of zero, though this isn't always the case. For example, in some cases, bonds are structurally rich, and the rich/cheap indicator will revert around a number that reflects this structural richness.

In other cases, the rich/cheap indicator won't exhibit any particular mean reversion at all. While we would be reluctant to assume that the rich/cheap indicator is non-stationary, given the economic implications of this inference, the failure for a time series to exhibit clear mean reversion makes it difficult for us to estimate the speed of mean reversion, even if we have persuasive reasons *a priori* for assuming the indicator to revert around a mean.

Z-Scores and T-Stats

In our experience, many analysts model the mean reversion of rich/cheap indicators by calculating the number of standard deviations by which the indicator differs from its long-run mean. For example, if a bond currently appears 10 cents rich, and if its average degree of richness has been zero, and if the standard deviation of the rich/cheap indicator for that bond is 5.0, then a Z-score or T-stat[3] is calculated for the bond of 2.0, by subtracting the mean from the current value and dividing the result by the standard deviation of the rich/cheap indicator. In this case, $\frac{10-0}{5} = 2$.

The clear problem with this approach is that it ignores the information the data contain regarding the speed with which the rich/cheap indicator tends to revert toward its mean. For example, if the rich/cheap indicator for the bond in our example bond appears to be independently and identically distributed each day, then our expected value for the rich/cheap indicator the next time this bond is observed is zero, regardless of the current value of the indicator.

On the other hand, if the rich/cheap indicator for our bond has exhibited slow mean reversion, say, with a half-life of 200 days, then our expectation for tomorrow's rich/cheap indicator for the bond should be virtually identical to today's value for the indicator.

Knowing the Z-score is 2.0 in this example tells us almost nothing about the value we should expect for the rich/cheap indicator for this bond tomorrow.

Mean Reversion

In most cases, there are strong *a priori* reasons for believing that rich/cheap indicators for bonds tend to be mean reverting. And in our experience, the mean reversion of these indicators is confirmed as an empirical matter as well.

As a result, we suggest applying the mean reversion models of Chapter 2 to the rich/cheap indicators obtained in these curve-fitting exercises.

For example, we find it useful to report the half-lives of these rich/cheap indicators, assuming they follow stochastic differential equations with linear drift coefficients, as with the Ornstein–Uhlenbeck process. More generally, we find it useful to calculate the ex ante Sharpe ratios of the rich/cheap indicators on various horizons, such as two weeks.

---

[3]The term *Z-score* typically refers to the case in which a demeaned normal random variable is standardized by a *known* standard deviation, in which case the resulting variable is also normal and can be compared to values in a standard normal table. The term *T-stat* refers to the case in which a demeaned normal random variable is standardized by a standard deviation that must be *estimated*. In this case, assuming the observations have been drawn from a normal distribution, the estimate of the variance will have a Chi-squared distribution. And the ratio of a normal variate to the square root of a Chi-square variate has a student-t distribution. In applications, we almost always need to estimate the standard deviation, in which case the student-t distribution is more appropriate.

Applications

Trading Bond Switches and Butterflies

One of the main reasons for a relative value analyst or trader to identify rich and cheap securities is to identify attractive relative value bond trades. For a hedge fund trader, this might mean establishing a short position in one bond against a long position in a nearby bond. For a portfolio manager at a pension fund, this might mean selling an existing long position in one bond and using the proceeds to purchase a nearby bond considered to offer greater value. We'll use the generic term *bond switch* for each of these trades. When a cheap (rich) bond is purchased (sold) against positions in two other bonds, one with a lesser maturity and one with a greater maturity, we use the generic term *bond butterfly*.[4]

The implicit assumption often made when conducting rich/cheap analysis is that bonds that are currently rich should be expected to cheapen and that bonds that are currently cheap should be expected to richen. However, this need not be the case, and the careful relative value analyst will try to identify the reasons that a bond is trading rich or cheap so as to form a reasonable expectation about the prospects for the bond in the future. For example, a bond that has begun to be squeezed in the repo market may have a spot price that appears expensive relative to other bonds, but it's quite possible that the squeeze will intensify before it weakens, to the detriment of a trader who has taken a short position. To protect against this and similar possibilities, we suggest taking care to understand changes in relative valuations rather than merely assuming that bonds will revert to fair value. It's not always possible to identify the reasons that a bond is rich or cheap, and to be honest it's not always necessary. But it's certainly prudent to make the effort.

Selecting Issues for Trade Expression

The rich/cheap analysis described here is also useful in identifying specific instruments for expressing views. For example, let's imagine that an analyst performed a principal component analysis of the yield curve, as per Chapter 3, and decided to implement a curve steepening trade between the two-year (2Y) and 10Y sectors. Further, let's imagine that he analyzed the term structure of swap spreads, as per Chapter 12, and concluded that bonds are likely to cheapen to swaps in the 10Y sector. As a result, he decides to express the 10Y

---

[4]The intention is that these switches and butterflies will involve bonds within the same sector of the curve. Otherwise, a switch between bonds with significantly different maturities would result in a position with significant curve exposure.

leg of the trade by shorting a bond in the 10Y sector. At this point, he could use the rich/cheap analysis in this chapter, perhaps combined with the mean reversion analysis in Chapter 2, to identify the specific bond in the 10Y sector to short.

Predicting New Issue Pricing

It's sometimes useful to predict the pricing of a new issue even before it's announced. For example, there have been times when newly issued German Schatze have been CTD into the Schatz futures contract. These typically would be issued according to a regular schedule, so the yet-to-be-announced bonds could affect the pricing of the futures contracts.

To take a view on the fair value of the futures contract even before the new issue is announced in this case, one could forecast the coupon and maturity date of the bond and forecast the extent to which the bond was likely to trade rich to the curve at the time it was issued. This would allow the analyst to assume a spot price and a coupon for the bond. From these, a conversion factor and a basis point value could be computed. By assuming a repo rate for the new issue, the analyst then could calculate the presumed converted forward price for the new issue, and the pricing of the futures contract could proceed along the lines discussed in Chapter 7.

Creating Generic Notional Benchmarks

There are times when a relative value analyst would like to track the price or yield of a notional benchmark (i.e. a bond that doesn't actually exist). For example, we may want to compare the constant-maturity yield of a 10Y bond trading at par against the 10Y swap rate. In that case, we'll need to create a synthetic or *notional* bond for this purpose.

Having a fitted curve of discount factors allows us to solve for the size of a coupon that will cause the price of our notional bond to be equal to par. This can be done numerically, but it also can be done algebraically via the discount function.

In particular, if Z_{10} is the price of a 10Y zero-coupon bond that pays one dollar at maturity, and if A_{10} is the value of an annuity that pays one dollar on each of the payment dates for the notional coupon bond in question, then the size of the coupon, C, that will cause our notional bond to have a fair or fitted price equal to par can be determined by the equation

$$100 = 100Z_{10} + CA_{10}$$

We can solve the equation for C to get

$$C = \frac{100(1 - Z_{10})}{A_{10}}$$

CONCLUSIONS

Our main innovation in this chapter is to place the rich/cheap analysis in the context of a regression, which is the tool of choice when forming expectations conditional on a particular set of information. These days, computing speeds tend to be sufficient for performing nonlinear regressions numerically in a real-time trading environment, allowing us to use a set of models that provide better fits to the data than models of the past, many of which relied on linear equations and/or simplifications. Having real-time fitted curves in the context of a regression allows us to use the resulting regression residuals as real-time rich/cheap indicators.

As swap spreads are used by many market participants as rich/cheap indicators, we'll assess their suitability as an alternative to fitted curves in Chapter 17. In summary, we'll find that only SOFR-asset swap spreads are (almost) free from the deficiencies of other types of swap spreads as rich/cheap measure. As a consequence, SOFR-asset swap spreads of basis swapped bonds can be used as an alternative global RV measure instead of or in addition to fitting curves through basis swapped bonds.

However, the switch to SOFR as the reference rate has introduced structural breaks in the time series of swaps, as highlighted in the Preface. Hence, even if fitted curve models may not be the only alternative for rich/cheap analysis in the presence of SOFR swaps, they are of particular relevance for generating constant maturity government bond time series as an alternative to swap data. By contrast, EURIBOR swaps provide time series with less structural breaks for historical analysis in EUR, but no good alternative for rich/cheap assessments.

In addition, regression residuals versus a fitted curve are preferable to swap spreads as rich/cheap indicators in a time-series context as well. For example, the means of our regression residuals are presumed to be zero. As a result, we can model the residual of each bond as a mean-reverting process over time, allowing us to characterize the speed with which bonds tend to return to their fitted values.

In contrast, the fair swap spread for a particular bond can change over time, for all the reasons cited in Chapter 17, which include unobservable factors, such as the cost of equity capital for banks. As a result, it's difficult, if not impossible, to quantify the speed with which misvaluations correct when these misvaluations are identified using swap spreads. This is yet another reason we suggest using fitted curves rather than swap spreads as relative value indicators for bonds. Nevertheless, rich/cheap analysis can play a role in determining which swap spreads are likely to widen and which are more likely to narrow.

CHAPTER 9

An Analytic Process for Government Bond Markets

INTRODUCTION

Having described several statistical and financial models separately, this chapter outlines a possible combination into an analytic process for government bond markets. At this stage, we'll limit the discussion to one single government bond market, for example, Bunds, and explain the additional elements from cross-currency relationships in Chapter 17.

In broad conceptual terms, the task of an analyst could be described as extracting the *relevant* information for trading and investing from the multitude of government bond prices. He could approach this task in two steps, i.e. on two levels of abstraction:

- Use fitted curves to generate constant maturity time series.
- Use PCA to extract factors from the constant maturity time series.

As explained in Chapter 3, PCA factors can guide maturity selection; once the maturities are selected, going back to the fitted curve model can help choosing the best specific bonds. For example, based on the PCA step-by-step guide in Chapter 3, the analyst may decide to enter into a long 5Y, short 2Y and 7Y butterfly on the Bund curve and then look at the rich/cheap figures from the fitted curve to select the cheapest 5Y and the richest 2Y and 7Y Bunds. In this set-up, the fitted curve is thus used both at the beginning of the analytic process, generating the input variables into the PCA, and at its end.

In addition, at various points of the analysis, mean reversion models can support the assessment of the relative risk and return of possible trades.

STEP 1: FITTED CURVES

The fitted curve model described in Chapter 8 provides several important functions in the analytical process:

- Its constant maturity time series are the input variables into (PCA) curve analysis.

- Already in isolation, it identifies opportunities for "micro" bond switches, for example, between different 5Y Bunds, such as a deliverable and a non-deliverable issue, or 5Y Bunds and 5Y OBLs, etc. In combination with a curve trade, this information can be used for asset selection at the end of the process.
- By using our approach to simultaneously calculate the fitted curve and adjust for external explanatory variables, such as issuance size, both the fitted curve and the rich/cheap measure are not affected by external influences. And these isolated external influences can be analyzed separately, for example, by looking at a time series of the benchmark premium. This also allows incorporating market information, for example, about flow and benchmarks, into the analytic framework.

STEP 2: PCA FOR MATURITY SELECTION AND CURVE TRADES

Using the constant maturity time series as input, PCA adds another level of abstraction and allows analysis of the Bund market via its uncorrelated factors. Rather than dealing with 100 specific bonds, we can assess the overall level, non-directional slope, etc. of the Bund market in general and base our curve trading on this aggregated information. For example, a long-only fund can look at 1-factor PCA residuals in order to identify the cheapest maturity segment, given the current overall yield level.

In addition, as the external variables of the fitted curve model allow the incorporation of market information (such as benchmark status), the factors allow the analysis to be linked to macroeconomic variables, as illustrated in Table 3.1. One could, for example, assess the impact of a change in inflation on the PCA factors and hence on the trading strategy.

The factors of a PCA are also a suitable input for automatically monitoring market opportunities. For instance, one OU process could be calibrated to each of the first three factors of a PCA on the Bund curve and return a signal if a pre-defined expected Sharpe ratio is exceeded. We have monitored the global markets for trading opportunities in this manner for many years, running PCAs on a variety of different input variables (commodities, currencies) and assessing their factors automatically via an OU process. Of course, this highlights only candidates for possible trades, which require further analysis – and maybe also other mean reversion processes than OU. However, due to its ease of implementation, OU remains a natural choice for monitoring a large number of possible trades in real time.

STEP 3: FITTED CURVES FOR BOND SELECTION

Working backwards from higher to lower levels of information aggregation, the fitted curve model can now again be used to select the cheapest or

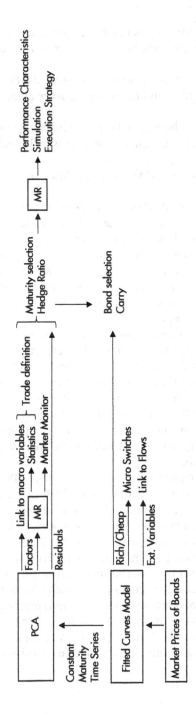

FIGURE 9.1 Combination of models into a possible analytic process for government bond markets.
Source: Authors.

185

richest bonds in the maturity segments bought or sold – adjusting for the effects of external influencing variables. This corresponds to step 11 of the guide in Chapter 3.

Once the individual bonds have been determined, the PCA results can be transferred to this level, corresponding to step 12 of the guide in Chapter 3:

- The PCA hedge ratios, which have been calculated on constant maturity time series, as outlined in Chapter 3, need to be adjusted to the BPVs of the individual bonds.
- With the hedge ratio of the individual bonds, the carry can be calculated.

By contrast, in order to avoid rolldown problems, the mean reversion characteristics should still be assessed via constant maturity time series. And at this stage of the analytic process, it is advisable to consult other models than OU as well: as mentioned in Chapter 2, the assumption of a constant variance may lead to overestimating the Sharpe ratio. Hence, assessing the mean reversion characteristics of the specific trade could be done via the bucketing method, for example, which brings elevated levels of variance at elevated levels of the trade to the attention of the analyst.

The (bucketing) mean reversion model calibrated to the trade can now be used to assess its expected performance characteristics, such as half-life and first passage time density, and to find the best execution strategy (target, stop loss, scaling), as outlined in Chapter 2. Moreover, the multi-variate mean reversion models discussed in Chapter 4 offer insights into the correlation characteristics, thereby providing also a framework for estimating the impact of adding the trade to an existing portfolio of positions.

Figure 9.1 attempts a graphical summary, with "MR" denoting the relevant mean reversion models.

As an alternative to the process outlined here, where MVOU is treated as a possible complement in step 3, it could replace PCA as the central element in step 2. In this case, the correlation and mean reversion characteristics of the constant maturity time series from step 1 are modeled directly via MVOU and the signals for potential trades are given by the deviations from its forecasts. And again, the richness and cheapness of individual bonds versus the fitted curve can then support the asset selection process in step 3. While this approach has the benefit of using one uniform model-framework for steps 2 and 3, sticking with PCA provides the intuitive insights from eigenvector interpretation and the link between factors and macroeconomic variables. In the end, each analyst will have to find that combination of models in an analytic process which best fits his goals and his way of thinking about markets.

CHAPTER 10

Overview of the Following Chapters

Asset Swaps, Basis Swaps, Credit Default Swaps and Their Mutual Influences

Chapters 10–18 discuss asset, basis, and credit default swaps as well as their combinations and mutual influences. The complexity of the subject is reflected in a rather complex structure of the following chapters, which contain many interdependencies. We therefore start the 'swap block' of chapters with a map intended to help guide the reader through that maze.

The key to analyzing swap spreads of bonds is to consider bonds as a swap between the fixed rate given by the coupon and the floating rate given by the repo rate. From that perspective, buying a bond and simultaneously financing it via the repo market are equivalent to entering into a receive coupon (fixed) versus pay repo (floating) swap, with the maturity of the swap being determined by the maturity of the bond (likewise for the payment frequency of the coupon; we assume overnight repo financing unless stated differently). Chapter 11 contains an overview of the repo market.

This key opens the door to understand and price asset swap spreads of bonds: conceptually, buying a bond means receiving the coupon and paying the repo rate, while an asset swap exchanges the coupon rate against the reference rate of the swap.

- For the hypothetical case of the reference rate of the swap being the (overnight) repo rate of the individual bond, the cash flows of the asset swap match those of the bond financed in the repo market – and hence the asset swap spread should be zero from the perspective of funding rates (additional perspectives such as credit exposure will be considered below).
- For the more realistic case of asset swapping a US Treasury, the reference rate of the swap is SOFR. Hence, the swap spread of US Treasuries can be considered as a repo–SOFR basis swap over the life of the bond. In other words, buying a US Treasury financed in the repo market and asset

187

swapping it results in paying the individual repo rate of the bond versus receiving SOFR. This is due to the statement above: The bond is a receive coupon versus pay repo position, the asset swap is a pay coupon versus receive SOFR position. Thus, the asset swap spread of US Treasuries can be analyzed by looking at the spread between the repo rate of individual bonds and SOFR. While specialness may cause a difference between the two (unlike in the hypothetical example above), they are usually quite close and hence the asset swap spreads of US Treasuries could be expected to be close to zero – again, speaking from the perspective of different funding rates only.

- Finally, consider asset swapping a German Bund into 3M EURIBOR. This results in a pay repo versus receive 3M EURIBOR basis swap over the life of the bond. When analyzing this asset swap spread, one therefore needs to deal with two types of differences between the funding rates. First, there is a difference regarding the term: While the overnight repo financing matches SOFR, this asset swap involves swapping between overnight and 3M term rates. Second, there is also a difference regarding the type of the funding rate: while both repo and SOFR are secured reference rates, this asset swap involves swapping between a secured and an unsecured rate. As a consequence, the asset swap spread of the German Bund depends on the repo–LIBOR spread and its driving forces. For example, due to the different BIS treatment of secured and unsecured loans, the higher the cost of equity, the lower[1] the asset swap spread should be.

In summary, asset swapping a bond results in a spread position between its repo rate and the reference rate of the swap. One important element of asset swap spread analysis therefore consists in understanding the different types and terms of reference rates. The 'swap block' of chapters starts correspondingly with an overview of the reference rates and the driving forces of their spreads in Chapter 11.

This is the foundation to assess the driving forces and fair value of asset swap spreads *from a funding perspective* in Chapter 12. Using the example of the Bund from above, we can determine a fair value for the GC–LIBOR basis swap by considering the different capital requirements among others and then add the specialness component via a repo–GC basis swap. While these basis swaps do not trade, we are in a position to price them and thereby obtain the fair value for the Bund asset swap spread from a funding perspective.

Apart from the funding rate, an asset swap also exchanges the credit exposure of both legs: buying a Bund and asset swapping it into EURIBOR involve both the default risk of Germany and the default risk of LIBOR panel

---

[1]We use the convention Reference Rate + X for the asset swap spread X. For example, when a Bund quotes at EURIBOR −10 bp, the asset swap is −10 bp (not +10 bp). Under this convention, a richening of bonds versus swaps results in lower asset swap spreads.

banks. Under some simplifying assumptions (such as ignoring counterparty risk, haircuts, and margining), one may conceptually consider an asset swap as a set of two swaps: first, a swap between funding rates, and second, a swap between credit risk. Adding this second element to the analysis, one can explain the usually upward-sloping term structure of swap spreads by the default risk of high-quality issuers increasing over time. Moreover, the perspective on asset swaps as incorporating a credit swap naturally establishes a link to credit default swaps (CDS).

At this point, we have formulated the proposition to analyze and price asset swap spreads as a combination of a funding and a credit swap, i.e. via assessing the difference of the funding rates and the credit exposure involved. Do we capture most of the driving forces of asset swap spreads or do we miss important elements? Figure 10.1 answers this question graphically. Verbally: we provide evidence that the credit component does indeed capture several of the influences typically being considered as driving forces of asset swap spreads. More issuance of government debt and factors depending on the economic cycle such as unemployment are correlated to the credit quality of the state. On the other hand, asset swaps are also influenced by factors which are hard to capture via cash-flow analysis and no-arbitrage principles, such as the need of banks to hold bonds to meet capital requirements or to obtain certain benefits. These factors are by nature difficult to observe and to quantify and we address the impact on swap spreads (analysis) in Chapter 18.

The task of analyzing swap spreads becomes even more complex and interesting when considering that all asset swap markets are linked via basis swaps. This results in mutual dependencies and influences of all global bond and swap markets – and means that an individual bond swap spread or an individual basis swap should never be analyzed in isolation. One can draw Figure 10.1 for every currency, as a start, say, for US Treasuries and German Bunds. The funding rates of the two, SOFR and EURIBOR, are exchanged in a cross-currency basis swap (CCBS), which thereby introduces a link between both markets. This has several key consequences:

- One can swap every bond into any reference rate in any currency (and with any coupon payment frequency). Hence, it is insufficient to assess

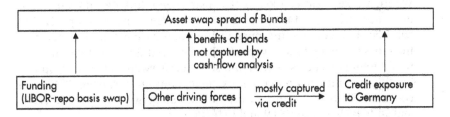

FIGURE 10.1 Driving factors of asset swap spreads.
Source: Authors.

Bunds only versus EURIBOR as they can also be priced versus SOFR. In fact, if basis swapped Bunds appear cheap versus SOFR compared to US Treasuries, it is likely that investors will switch from Treasuries into Bunds, thereby causing them to richen also versus EURIBOR. An analyst who does not consider this link and limits his perspective to EUR has no chance of understanding these moves caused by global asset allocation flows.

- It is possible to use USD SOFR par asset swap spreads of basis swapped bonds as a universal rich/cheap indicator for every bond.

Moreover, the credit element is obviously correlated to the CDS – which adds another link and connects all bond (asset and basis) swap and credit default swap markets worldwide. Figure 10.2 illustrates this statement, as does the following example from our daily experience as analysts: at a time when the SOFR swap spreads of basis swapped JGBs traded close to the Japanese CDS, a tightening of the latter forced JGBs to richen versus SOFR. This enticed investors to switch from basis swapped JGBs into Bunds, causing more negative EURIBOR swap spreads of Bunds. Hence, while neither the EUR funding conditions nor the German credit quality changed, a move in the Japanese CDS had the effect of Bunds richening versus EURIBOR. This cannot be captured by looking at the EUR universe in isolation (Figure 10.1), but only by considering the links to other markets as well (Figure 10.2).

Keeping track of the multitude of links is a complex but worthwhile task, which yields many insights. This is one important goal of the following chapters:

- Since CDS have observable market prices, the idea is to use them in the model for swap spreads as a measure for the credit risk of government bonds. However, due to involving an FX component and in case of physical delivery also a delivery option, sovereign CDS are not a pure measure for credit risk. The foremost task is therefore to extract the pure credit information from the CDS market in order to be able to use it as input in the swap spread formula. Chapter 13 tries to complete this task as well as possible in the current situation and additionally discusses other applications of CDS in RV analysis and trading.
- We then take a closer look at the instruments linking different funding rates: Chapter 14 treats the intra-currency basis swaps (ICBS) between different funding rates in the same currency and Chapter 15 the cross-currency basis swaps (CCBS) between different funding rates in different currencies. Through a set of basis swaps one can swap any funding rate into any other. For example, one can start from SOFR and construct EURIBOR synthetically via a CCBS between SOFR and ESTR and an ICBS between ESTR and EURIBOR.

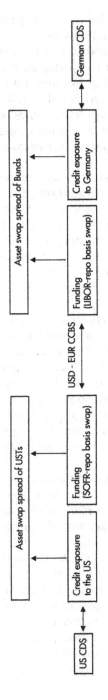

FIGURE 10.2 Mutual influences between the driving factors of asset swap spreads.
Source: Authors.

- We are then prepared to combine the building blocks and to analyze their mutual influences in Chapter 16. By using asset and basis swaps, every bond can be expressed as a spread versus USD SOFR, which is therefore a universal yardstick for comparing all global bonds and the basis for asset allocation and funding decisions. Likewise, the CDS also measures every bond as a spread versus USD SOFR. Using the insights from Chapter 13, we present arbitrage relationships between both. Finally, we combine all relationships into a formula expressing the links between local swap spreads, USD swap spreads, basis swaps, and the CDS.

At the end of this journey, we hope the reader will be in a position to assess the mutual influences between asset swaps, basis swaps, and CDS. This remains a complex problem, as a move in one variable can cause a move in several other variables. In the example above, the switch from basis swapped JGBs into Bunds, which caused a richening of Bunds versus EURIBOR, could have also caused a less negative USD-EUR CCBS (without Bunds richening versus EURIBOR). This situation is somewhat similar to the three-body problem in physics. Fortunately, the arbitrage relationships provide some firm boundaries and orientation.

Chapter 17 presents two options for assessing the relative value between bonds in different currencies. The first method asset and basis swaps every bond in a fixed rate note in a given currency and then applies the fitted curve model from Chapter 8. The second method asset and basis swaps every bond in a SOFR floating rate note, i.e. applies the universal yardstick "SOFR par asset swap spreads of basis swapped bonds" as a universal rich/cheap indicator for bonds. Since only par asset swap spreads with SOFR as the reference rate solve (almost) all deficiencies of asset swap spreads with LIBOR as the reference rate, the second method is only advisable in USD, while the first method can be used in any currency.

All of the above has been based on thinking about asset swap spreads as a combination of a funding and a credit swap (Figure 10.1). While we will provide evidence that this captures many of the actual swap spread moves, some depend on variables, that vary with the circumstances. Haircut funding costs are important examples, which need to be incorporated into swap spread models in order to obtain realistic results (see Figure 12.4) but vary significantly between different market participants. Also important are shadow costs, which are individually different and practically impossible to observe or estimate. Unfortunately, the impact of regulation on markets has generally increased over the last few years, making an already complex task even harder. The final chapter of the 'swap block' (Chapter 18) mentions some consequences for swap spread analysis and concludes that, despite all efforts, only partial and approximative predictions are realistic.

CHAPTER 11

Reference Rates

OVERVIEW OF GLOBAL REFERENCE RATES

Until the financial crisis of 2008–2009, the main reference rate in all major markets was LIBOR or a similar rate, i.e. an unsecured term rate. When the credit risk of banks increased during the financial crisis, lenders favored shorter terms in order to minimize credit exposure. The natural endpoint was overnight (O/N) lending and correspondingly a higher volume in overnight indexed swaps (OIS). In addition, following the LIBOR rigging scandal, regulators entered the scene and decided on the reference rate by bureaucratic fiat.[1] Depending on the jurisdiction, the goals and perseverance of regulators were different, leading to different types of reference rates in the major markets:

- In the US, LIBOR was terminated and SOFR (secured overnight financing rate) officially promoted as main reference rate. SOFR is calculated by the Fed based on overnight repo transactions, hence a secured O/N rate. The Fed Funds, an unsecured O/N rate, continues to exist.
- In the eurozone, by contrast, LIBOR was reformed and continues to serve as an unsecured term reference rate. In addition, ESTR, the EUR O/N index average based on unsecured bank lending and being determined by the European Central Bank (ECB), has been introduced as the replacement for EONIA.
- In Japan, the situation is similar to Europe: whereas LIBOR has been terminated, the domestic version, TIBOR, continues to provide an unsecured term reference rate, while TONAR serves as unsecured O/N reference rate.
- In the UK, LIBOR was terminated and SONIA, the GBP O/N index average based on unsecured bank lending and being determined by the BoE, is the only common reference rate.

---

[1]Huggins and Schaller (2022), Introduction.

TABLE 11.1   Most Common Reference Rates in the Major Markets

	Unsecured term	Unsecured O/N	Secured O/N
USD	—	(Fed Funds)	SOFR
EUR	EURIBOR	ESTR	—
JPY	TIBOR	TONAR	—
GBP	—	SONIA	—

Table 11.1 classifies these reference rates by their length (term[2] or O/N) and type (unsecured or secured). Table 11.1 represents a snapshot of the situation at the time of writing (September 2023), which may evolve in future. Also, as swaps are over-the-counter (OTC) products, other reference rates than those listed can be agreed upon, for example, the ECB policy rate, but these instances are rare and likely to decrease further due to the increasing standardization of swaps by exchanges.

Summarizing the description above in terms of Table 11.1, the starting point was the left column, the unsecured term rate LIBOR. The transition worked generally from the left to the right, but the final goal and the continuation of LIBOR were different in the individual markets. As a consequence, there currently exist three different sorts of reference rates: unsecured term (LIBOR-like) in EUR and JPY, unsecured O/N in all markets, and secured O/N (SOFR) in the US only.

Table 11.1 is the foundation for the discussion of asset and basis swaps in the following chapters:

■ Depending on the reference rate used in an asset swap, there are three different types: the fixed coupon payments of a bond can be swapped in LIBOR, or in an unsecured O/N rate such as ESTR, or (in the US) in SOFR. Due to the differences in reference rates relative to the financing rate of the bond (repo), these three swap spreads are different and require different analysis tools. For example, SOFR is by construction closely linked to the repo rate and hence the influence of different funding rates is usually close to zero for asset swap spreads of US Treasuries versus SOFR (i.e. using SOFR as reference rate in the asset swap). In contrast, asset swap spreads of Bunds versus 6M EURIBOR involve both a difference in term (O/N repo versus 6M LIBOR) and in type (secured repo versus unsecured LIBOR). A model for the repo–LIBOR spread is therefore an essential part

---

[2]Strictly speaking, also O/N is a "term" with length of one business day. However, we reserve the term "term" for longer periods, such as 1M or 6M.

for analyzing asset swap spreads of Bunds versus EURIBOR and will be presented later in this chapter.

■ Intra-currency basis swaps (ICBS) exchange the reference rates listed in different columns of the same row (currency) as well as between different terms of the same cell in the first column (e.g. between 3M and 6M LIBOR). Cross-currency basis swaps (CCBS) exchange the reference rates listed in different rows (currency). Since practically all CCBS use SOFR as one leg and a secured reference rate exists only in the US, CCBS also involve a switch between columns, i.e. between unsecured and secured lending. An understanding of the spreads between different reference rates is therefore also vital for analyzing basis swaps.

Given the classification by the two criteria, term or O/N and unsecured or secured, there are four possible combinations, with one of them, secured term reference rates, being absent from Table 11.1. When US regulators decided to switch to secured reference rates, given the concentration of liquidity in the repo market in O/N, they naturally chose a secured O/N rate, i.e. SOFR. Together with the termination of LIBOR, this resulted in term reference rates being absent from the US market, which posed major difficulties for many market participants and made them reluctant to transition from LIBOR to SOFR. As a compromise between the goal of policy makers (SOFR) and the needs of the market (a term rate such as LIBOR), SOFR term rates became popular. Specifically, the CME Group calculates 1M, 3M, 6M, and 12M term rates from SOFR futures prices. From the viewpoint of the average market participant, such as a corporate treasurer, the reference rate has therefore evolved along the curve depicted in Figure 11.1.

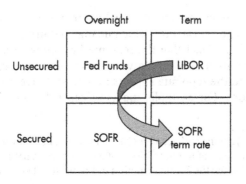

FIGURE 11.1   Evolution of the USD reference rate.
Source: Authors.

While the introduction of a SOFR term rate satisfied the immediate needs of market participants and thereby supported the transition from LIBOR, regulators continue to favor O/N SOFR as reference rate and thus prohibit a secondary market for the term rate. Without a secondary market, the SOFR term rate cannot be practicably used as reference rate for swaps.[3] Consequently, our discussion is limited to the three types of asset swap spreads corresponding to the three columns of the reference rate in Table 11.1.

The rest of the chapter first reviews the repo market and SOFR constructed from it, before presenting a model for the spread between repo and unsecured rates.

OVERVIEW OF THE REPO MARKET[4]

A repurchase agreement, or repo, in its most basic form is a type of secured loan. One party lends money for a specified term to a second party, who posts collateral to the first party for the duration of the loan and who pays an agreed interest rate – the repo rate – to the first party on the funds lent. The collateralization by a bond, usually of very high quality like US Treasuries, is different from unsecured lending, such as LIBOR, and tends to result in most observed repo rates being lower than comparable rates involving unsecured, private-sector lending. This difference also leads to repo transactions being assigned lower risk weightings by the Bank for International Settlements (BIS) (0% in the case of US Treasuries) and thereby to lower capital costs. Hence, the motivation for the borrower in the repo market is usually lower interest rates than in unsecured lending markets such as Eurodollar; the motivation for the lender in the repo market is a significant reduction in credit risk and a lower cost of capital.

In addition, the lender can be motivated by receiving a specific bond as collateral in the repo transaction, which he may require to cover a short position in this bond. The fact that the repo markets allows traders to establish short bond positions makes repo a vital component of many relative value trades. As a result, the repo rate appears in many relative value relations and arbitrage equations. For example, the 'classical' RV trade of buying a bond

[3]See Chapter 3 of Huggins and Schaller (2022), for a detailed description and an analysis of the consequences of the prohibition of a secondary market for the SOFR term rate and of scenarios for the future evolution of the tension between policy goals and market needs.
[4]The section is a slightly modified version of the first section of Chapter 1 of Huggins and Schaller (2022).

future versus selling a deliverable bond (net basis) described in Chapter 7 requires establishing and maintaining the short position in the bond until the delivery date of the future – and therefore its repo rate is part of the net basis. Vice versa, relationships between deliverable bonds can be expressed by the implied repo rate, i.e. that repo rate, which would result in a particular bond becoming CTD (cheapest-to-deliver).

The vital function of the repo market for RV trading also means that RV relationships can exert at times a significant influence on the repo market. Using the example of net basis trading, in case of the future trading cheap relative to its CTD, buying the future versus selling the CTD is an attractive arbitrage, whose execution requires establishing the short position in the CTD via the repo market. This situation often results in traders being willing to lend at lower rates, if they receive the CTD as collateral. A borrower in the repo market can then enjoy an especially low rate, if he secures the loan with the CTD rather than general US Treasury collateral. Accordingly, the CTD and its repo rate are called "special," i.e. below the GC (general collateral) rate offered for loans, in which the borrower can choose any US Treasury as collateral. Apart from CTDs, specialness tends to occur in every bond for which there are significant short positions, which can be caused by RV trading or specific flow situations, such as in the aftermath of a new issuance. Accordingly, specialness tends to appear mainly for new issues, benchmarks, and deliverables, though it can occur in any bond.

If the lender in a repo transaction is unable to return the collateral to the borrower at maturity, this is called a "failure", which carries penalties. In order to avoid the risk of failures, in addition to the bilateral repo lending described above, tri-party repo can be used, where a custodial bank (as the third party to the repo transaction) holds the collateral. In tri-party repo, no specific bonds can be selected as collateral, so that the tri-party repo rate can be considered as a GC rate with almost no risk of failure. For this reason, the distribution of tri-party repo rates on any given day tends to be narrower than the distribution of bilateral repo rates. Particularly low rates tend to be excluded owing to the absence of special collateral effects and/or the risk of counterparty failures. On the left side, it excludes the special repo rates and any premium charged for the possibility of the counterparty failing.

REPO RATES IN GREATER DETAIL

Unlike LIBOR and OIS rates, repo rates apply to loans that are secured by collateral. While the collateral enhances the security of the loan, it also introduces some additional issues of which the relative value analyst should be aware.

Repricing

Once the initial exchange of repo funds and repo collateral has been made, it's possible, even likely, that the value of the collateral will change before the end of the repo agreement. If the value of the collateral increases, the lender will be holding more collateral than is required to secure the loan and will be asked to return the surplus collateral. If the value of the collateral decreases, the lender will be holding less collateral than is required to secure the loan, and the borrower will be required to post additional collateral. This process is referred to as repricing and occurs throughout the term of the repo transaction along terms set out in the initial repo documentation.[5]

Repricing is an issue too often neglected by analysts when calculating carry and cash flows. For example, imagine a trader has purchased bonds financed via a term repo transaction and has sold bond futures against the long bond position. If the price of the bonds declines, the repo counterparty is likely to ask for more collateral. At the same time, the price of the futures contracts is likely to have decreased, resulting in a positive inflow of cash in the futures margin account. The cash in the futures margin account can be provided directly to the lender to satisfy the call for additional collateral, or the cash could be used to purchase additional bonds, which could be used as collateral. Either way, the additional transaction is likely to have at least some impact on the interest receipts and/or payments made by the trader.

Many larger financial institutions have collateral management desks that consolidate the process of posting collateral, including repricings, insulating the bond trader from the need to worry about these considerations. But that won't be the case for every trader. And even traders who benefit from a central collateral management operation should be aware of the mechanics affecting the financing of their positions.

Specialness

Repo desks typically accept a large number of bonds as collateral for a repo loan, with no real preference for any specific issue. We refer to such bonds as 'general collateral' (GC). However, there are some scenarios where a repo desk or the market in general will have a preference for a particular bond.

For example, consider a scenario in which a trader has borrowed a particular bond from a repo desk so that he could sell the issue short. The repo desk will need to acquire this bond in the market on or before the day it is scheduled

---

[5]The rules governing acceptable collateral usually are negotiated between counterparties and will specify which instruments are acceptable as collateral and under what conditions repricing is to occur.

to be returned to the original counterparty who previously submitted the bond as collateral.

It may be a simple matter for the repo desk to find that bond and persuade another of its clients to provide that bond as collateral. But that won't always be the case. If the repo desk is finding it difficult to obtain the bond, it can offer to lend funds at a reduced interest rate for any borrower who is able to provide that bond as collateral. In this case, we say the bond has become 'special collateral.' Equivalently, we may say that the bond has 'gone special.'

A bond that confers a borrowing advantage to its owner is worth more than a bond that is trading as GC in the repo market. As a result, for traders to be indifferent between the two bonds, the bond that is special in the repo market needs to trade with a spot price that is greater than that of the GC bond by an amount that exactly offsets the advantage the special bond provides in the repo market.

Some bonds are more likely than others to experience periods of specialness. For example, bonds that are deliverable into futures contracts are more likely to be special than other bonds. Even if a bond isn't part of a futures delivery basket at the moment, the prospect that it will become eligible for delivery and possibly experience a period of specialness may give it additional value in the spot market today. In this sense, repo specialness is asymmetric and therefore exhibits some similarities with call options.

Owning a bond that becomes special is a bit like winning the lottery in this sense. And the price premium that a bond enjoys in the spot market is related to the likelihood and extent of any specialness it might enjoy over its life.[6]

Repo 'Fails'

In the above example, a repo dealer lent a particular bond to a trader who wished to sell the issue short. In this transaction, the trader was lending money, and the repo dealer was lending the bond as collateral to this trader, who was able to sell the bond in the spot market.

The repo dealer in this example was able to provide the bond to the trader because it previously had been posted to the dealer as collateral for another transaction. And at some point, the dealer will need to return this bond to the original counterparty.

Of course, one possibility is that the dealer will receive the bond from the short-seller before he's scheduled to return it to the original counterparty. But that need not be the case. For example, the repo dealer may have entered into a term repo with the short seller for a date that falls after the date on which the collateral is scheduled to be returned to the original counterparty.

---

[6]For more on repo specialness, see Darrell Duffie (1996), Special Repo Rates. *Journal of Finance*, **51**(2), 493–526.

In that case, the repo dealer will have to find the bond elsewhere – perhaps in the portfolio of another customer or perhaps from the street (e.g. through an interdealer broker).

If the repo dealer has trouble finding the bond, he can provide an incentive to the market by lowering the repo rate on the bond. If he's having considerable difficulty, he may have to lower the repo rate quite a bit.

But in some circumstances, despite his best efforts, the dealer simply may not be able to find the bond in time to return the bond to the original counterparty. In that case, the dealer is said to have 'failed' to the original counterparty.

Repo failures typically carry a penalty to provide an incentive against failure, and these penalties have varied over time and in different markets. In some markets, failure could result in a suspension of the repo desk from the market. In some markets, the failure penalty was that the person borrowing money could hold onto the funds at an interest rate of zero until the collateral was returned. Of course, this penalty is more effective when interest rates are high than when they're low.

Haircuts

Since government bond prices can be volatile, repo transactions often require the party borrowing cash to post as collateral bonds having a somewhat greater market value than the cash being lent. The difference between the value of the cash and the value of the bonds is referred to as the haircut of the collateral.

If repo counterparties can fund the haircuts at the repo rate, then the haircuts should be of no consequence when considering valuations along the curve. However, if repo counterparties have to fund the haircuts at a cost of capital in excess of the repo rate, then these haircuts may have some effect on the relative pricing of bonds across the curve.

Haircuts can have a considerable impact on the economics of repo transactions and depend both on changing haircut schedules and on the specific funding situation of individual market participants. Chapter 18 provides more details and examples.

We'll also find that haircuts can have a considerable impact on swap spreads and hence need to be included in models in order to obtain realistic predictions (see Figures 12.4 and 17.2) – which is a difficult task, given that the haircut funding costs of the marginal market participant cannot be observed.

Right of Substitution

In some cases, the party who borrows cash and provides collateral will retain the right to substitute new collateral for existing collateral during the course of the repo loan. In this case, we say that the borrower has the *right of substitution*.

The right of substitution is an option that benefits the cash borrower in the event that the bonds submitted as collateral become special during the term of the repo transaction. Like most options, its value ex ante depends on the extent to which the bonds in question are likely to 'go special.' As this right is valuable to the party borrowing cash, the owner of this right pays for it by agreeing to pay a higher repo rate to the party lending the cash.

Many analysts ignore the right of substitution in their calculations, and we admit that the issue may seem a bit esoteric in many cases. But there are times when additional relative value can be derived by being smart about this issue, and we suggest being aware of the issue when looking carefully at repo calculations.

Credit: Counterparty and Collateral Combined

One of the key features of repo transactions is that they rely on more than a single source of credit. For example, for a lender of cash in a repo transaction not to get paid requires that the borrower default at the same time that the collateral drops precipitously in value.

Consider the case of a US bank submitting German Bunds as collateral against a loan of EUR cash from a Japanese bank. If the US bank is unable to repay the EUR cash to the Japanese bank at the end of the repo transaction, the Japanese bank should be made whole as a result of the German Bunds it holds as collateral against the loan. The risk to the Japanese bank is that the German Bunds plummet in value at precisely the time the US bank goes bankrupt.

While this scenario is not impossible, it's typically viewed as being very unlikely, and most repo desks can manage this risk to some extent by judiciously diversifying collateral types with respect to counterparty.

For example, during the euro crisis, many international banks were wary about lending cash to Spanish banks in exchange for Spanish government bonds, given the apparent linkages between the sovereign and financial sectors in Spain. Instead, Spanish banks submitted their Spanish government bonds as collateral against loans of EUR cash from the ECB. If the Spanish banks need cash in other currencies, they've been able to use EUR cash as collateral against loans of cash in these other currencies, such as USD, in the form of shorter-term FX swaps or longer-dated cross-currency basis swaps.

Tri-Party or Custodial Repo

In a bilateral repo transaction, the party receiving collateral typically is able to make use of that collateral in a variety of ways. For instance, in the example above, the repo dealer lent bonds that he was holding as collateral to a trader, so that the trader could sell the bond short.

And as we continued with this example above, we saw that the repo dealer might be caught short himself, unable to return the bonds to the original counterparty, resulting in a repo fail.

To continue with this example, let's imagine that this repo dealer went bankrupt before being able to return the collateral to the original counterparty. In this case, the original counterparty may have to spend considerable time, effort, and money in order to replace the missing bonds. Many repo counterparties consider this risk to be small and manageable, but some participants in the repo market are concerned about it.

One way to mitigate this risk is to use a custodial bank to hold the collateral, in which case the custodial bank is a third party to the transaction, which is then referred to as a tri-party repo.

Most relative value analysts tend not to concern themselves with tri-party repos, but there are times when it's useful to consider the implications of tri-party vs. bilateral repo. For example, there have been times when haircuts on bilateral repo transactions have tended to be considerably wider than in the tri-party market. And as we've seen above, the size of any haircut applied in a repo financing typically impacts the all-in cost of carrying a position, as the haircut typically must be financed at a higher cost of funds.

SOFR

Based on the O/N repo market, the Fed calculates and publishes SOFR, the main reference rate in the US. For the details of this process, we refer to Chapter 1 of Huggins and Schaller (2022), and the illustration in Figure 11.2. Note that due to the exclusion of (most) special repo rates during the calculation process, SOFR is usually close to the GC repo rate. Hence, the spread between SOFR and the repo rate of a specific bond is mostly driven by the specialness of that bond and therefore close to zero for the majority of Treasuries.

A major problem of the new reference rate was the tendency for SOFR to exhibit spikes, especially around the end of quarter. On some days, SOFR quoted more than 20 bp above Fed Funds. A secured rate trading above an unsecured rate is an obvious arbitrage opportunity (particularly when executed with the same counterpart). But with banks being subject to balance sheet constraints and regulatory restrictions (see Chapter 18), the threshold for them to execute this arbitrage can be quite high, especially at the end of quarter. Realizing the problem that banks were unable to fulfill their role as arbitrageur and provide liquidity in the repo market precisely at those times when they would be needed most, the Fed decided to take over that function and announced on July 28, 2021, the implementation of a standing repo

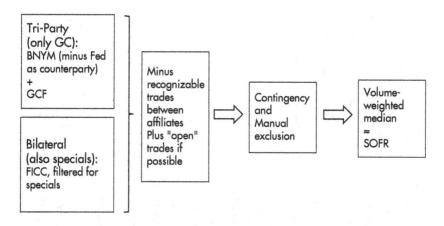

FIGURE 11.2   SOFR calculation.
Source: Huggins and Schaller (2022).

facility (SRF). The SRF provides liquidity to the repo market independent of the balance sheet constraints of banks, with the minimum rate usually being set at the top of the current policy window. In other words, via its repo facility the Fed has introduced the SRF rate (SRFR) as a constraint, i.e. SOFR $\leq$ SRFR. This had the desired effect and spikes in SOFR have since then disappeared, as shown in Figure 11.3.

However, while the SRF was successful in suppressing spikes, it has introduced a structural break in the SOFR time series before and after the Fed repo facility existed, i.e. without and with the constraint SOFR $\leq$ SRFR. This causes a problem for analysts requiring a long-term time series of swap rates as basis for their job. In case a ten-year history of USD swap rates is needed, the analyst deals with three different types of reference rates for the swap: LIBOR, SOFR pre-SRF, and SOFR post-SRF. While he may apply ad hoc "solutions" such as adjusting for the average spread between LIBOR and SOFR during the period both traded, we know no method to generate long-term time series for USD swap rates, which can be used as input for analysis requiring a high degree of precision.

Given this situation, we therefore recommend using constant maturity par rates calculated via a fitted curve model as input for RV analysis in those countries, where swaps have experienced structural breaks. For the US in particular, it seems advisable to apply the fitted curve model described in Chapter 8 to generate a time series of par rates for synthetic constant maturity Treasuries, for example, 2Y, 5Y, and 10Y. While this involves some effort, it avoids basing the analysis on swap rate time series with structural breaks.

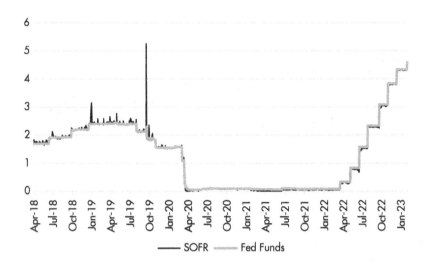

FIGURE 11.3 Evolution of the USD reference rate used by most market participants. *Source:* Authors, from data provided by the Fed on www.newyorkfed.org. Disclaimer: these reference data are subject to the Terms of Use posted at newyorkfed.org. The New York Fed is not responsible for publication of the reference data by the Authors and Wiley and does not endorse any particular publication, and has no liability for your use.

DRIVING FORCES OF THE SPREAD BETWEEN DIFFERENT REFERENCE RATES

As illustrated in Table 11.1, asset and basis swaps involve a number of different reference rates. An understanding of the spread between them is therefore a key element in the analysis of asset and basis swaps provided in the following chapters. According to the classification of reference rates by the two criteria, secured or unsecured and term or O/N, this task can be broken down into two components:

- Understanding the driving forces between unsecured O/N and secured O/N reference rates, i.e. the second and third column of Table 11.1. The different BIS risk weighting results in a significant benefit of secured lending. While secured lending also improves the credit exposure, the difference is usually negligible for O/N lending to contributing banks. Hence, the main advantage of secured lending emerges *indirectly* via capital requirements rather than *directly* via less default risk. Correspondingly, the spread between secured and unsecured O/N rates is mainly a function of the cost of capital: the higher the cost of capital, the higher the preference for secured lending with 0% BIS risk weighting.

- Understanding the driving forces between unsecured term and unsecured O/N rates, i.e. the first and second column of Table 11.1. As both have the same BIS risk weighting, the cost of capital has no impact on this spread. On the other hand, the longer the term, the higher the credit risk: whereas lending to a contributing bank on an O/N basis may involve negligible credit exposure, the default risk may become considerable for a 6M term.

With some simplifications, one can therefore say that the spread between secured and unsecured O/N rates is driven by the cost of capital, while the spread between unsecured O/N and term rates is driven by credit. Using this conceptual approach, we will now fill in the details.

THE SPREAD BETWEEN SECURED AND UNSECURED LOANS AS DRIVEN BY CAPITAL REQUIREMENTS

In most regulatory jurisdictions, the capital requirements that banks face for unsecured loans are different from the requirements they face for secured loans. These requirements typically conform to the Basel directives, which have evolved over time since the Basel capital accords of 1998.

In general, unsecured lending between banks carries a risk weighting under Basel rules. The precise risk weights depend on a variety of factors but usually involve a minimum risk weighting of 20% in most cases. So, for example, an asset with a 20% risk weight would require capital of 1.6% for a bank with a core capital requirement of 8%. In this case, 1.6% of the interbank loan needs to be funded at the lending bank's cost of equity (or other core) capital. The Bank for International Settlements' (BIS) risk weighting for a secured repo transaction, however, is less in most cases. In fact, for repos involving high-quality government bonds as collateral, the BIS risk weighting is zero in many jurisdictions.

Independent of the actual credit risk – which may well be negligible for lending O/N to high-quality banks – these capital requirements introduce a significant benefit for lending on a secured basis. Assuming a bank has a cost of equity of 10%, lending unsecured results in $10\% * 1.6\% = 16\,bp$ capital costs. Hence, this bank would prefer (speaking from a funding perspective only) lending secured until the repo rates are more than 16 bp below the rates for unsecured lending. If this bank is the marginal market participant, the spread between unsecured (e.g. Fed Funds or ESTR) and (GC) repo rates should therefore be 16 bp (again, seen only from a funding perspective).

As a starting point, one can therefore estimate the spread between unsecured and secured O/N rates by $g*q*d$, where g is the cost of equity capital, q is the BIS risk-weighting for interbank loans, and d is the BIS guideline for the capital adequacy ratio for a 100% risk-weighted asset (typically 8%).

Since both the cost of equity of individual banks and the marginal market participant are impossible to observe ex ante, this formula can seldom be used for exact quantifications. However, it explains the qualitative relationships observed: in times of stress in the banking sector, the cost of bank capital increases, hence the bank's preference for repo lending increases, hence the asset swap spread of government bonds versus LIBOR or euro short-term rate (ESTR) decreases.[7]

While changes in g are difficult to quantify, changes in the other variables, q and d, are obvious. In case of discussions about reforming the BIS rules, this formula therefore allows exact predictions. As a hypothetical example, if an increase of the capital adequacy ratio for 100% risk weighted assets (i.e. d) from 8% to 12% was proposed, one could easily forecast Bund asset swap spreads versus LIBOR or ESTR to decrease by 50%, for example, from −20 bp to −30 bp. Note that, in contrast, asset swap spreads versus SOFR are not affected by changes in any of the three variables, g, q, and d.

We will expand this approach to a model for the repo–LIBOR spread by adding a credit component, which we discuss next. Moreover, following the financial crisis, additional capital requirements have been introduced, which vary by jurisdiction and market participant, as discussed in Chapter 18. The general approach developed here therefore potentially requires modifications to reflect the specific regulatory framework.

THE SPREAD BETWEEN UNSECURED O/N AND TERM RATES AS DRIVEN BY CREDIT EXPOSURE

The Effect of Short Rate Expectations

The most obvious effect of a longer tenor is that expectations of future short rates are reflected in LIBOR, whereas expected future short rates are not incorporated into O/N rates.[8] Over long periods of time, short rates appear to

---

[7]We use the convention Reference Rate + X for the asset swap spread X. For example, when a Bund quotes at EURIBOR −10 bp, the asset swap is −10 bp (not +10 bp). Under this convention, a richening of bonds versus swaps results in lower asset swap spreads.
[8]Strictly speaking, the expectation of high short rates in the remainder of a current reserve maintenance period could induce banks to pay a higher rate on overnight funds, but since this effect is symmetric and not systematic it will not be addressed in this analysis.

increase as often as they decrease, so this effect should not explain persistent differences between O/N rates and LIBORs over long periods of time or persistent differences between longer-dated LIBOR and OIS swap rates.

The Effect of Interest Rate Compounding

Another difference is that O/N rates must be compounded in order to be compared to LIBORs of longer tenors. For example, even if O/N rates were certain to be 5% every day for an entire year, the six-month (6M) LIBOR rate would be 4–5 basis points (bp) above this rate to reflect the difference in the compounding frequencies.

The Effect of Interest Rate Compounding Convexity

One additional conceptual difference relates to the fact that compounding of any frequency introduces a convexity that links interest rate volatility to the expected growth rate in overnight deposits. For example, consider two scenarios in which the expected O/N rate was 5% indefinitely: one in which the volatility around this rate was high, and another in which the volatility of the O/N rate was low. In each scenario, an investor makes the same initial deposit, which is re-invested every night at the prevailing O/N rate in each scenario for an investment horizon of six months.

The expected terminal value of this deposit is greater in the high-volatility scenario than in the low-volatility scenario, simply due to the convexity inherent in the compounding process. All things being equal, longer-term rates should be lower in high-volatility environments than in low-volatility environments. And in the presence of any volatility at all, there is a conceptual downward bias in longer-term rates for this reason. In theory, this convexity effect might lower LIBORs relative to OIS rates. However, the magnitude of this effect for the tenors considered here is very small (much less than a basis point), and this effect will not be addressed further in this book.

The Effects of Risk and Term Premia

Of course, risk premia and term premia are often invoked to explain the difference between overnight rates and rates with longer tenors. These terms are often used by market analysts as catchall terms to refer to the additional return or yield that investors might demand to be compensated for various risks.

In this book, these terms are reserved for more academic usage. In particular, these premia refer here to the compensation that investors demand in the expected return for accepting systematic risks (e.g. consumption risk) resulting from the covariance between the marginal utility of the investor and the return of the asset.

Though a truly comprehensive analysis would include these sorts of risk and term premia, they will not be considered explicitly in this book, for two reasons. First, these premia are not observable ex ante, and a comprehensive treatment of these premia is simply beyond the scope of this book.

Second, this book deals primarily with the systematic difference between interest rates along three yield curves with maturities of up to fifty years in some cases. It's unlikely (though not inconceivable) that these risk and term premia could explain temporary anomalies between spreads in isolated and long-term segments of these yield curves.

The Effect of Default Risk

Perhaps the most important reason for the systematic difference between LIBOR and OIS involves default risk. The OIS rate is the interbank rate for overnight lending between banks, all of which are healthy on the day the transaction is initiated. The scope for a bank to transition overnight from being healthy to being bankrupt is fairly limited. In contrast, there is greater scope for a healthy bank to transition to bankruptcy over, say, six months, a common tenor for LIBOR. By using OIS rather than term lending, the lender can reassess the credit quality of his counterpart every day and in case of emerging signs of stress immediately select a different borrower for the next day. This ability greatly reduces the credit exposure even for unsecured rates.

As this concept is particularly important, we'll reiterate the importance of these credit 'refreshes.' If an investor lends at the 6M interbank deposit rate, he subjects his deposit to the possibility that the borrowing bank will default at some point during those six months, and his deposit rate reflects that risk. If, as an alternative, he sticks with one-month deposits, which he rolls five times after the initial deposit, then he subjects his deposit to less default risk, since an institution whose credit deteriorates after, say, three months can be avoided when rolling the deposit in the latter scenario, while our investor would be subject to this credit deterioration in the former scenario.

In other words, 6M LIBOR reflects the risk that institutions in the LIBOR fixing panel might default during those six months. But by dealing with LIBORs of lesser tenors, we limit the extent of default risk, as subsequent LIBOR fixings are in some sense 'refreshed' by the fact that poor credits are removed from the fixing panel. So exposure to two 3M LIBORs in sequence will expose a trader to less credit risk than will a single 6M LIBOR. And a series of overnight index swaps will subject the trader to far less credit risk, as each overnight rate in the sequences exposes the trader only to one day's worth of credit risk.

The implication here is quite important. As credit conditions in the banking sector deteriorate, LIBORs should increase relative to OIS rates, all things being equal. And, of course, this is precisely the behavior observed in practice.

COMBINING THE DRIVING FORCES CAPITAL REQUIREMENTS AND CREDIT EXPOSURE INTO A MODEL FOR THE REPO–LIBOR SPREAD

This chapter started with a classification of the reference rates, before assessing the most important driving forces of the spreads between them: the cost of capital for the spread between secured (repo) and unsecured (Fed Funds, ESTR) O/N rates, the credit exposure for the spread between unsecured O/N and term rates (LIBOR). Combining both, we can expand the simple formula from above ($g*q*d$) with credit terms to a model for the repo–LIBOR spread, i.e. between the third and first column of Table 11.1. This will be the basis for pricing asset swap spreads of bonds versus LIBOR in Chapter 12: the funding difference and the credit exposure of the floating leg are already covered by the model, hence only the credit exposure of the fixed leg (the sovereign issuer) still needs to be added.

Assume a bank[9] wants to make a loan for a single period. If the loan is to be secured via repo collateral, the pre-tax return at the end of the period will be $[1 + R]$, where R is the repo rate for this single period. Assuming the loan is collateralized with a high-quality government bond, the bank can use a low-cost source of funds (e.g. bank retail deposits) to provide for the loan. If the cost of this capital is given by b, the cost of the loan is $[1 + b]$. The profit on this transaction is then $[1 + R] - [1 + b]$.

If the bank makes an unsecured interbank loan instead, it will have to finance dq of this loan at its higher cost of equity capital, g, where q is the BIS risk-weighting for interbank loans and d is the BIS guideline for the capital adequacy ratio for a 100% risk-weighted asset (typically 8%). The cost of capital will then be given by the expression:

$$(1 - qd)[1 + b] + qd[1 + g]$$

---

[9]This model is constructed from the perspective of a bank lending cash. We ignore any possible impact of haircuts for simplicity at this point. From the perspective of the bank, this would be valid, for example, in a case in which the loan was over-collateralized with government bonds, with the borrower of cash receiving any interest payments on the bonds.

Now, we add the credit component. If the probability of default is given by p, and the recovery percentage is given by c (percentage of terminal liability recovered rather than percentage of the current market value), then the expected return of the interbank loan L is given by:

$$pc[1 + L] + (1 - p)[1 + L]$$

Then the expected profit is given by:

$$pc[1 + L] + (1 - p)[1 + L] - (1 - qd)[1 + b] - qd[1 + g]$$

Assuming that the default probability is a risk-neutral default probability (i.e. it already incorporates the effect of any covariance-related risk premia), the expected profits of the secured and unsecured transactions can be equated to obtain an expression relating LIBOR and the repo rate. In particular:

$$[1 + R] - [1 + b] = pc[1 + L] + (1 - p)[1 + L] - (1 - qd)[1 + b] - qd[1 + g]$$

This equation can be solved in terms of LIBOR.

$$L = \frac{R}{1 - p(1 - c)} + \frac{p(1 - c)}{1 - p(1 - c)} + \frac{qd(g - b)}{1 - p(1 - c)}$$

The first term on the right-hand side of this equation is an amount to act as insurance against the default on the interest payment. In the degenerate case that $R = 0$, there is no interest payment against which to insure, and this term equals zero. And in the case that the recovery rate in the event of default is 100% (again, as a percentage of terminal value rather than nominal value), then the denominator in the first term equals 1, in which case this term contributes nothing to the repo–LIBOR spread. And if $p = 0$, so there is no probability of default, then the denominator of this expression is also 1, and this first term contributes nothing to the spread.

Note also that as long as there is some probability of default ($p > 0$) and the recovery value, c, is less than 100%, the denominator of this first term is less than 1, so that LIBOR increases at a rate faster than the repo rate. As a result, the difference between LIBOR and repo in general should be an increasing function of interest rates, all things being equal.

The second term on the right-hand side of the equation is an amount to insure against the principal of the loan. Note that this term equals zero if the recovery value is 100% ($c = 1$) or if the default probability is zero ($p = 0$).

The third and final term on the right-hand side of the expression reflects the additional amount that needs to be charged to compensate for the higher cost of equity capital on the portion of the unsecured loan that needs to be funded with core capital to satisfy the bank's regulatory capital requirement. If the cost of equity capital, g, happens to be the same as the marginal cost of borrowed funds, b, then this term is zero. Likewise, if the regulatory risk weighting for the unsecured loan is zero ($g = 0$) or if the capital adequacy ratio is zero ($d = 0$), then this term is also zero.

Overall, this equation explains and quantifies the empirically observed behavior of the difference between LIBOR and repo ($L - R$), which is

- an increasing function of the level of interest rates;
- an increasing function of the cost of core capital;
- an increasing function of required capital ratios.

CHAPTER 12

Asset Swaps

GENERAL CONCEPT

When looking at investing in a government bond from the viewpoint of a derivative, it appears to be a swap between the coupon as fixed rate and the repo as floating rate: until the maturity of the bond, one can finance the investment by using the bond as collateral in the repo market, i.e. by paying its repo rate (e.g. rolling O/N). Hence, investing in a bond and funding the position until maturity in the repo market is in principle the same as a pay repo–receive coupon swap (whose tenor is given by the maturity of the bond).

This derivative-like perspective on a bond makes it easy to compare bonds with swaps: Imagine that at the same time as investing in the bond we enter into a swap agreement paying fixed and receiving floating. If we choose the dates and size of the fixed payments in the swap to match the coupon dates and size of the bond – which is what happens in an asset swap – the fixed payments cancel out.[1] Thus, the combination of a bond and a swap in an asset swap results in a pay repo of the bond versus receive the floating rate of the swap position. In case the floating rate of the swap is LIBOR, an asset swap can therefore conceptually be thought of as a repo–LIBOR basis swap over the life of the bond. And the asset swap spread, i.e. the amount added to the floating rate of the swap position,[2] can be determined (in part) by the fair value of a repo–LIBOR basis swap. In other words, the asset swap spread includes the market price compensating for the privilege to fund at repo rather than LIBOR. While these basis swaps do not trade, we can price them via the model

---

[1]In order to focus on the big conceptual picture, we need to abstract from several complicating features, such as bonds not trading at par, different daycount conventions, etc. These features will be added subsequently.

[2]This definition results in the convention Reference Rate + X for the asset swap spread X. For example, if a Bund quotes at EURIBOR −20 bp, its asset swap spread is −20 bp (not +20bp). Under this convention, a relative richening of bonds versus swaps corresponds to decreasing asset swap spreads. In line with this convention, the funding difference of asset swap spreads versus LIBOR is given by a repo–LIBOR (not LIBOR–repo) basis swap.

presented in Chapter 11 and thereby obtain a starting point for pricing asset swap spreads: the fair value of the repo–LIBOR basis swap, using the anticipated repo rates and maturity of a specific bond, is one component of the fair value of the asset swap spread of that bond.

This is a conceptual approach[3] to asset swap spreads, which directly and causally captures the different funding rates for bonds (repo) and swaps and allows the application of cash-flow arbitrage principles to asset swap spread pricing: since an asset swap matches the fixed payments of the bond and swap, the asset swap spread can be determined as fair value of the basis swap between the two floating rates, i.e. repo and the reference rate used in the floating leg of the swap.

Apart from exchanging funding rates, an asset swap also exchanges credit exposure: investing in a bond exposes one to sovereign default risk, while a swap with LIBOR as reference rate exposes one to bank default risk. In other words, an asset swap matches the fixed cash flows and exchanges the floating cash flows, but these cash flows are subject to different credit risk.

Adding the credit perspective to the funding perspective from above, we can compare the two sides of an asset swap, choosing LIBOR as example for the reference rate:

- The holder of the bond is subject to the default risk of the issuer. In case of a sovereign default, despite losing the principal, he still needs to serve his fixed payment obligations in the asset swap, but will not receive the matching coupon payments from the bond anymore.
- If he takes the other side of the asset swap, i.e. he will receive fixed/pay floating, he needs to generate the floating payments, i.e. LIBOR, by lending unsecured to (LIBOR panel) banks. Again, in case of the borrower defaulting, despite losing the principal, he still needs to serve his floating payment obligations in the asset swap, but will not receive the matching LIBOR payments anymore.

Altogether, one can consider an asset swap as a combination of a funding swap and a credit swap:

- An exchange between the funding rate of the bond (repo) and the reference rate of the swap, i.e. a repo–swap reference rate basis swap over the life of the bond
- An exchange between the credit exposure to the bond issuer and to the counterparties in the money market.

---

[3] In the first edition of this book, we compared this "modern" with the "old" approach. By now, this is more of historic interest and has therefore been omitted from the second edition.

As argued in Chapter 11, the credit risk to counterparties in the money market is usually negligible for rolling O/N loans. Note that the credit 'refreshes' in the money market are a significantly different feature from the credit exposure of a bond investment: buying and holding a 10Y government bond expose one to the same counterpart for the next decade. Hence, the credit exposure on the floating side is in practice usually only relevant for swaps with LIBOR as the reference rate. And as it has already been incorporated into the model for the repo–LIBOR spread from Chapter11, this model covers both the funding aspects and the credit aspects of the floating side.

With an asset swap combining a funding and a credit swap, it can be priced by expanding the funding model with a credit component:

- The model for the spread between different reference rates gives a fair value for the repo–swap reference rate basis swap, i.e. the *funding component* of swap spreads.
- Adding the *credit component* of swap spreads on the *floating side* only needs to be done in case of LIBOR as reference rate and has already been done in the repo–LIBOR model at the end of Chapter 11.
- Hence, only the *credit component* of swap spreads on the *fixed side*, i.e. the exposure to sovereign default risk, still needs to be added to the model.

If the credit default swap (CDS) was a pure measure of default risk, one could complete the task of building a pricing model for asset swap spreads by simply adding it to the fair value of the repo–swap reference rate basis swap, i.e.

Asset swap spread = Fair value of the basis swap between repo and the reference rate of the swap (from model) + CDS (from market),

in the case of LIBOR thus:

Asset swap spread = repo–LIBOR basis swap (from model) + CDS (from market).

Unfortunately, the elegance of this concept is tainted by the fact that the CDS is not a pure measure of default risk and therefore requires adjustments before being used in the formula above. This is a complex topic, which occupies Chapter 13. Previewing the results from Chapter 13 (and keeping the caveats under which they are derived in mind), the formula will read:

Asset swap spread = Fair value of the basis swap between repo and the reference rate of the swap (from model) + Adjusted CDS,
with *Adjusted CDS = CDS (from market) * 0.45 for cash-settled CDS and Adjusted CDS = CDS (from market) * 0.39 for CDS with physical delivery.*

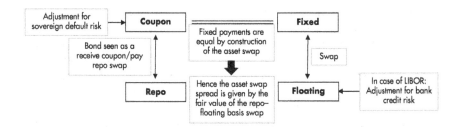

FIGURE 12.1 Conceptual approach to asset swap pricing.
Source: Authors.

Before applying the general concept to the different types of reference rates and discussing further additions, it may be useful to reflect on its fundamental principles. On a very basic level, we have considered only the cash flows of an asset swap. While this is the precondition to apply no-arbitrage principles, it also excludes features not accessible via cash flow analysis from the onset. These features, for example, the regulatory benefits of holding bonds, therefore need to be treated separately in Chapter 18, after the cash flow-based models will have been completed. Looking at the cash flows of an asset swap and thinking of a bond like a swap between fixed (coupon income) and floating (repo financing), we applied a no-arbitrage principle by arguing, that as the fixed cash flows match by construction of the asset swap, also the floating cash flows should match, hence that the asset swap spread should be equal to the fair value of the repo–swap reference rate basis swap over the life of the bond. This argument is illustrated by the fat arrow in Figure 12.1. Having captured the funding element of asset swaps, we have then turned our attention to the different credit exposure and found that while the cash flows match in case of no default, they are subject to different default risk. In order to maintain the cash flow-matching in the presence of default risk, corresponding adjustments are required: the adjustment for the credit exposure to LIBOR has already been incorporated in the model for the repo–LIBOR spread, while the adjustment for the credit exposure to bond issuers can be done by adding the CDS (subject to the modifications in Chapter 13).

APPLICATION OF THE GENERAL CONCEPT TO PRICE THE THREE TYPES OF ASSET SWAPS

As discussed in Chapter 11, there are three types of swaps, depending on the reference rate used on the floating side and therefore also three types of asset swap spreads, all of which can be considered as special cases of the general concept and which will now be treated individually.

Swap Spreads Versus SOFR

In case of the floating rate of the asset swap being SOFR, the asset swap spread ("ASW") of a bond versus SOFR (the "SOFR–ASW") is given by the following special case of the general formula above:

SOFR–ASW = repo–SOFR basis swap + adjusted CDS.

As mentioned in Chapter 11, due to the calculation process of SOFR, most special repo rates are excluded. Hence, SOFR is generally close to the GC rate. Still, deviations between SOFR and GC can arise from several sources, including:

- Since only FICC transactions below the volume-weighted 25th percentile are removed, in case more repo trades at special rates take place during a certain day, some of them enter the SOFR calculation.
- Due to the additional constraint SOFR $\leq$ SRFR, SOFR could be lower than GC transactions in the actual market. This difference is likely to be mitigated by the SRFR influencing the repo market – as long as there is enough arbitrage capital available.

If we assume – subject to the caveats just mentioned – *SOFR = GC*, then the repo–SOFR basis swap equals a repo–GC basis swap, i.e. a daily exchange between the repo rate of the specific bond used in the asset swap and the GC rate. This is precisely the specialness of the bond and the formula is thus

SOFR–ASW = repo–GC basis swap (specialness) + adjusted CDS.

In case of SOFR–ASW and under the assumption SOFR = GC, the funding element of the asset swap is therefore simply the specialness of the bond, and the fair value of the SOFR–ASW is given by the expected specialness of the bond over its entire life (plus the adjusted CDS). In other words, a SOFR–ASW exchanges every day the repo rate of a specific bond versus the GC rate. In case of the bond trading GC, the value of this exchange is zero. In case of the bond trading special, the spread to GC, i.e. its specialness, is exchanged. Hence, the fair value of the repo–GC basis swap used in the ASW formula is given by the sum of the discounted (O/N-)specialness of the bond for every day of its remaining life.

One can estimate the evolution of specialness over the life of a bond by looking at its predecessors. For example, Bunds trade typically special as 10Y benchmark immediately after issuance and as deliverables into the Bund and Bobl future contracts. In this way, the fair value of the repo–GC basis swap

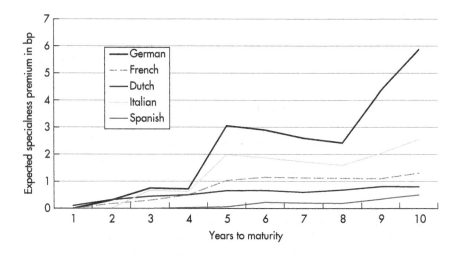

FIGURE 12.2 Historical average for the GC–repo basis swap for different EUR sovereign issues.
Source: ABN Amro, reproduced with permission from RBS.

(i.e. the expected specialness premium) can be calculated by using historical repo specialness data and assessing how special a bond of a certain issuer and with a certain maturity is expected to become over its life. The result, based on ABN Amro's database for repo rates, which was first published in our ABN Amro Research note "Many EUR sovereign default swaps are undervalued" from 17 April 2002 and is reproduced here with kind permission from RBS, is depicted in Figure 12.2. The effect of the Bobl and Bund futures contracts on the expected specialness is clearly discernible. Note that the formula above uses the negative values from Figure 12.2.

For a bond without any periods of (expected) specialness during its remaining life, its funding rate (repo) is always GC, and thus the fair value of the funding component of its SOFR–ASW is zero. This is a consequence of SOFR being by design close to the funding rate of government bonds: Unlike LIBOR, an unsecured term rate, SOFR is a secured O/N rate, calculated from the transactions in the repo market.

The transition from LIBOR to SOFR has therefore resulted in the proximity of the funding rates for bonds and the reference rate of swaps. The funding difference involved in asset swaps and expressed as repo–SOFR basis swap in the formula above is hence limited to the specialness of specific bonds and usually rather close to zero.

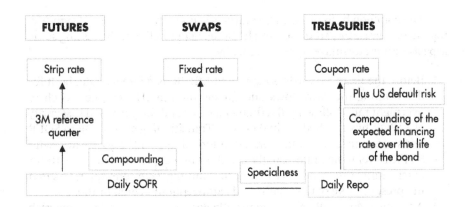

FIGURE 12.3 Integration of SOFR into a term rate in the US future, swap and bond markets.
Source: Huggins and Schaller (2022).

This observation is part of a larger picture,[4] which can be described as convergence of the bond, swap and future markets in the US due to the transition to SOFR (Figure 12.3):

- 3M SOFR futures compound consecutive 3M forward periods of SOFR into a forward rate and hence the SOFR future strip into a term rate.
- Swaps with SOFR as floating leg exchange SOFR versus a fixed term rate.
- Treasuries can be considered as exchanging their funding rate at (a level close to) SOFR versus their coupon payments.

Hence, all three instruments, futures, swaps, and Treasuries, can be seen as (slightly different) ways to compound the same reference rate, daily SOFR values (or, in case of Treasuries, the repo rate, which is typically close to SOFR), into a term rate. Allowing for some imperfection in order to express the conceptual similarity, one could say that future strips, swaps with SOFR as reference rate and Treasuries all combine the same underlying SOFR into term rates. Abstracting from the technical differences, one might therefore consider all three instruments to be essentially the same, i.e. market prices for a certain future segment of daily SOFR.

---

[4]Chapter 9 of Huggins and Schaller (2022) discusses this topic in detail. The next few paragraphs contain some excerpts.

The common basis of the three markets leads to the advantage of simplifying the relationships, arbitrage, and hedging, between them. Expressing some aspects of this advantage more specifically:

- Before the financial crisis, swaps used LIBOR as reference rate, both for determining the cash flows and for discounting. Hence, the switch to overnight rates following the financial crisis and the perceived insecurity of LIBOR has resulted in dual curves. Transitioning everything to SOFR reinstates the clean and easy situation of the old days: swaps with SOFR as reference rate usually use the same curve, i.e. SOFR, both for determining the cash flows and for discounting. One consequence is that the present value of the floating side at inception is equal to 100.
- And the daily SOFR values are usually compounded for calculating cash flows and discount factors in the same manner as the settlement price of 3M future contracts. Hence, the SOFR future strip applies in principle the same calculation as swaps with SOFR as reference rate. This link allows using SOFR futures as alternative to swaps, for example, for hedging US Treasuries. One consequence is the increase in liquidity and decrease in hedging costs. In order to establish this nice principle in practice, different payment frequencies (e.g. 3M for futures and 6M for Treasuries) and daycount conventions (usually actual/360 for money market and actual/actual for Treasuries) need to be addressed. Moreover, as an OTC product, the swap counterparties can agree to all sorts of discounting curves and payment times. For example, swaps with SOFR as reference rate cleared by the CME have a 2-day payment delay. On top of all this come the issues of date mismatches between the coupon periods and the reference periods of SOFR contracts.[5]
- And as we have just seen, the migration to asset swaps with SOFR as reference rate eliminates the basis between unsecured and secured rates inherent in asset swaps with LIBOR as reference rate. Assuming a Treasury to always fund at SOFR (in particular never becoming special) and ignoring credit exposure, payment frequency and daycount differences, the transition to SOFR allows considering swaps and bonds to be conceptually the same: an exchange of an overnight secured funding rate (SOFR) into a term rate. The future, swap, and bond markets are three different places to get a price for the same collections of future SOFR values, for example, over the next two years. Another way to express this link is to say that under these assumptions, the contribution of funding differences to the asset swap spreads of Treasuries is zero.

---

[5] Chapter 7 of Huggins and Schaller (2022).

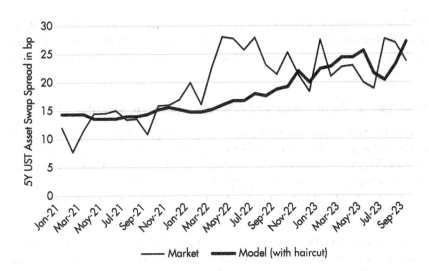

FIGURE 12.4 Actual SOFR–ASW of 5Y US Treasuries versus the model forecast. *Source:* Authors.

Data period: Mid-monthly data from January 2021 to September 2023. As the CDS quotes infrequently, some interpolation assumptions were required.

Moving from theory to practice, Figure 12.4 compares the model forecast with the actual evolution of SOFR–ASW for 5Y US Treasuries. In order to minimize the structural break from the introduction of the standing repo facility (SRF) (see Chapter 11), we have chosen data points around the middle of each month, avoiding the spikes at quarter end pre-SRF.

It turns out, that without including the haircut financing costs, the model systematically underestimates the SOFR–ASW level. Hence, adding a term for haircut costs by assuming reasonable funding rates is vital to achieve the good fit to the market visible in Figure 12.4. Applying the haircut of 2% shown in Table 18.1 and a funding rate of 5% above SOFR results in 10 bp haircut costs. Actually, one could also pursue the opposite direction and estimate the haircut (financing) costs of the marginal market participant via the spread between actual and modeled SOFR–ASW. At the time of writing (September 2023), this estimate would have been 8 bp.

Once the haircut costs are added to the model value, it follows the actual market quite well. The only exception has occurred at the beginning of 2022, when the actual SOFR–ASW exceeded the model value (with haircut) by about 10 bp. Since this deviation has coincided with a strong sell-off in the Treasury market and disappeared afterwards, it seems to be an indication of a flow-related market mispricing rather than of a problem with the model.

While the empirical data for testing SOFR–ASW models is too short to draw definite conclusions, so far the model seems to reflect actual market behavior: readers are encouraged to repeat this test once more data will have become available.

Swap Spreads Versus Unsecured O/N Rates (OIS Swap Spreads)

In case of the floating rate of the asset swap being an O/N rate (we use ESTR in the following expressions, which hold true for other O/N rates as well), the asset swap spread of a bond versus ESTR[6] (the "ESTR–ASW") is given by the following special case of the general formula above:

ESTR–ASW = repo–ESTR basis swap + adjusted CDS.

The repo–ESTR basis swap can be thought of as consisting of two components: first, a repo–GC basis swap, second, a GC-ESTR basis swap. Seen from this perspective, it extends the repo–GC basis swap (specialness) applied in the formula for SOFR–ASW with a basis swap between secured (GC) and unsecured (ESTR) O/N rates.

As ESTR–ASW contain the funding difference between secured (repo) and unsecured (ESTR) rates, they are driven by the capital treatment discussed in Chapter 11. This is a difference to SOFR–ASW, which are independent of the cost of capital and BIS rules, explaining the usually higher level and volatility of ESTR–ASW compared to SOFR–ASW.

Under the assumption that also unsecured O/N rates involve a negligible credit risk, ESTR–ASW can be priced by using the simple formula $g*q*d$ for the funding difference, i.e. the fair value of the GC–ESTR basis swap, and adding both the expected specialness as explained above and the adjusted CDS level.

In contrast to the convergence of the markets for swaps and government bonds in the US described above, the transition from the unsecured funding rate LIBOR to the secured funding rate SOFR has caused a divergence of the markets for swaps and corporate bonds. Actually, hedging a corporate bond with a swap using SOFR as reference rate now involves the same unsecured versus secured basis, which was involved in hedging government bonds with swaps using LIBOR as reference rate.

Hence, if asset swaps or swap hedges which do not involve the secured–unsecured basis are desired, swaps with SOFR as reference rate can be used

---

[6]When combined with a USD-EUR CCBS, also Treasuries have ESTR–ASW and EURIBOR–ASW. And the other way round, basis swapped Bunds also have SOFR–ASW.

for government bonds and swaps with Fed Funds (in case of the US) as reference rate can be used for corporate bonds. Both (asset) swaps are connected through the SOFR–Fed Fund basis; as a result of the convergence shown in Figure 12.3, the SOFR–Fed Fund future spread contracts provide a market price and a cheap way to hedge this basis.

Swap Spreads Versus LIBOR

In case of the floating rate of the asset swap being LIBOR, the asset swap spread of a bond versus LIBOR (the "LIBOR–ASW") is given by the following special case of the general formula above:

$$LIBOR\text{–}ASW = repo\text{–}LIBOR\ basis\ swap + adjusted\ CDS.$$

The repo–LIBOR basis swap can be thought of as consisting of three components: (1) a repo–GC basis swap, (2) a GC–ESTR basis swap, and (3) an ESTR-LIBOR basis swap. Seen from this perspective, it extends the repo–GC basis swap (specialness) applied in the formula for SOFR–ASW with a basis swap between secured (GC) and unsecured (ESTR) O/N rates *and* with a basis swap between unsecured O/N (ESTR) and term (LIBOR) rates.

In comparison with SOFR–ASW, LIBOR–ASW depends in addition to the specialness element also on the secured–unsecured spread and hence the capital considerations *and* on the O/N–term spread and hence on a non-negligible credit exposure to the money market counterparties. LIBOR–ASW should therefore be priced by using the model for the repo–LIBOR spread (including the credit element) for the funding difference, i.e. the fair value of the GC-LIBOR basis swap, before adding again both the expected specialness as explained above and the adjusted CDS level.

Taking a step back and overviewing the three special cases of the general concept, one realizes how the increasing difference between repo and the reference rate of the swap (first SOFR, then ESTR, finally LIBOR) results in the elements driving the asset swap spread to increase, with the calculation being expanded accordingly. Apart from the credit exposure of the bond issuer (and driving factors not captured in the model) involved in every type of swap spread, SOFR–ASW only depends on the expected specialness, ESTR–ASW also on the capital treatment driving the secured–unsecured basis, LIBOR–ASW also on the term risk. From this viewpoint, the evolution of reference rates summarized in Table 11.1 in the opposite direction (from LIBOR to SOFR) can be considered as removing one difference between the funding of bonds and swaps after another, with the convergence of the markets depicted in Figure 12.3 as the goal.

The increasing number of driving forces is reflected in a usually increasing volatility when moving from SOFR–ASW via ESTR–ASW to LIBOR–ASW. The variable CoE is particularly prone to sharp moves, but affects only ESTR–ASW and LIBOR–ASW, not SOFR–ASW. This is one reason why the ASW of Bunds versus ESTR and LIBOR tends to be more volatile than the ASW of US Treasuries versus SOFR shown in Figure 12.4. Chapter 16 will combine these two observations and discuss how the relative stability of SOFR–ASW of US Treasuries and of their spread to basis swapped Bunds results in most of the volatility of the ESTR–ASW and LIBOR–ASW of Bunds being usually absorbed by volatile basis swaps (and vice versa).

TERM STRUCTURE OF SWAP SPREADS

Summarizing the discussion above, Table 12.1 exhibits the driving factors of the different types of asset swap spreads.

By assessing the term structure of each of the driving factors one can predict the term structure of the asset swap spread curve:

- The credit risk of bond issuers has a term structure, which can, for example, be calculated by multiplying the yearly rating transition matrix with itself. It turns out that for issuers starting with a good rating (as is the case for the sovereign issuers considered in this book), the default risk increases over time. This is also reflected in the market price for that risk, i.e. the adjusted CDS quotes. While liquidity in the government CDS market is concentrated in 5Y, rare quotes for shorter or longer maturities are regularly lower or higher. In line with this observation, the asset swap spread curves tend to be upward-sloping. The SOFR–ASW curve of Treasuries usually starts around zero (as explained above) and then becomes more and more positive, which can (partly) be explained by the increasing credit exposure to the US: the longer the maturity, the higher

TABLE 12.1 Driving Factors of the Different Types of Asset Swap Spreads

Driving factor of	SOFR–ASW	OIS–ASW	LIBOR–ASW
Credit risk of bond (CDS)	Yes	Yes	Yes
Specialness	Yes	Yes	Yes
Capital requirements	No	Yes	Yes
Money market term (risk)	No	No	Yes

the chance for the US credit quality to deteriorate – while being stuck with the bond without the feature of credit 'refreshes.' The LIBOR–ASW curve of Bunds usually starts with negative values (reflecting the capital requirements) and then also increases. If and where it reaches positive values depends on the relationship between the CDS curve of Germany and the unsecured–secured basis on a given day.

- The specialness also has a term structure, as depicted in Figure 12.2. Since specialness is mostly caused by benchmark and delivery status, it usually increases with the maturity of the bond. Hence, the longer the bond, the higher its expected specialness and thus the lower (in case of LIBOR–ASW of Bunds usually more negative) the asset swap spread. Specialness is therefore a driving factor which imposes a term structure opposite to the credit exposure. For example, with an unsecured–secured basis of 16 bp (using the example given in Chapter 11) and an adjusted 10Y German CDS level of 15 bp, the ESTR–ASW of a 10Y Bund should be −16 bp + 15 bp − 6 bp = −7 bp, with the term "−6 bp" taken from the average specialness shown in Figure 12.2.
- Since the capital requirements are the same for any maturity (for the instruments considered here), the unsecured–secured basis has no term structure. Using the example from Chapter 11 again, for a cost of capital of 10%, that basis is −16 bp for all maturities. Only in case of expected future changes to one of the three variables, cost of equity, risk weighting, and core capital ratio, would there be a term structure to the basis as well. For instance, if a change to the cost of capital or to the BIS rules was expected to occur in two years, the unsecured–secured basis would exhibit a term structure from that point in time onwards.[7]
- The term (risk) involved in LIBOR–ASW is the same for all bond maturities and does not contribute to the term structure of LIBOR–ASW.
- In addition, also the haircut schedules usually have a term structure, which influences all three asset swap spread curves. While the exact quantity depends on the financing costs of the haircut, as the haircuts typically increase with the maturity of the bond, this factor generally supports steeper swap spread curves. In fact, we'll see that the exceptionally steep haircut schedule of the BoE (Table 18.2) is partly responsible for the exceptionally steep SOFR asset swap spread curve of basis swapped Gilts (Figure 17.2).

---

[7]At the time of writing, we have found no basis for such expectations in the BIS documents.

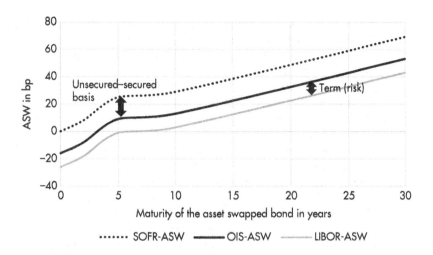

FIGURE 12.5 Schematic relationship between the three asset swap spread curves. *Source:* Authors.

Cutting through Table 12.1 by columns rather than rows, we can determine the term structure of the different asset swap spread curves and find that all driving factors with a term structure are already reflected in the SOFR asset swap spread curve. Hence, all three swap spread curves are usually parallel shifts of the same slope and curvature (Figure 12.5). In more detail:

- The SOFR asset swap spread curve depends on the term structure of the CDS, specialness, and haircut curves. It typically starts at zero and is upward-sloping due to the increasing default risk and haircuts, which is somewhat mitigated by the expected specialness also increasing with the maturity.
- The OIS asset swap spread curve additionally depends on the unsecured–secured basis. In the absence of expected future changes to the cost of capital or BIS rules, this basis has no term structure. Hence, the OIS asset swap spread curve typically has the same shape as the SOFR asset swap spread curve, just starting from a lower (negative) level as given by the basis.
- The LIBOR asset swap spread curve additionally depends on the term (risk), which also has no term structure. It therefore exhibits typically the same shape as the other two, just starting from an even lower (negative) level, which also reflects the term (risk).

CYCLICALITY OF SWAP SPREADS

In the same way that we have just screened the influencing factors of swap spreads listed in Table 12.1 for term structures, we can now assess their cyclicality[8]:

- The credit risk of bond issuers exhibits a clear cyclicality: in a recession, tax revenue decreases and social benefit payments increase, negatively affecting the credit quality of a state. This is a major driving force behind the cyclicality of swap spreads, which explains their tendency to increase in times of a recession. Using the terminology from the note and the fact that recessions are typically accompanied by decreasing interest rates,[9] one could therefore call swap spreads (with the convention Reference Rate +X) "counter-cyclical." The next section outlines that the impact of many cyclical and counter-cyclical variables, such as bond issuance and unemployment, on swap spreads can be captured in our model via the credit component.
- We see no theoretical or empirical reason to assume cyclicality of repo specialness.
- If a recession is accompanied by a banking crisis, it is conceivable that it leads to (speculation about) more restrictive BIS rules, such as higher core capital ratios. This effect would result in lower swap spreads, i.e. be cyclical, and hence counteract the counter-cyclical impact of the credit risk of bond issuers. By contrast, if the recession leads to a sovereign downgrade, the bond may lose its 0% risk weighting, which would result in higher swap spreads and hence reinforce the counter-cyclical impact of the credit risk of bond issuers. While these events could have a material impact on swap spreads, they have been historically rare.
- As discussed at the end of Chapter 11, the difference between LIBOR and repo is an increasing function of the level of interest rates and of the probability of default of LIBOR panel banks (as well as the recovery ratio). In case of a recession leading to lower rates, for example, due to monetary stimulus, LIBOR–ASW can thus be expected to increase since the funding

---

[8]The term "cyclicality" refers to any correlation (positive or negative) of a time series to macro-economic cycles. Positive correlation of a time series to the level of interest rates is called "cyclical," negative correlation "counter-cyclical."

[9]There are exceptions such as stagflations. Actually, the current economic downturn coincides with rising interest rates. We therefore prefer to speak of the behavior of swap spreads in a "recession" rather than in a "low rate environment."

advantage of holding bonds decreases. By contrast, if the recession leads to a higher (perceived) probability of default of LIBOR panel banks, for example, due to their borrowers experiencing trouble or their collateral dropping in value, LIBOR–ASW should decrease. If both effects occur simultaneously, they could net out or one of the two sides, counter-cyclical or cyclical, could prevail, mainly depending on the extent to which banks are affected by the recession.

- If a recession is accompanied by stress in the financial sector, it is probable that haircuts will be increased and that at the same time the cost of financing them will go up. Both effects support increasing swap spreads in a recession and hence reinforce the counter-cyclical impact of the credit risk of bond issuers.

Altogether, in a recession, swap spreads tend to increase due to the worsening of the credit quality of the bond issuer and the tightening haircut schedules (and financing conditions). The impact of a recession on swap spreads via BIS rules and repo–LIBOR spreads is less clear and can work both ways. As a result, while there is a general tendency for swap spreads to be counter-cyclical (increasing during a recession), their behavior during a specific economic cycle depends on the extent to which the recession affects the banking sector. For example, if a recession starts with a banking crisis, it is possible that the worsening credit quality of banks will cause a decrease in LIBOR–ASW, which might be followed by an increase as the recession continues and ends up also affecting the sovereign credit quality (and leads to larger haircuts).

Cutting through Table 12.1 by columns, we note that SOFR–ASW are only affected by counter-cyclical factors (and the non-cyclical variable specialness): both the credit quality of sovereign issuers and haircuts support higher SOFR–ASW in a recession. OIS–ASW and in particular LIBOR–ASW are subject to additional influencing factors, which can include cyclical ones. Hence, one may expect the counter-cyclical behavior of SOFR–ASW to be more pronounced and more predictable than that of LIBOR–ASW.

Moreover, since the financial crisis the credit quality of sovereign issuers has been subject to more scrutiny, as reflected in higher and more volatile CDS levels even for the US and Germany. In terms of Table 12.1, this means that the counter-cyclical factor "credit risk of bond" has gained increasing influence on swap spreads. Consequently, the counter-cyclical behavior of all types of swap spreads has generally increased. And as the transition to SOFR limits the factors influencing swap spreads to counter-cyclical ones, it seems reasonable to anticipate an even clearer and stabler counter-cyclical picture of SOFR–ASW in future, compared to the large variety of patterns displayed by LIBOR–ASW some years ago.

As there has been no full macro economic cycle since the transition, we cannot provide comprehensive empirical evidence for the theoretical forecast of counter-cyclical SOFR–ASW based on our model. At least the semi-cycle shown in Figure 12.4 is in line with it: during the recent economic downturn both the SOFR–ASW of US Treasuries and the CDS level of the US have increased. Unlike in a usual recession, this has occurred against the background of rising interest rates and hence been cyclical. But the argument above has been based on a recession in general and holds true independent of the direction of interest rates, i.e. whether increasing SOFR–ASW during an economic downturn are accompanied by falling (usual) or rising (unusual) yields.

DRIVING FORCES OF SWAP SPREADS CAPTURED IN OUR MODEL

Many analysts use a different approach to assess swap spreads and regress them empirically versus a number of explanatory variables. A typical result could be that swap spreads tend to be higher in times of larger bond issuance, leading them to include Treasury supply as an explanatory variable in a (multiple) regression model for swap spreads.

Most cyclical and counter-cyclical variables are linked to and some of them even caused by the credit quality of the sovereign issuer. This is quite obvious in case of the amount of Treasury supply: the worse the situation of state finances, the larger the debt issuance. Likewise, the higher the unemployment, the lower the tax revenue and the higher the social benefit payments, thus the worse the government's credit situation. In other words, cyclical and counter-cyclical variables like the unemployment rate and government bond supply are both serving as proxies for any credit risk that is reflected in the prices of US Treasury bonds.[10]

Consequently, we claim that our financial model for asset swap spreads not only offers deeper causal insights than a superficial correlation exercise, but also incorporates most of the cyclical and counter-cyclical variables correlated to swap spreads (in particular the amount of bond issuance) via the adjusted CDS level (see Figure 10.1). We see therefore no reason to expand our model with cyclical or counter-cyclical variables, which can reasonably be linked to the credit risk of the government.

---

[10]We'd like to thank Antti Ilmanen for making this point.

DRIVING FORCES OF SWAP SPREADS NOT CAPTURED IN OUR MODEL

On the other hand, there are a number of driving forces, which are not covered by the conceptual approach of our model. This section provides a (probably incomplete) list of these elements, some of which can and should be added to our model when necessary. In fact, the remaining chapters of the "swap block" will largely be occupied with expanding the asset swap spread concept founded here.

Bonds Trading Away from Par

The presentation of the concept above tacitly assumed par-coupon bonds. The situation becomes a bit more complex in the case of bonds trading at a discount to par, as we'll see in Chapter 17. But fair swap spreads for off-coupon bonds can be calculated by first calculating a fair swap spread for a par-coupon bond and then determining the fair yield spread between the par-coupon bond and the off-coupon bond.

Also, we ignored some of the real-world issues in the repo market. For example, current par-coupon bonds are likely to trade away from par at some point, in which case they will be re-priced in the repo market, as we discussed in Chapter 11. If the swap spread for the bond remains constant, then the NPV of the swap is very likely to move in the opposite direction and by a similar magnitude. Provided the swap is being margined (as almost surely will be the case), then the change in margin for the swap is very likely to offset the change in margin for the bond. For example, if cash were acceptable as margin for the bond position and the swap position, then we could shift the cash from our swap margin account to our repo margin account, and vice versa. However, the swap spread is likely to move over time as well, in which case there will be times when our repo margin and swap margin don't offset.

Insurance Properties of Swap Spreads

So far in our discussion, we've addressed the notion of random and time-varying asset swap spreads by focusing on the expectation of funding and credit spreads over the lives of the bonds. In theory, we might also care about the covariance between these swap spreads and the marginal utility of a typical investor, which is an impact on swap spreads not captured in our model and not treated in the remaining chapters.

When considering this issue, it's useful to draw an analogy to popular types of insurance contracts, such as fire insurance. For most homeowners, the expected return on a fire insurance policy is negative, in that they are required to pay more in insurance premiums than the payouts they expect to receive from the policy, given the likelihood of a fire. Nevertheless, most homeowners are happy to buy fire insurance because the payouts from a policy come at precisely the time that the homeowner most needs money to rebuild a home destroyed by fire. In other words, the covariance between the payout and the homeowner's marginal utility is relatively high.

As discussed above, swap spreads are subject to a number of cyclical and counter-cyclical forces and hence correlated with the marginal utility of the typical investor. For example, in a recession, when banks are at a higher risk of experiencing stress, swap spreads (at least SOFR–ASW) typically increase. In order to assess their covariance to marginal utility, the volatility of swap spreads and marginal utility also needs to be considered: As volatility is usually higher in times of a recession, we'd expect the insurance component of swap spreads to be greater during times of recession than it would be when the economy was expanding.

As a result, a "fair" swap spread might also reflect the extent to which the spread is correlated with factors investors may want to hedge. For example, a bank may have a preference to reverse asset swap bonds, because the (SOFR–)ASW is likely to widen in bad times. Of course, the range of considerations here will be quite complex. For example, if the fortunes of the bank's swap counterparty are likely to be correlated with the macroeconomy, this factor may affect the bank's willingness to enter into the swap agreement as well. But the point underlying both issues is that the performance of the swap may be correlated with things that the bank may wish to insure. And just as insurance policies tend to be priced so that the providers of insurance can expect to make a profit, so should we expect swaps to be priced so that the providers of insurance can expect to make a profit.

While the potential impact of the insurance properties of swap spreads on their pricing cannot be denied, it cannot be observed or modeled: if a subset of market participants finds that reverse asset swapping bonds helps insure against macroeconomic risk, how are the other market participants even to know of this, let alone incorporate it into their own analysis? Like the shadow costs discussed in Chapter 18, this is therefore a driving force which necessarily remains outside any model framework.

Global Influences via the CCBS

By construction, our model looks at the situation in one currency only and we can repeat our exercise for each currency. But due to the existence of CCBS linking all currencies, the swap spreads and their modeling in a given currency are subject to influences from all other swap spread markets.

This means that we cannot simply multiply our model and have one model for the US, a separate one for the eurozone, etc., but that we need to consider at the same time the mutual links via the CCBS between all of them. This is an essential, relatively complex but also worthwhile task, which is the subject of Chapter 16.

Repo Haircuts and Other Individual Factors

While we have included repo haircuts in the qualitative discussions of term structure and cyclicality, we have not included them in our quantitative formula. The reason for this decision is the fact that both the financing costs of repo haircuts and the applicable haircut schedule can vary significantly between individual market participants. Conceptually, one can think of the formula above as representing "the" swap spread, using only input variables which tend to be rather similar for most typical market participants,[11] which then needs to be adjusted with individually different parameters, such as the haircut, in order to obtain "your" swap spread.

These impacts of individual factors, including haircuts, on swap spreads will be the subject of Chapter 18, helping the reader to adjust the general pricing formula according to his specific circumstances.

Altogether, the model presented in this chapter is only the foundation for expansions and modifications in the following chapters. The increasing complexity reflects the complex interdependencies established by the CCBS and the tricky features of the CDS, among others. Unfortunately, already the core model of this chapter contains an unobservable variable (the cost of equity) and while most of the subsequent additions are observable (like ICBS and CCBS), the adjustments of the CDS will involve some more assumptions based on only a few market observations during defaults. Fortunately, we will encounter on our journey through this web of complex relationships and partly unobservable variables some hard and clear boundaries, specifically the arbitrage inequality in Chapter 16.

---

[11] As also the CDS quotes can vary depending on the credit standing of the counterpart, it is hard to draw a scientifically precise line between individual and non-individual factors.

CHAPTER 13

Credit Default Swaps

INTRODUCTION

Credit default swaps (CDS) have the advantage of providing observable market prices for credit exposure. We have exploited this advantage by using them as input into our swap spread model in Chapter 12. Unfortunately though, they are not a pure measure of credit risk, but in the case of sovereigns also involve an FX component and in case of physical delivery a delivery option. The first task of this chapter is therefore to assess the contribution of these elements to the observed CDS prices, allowing us to extract the pure credit information from the CDS quotes and to use them as input variable "adjusted CDS" in our swap spread model.

In principle, the data needed to adjust for the FX component and the delivery option are observable ex ante (unlike the CoE, for instance). However, as a consequence of the scarcity of CDS quotes in the domestic currency and of relevant sovereign defaults, there are only a few observations. The adjustments are therefore based on a few data points only and can be improved by adding more observations in future. The best estimation for the 'adjusted CDS' input variable currently possible given the rare observations seems to be:

- The 'pure' credit risk amounts to 45% of the CDS quote observed in the market in case of a sovereign CDS with cash settlement.
- The 'pure' credit risk amounts to 39% of the CDS quote observed in the market in case of a sovereign CDS with physical delivery.

In relation to Chapter 12, this chapter thus provides (an imperfect estimation for) the input variable 'adjusted CDS' for the swap spread model. In the following chapters, this model will be expanded with the global links established by the CCBS. One result will be the ability to express any bond in any currency via a combination of asset&basis swaps as a swap versus USD SOFR. As this is conceptually very similar to a CDS, which also expresses any bond as a spread versus USD SOFR, it is natural to compare the two. CDS will therefore reenter the stage in Chapter 16 discussing the RV relationships between asset, basis and credit default swaps. Specifically, by comparing the USD ASW with the CDS (i.e. by comparing credit risk reflected in the bond market *relative* to credit risk reflected in the CDS market), one can detect relative value opportunities, exploiting the *different assessment* of the same credit risk in bonds and in CDS, while being hedged against the absolute level of credit risk.

Apart from being a driving force of swap spreads, CDS are also an interesting asset class of their own:

- CDS markets exhibit intrinsic relationships, which are well suited to be analyzed and traded via PCA.
- By subtracting (adjusted) CDS from bond yields, one obtains a proxy for risk-free government yield curves. This is the basis for several analytical insights and relatively new RV trading strategies.

These two points are the subject of the second part of this chapter, which can be skipped by readers focused on understanding swap spreads.

STRUCTURE OF A CDS

A CDS contains information about a bond issuer's credit risk, but not in a clean form. Rather, a CDS presents the information about credit risk in connection with other elements, which arise from its structure and legal specifications. Here, we briefly discuss the specifications of the CDS as far as they are relevant for the potential distortion of the credit information. We shall find that the credit information in a CDS is given:

- together with information about the delivery option (DO) in case of CDS with physical delivery;
- potentially in a different currency than the bond covered by the CDS.

Then, we address these two issues separately and investigate how these two factors can be priced and thus how the clean information about credit risk can be extracted from the CDS quotes observed in the market.

A CDS on a bond issuer exchanges floating payments (usually quarterly[1]) of the premium (which we shall also denote with the term "CDS") for the right to deliver a bond of the issuer for payment of its par value in case of a default of the issuer. We shall refer to paying the premium and enjoying the right to deliver the bond for payment of principal in case of a default as "buying" or "being long" the CDS.

---

[1]Since CDS are over-the-counter products, any terms can be agreed on. We focus on the most common terms.

The usual specifications of a CDS result in the following features, which overlay the credit information in a CDS with other elements:

- There are two types of CDS depending on the form of compensation in case of a default. In cash-settled CDS, the buyer of the CDS receives a payment to compensate for the loss of holding a bond of an issuer in default. There are several ways to determine the amount of the loss and hence of the compensation, such as an auction or a poll among dealers. By contrast, the buyer of a CDS with physical delivery has the right to deliver *any* bond (as defined in the contract) of the defaulted issuer to the seller in exchange for receiving the par value. Since he can select the bond he delivers, CDS with physical delivery contain a delivery option, unlike cash-settled CDS. For sovereign CDS, physical delivery seems to be more common and unless otherwise stated we assume physical delivery.

  For corporate CDS, on the other hand, there seems to be a general tendency to move away from physical delivery: with CDS becoming popular and their outstanding volume increasing relative to the size of outstanding bonds of the defaulting issuer, physical settlement has an increasingly distorting impact on bond prices, since it artificially increases demand for the bonds of defaulting issuers, just for them to be delivered into CDS contracts. Actually, in the case of more CDS contracts (net) than bonds being outstanding, the need to deliver a bond in order to receive payment from the CDS contract should theoretically result in the bonds of a defaulting issuer trading at par. This problem of physical delivery has supported the transition to cash settlement for corporate CDS – though it has its own set of problems. For sovereign issuers, the amount of bonds is much larger relative to the net position of CDS contracts, which may explain why the transition to cash settlement is not as significant as for corporate issuers.

- CDS contracts with physical delivery usually do not specify which bond needs to be delivered in the event of default but rather allow any of the issuer's bonds to be delivered into the CDS contract. This results in a delivery option (DO), similar to a bond futures contract, though in this case the buyer of CDS is long and the seller of CDS is short the DO. If we own a bond and a CDS on its issuer, in the event of default we can deliver our bond in exchange for our principal. But we also could sell our bond, buy another bond of the same issuer, and then deliver that bond into the CDS. If the other bond is cheaper than the one we originally held, we realize a profit.

- In most cases, the CDS terminates when an issuer defaults, even if the stated end date of the CDS is still in the future. For example, if we hold a 10-year (10Y) bond and hedge it with a 10Y CDS, and if the bond issuer defaults after five years, then we can deliver the bond into the CDS in exchange for the bond principal at the time of default rather than waiting until the maturity of the bond. In contrast, cash flows of other instruments traded in conjunction with the bond, such as asset swaps and basis swaps, would not end in the case of default by the issuer. In our example, if we hold a 10Y *asset-swapped* bond and hedge it with a 10Y CDS, and if the bond issuer defaults after five years, then we receive the principal from the CDS counterparty after five years, but we'll no longer receive the bond cash flows that we had matched against our open asset swap position. Thus, we would need to take our principal and reinvest it at the prevailing interest rate after five years in order to fulfill the remaining asset swap contract. Obviously, this introduces an interest rate risk in case of a default.

- Unlike corporate CDS, sovereign CDS usually[2] pay the principal of a defaulted bond *in USD*. For example, the typical Japanese CDS gives the buyer the right to deliver in case of a default any JGB and to receive the notional value of the CDS, which is trading in USD. This agreement therefore amounts to receiving the par value of the JGB in USD at the USD–JPY exchange rate defined when entering the CDS, hence pre default. We refer to the currency in which the principal of a defaulting bond is paid to the buyer of a CDS contract as the settlement currency or *denomination* of the CDS. As a consequence, a non-USD-denominated bond and a USD-denominated CDS assess the credit risk *in different currencies*.

In the likely case of the currency of a defaulting country weakening this can result in overcompensation for the CDS buyer. The holder of a USD-denominated CDS will not only get his principal back but very likely receive the principal in a stronger currency. This results in an additional profit, which should be reflected in the pricing of the CDS. In fact, if CDS denominated in local currencies trade at all, they tend to quote at a tighter premium than USD-denominated CDS on the same issuer.

Combining this point with the previous one leads to a specific issue when a 10Y *asset&basis swapped* bond in local currency is hedged with a 10Y *USD-denominated* CDS. A default after five years results in payment of the principal in USD at the FX rate pre default, while the asset&basis swap contracts remain unaffected and require service of the cash flows in local currency. In this case, the default results not only in an open interest rate exposure but also in an open FX exposure, since we need to exchange our USD back into local currency in order to serve the payment obligations in the ASW and CCBS. If the local currency weakens in the event of a

---

[2]There are JPY-denominated CDS contracts on Japan and EUR-denominated CDS contracts on Italy trading, but liquidity is rather poor. The only exceptions are CDS contracts on the US, which are usually denominated in EUR.

default, we can obtain an additional profit, since through the CCBS and CDS we are over-hedged against the weakening currency.

- Other specifications with a potential impact on the pricing of a CDS include the treatment of coupons, margin and collateral requirements, consideration of the time value for the settlement process, and the potential difference between the frequency of coupon payments and CDS premium payments.

Trying to strip out the pure credit information from the CDS quotes observed in the market, we need at least to obtain a fair value for the DO and the impact of having the CDS and the bond denominated in different currencies. The next two sections address the issues involved in this task.

Delivery Option

Pricing the DO requires two things, a model and historical data. For the first ingredient one could replicate the DO model for bond futures contracts from Chapter 7 for the delivery situation of a CDS. As discussed in Chapter 7, this model requires the price spread volatility of deliverables as an input variable, and its results will largely depend on this input.

While the issues regarding modeling have been solved in Chapter 7, we need to estimate a realistic price spread volatility for deliverables in case of a default and face the basic problem that there are little to no precedents of *relevant* defaults. While the yield spread volatility between cheapest-to-deliver (CTD) candidates in the current Bund futures contract can be estimated by the yield spread volatility between CTD candidates in previous contracts (see Figure 7.4), which historical precedents could we use to get an idea about the price spread volatility between Bunds in the event of a German default?

Using the price spread volatilities between the bonds of defaulting Latin American countries as inputs, our model returns an average DO value of 6 dollars per 100 dollar par CDS contract *in the event of default*. This might mean that about 6% of the CDS quote observed in the market could be due to the DO. However, the significant standard deviation of the DO in the case of Latin American defaults suggests that defaults and the DO value they produce are hardly comparable, even within the Latin American sovereign universe. And using the price spread volatility between a handful of Argentinean or Ecuadorian bonds as an estimate for the price spread volatility between German issues in case of a default is obviously even more problematic.[3]

---

[3]The data situation is better in the US credit universe; but, again, would the default of a corporation be a relevant precedent to assess the expected price spread volatility in case of a bank defaulting, which involves completely different considerations (e.g. between senior and subordinated debt)?

From a practical perspective, the adjustment for the DO seems with 6% relatively small, especially in comparison with the adjustment of the FX component discussed next. Hence, in the absence of a better alternative, we usually assume this value of 6% – while seeing in every sovereign default the positive side of an opportunity to improve this estimate further.

Difference in Settlement Currency

In order to illustrate the value of the FX component, imagine we are long a five-year (5Y) asset&basis swapped JGB and a CDS on Japan, and after three years into the trade Japan defaults (Figure 13.1). We can deliver the JGB into the CDS and receive our initially invested USD principal back. However, we still need to serve all cash flows in the outstanding swap agreements. In particular, at maturity of the cross-currency basis swap (CCBS), we need to pay the JPY principal, which we thought to match with the JGB principal repayment. Since we now lost our JGB (to receive USD ahead of time), we need to replicate the JPY cash flows by exchanging the USD we received from the CDS back into JPY and invest that capital again in JPY in order to generate the JPY cash flows needed to serve the remaining payments in the outstanding ASW and BSW. Thus, entering into an asset&basis swapped JGB

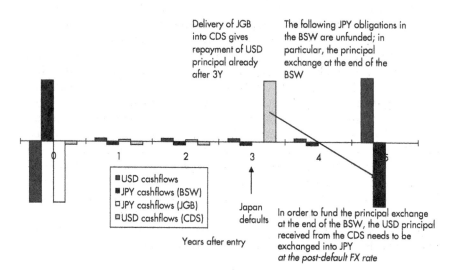

FIGURE 13.1   Cash flows in an investment into a 5Y asset&basis swapped and default protected JGB, with default after three years.
Source: Authors.

and a CDS on Japan includes entering into an *exposure to a JPY weakening conditional on a Japan default.* If the JPY weakens, say, from 80 to 160, following default, we can reproduce the JPY cash flows[4] we need to serve the CCBS with just half the USD we received from the CDS payment, keeping the remaining half as extra profit. This also affects the arbitrage positions between asset&basis swapped bonds and the CDS discussed in Chapter 16.

Similarly to the DO, when pricing the portion of the CDS due to currency effects, we face two issues:

- which pricing model to use;
- which parameters to use (e.g. which impact of credit risk on the FX rate should we assume?).

While we do not intend to participate in the ongoing academic discussion about the pricing model, we propose an original approach, modeled on the delta hedging of an option. The goal is not to present a solution but rather to gain a framework for illustrating the problems.

As starting point for the construction, we buy a USD-denominated CDS on Japan and sell a JPY-denominated CDS on Japan with the same end dates. Then, in case of a default, we can take the bond we are delivered and deliver it against receiving USD at a pre-defined FX rate. Assuming the yen weakens in the event of a default, we realize the difference between the pre- and post-default FX rate as profit. For example, if the JPY was to weaken from a pre-defined 80 to 160 in the event of default, our CDS spread position would be a binary option which pays us $50 in the event Japan defaults. Then, the fair difference between the CDS settling in USD and the CDS settling in JPY would be given as the annuity value of the fair value of that binary option.

Alternatively to pricing a binary option, we could replicate the delta hedging of the Black–Scholes framework, increasing a long JPY/short USD position as the credit risk of Japan (as measured by the CDS) increases. Then, in the event of no default, we have no FX position. But in the event of default (i.e. a default probability of one), our FX hedge covers the full long USD/short JPY position we get from settling the CDS spread. As in the case of delta hedging an option, this transfers the profit from the payoff at expiry to the profit from continuous adjustments of the hedge ratio. We can buy JPY when the default risk of Japan is high (and thus the JPY is expected to be cheap) and sell

---

[4]Of course, we face the risk that we cannot generate JPY cash flows at the original yield level. However, the gain from a weakening currency in case of its issuing government defaulting is likely to be much bigger than any potential losses from moves on the yield side.

JPY when the default risk of Japan is low (and thus the JPY is expected to be rich). Consequently, the fair value for the CDS spread (i.e. for the overcompensation through USD-denominated CDS) is a function of the *default probability volatility*. In other words, the higher the volatility of the CDS, the higher the premium of USD-denominated versus JPY-denominated CDS should be.[5]

Given the current stage of modeling the CDS, to our knowledge, there remain significant hurdles on the way to a consistent pricing of the overcompensation through USD as settlement currency (which we also refer to as the "FX component"). In particular, as our delta-hedging approach does not seem to have entered the academic discussion, it remains unclear whether and how it can be reconciled with the binary option approach.

An even bigger problem is posed by the estimation of the input variables in any model, just as in the case of the DO (where at least the model issue could be adequately addressed):

- How much should the currency of a defaulting country be expected to weaken?
- Does this weakening occur linearly as the credit risk increases, or are there jumps in the process?
- How can influences on the FX rate other than credit risk be excluded from the analysis?[6]
- What is the correlation between the default probability (and thus the FX rate) and the volatility of the default probability?

Again, one could look at historical precedents of sovereign defaults. But it is of no practical value to use the weakening of the Argentine peso as an estimate for the weakening of the JPY in case of a default, given the difference in foreign reserves, among others. Actually, if someone were to argue for the JPY to appreciate against the USD in case of Japan defaulting, due to Japan being forced to repatriate its large USD reserves, we could not refute this argument with certainty.

If it is possible to reasonably doubt even the *direction* of the currency movements of defaulting developed countries, there is little hope of achieving consensus about the *size* of the weakening of a currency in the event of default. Actually, one might even try the other way round. If quotes for

---

[5]As far as we are aware, this approach has not been discussed or formalized. Its implications for CDS pricing therefore remain unknown. However, our preliminary model based on this approach suggests that it could be a major driving force for CDS markets which exhibit a high volatility, such as Portugal during the euro crisis.
[6]Imagine that in the CDS spread construction from above the Japanese credit risk does not change but that the USD weakens due to an unrelated factor (e.g., China selling its US Treasuries).

the JPY-denominated CDS were available, one could translate the spread between the USD-denominated and the JPY-denominated CDS on Japan into the market-implied FX level in the event of default.[7]

Altogether, for pricing the FX component there is neither a consensus about the model nor an estimate for its parameters. This may explain the low liquidity for CDS without FX component, for example, for CDS on Japan settling in JPY. The scarce observations for these CDS without FX component known to us fall in a range between 30% and 60% of the quotes for CDS with FX component, i.e. the standard specifications. For example, if the usual CDS on Japan settling in USD trades at 100 bp, the CDS settling in JPY may be quoted in a range between 30 bp and 60 bp – which is a rare event and leads to two conclusions:

- Using the middle of the range, its level of only 45% suggests that the FX component is indeed a major factor in sovereign CDS prices. Adjusting for it – however imperfectly – is therefore vital. If we were simply using the unadjusted CDS quotes in our ASW model, we are likely to overestimate the actual credit risk of bonds by more than twice the actual amount. In the example of Japan above, our model would overestimate the fair JGB ASW by 55 bp, i.e. the amount of the CDS on Japan which reflects the FX component rather than the credit exposure of an asset swapped JGB, which is only 45 bp (ignoring the DO for the moment).
- The large width of the range may be a consequence of the missing pricing model, making traders reluctant to quote CDS without FX component at all; and in case they are forced to make an exception, they have little guidance from a pricing tool, need to apply a rough rule of thumb, with the results being widely distributed between 30% and 60%. Hence, using the middle of the range to adjust the CDS quotes in our ASW model is very likely to be an imprecise estimate. In case of an evolution of the pricing models allowing traders to quote CDS without FX component more frequently and more precisely, this will be a welcome opportunity to improve the adjustment.

Extracting the 'Pure' Credit Information from CDS Quotes by Adjusting for the DO and FX Component

The advantage of the CDS (versus fundamental credit analysis) is that it is a *quantitative*, traded variable. The disadvantage is that it is a variable that combines credit information with other elements. Before using the

---

[7]Under some assumptions for the probability distribution of default.

CDS quotes as input variable in RV relationships such as our ASW model, it is therefore necessary to extract the pure credit information from the CDS by adjusting for the fair value of its other elements, the DO and the overcompensation from USD as settlement currency. We found that for both adjustments – though they are in principle observable ex ante, unlike the variable cost of equity – there are only very few observations. Still, in the absence of a better alternative (such as a fundamental model for the FX component), we need to base our estimations on them and aim for gradual improvements as more and more observations[8] become available.

Given the information currently available to us, we might use the following adjustment to the CDS prices (with FX component) from the market in order to translate observable market prices in an estimate for the 'pure' credit risk of sovereign issuers, i.e. the input variable required in our swap spread model:

- All sovereign CDS with an FX component, i.e. all CDS usually traded, should be adjusted for this element in their prices, which is estimated to amount on average to 55% of the CDS quote observed. Hence, the CDS adjusted for the FX component = CDS quote observed (with FX component) * 0.45.
- Sovereign CDS with physical delivery, i.e. most of them, also need to be adjusted for the DO, which is estimated to amount to 6% of the CDS quote observed. Assuming independence between the DO and the FX component, another 6% of the full CDS quote need to be subtracted from the CDS adjusted for the FX component. Hence, the CDS adjusted for the FX component and DO = CDS quote observed (with FX component and DO) * 0.39.

Some RV relationships such as the ASW model require a quantitative estimation of the sovereign credit risk. Given the uncertainty of the quantification in an environment of scarce observations, it seems prudent to assess hedges and trades based on these RV relationships under several estimations for the DO and FX component. When thinking about a JGB swap spread trade in the example above, one could price it under three different input variables for the 'adjusted CDS,' at the bottom (30 bp), in the middle (45 bp), and at the top (60 bp) of the range. If it appeared attractive under all three scenarios, we would feel more comfortable than if it only worked at the bottom of the range.

---

[8]It is possible that analysts with good access to CDS traders can already produce better estimates from more observations than the authors.

Other RV relationships rely on qualitative statements only. For example, even without quantifying the DO or the FX component, we can say that neither of the two should be negative and that thus the 'pure' credit risk should not be higher than the CDS quote representing the combination of credit risk, DO, and FX component. The arbitrage inequality presented in Chapter 16 will only rely on such a qualitative statement and thereby remain unaffected by the quantification problems, which will contribute to its firmness.

OTHER APPLICATIONS OF CDS: TRADING CDS VERSUS OTHER CDS AND VERSUS BONDS

Apart from fulfilling the function as input variable for credit exposure in pricing formulae, CDS are interesting both as a separate class of financial instruments and in relation to their underlying bonds. These two approaches are different from a conceptual perspective, lead to different trades and are covered in different parts of the book: the rest of this chapter looks at the intrinsic relationships of CDS as separate asset class, while Chapter 16 will connect sovereign CDS with the sovereign bonds asset&basis swapped into USD.

Conceptually, one can price any instrument either versus instruments of the same type or versus other instruments. In the first case, one evaluates the intrinsic, typically statistical, properties of the instrument; in the latter, one assesses how the same information is expressed through different instruments. We can use this conceptual difference to classify CDS pricing models and trades (and shall use it later on to classify option pricing models and trades):

- In this chapter, we analyze the CDS in isolation of its relationship to other markets. Thus, we are mainly concerned with the statistical properties between CDS quotes, for example, with the factor structure of a CDS curve (different maturities of a CDS on the same issuer) and with the factor structure of the CDS market on euro sovereign issuers (same maturity of CDS on different euro governments). As far as we are aware, this approach is less commonly applied by market participants. Consequently, we often find more relative value opportunities in these 'neglected' statistical relationships within the CDS market than in the well-analyzed link of the CDS to swap spreads.
- Since both bond yields and CDS quotes are driven to some extent by the credit quality of the bond issuer, one can compare the way the information is expressed in both markets, derive the 'fair' CDS quote by the bond yields (or, vice versa, the 'fair' bond yields by the CDS quotes), and exploit

potential mismatches by trading bonds against CDS. Because CDS express the sovereign default risk as a spread over USD SOFR, this comparison needs to be done against the SOFR-ASW of sovereign issues asset&basis swapped into USD. Turning this general concept into a trading strategy that works in practice requires taking into account the elements other than credit that also impact swap spreads and CDS. This work will be completed in Chapter 16, after the basis swaps will have been introduced in the next chapters.

Before starting with the statistical analysis of CDS, a word of caution is required: when considering CDS in isolation from its relationship to bonds, it is easy to lose sight of the issues involved in the event of default. And in fact, sometimes the CDS market seems to trade *as if these issues did not exist.* For example, trading occurs without the two partners being concerned about the inability to price the FX component. And as long as there is no default, this abstract treatment of CDS as a statistical time series without connection to bonds (thus also in abstraction from the problems of the connection between CDS and bonds) works well. A 5Y-10Y CDS curve trade, for example, can be assessed by its statistical properties and traded just like a yield curve position. And if mean reversion occurs before default, it is unlikely that this abstraction will cause any problems. However, in the event of a default, the abstract treatment of CDS can no longer be maintained; when faced with the physical delivery of a bond, at the latest, the relationship of a CDS to the bond market can no longer be ignored.

Accordingly, we shall begin our treatment of CDS on an abstract basis, using statistical methods to derive trading strategies within the CDS market. Then, we shall analyze the way those strategies are likely to fare in the event of a default and restrict our positions to those that can be expected to perform well in the event of no default (due to their statistical properties) and to be unaffected by potential problems in case of a default (e.g. by not being short the DO).

In addition, every comprehensive CDS analysis should include fundamental credit analysis. While this is outside the scope of this book, it should be part of the assessment of credit risk.

A PCA ON THE CDS CURVE

Figure 13.2, Figure 13.3, and Figure 13.4 depict the results of a PCA of the Italian CDS curve during the euro crisis (2Y, 5Y, and 10Y USD-denominated CDS quotes, weekly level data from January 2006 to August 2012).

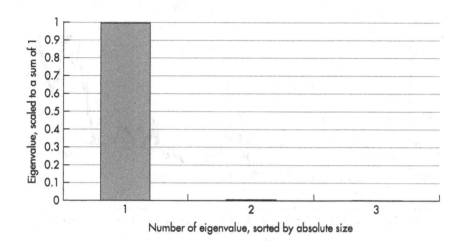

FIGURE 13.2   Scaled eigenvalues of a PCA on the Italian CDS curve.
Sources: data – Authors, Bloomberg; chart – Authors.

Data period: 1 Jan 2006 to 26 Aug 2012, weekly data.

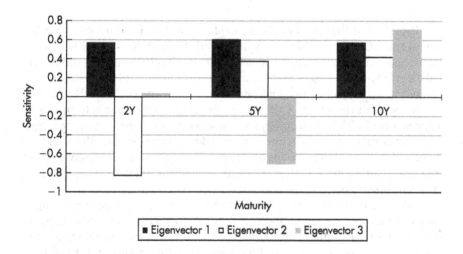

FIGURE 13.3   First three eigenvectors of a PCA on the Italian CDS curve.
Sources: data – Authors, Bloomberg; chart – Authors.

Data period: 1 Jan 2006 to 26 Aug 2012, weekly data.

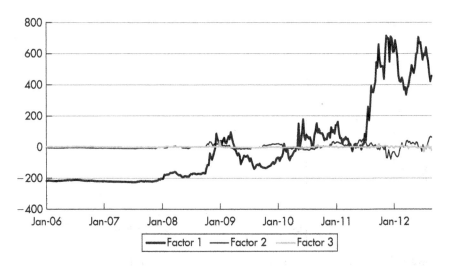

FIGURE 13.4   First three factors of a PCA on the Italian CDS curve.
Sources: data – Authors, Bloomberg; chart – Authors.

Data period: 1 Jan 2006 to 26 Aug 2012, weekly data.

It turns out that the first factor explains 99.5% of the overall variation across the CDS curve. This is a typical result for a PCA run on CDS curves (same issuer, different maturities) and indicates that CDS curves exhibit basically a single-factor structure. It means that the whole CDS curve contains in essence just one piece of information (factor 1, the overall CDS level), and that, given one maturity on the CDS curve, the whole maturity spectrum can be reconstructed with high accuracy (by the sensitivities of the first eigenvector). This statistical property is in line with anecdotal evidence about the pricing of CDS traders. They tend to focus on the most liquid maturity (usually 5Y) and to adjust their quotes for other maturities as a linear function of the moves in the most liquid one.

Like the example of Italy above, CDS curves typically display a single-factor structure, which is indicative of a market in an early stage of development.[9] The theoretical conclusion is that the credit risk element in bond yields cannot explain the three-factor structure observed in bond yield curves.

Thus, the three-factor structure of bond yield curves must arise from the risk-free yield curve (e.g. from inflation expectations) rather than from the default risk element.

---

[9]See Chapter 3 for more details on PCA.

The practical consequence for trading the CDS curve is that there is little scope for relative value trades across CDS curves. For example, a 5Y-10Y CDS curve trade *unaffected* by directional impacts on the CDS curve (i.e. a position on factor 2) faces the problem of a low range of factor 2 (since 99.5% of the variance across the CDS curve is already explained by directional impacts), which means that the potential profit from relative value trades on the CDS curve is usually too small to cover the relatively high bid–offer spreads. Hence, relative value considerations can only play a role in selecting the best maturities for expressing directional views on the CDS curve. In the example above, an investor who wants to position for a decrease of the Italian CDS in general (factor 1 decreasing) can enhance his profit by expressing his view through selling 5Y or 10Y rather than 2Y Italian CDS (given the shape of the second eigenvector and the fact that factor 2 is positive).

While a single-factor structure for the CDS curve as in the example above is typical, there are some exceptions when more than just one point on the CDS curve is actively and independently traded. In these instances, one can observe a richer factor structure and deploy the entire arsenal of statistical yield curve analysis outlined in Chapter 2 and Chapter 3 to the CDS curve as well.

Among relative value traders focusing on the CDS, it is common to strip out the implied default probabilities from CDS curves and scan the result for anomalies, in particular for negative implied default probabilities. While there is nothing wrong with this approach, we recommend complementing it with the additional perspective from a statistical analysis along the lines above.

A PCA ON THE EUR SOVEREIGN CDS UNIVERSE

While CDS curves on different maturities of the same issuer usually display single-factor structures, a set of CDS of different issuers, with the same maturities, can exhibit a richer factor structure and thus allow a wider variety of trades, in particular also relative value trades, which are hedged against factor 1 (i.e. the overall level of CDS quotes) and exploit meaningful higher factors. A natural application for a PCA on CDS of the same maturity (here 5Y) covering different sovereign issuers is an analysis of the euro universe (again using the time period of the euro crisis as a valuable case study), with the results being shown in Figure 13.5 and Figure 13.6.

It turns out that the first factor, explaining 92% of overall variation in the EUR sovereign CDS market, represents the overall level of CDS in the Eurozone. Thus, factor 1 can serve as a measure of the market's perception of sovereign credit risk in the Eurozone in general. The sensitivities to factor 1, given by the first eigenvector, show the extent to which a specific country is affected by a general worsening (or improvement) of the euro crisis.

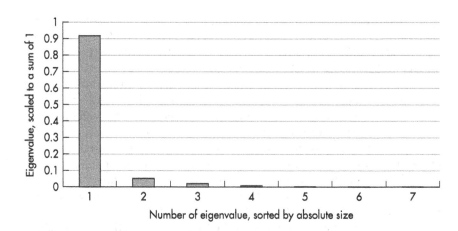

FIGURE 13.5 Scaled eigenvalues of a PCA on CDS quotes for EUR sovereigns. *Sources:* data – Bloomberg; chart – Authors.

Data period: 4 Mar 2009 to 26 Sep 2012, weekly data.

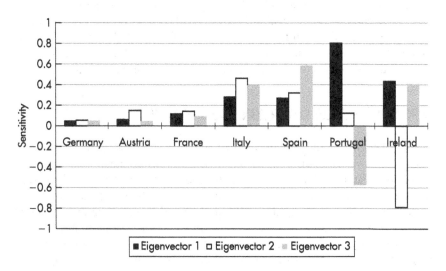

FIGURE 13.6 First three eigenvectors of a PCA on CDS quotes for EUR sovereigns. *Sources:* data – Bloomberg; chart – Authors.

Data period: 4 Mar 2009 to 26 Sep 2012, weekly data.

The qualitative results are unsurprising, with Germany being less affected than Austria, Austria less than France etc. Figure 13.6 offers the additional insight into the quantitative relationships. An overall worsening of the crisis that leads to a 10 bp (basis point) widening of German CDS usually leads to a 26 bp widening of French CDS, a 64 bp widening of Italian CDS and so on, with the relationships being given by the quotients of the sensitivities to the first factor. It is interesting to note that the inclusion of non-European countries in the PCA does not change the results significantly; in particular, no "euro-block" is evident (i.e. there is no eigenvector grouping together all euro countries through positive sensitivities versus all non-euro countries through negative sensitivities). Thus, euro sovereigns seem to be priced in the CDS market as individual countries, not as part of a euro-block.

The higher eigenvectors have positive entries for all countries except one. Thus factors 2 and 3 are country-specific factors, measuring the differentiation of a particular country's CDS versus the overall CDS level given by factor 1. As it happens, a country has a specific factor (with some meaningful eigenvalue), if and only if it is a bailout country (Portugal and Ireland). Hence, the PCA decomposes the EUR sovereign CDS market into its general level, subject to the overall worsening and improvement of the crisis (factor 1), and into the pricing action subject to the bailouts of specific countries (factors 2 and 3). Using this framework, a particular move in the CDS market can thus be attributed to the different pricing mechanisms as expressed by the eigenvectors. For example, a narrowing of Irish CDS quotes can be decomposed into the part due to a general improvement of the euro crisis (factor 1) and into the part due to Ireland-specific developments (factor 2).

While this is a reasonable result, it also means that "pure" relative value trading on the whole EUR CDS universe is hardly possible. Factor 1 represents the overall crisis and factors 2 and 3 country-specific developments, both of which are highly influenced by political decisions. For example, European Central Bank support drives factor 1 lower, while bailout programs in Ireland cause factor 2 to increase, and civil unrest in Portugal results in a drop of factor 3. If the analyst has a view on political developments, the PCA can guide toward the best expression: 1-factor residuals show the best country with which to express a general expectation about the euro crisis worsening or improving. And the PCA hedge ratios allow expressing a view on country-specific developments cleanly, isolating a trade on factor 2 or 3 (e.g. a view that Ireland will improve *relative* to other EUR sovereigns) from the overall level of the euro crisis (factor 1).

If the analyst has no political view and is looking for "pure" relative value trading opportunities, he should exclude the bailout countries from the PCA input data. This allows factors 2 and 3 to reveal the relative value mechanisms across the EUR sovereign CDS market, irrespective of the

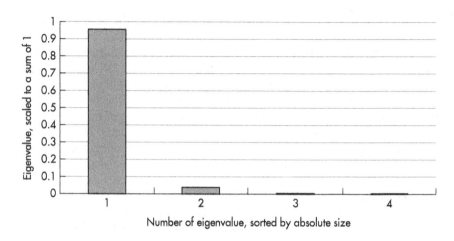

FIGURE 13.7   Scaled eigenvalues of a PCA on CDS quotes for core EUR sovereigns. *Sources:* data – Bloomberg; chart – Authors.

Data period: 6 May 2009 to 26 Sep 2012, weekly data.

political developments in a bailout country. Figure 13.7 and Figure 13.8 show the results of a PCA on the EUR sovereign CDS market, which has been restricted to the core countries Germany, France, the Netherlands, and Austria.

Like the PCA of the whole EUR sovereign CDS universe, the first factor represents the overall CDS level, producing a fever chart for the EUR crisis (Figure 13.9). Also, the relative sensitivity of individual countries as given by the first eigenvector is very similar to the first PCA. Unlike the first PCA, however, there are no country-specific factors anymore. Rather, factor 2 groups together Germany and France (negative sensitivities) and the Netherlands and Austria (positive sensitivities) and can thus be interpreted as "big versus small core country" factor. The scaled eigenvalues (Figure 13.7) suggest that the differentiation between big and small countries is in fact the only powerful mechanism (besides the overall CDS level represented by factor 1) in the core CDS market. And since the size of a country is independent of political influence, factor 2 of the core PCA can be considered a basis for "pure" relative value trades. This is further supported by the high speed of mean reversion of factor 2 (Figure 13.9). The differentiation between big and small core countries appears to be like statistical noise – unlike the differentiation of bailout versus non-bailout countries, which is subject to long-term (slow speed of mean reversion) political (little value of statistical models) decisions.

Thus, trades on factor 2 of the core PCA can justifiably be treated as 'pure' relative value positions, exploiting the statistical properties like mean reversion and being hedged (through PCA hedge ratios) against factor 1

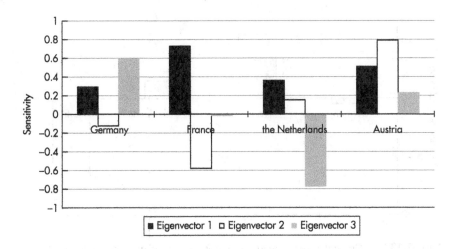

FIGURE 13.8 First three eigenvectors of a PCA on CDS quotes for core EUR sovereigns.
Sources: data – Bloomberg; chart – Authors.

Data period: 6 May 2009 to 26 Sep 2012, weekly data.

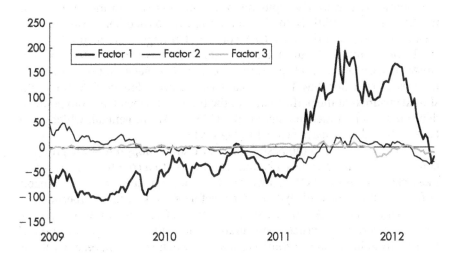

FIGURE 13.9 First three factors of a PCA on CDS quotes for core EUR sovereigns.
Sources: data – Bloomberg; chart – Authors.

Data period: 6 May 2009 to 26 Sep 2012, weekly data.

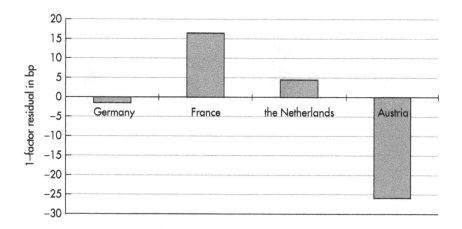

FIGURE 13.10   Current 1-factor residuals of a PCA on CDS quotes for core EUR sovereigns.
Sources: data – Bloomberg; chart – Authors.

Data period: 6 May 2009 to 26 Sep 2012, weekly data; "current" as of 26 Sep 2012.

(i.e. politically driven developments of the euro crisis and their impact on the CDS market). With factor 2 being currently considerably away from its mean, big core countries have CDS spreads that appear too high relative to small core countries. Figure 13.10 suggests that selling French versus buying Austrian CDS offers a 42 bp profit potential. The hedge ratio is given by the first eigenvector (buy 1.4 Austrian CDS for every French CDS sold) and should ensure that the performance of the trade is independent from political developments and their impact on the CDS market in general, which have caused the wild swings of factor 1 in Figure 13.9.

Of course, a risk to the position is that France drops out of the group of core countries and becomes a bailout country (with a country-specific factor like Ireland in the first PCA). However, given the high speed of mean reversion of factor 2, the trade is likely to perform before slow-moving macroeconomic events cause the market to reassess the status of France in the core group. Also, an investor concerned about France could still exploit the deviation of factor 2 from its mean by selling German or Dutch versus Austrian CDS, for an expected profit of 23 or 29 bp.

While a statistical analysis like the PCA above can provide interesting insights into the structure of CDS markets and lead to their exploitation through profitable relative value trades, we need to keep in mind that we are operating in an abstract world, assumed to be free from potential pitfalls. At the end of this chapter we shall describe ways to address these issues.

Other applications worth investigating along the same lines include the CDS quotes of a set of corporations of the same sector, or of the same country, or over different sectors, or over different countries.

Overall, we consider the CDS market as an excellent field to apply PCA, since:

- PCA can structure the information from a multitude of different bond issuers (different country, different rating, different sector) in the form of a few relevant factors, at the same time revealing significant interpretations.
- PCA thereby gives the basis for relative value trades within the credit universe, that is for exploiting mismatches between different issuers while being hedged against overall moves in the CDS market.

A PCA ON RISK-FREE BOND YIELDS

Combining CDS with their underlying bonds, one can create, analyze, and trade a proxy for risk-free government yield curves. This is another application of CDS which offers rather new analytical perspectives and RV trading strategies.

The theoretical benefit of this exercise is that we become able to analyze the factor structure of risk-free yield curves. In addition, we shall find that the statistical properties of risk-free yield curves are superior to those of unadjusted yield curves. In particular, problems like correlation between factors of a PCA during subperiods tend to be much less pronounced when using risk-free yield levels as input data.

On the practical side, analyzing the risk-free yield curve (i.e. the difference between the yield and CDS curve) gives insights into the pricing mechanisms of the bond yield curve *relative* to the CDS curve. These insights can then be translated into relative value positions on the yield versus CDS curve, for example, a steepening position on the JGB curve *relative* to the Japan CDS curve. What has been said above about applying PCA analysis to the CDS market is true for applications of PCA to risk-free bond yield curves as well: being among the first to gain insights into new types of relative value relationships, as in the shape of the bond yield curve *relative to* the CDS curve, suggests high returns from trading strategies based on these insights.

One has two different options to create synthetic risk-free bond yields by subtracting the CDS from the "normal" bond yield as traded in the market:

- Subtracting the adjusted CDS, i.e. without the DO and FX component as described above, gives a proxy for the risk-free yield curve. The bond yield can be considered a combination of the risk-free yield plus information about the market's assessment of its credit risk. Thus, subtracting the adjusted CDS quotes, i.e. only that part of the CDS quotes which actually represents credit exposure rather than optionality, from the bond yield can be considered an expression of the risk-free yield level. If the goal is only analytical, this option seems the natural choice. However, when also applied for trading, using the adjusted rather than the "full" CDS subjects the trading strategies to the significant risk of misestimation of the DO and FX component. Specifically in case of default, misestimation of the DO and FX components can lead to being underhedged. Imagine that in the situation of Figure 13.1 we estimated the JPY to weaken by 50% in case of default and therefore bought only 0.5 CDS per JGB (and assume a cash settlement). If default occurs and the JPY actually weakens by that amount, 0.5 CDS per bond are sufficient; but if the JPY weakens less than expected (maybe due to the large foreign reserves), we are underhedged.

■ Subtracting the full (unadjusted, i.e. as observed in the market) CDS, i.e. the credit information together with the DO and FX component, results in an analytically inferior proxy for the risk-free bond yield, since it also contains information about the expected weakening of the FX rate of a defaulting country, for instance. On the other hand, given the nature of current CDS specifications, this is the only way to obtain trades which are sure to avoid the risk of being underhedged in case of default. We will use the definition "Risk-free yield = bond yield minus (unadjusted) CDS" in this section and end it by highlighting the pitfalls introduced by it.

Figure 13.11, Figure 13.12, and Figure 13.13 display the results of a PCA on the risk-free BTP (Italian government bond) yield curve in comparison with the PCA on the usual BTP yield curve. Note that the data input starts in 2006, that is it covers both a period when CDS were close to zero and exhibited virtually no volatility (see Figure 13.4) and a period when CDS quotes became a major driving force of bond yields. These results are typical and appear in a similar form in the US Treasury and JGB markets (and hence the outcome is not limited to Eurozone sovereigns), though the quantitative impact of the adjustment is sometimes less than in the case of Italy.

Starting the discussion of the results from the theoretical side, the data period covers the pre-crisis situation (2006, 2007), when credit considerations had a negligible impact on BTP yields. Actually, before the crisis, market participants usually considered these government bonds as risk-free and thus there was little difference between the two PCAs until 2008. (See Figure 13.12.) Starting in 2008, however, this assumption was revised and credit quality became a major driving force of government bond yields. Consequently, the two PCAs show a distinctly different behavior from 2008 onwards. (See Figure 13.12 and Figure 13.13.)

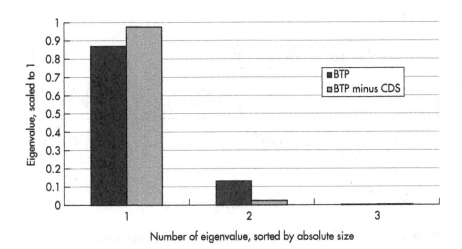

FIGURE 13.11 Scaled eigenvalues of a PCA on the risk-free BTP yield curve in comparison with those of a PCA on the BTP yield curve.
Sources: data – Authors, Bloomberg; chart – Authors.

Data period: 1 Jan 2006 to 26 Aug 2012, weekly data.

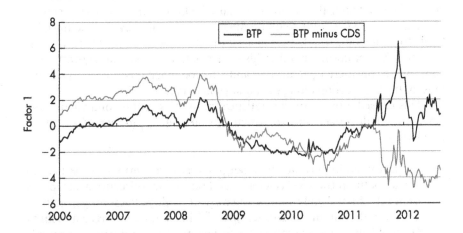

FIGURE 13.12 First factor of a PCA on the risk-free BTP yield curve in comparison with the first factor of a PCA on the BTP yield curve.
Sources: data – Authors, Bloomberg; chart – Authors.

Data period: 1 Jan 2006 to 26 Aug 2012, weekly data.

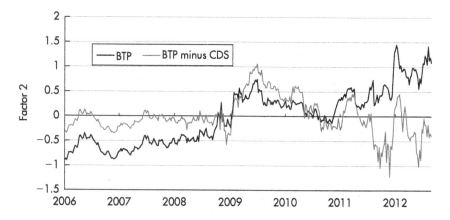

FIGURE 13.13   Second factor of a PCA on the risk-free BTP yield curve in comparison with the second factor of a PCA on the BTP yield curve.
Sources: data – Authors, Bloomberg; chart – Authors.

Data period: 1 Jan 2006 to 26 Aug 2012, weekly data.

Moreover, the PCA of risk-free bond yields always uses default-free data, both before and after the credit crisis started. On the other hand, the benefit of excluding impacts from credit on the bond yield curve by subtracting CDS levels could introduce statistical noise if the CDS quotes were erratic. By contrast, the PCA of normal bond yields covers both a period when government bonds were considered default-free and a period when credit concerns drove most of the price action along the bond yield curve.

This caused a break in the statistical properties of the bond yield curve when the credit crisis started, which is visible in a number of statistical problems.

■ Perhaps most important, the emerging credit concerns in 2008 had an impact both on the level (factor 1) and on the non-directional steepness (factor 2) of bond yield curves, since credit quality affects longer maturities more than it affects shorter ones.[10] This is the main reason behind the problem of correlation between factors 1 and 2 during subperiods

---

[10]This statement can be backed up with ratings transition matrices, which show that the yearly default probability increases with the length of exposure – unless the credit quality is very bad at the beginning, which was not the case for the sovereign examples used here.

of PCAs spanning pre-crisis and post-crisis data. We have discussed in Chapter 3 that this is a major pitfall for PCA-based trades. Thus, we are excited to find that by using risk-free bond yields as input variables we can exclude by construction the impact of credit on every factor of the PCA and thereby also get rid of a major source of problematic correlation between PCA factors in subperiods.[11] Proving this important point, we display in Figure 13.14 the correlation between factors 1 and 2 in the subperiod since 2010 of a PCA using normal BTP yields and of a PCA using risk-free BTP yields since 2006 as input. We observe that the problematic correlation between factors 1 and 2 of a PCA using normal BTP yields (Figure 13.14, top graph; compare also with Figure 3.23) is largely absent in a PCA using risk-free BTP yields (Figure 13.14, bottom graph).

- Thus, a shift in credit regime causes a correlation between factor 1 and factor 2 in a PCA of normal bond data (in the subperiod following the shift in credit regime). This results in factor 2 being driven in large measure by the directional factor 1 following a change in credit assessment. Intuitively speaking, part of the explanatory power of factor 1 shifts to factor 2, destroying its interpretation as non-directional steepness and the performance of any relative value trades based on it.

- Correspondingly, the explanatory power of the first factor decreases significantly. (See Figure 13.11.) Using risk-free yield levels, however, maintains a high explanatory power of the first factor. In fact, the results of a PCA on risk-free yield levels are very similar to those of a PCA of normal bond yields, which uses only data pre-crisis or only data post-crisis. (Compare the charts above with those in Chapter 3, in particular, Figure 13.11 with Figure 3.4.) In a manner of speaking, subtracting CDS quotes from bond yields maintains the usual three-factor structure of bond yield curves *independent of credit impacts*. While we have seen above that the credit component does nothing to *explain* the three-factor structure of bond yield curves, accounting for it can *maintain* the normal mechanisms of yield curves also in times of major shifts in the assessment of the credit quality of government bonds. The first factor loading of the CDS curve actually seems to have precisely the shape needed to correct the three factor loadings of the bond curve, so that they remain stable in changing credit regimes.

This is a crucial condition to conduct analysis in times of shifting credit assessments – and to construct trades which are hedged against their impacts on the bond yield curve. Imagine we had put on a 2Y-10Y

---

[11]Of course, there can still be a correlation between factors in subperiods for other reasons and we advise to check for it also when running a PCA on risk-free yields.

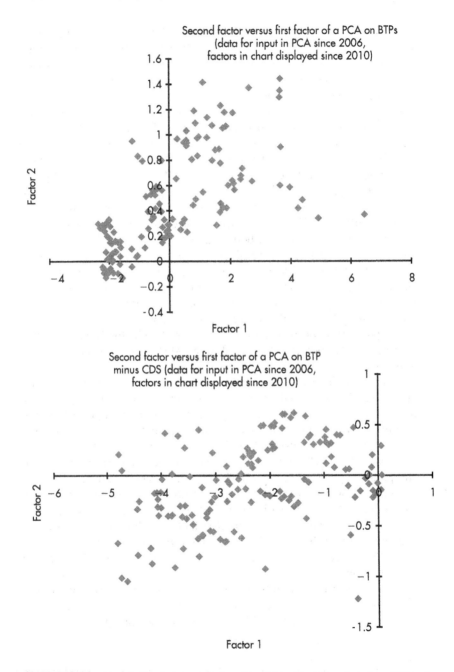

FIGURE 13.14 Correlation between factors 1 and 2 in the subperiod since 2010 of a PCA using BTP yields and of a PCA using risk-free BTP yields.
Sources: data – Authors, Bloomberg; chart – Authors.

Data period: 3 Jan 2010 to 26 Aug 2012, weekly data.

BTP curve trade based on pre-crisis PCA hedge ratios (without any credit impact in the data). Our actual P&L would be a function of an unforeseen impact of credit quality on both the hedge ratios and the yield curve dynamics.

■ Likewise, the explanatory power of the first factor of a PCA on normal BTP data not only decreases generally in times of a shift in credit quality but its impact also becomes unevenly distributed over the yield curve. The explanation can again be found in the correlation between factors 1 and 2 following a shift in credit regimes. Now factor 2 contains part of factor 1, but the second eigenvector differentiates across the yield curve, causing a decrease of the explanatory power of factor 1 in a specific sector of the curve. This effect is summarized in Table 13.1, which compares the correlation of factor 1 of a normal and a risk-free PCA to different points on the yield curve.

TABLE 13.1 Correlation between Different Points on the Yield Curve and the First Factor of a PCA on BTP Yields and a PCA on Risk-Free BTP Yields

	BTP	BTP minus adjusted CDS
2Y	0.95	0.99
5Y	0.98	1.00
10Y	0.79	0.96

It turns out that the first factor of a PCA on normal BTP data has only limited explanatory power at the long end of the BTP curve. The PCA on risk-free data returns significantly better results; the explanatory power of the first factor over the BTP minus adjusted CDS curve over the five turbulent years during the euro crisis is comparable with a traditional PCA before the crisis and as evenly distributed over the yield curve.

■ Factor 2 exhibits a significantly higher speed of mean reversion in the risk-free PCA. Intuitively, this can be understood by the fact that in the case of the PCA on normal BTP data some of the directional moves (with low speed of mean reversion) usually explained by factor 1 become part of factor 2 due to the shift in credit regimes. By contrast, factor 2 of the risk-free PCA does not need to bear any elements of factor 1 (reflected in a lower-scaled second eigenvalue in Figure 13.11) and shows therefore a speed of mean reversion typical for a factor 2 of bond yield curves in the absence of credit regime shifts (compare, e.g. Figure 13.13 with Figure 3.13).

- While CDS moves may sometimes on the surface appear to be irrational or erratic, the good PCA results suggest that they follow a rather stable, predictable pattern. This alleviates our concern regarding the use of risk-free data obtained by subtracting CDS quotes as inputs into statistical models.
- When (normal) bond yields approach their lower boundary (such as 0% or the ECB buying limit), their volatility tends to decrease, leading to unstable eigenvectors, particularly at the short end, particularly when accompanied by unusual monetary policy (see Figure 3.24 and Figure 3.25). This is a problem that can affect hedge ratios, for example. On the other hand, bond yields minus CDS are not bounded by zero and can therefore exhibit a higher volatility also in low-yield environments. This leads to a better stability of eigenvectors at the short end. Hence, using risk-free bond yields is an alternative to using shadow rates as discussed in Chapter 6 as input into a PCA in times of extremely low rates.

Turning from the theoretical benefits of risk-free bond yields to their practical exploitation, we observe that factor 2 of a PCA of risk-free BTP yields is away from its mean (Figure 13.15). This means that the BTP yield curve is too

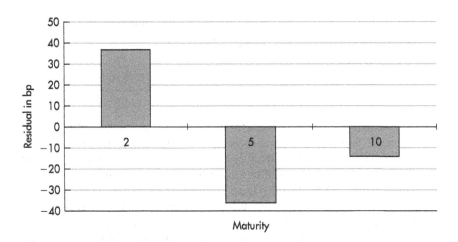

FIGURE 13.15 One-factor residuals of the PCA on risk-free BTP yields.
Sources: data – Authors, Bloomberg; chart – Authors.

Data period: 1 Jan 2006 to 26 Aug 2012, weekly data; "current" as of 26 Aug 2012. Note that the result is not materially affected by using shorter data periods (e.g. only post-crisis data). This is in line with the discussion above and a contrast to a PCA on normal BTP yields.

flat relative to the Italian CDS curve. In other words, steepening positions of the risk-free BTP yield curve (buying short end BTPs and short maturity Italy CDS versus selling long end BTPs and long maturity Italy CDS) are attractive. As always, one can choose the statistically most attractive expression for steepening positions on the BTP relative to the CDS curve by looking at the one-factor residuals.

One might therefore consider a 2Y-5Y steepener as a candidate for a trade idea. This would involve selling 5Y BTPs and 5Y CDS versus buying 2Y BTPs and 2Y CDS, with the hedge ratios being given by the first-factor sensitivities (resulting in a ratio of roughly 5:3 for the 2Y:5Y instruments).

Note that this trading opportunity does not show up in a PCA on the normal BTP curve. Hence, it arises from the *relationship* between the yield curve and the CDS curve, which is only visible through the risk-free PCA. The 2Y-5Y BTP curve is too flat *relative to the CDS curve*. The fact that few analysts consider the steepness of bond yield curves in relation to the CDS curve may help explain the unusually large profit potential of 73 bp for a relative value position on the yield curve.

PITFALLS

We can thus use the CDS to make statistical models work also in an environment of unstable credit risk. On the other hand, this introduces the particular features of the CDS, in case of using unadjusted CDS levels in particular the DO and FX components, and we recommend checking any trading strategy derived by statistical models on the CDS market for the following problems:

- **FX component.** If the CDS is denominated in a different currency than the government bond it protects, the holder of a long CDS position profits from the currency of the defaulting government weakening in case of default (and vice versa). For example, in the 2Y-5Y steepening trade discussed above, the notional weights (long 5:short 3) give us a net long position in the Italian CDS, thus in that case we seem to be on the profitable side of the FX exposure in case of default. Had the trading strategy resulted in a net short position of the CDS, on the other hand, we might have chosen to assess the profit potential and the expected holding horizon of the trade versus different estimates for the unquantifiable potential loss from the EUR weakening in case of an Italian default.
- **Delivery option.** Similarly, the net long or short position in the CDS decides about whether we are net long or short the DO in case of a default.

Again, in our example, we are net long the CDS, thus also the DO, and have passed this check. As a general rule, being net long, the CDS usually results in being on the safe side of potential issues surfacing in case of a default.

- **Repo.** What is the expected value of the bonds involved in the repo market? When approaching default, repo markets may well become dysfunctional, driving the actual costs away from the estimation. How would this affect the overall position?

- **In case of euro sovereign bonds being involved, the redenomination risk.** While the CDS is and remains USD-denominated, BTPs might be repaid in lira.[12] Thus, we face the problem that by construction of the bond versus CDS curve trades, if we are net long the CDS (which is the "safe side" concerning the FX component and DO), we are also net long the lira in case of BTP redenomination. In the example above, if Italy redenominates in lira and this does not fall under the default definition of the CDS, the steepener with a notional ratio of long 5:short 3 is exposed to a lira weakening. An investor assigning a significant probability to this risk may therefore want to use CDS treating redenomination as default, or, if these are too expensive, to refrain from applying these trading strategies to euro sovereign bond curves. For example, he could also enter a 2Y-10Y flattener on the risk-free JGB yield curve for an expected profit of 47 bp and then assess whether the exclusion of redenomination risk (or the saving on the cost for CDS covering it) was worth the loss of a 26 bp profit potential (and the bigger distance between the two points on the yield curve).

As a general note, given the high speed of mean reversion for most (good) relative value trades, chances are high that in reality they will not be subject to these problems. In other words, if the expected holding horizon of a statistical trade involving the CDS market is shorter than the time period over which issues arising from default can reasonably be expected to occur, then one can justify ignoring the potential problems and analytically treating trades involving CDS as if those problems did not exist. As mentioned in Chapter 1, one then has a useful but not necessarily theoretically rigorous statistical model for CDS trades. Still, we would like trades involving CDS to work also in the event of default and therefore advise checking for the above points, even when a high speed of mean reversion makes it unlikely that a real default will test our performance in this task.

---

[12]Whether redenomination counts as default has been discussed extensively and depends on the specifications of the individual CDS agreements.

CONCLUSION

- CDS can be priced either against other CDS through a statistical model or against the underlying bond as outlined above or against asset&basis swapped bonds through a financial model, covered in Chapter 16.
- The CDS curve over different maturities often exhibits a single-factor structure and thus permits little room for relative value trades.
- A PCA of the CDS of different issuers reveals the pricing mechanisms and potentially attractive relative value trading opportunities. For example, it segments the CDS of euro sovereigns into bailout and no-bailout countries, and the core group according to the size of the bond markets.
- A PCA of risk-free yield curves can alleviate some of the statistical deficiencies of a PCA of normal yield curves. Moreover, at times it detects significant relative value opportunities between the shape of the yield curve and the shape of the CDS curve.
- Since the DO and FX component of a CDS may be part of a curve trade on risk-free yields, every trading position involving the CDS should be assessed from the viewpoint of its performance in the event of default for a reasonable range of different values for the DO and the FX component.

CHAPTER **14**

Intra-Currency Basis Swaps

DEFINITION

An intra-currency basis swap (ICBS) is a derivative security in which each of the two parties agrees to pay the other a different floating rate, with both rates denominated in the same currency. For example, one party might agree to pay six-month (6M) LIBOR to the other party in exchange for being paid 3M LIBOR less a spread.

As described in Chapter 11, the transition away from LIBOR over the last decade has resulted in additional or alternative reference rates, such as unsecured overnight (O/N) rates and secured overnight financing rates (SOFR) in the US. Correspondingly, the ICBS definition has been extended: While it formerly referred to basis swaps between different LIBOR tenors only, it now also includes basis swaps between unsecured O/N rates and LIBOR (in those markets where LIBOR still exists) and between unsecured O/N rates and SOFR in the US.

In terms of Table 11.1, ICBS can thus be defined as basis swaps between two different reference rates in the same currency, i.e. in the same row, including basis swaps between two different terms of the same reference rate, i.e. LIBOR shown in the left column. Of particular importance are the following three ICBS:

- In Europe and Japan, ICBS between different tenors of EURIBOR and TIBOR.
- In Europe, ICBS between EURIBOR and ESTR. This basis swap plays an essential role in constructing a basis swap between SOFR and EURIBOR and hence in the following chapters. Reflecting its importance, while ICBS are usually over-the-counter (OTC) products, CME offers clearing for a standardized version of the EURIBOR-ESTR ICBS.
- In the US, ICBS between SOFR and Fed Funds. This ICBS covers the secured–unsecured basis and therefore has the vital function of providing a market price for that funding spread. In case of using swaps with SOFR as reference rate for asset swapping Treasuries and swaps with Fed Funds

as reference rate for asset swapping US corporate bonds (as discussed in Chapter 12), this ICBS connects both. Since there is also a market for spread future contracts between SOFR and Fed Fund futures with margin offset, this ICBS can be cheaply hedged and replicated via futures.

PRICING OF ICBS

Per definition above, pricing ICBS is a direct application of the models provided in Chapter 11 assessing the fair value of the spread between different reference rates in the same currency. Specifically:

- ICBS between different tenors of EURIBOR and TIBOR are driven by the term (risk), which includes a minor effect for short rate expectations, a minor effect due to interest rate compounding frequencies, and a catchall term that often is referred to as "risk premia." The main driving force is the perception about the credit risk of (LIBOR panel) banks: The higher this risk, the more valuable the credit 'refreshes' explained in Chapter 11. In case of a banking crisis, the value of the option to switch counterparties after 3M rather than being stuck with one borrower for 6M increases and so does the 3M-6M LIBOR ICBS.
- ICBS between LIBOR and unsecured O/N rates can be priced in the same framework of term (risk). With O/N rates taking the advantage of credit 'refreshes' to the practical maximum, the ESTR-6M EURIBOR ICBS usually quotes above the 3M-6M EURIBOR ICBS (and the ESTR-3M EURIBOR ICBS), with the spread between both increasing as the perception of bank credit risk deteriorates.
- ICBS between SOFR and Fed Funds reflect the secured–unsecured basis, which is a function of the cost of capital (and the capital requirements). In a banking crisis, the cost of capital of banks is usually highly correlated to the perceived credit risk of banks. In these situations one can therefore expect the ICBS between different unsecured reference rates (e.g. ESTR and 3M EURIBOR) and the SOFR–Fed Fund ICBS to rise. Given the current situation of global reference rates, there is no ICBS between secured O/N rates (SOFR) and unsecured term rates (LIBOR). Thus, ICBS pricing models do not require the full repo–LIBOR model (including term risk), but can apply simpler versions, as outlined in Chapter 11.

To provide intuition about the impact of perceived credit risk of banks on the pricing of ICBS, Figure 14.1 shows the five-year (5Y) basis swap spread between 3M EURIBOR and 6M EURIBOR during the subprime and euro crises. The positive spread shown in Figure 14.1 depicts the spread attached

FIGURE 14.1 5Y basis swap spread between 3M EURIBOR and 6M EURIBOR.
Sources: data – Bloomberg; chart – Authors.

to the 3M rate in this case. For example, in June of 2010, one could agree to pay 6M EURIBOR for five years in exchange for receiving 3M EURIBOR + 18 basis points (bp) for five years.

A few points to note:

- The basis swap was almost always within 1 bp of zero prior to the onset of the subprime crisis in July of 2007.
- Subsequent to the onset of the crisis, the spread widened considerably, reflecting the perception that the risk of bank default had increased.

To further illustrate the relation between the level of the EUR 3M/6M basis swap and overall perceptions of crisis-related credit risks, we show the 5Y EURIBOR 3M/6M basis swap along with the euro exchange rate in Figure 14.2. In Figure 14.3, we show this ICBS along with the 5Y basis swap between 3M EURIBOR and 3M USD LIBOR.

Prior to the onset of the subprime crisis, there was no correlation between the euro and the ICBS, but after the onset of the crisis, the correlation between these two variables has been 0.68.

Prior to the onset of the subprime crisis in July of 2007, the two basis swaps were both very close to zero. Subsequent to the start of the crisis, the spreads have tended to widen and narrow together. Over the entire period,

FIGURE 14.2   EUR exchange rate and 5Y basis swap spread between 3M EURIBOR and 6M EURIBOR.
Sources: data – Bloomberg; chart – Authors.

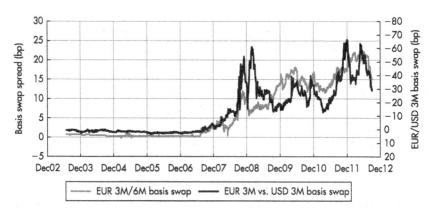

FIGURE 14.3   5Y basis swap spread between 3M EURIBOR and 6M EURIBOR and 5Y basis swap between 3M EURIBOR and 3M USD LIBOR.
Sources: data – Bloomberg; chart – Authors.

the correlation between these two variables has been -0.62. (The convention is to quote the EUR 3M vs. USD 3M basis swap as a spread to the EUR leg, and the cross-currency basis swap is shown on an inverted axis in Figure 14.3.)

The correlation between ICBS, especially those covering the secured-unsecured basis, and cross-currency basis swaps (CCBS) has been stable over the years, reflecting the link via a causal relationship: in times of higher (perceived) credit risk, for example, due to stress in the banking sector, the

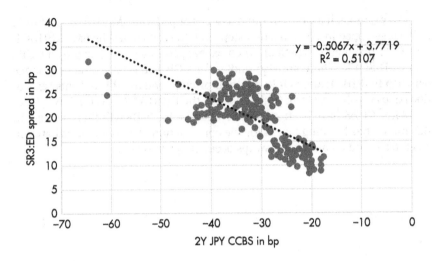

FIGURE 14.4 Regression of the 3M SOFR versus Eurodollar future spread against the 2Y USD–JPY cross-currency basis swap.
Source: Huggins and Schaller (2022).

preference for both secured versus unsecured lending and for keeping funds in the US banking system increases. Exploiting this relationship shown in Figure 14.4, Chapter 4 of Huggins and Schaller (2022) presents a model for the ICBS (as traded in SOFR versus Eurodollar or Fed Fund futures) relative to the CCBS. One application of this model is the possibility of replacing the capital-intensive CCBS in some relative value (RV) trades (which do not require the actual exchange of principal) with cheaper spread future contracts.

Chapter 15 will use the secured–unsecured basis as one input variable for pricing CCBS – as this chapter does for the ICBS and Chapter 12 did for swap spreads.

ROLE AS BUILDING BLOCKS

ICBS are of interest in their own right, as instruments for hedging various transactions, as a means for trading perceptions of credit risk in the banking sector and as a market price for the secured–unsecured basis. In addition, they fulfill an essential role as a building block for other structures, primarily bonds that are cross-currency basis swapped into other currencies.

For example, if a German Bund asset swapped into 6M EURIBOR should be basis swapped in USD, in a first step, an ICBS exchanges the 6M EURIBOR into ESTR payments, which are then exchanged in a second step by a CCBS into USD SOFR. There are also quotes for CCBS offering a direct exchange between EURIBOR and SOFR, but their pricing (and usually also their execution) does involve the term (risk) given by the EURIBOR–ESTR ICBS.

After CCBS have been treated in Chapter 15, ICBS will then be used in this manner as building blocks for the construction of combinations between asset, basis and credit default swaps occupying Chapter 16.

Cross-Currency Basis Swaps

DEFINITION

A cross-currency basis swap (CCBS) exchanges two reference rates in different currencies. In terms of Table 11.1, it therefore links two different rows. In practice, all CCBS have USD as one leg; for example, a CCBS between ESTR and TONAR is executed as a combination of two CCBS, one between ESTR and SOFR and one between SOFR and TONAR. The transition from LIBOR to SOFR in the US therefore resulted in CCBS now (almost) always[1] involving different types of reference rates as well, the secured O/N rate SOFR in USD and an unsecured (O/N or term) rate in EUR, JPY, or GBP. In terms of Table 11.1, this corresponds to the CCBS involving a switch between both rows and columns.

This chapter starts with outlining the situation before the transition, i.e. assumes LIBOR as reference rate in all currencies, and then explains the impact of the transition on the instruments and their pricing.

FX Swap

In a spot FX transaction, two parties exchange two currencies immediately upon agreement of the exchange rate.

In a forward FX transaction, two parties agree on an exchange rate and on a date in the future on which the two currencies will be exchanged.

The relation between the spot exchange rate and the forward exchange rate typically precludes arbitrage opportunities, in accordance with the standard equation:

$$F_{\frac{USD}{EUR}} = \frac{1 + R_{USD}}{1 + R_{EUR}} S_{\frac{USD}{EUR}}$$

---

[1]Being an OTC product, CCBS between SOFR and the ECB policy rate, i.e. another secured reference rate, are theoretically conceivable, but do not appear to play a major role in the market.

where

$S_{\frac{USD}{EUR}}$ is the number of US dollars that can be exchanged for one euro in the spot market;

$F_{\frac{USD}{EUR}}$ is the number of US dollars that can be exchanged for one euro three months forward;

R_{USD} is the *non-annualized* rate at which a bank could lend US dollars on an unsecured basis for three months;

R_{EUR} is the *non-annualized* rate at which a bank could borrow euros on an unsecured basis for three months.

If this condition were not satisfied, one could make arbitrage profits by borrowing euros, buying dollars in the spot market, lending the dollars, and selling the dollars forward – or by doing the opposite, depending on whether the forward rate was higher or lower than the forward exchange rate implied by this no-arbitrage equation.

The FX swap is a combination of the spot and forward transactions discussed above. In other words, the FX swap consists of the spot and forward transactions by which one would attempt to exploit the arbitrage in the event the equation above was not satisfied.

It's important to note the difference between an FX swap and an FX forward. In an FX forward, the two currencies are exchanged only on the forward date. In an FX swap, currencies are exchanged on both the spot date and on the forward date. As we'll see later in the chapter, the distinction is important for understanding the economic function of the FX swap, as it eliminates the FX exposure.

An FX swap can be conceptualized as consisting of three components:

1. an initial exchange of principal in two currencies;
2. a return at the swap end date of the principal exchanged at the start date;
3. a payment of interest in each currency at the swap end date, added to the principal returned.

Because the interest payments in step (3) typically differ in value, the exchanges of principal and interest payments at the end date of the swap constitute an effective forward rate that typically is different from the spot exchange rate.

FX swaps typically have tenors of up to one year. When the principal is to be exchanged for a period greater than a year, a CCBS is more typical. In fact, the CCBS can be thought of as an extension of the forward FX market to longer maturities – just as we have thought of the asset swap spread as a repo–LIBOR basis swap, i.e. an extension of the repo market to longer maturities.

Cross-Currency Basis Swaps

A CCBS is very similar to an FX swap in that it involves:

1. an initial exchange of principal in two currencies;
2. the return of this principal at the end date of the swap;
3. the interest payments in each currency to reflect the time value of the funds borrowed by each counterparty in the swap.

Where an FX swap involves payment of a single interest payment in each of the two currencies, a CCBS involves a stream of interest payments in each of the two currencies. Usually, both legs have floating payments. For example, before the transition a five-year (5Y) EUR/USD CCBS might involve quarterly payments of three-month (3M) USD LIBOR in exchange for quarterly payments of 3M EURIBOR. After the transition, it might involve quarterly payments of the compounded USD SOFR rate in exchange for quarterly payments of the compounded EUR ESTR rate. Being an OTC product, also fixed payments on one or both legs of the CCBS are conceivable. However, it is much more common to trade a CCBS with two floating legs and then add one (or two) (asset) swap between floating and fixed, i.e. to keep all (asset) swaps between floating and fixed free of currency exchanges. This book follows the market convention (and liquidity) and in Chapter 16 treats swaps between fixed rates in one currency and floating rates in another currency as a combination of a CCBS between two floating rates and an asset swap without currency exchange.

The key to understanding the CCBS is to keep in mind the three components of the swap:

1. an initial exchange of principal in each currency;
2. the return of principal in each currency at the end of the swap;
3. the interest rate payments during the swap paid to each counterparty to reflect the time value of money in that currency.

In these examples, we've discussed fixed and floating payments without reference to any spreads, while in practice CCBS typically are traded with an attached spread to reflect the balance of supply and demand. For example, one swap counterparty might agree to pay USD LIBOR in exchange for EURIBOR less a spread in order to provide sufficient motivation for a counterparty to engage in the swap. Usually, the "CCBS spread" is referred to simply by the name for the instrument and is called "CCBS" as well.

As a practical matter, the spread could be attached to either leg of the swap. For example, the same counterparty might agree to pay USD LIBOR plus a spread in exchange for EURIBOR. By convention, CCBS spreads tend to be quoted with reference to the non-dollar leg when the swap involves USD. For example, a 5Y CCBS quote of $-38/-37$ would mean that an investor could exchange dollars for euros by agreeing to pay 3M EURIBOR less 37 basis points (bp) and to receive 3M USD LIBOR for five years – or the investor could choose to receive 3M EURIBOR less 38 bp in exchange for 3M USD LIBOR for five years.

APPLICATIONS OF THE CCBS

As with any new asset class, it can be analyzed in isolation from others and screened for opportunities by statistical assessment of its intrinsic relationships. We have illustrated this in the case of CDS in Chapter 13 and in principle the same methods can be applied to the CCBS market as well. For example, the term structure of the CCBS curve(s) can be subjected to a PCA. While statistical analysis is always an important element of a comprehensive insight, the function of the CCBS to link the funding rates of different markets results in it being highly dependent on the flows between these markets and hence a bad candidate to be traded via statistical tools only. We will therefore provide an overview over some applications of the CCBS before discussing their impact on its pricing.

CONSTRUCTING ANY REFERENCE RATE FROM ANY OTHER

Via a combination of CCBS and ICBS, any reference rate globally can be swapped into any other. Once more in terms of Table 11.1, any cell can be connected with any other cell.

If one considers USD SOFR as the global benchmark due to it combining the safe haven currency with the safest reference rate practically possible, one can construct from this starting point all other USD reference rates via ICBS, all EUR reference rates via a USD–EUR CCBS (maybe together with a EUR ICBS), all JPY reference rates via a USD–JPY CCBS (maybe together with a JPY ICBS), etc. For example, in order to transform SOFR into EURIBOR, one could either use directly a USD SOFR–EURIBOR CCBS or alternatively a USD SOFR–EUR ESTR CCBS together with a ESTR–EURIBOR ICBS within EUR. Actually, even if one chooses the first option, it is likely that the broker will execute the trade via the second option.

Or taking the perspective of a German corporate funding at EURIBOR plus a spread, it can use the market quotes for ICBS and CCBS to calculate its funding costs against any reference rate worldwide. And if it finds that it can fund cheaper against another rate than against EURIBOR, the basis swaps enable exploiting this difference.

ISSUING FOREIGN BONDS WITHOUT FX EXPOSURE

An important function of a CCBS is to allow someone to engage in a transaction in a currency other than his domestic currency without taking FX risk. For example, an Italian issuer might issue bonds in USD and swap them into EUR via a CCBS in order to take advantage of a relatively large demand for his bonds among US investors. In so doing, he may be able to achieve a lower borrowing cost than he could achieve by issuing bonds in EUR.

In this example, there's nothing to prevent the issuer from simply selling bonds denominated in USD and then converting the proceeds to EUR, without engaging in any additional swaps. But in that case, the issuer is exposed to FX risk with respect to making payments of principal and interest in USD. To eliminate this FX risk, the issuer can engage in a CCBS immediately after issuing the bonds. The issuer receives EUR at the start of the swap, pays EUR at the end of the swap (equal to the maturity date of the bonds), and makes ongoing payments of EUR between the start and end dates.

Through the CCBS, issuers of debt can choose the currency in which they fund, independent of the denomination of their debt. For example, if an A-rated company funds in USD at LIBOR + 250 bp and in JPY at LIBOR + 150 bp, it has an incentive to issue Samurai bonds and to exchange its JPY into USD funding via the CCBS. If the CCBS were zero, it would realize about 100 bp funding advantage. Of course, the activity of Samurai issuers seeking to profit from this opportunity would be expected to pressure CCBS spreads and/or to widen JPY credit spreads so as to reduce the attractiveness of the opportunity.

INVESTING IN FOREIGN BONDS WITHOUT FX EXPOSURE

On the other side of the supply/demand balance, buyers of bonds can also choose the currency in which they invest, through the CCBS. For example, if a US Treasury bond trades at USD LIBOR −50 bp and a Bund at EUR LIBOR −20 bp (and both issuers are considered of the same credit risk), a USD-based investor might want to use the CCBS to obtain access to the EUR bond market without FX exposure. If the CCBS was equal to zero, he would realize a return of roughly USD LIBOR −20 bp, thus about 30 bp pick-up versus the US Treasury investment. Now, the activity of investors seeking to take advantage of that opportunity will drive the CCBS up and/or Bund swap spreads wider (more negative) relative to US Treasury swap spreads.

The CCBS level observed in the market therefore reflects the sum of global capital flows chasing the currency which offers superior funding and investment opportunities. For example, high credit spreads in USD relative to JPY could lead to an increase in Samurai issuance, driving the CCBS negative. This in turn might make basis swapped JGBs attractive on a USD LIBOR spread basis, generating flows that push the CCBS up again. Consequently, the pricing of the CCBS reflects the complex mixture of global funding and investment flows and can serve as a useful and quantitative indicator for these activities, which are often hidden from direct observation. Stated otherwise, the CCBS condenses the multitude of all cross-currency funding and investment flows into one easily observable and tradable number.

In abstract terms, basis swaps link global funding rates and therefore allow investors and borrowers to exploit global credit spread differences. And in a similar manner, global credit spread differences impact the level of the CCBS via global credit spread arbitrage.

Further impacts on the CCBS can arise from:

- Differences in yield curve steepness (carry) in different currencies. For example, a high carry difference between the Treasury and JGB yield curve typically prompts Japanese investors to increase their foreign bond holdings and to roll the FX hedge on a short-term (e.g. 1Y) basis. This mismatch between the maturity of the bond and of the CCBS results in a synthetic carry position along the US yield curve. Thus, whenever these carry positions are particularly attractive, demand for the short end of the CCBS curve tends to be affected.
- Hedging flows from structured products. Many structured products involve several currencies, and hence dealers require CCBS positions to hedge them. For example, the hedging flows of power reverse dual callables (PRDCs) introduce a link between the CCBS and the FX markets. When the FX rate moves, in particular through certain levels used in PRDCs, PRDC hedges need to be adjusted. Since most PRDCs are ultralong issues, this tends to affect 20Y and 30Y CCBS in particular.

Selecting the Banking System to Generate Money Market Returns

Imagine a USD-based institution that wants to invest its USD funds on a rolling 3M basis at the prevailing rate in the money market over the next five years. The most obvious possibility to achieve this modest goal is to simply choose every quarter a US LIBOR panel bank as counterparty to lend to. But the CCBS offers another way of achieving the same goal: enter into a 5Y CCBS, in this example the USD–EUR one, which exchanges the USD funds at the beginning into EUR. Then choose every quarter a EURIBOR panel bank as counterpart to lend the EUR funds to. This will generate EURIBOR cashflows, which the CCBS exchanges back into USD LIBOR cashflows. And at the end of the five years, the CCBS will also exchange the EUR principal back into USD at a pre-defined exchange rate. Hence, this second option seems like a complicated way to achieve the same result: every quarter a USD LIBOR income and after five years the same USD funds originally invested (also in case of using the CCBS without FX risk). But there are a few differences:

- Most importantly, while the final cashflows are the same, they are generated via different counterparties: US LIBOR panel banks in the first and EURIBOR panel banks in the second option. If the first are considered to be safer, there is higher demand for the first option.
- The CCBS spread subtracted from the EURIBOR payments. Together with the statement of the first point, the CCBS spread can therefore be considered as market price for the "privilege" of keeping funds in the US banking system rather than lending to counterparties abroad. If there was no preference, the CCBS spread should be zero from this perspective. The more demand for generating money market returns in the US relative to other countries, the more negative the CCBS spread, as compensation for those choosing the second option. Correspondingly, it shows a clear correlation to stress in the banking sector: the CCBS tends to become more negative whenever bank risk is deemed to increase. Interestingly, this was also true when the problems of the banking sector originated in the US during the subprime crisis: after a few days of slightly positive USD–EUR CCBS spreads, significantly negative values followed soon and persisted for long. This is in line with the perception of the US banking system as a relative safe haven for any sort of crisis.
- The second option also involves higher transaction costs, capital requirements and counterparty risk – not only from exposure to foreign banks to generate the money market returns but also from exposure to the counterpart of the CCBS, from whom the investor expects to get the USD principal back after five years. As the principal is exchanged in a CCBS, this results in a significant exposure to the counterpart: imagine the counterpart in the CCBS is a European bank and defaults during a euro crisis. The investor is then left with a depreciated EUR principal; while the CCBS has pre-defined the FX rate, the counterparty no longer exists. Collateral and margin agreements are therefore of particular importance for (the pricing of) CCBS.

PRICING OF THE CCBS

Summarizing the driving forces of the CCBS (other than intrinsic statistical relationships), it reflects at the same time:

- The sum of global capital flows chasing the currency which offers superior funding and investment opportunities; *and*

■ The market price for the privilege to generate money market returns in the US banking sector relative to foreign alternatives.

(Capital controls are obviously the main driving force of basis swaps between onshore and offshore. These basis swaps are not treated in this book, which assesses the flows between comparatively free markets only.)

Pricing the CCBS is therefore a complex task, which should reflect the complexity of its driving forces. At a minimum any pricing model should include the global asset swap spreads (e.g. of AA-rated corporate issuers) and a proxy for bank risk among its input variables. As proxy for bank risk, the secured–unsecured basis might be used, which offers the advantage of being closely linked to the cost of equity (an input variable into the swap spread model) but observable (e.g. via the price for SOFR–Eurodollar or Fed Funds future contract spreads) and of driving the ICBS as well. Figure 14.4 illustrates the relationship of that basis to the CCBS.

A starting point for modeling the USD–EUR CCBS could therefore be a multiple regression of its price versus the difference of swap spreads of AA-rated corporates in both currencies and versus the SOFR–Fed Funds future spread. Due to the mutual global influences, CCBS for the major currencies should be priced together. This expands the starting point to simultaneously optimizing the USD–EUR, USD–JPY, and USD–GBP CCBS versus the swap spreads of AA-rated corporates in USD, EUR, JPY, and GBP as well as the SOFR–Fed Funds future spreads.

In addition to setting up the pricing model framework, analysts of the CCBS need to be constantly aware of all global developments and their mutual links. In the following we will provide some typical illustrations, starting with the impact of different swap spreads of government bonds on the pricing of the 2Y JPY CCBS in 2002 and 2003. As depicted in Figure 15.1, when the swap spreads of US Treasuries narrowed relative to those of JGBs (i.e. when investing in US bonds became more attractive relative to investing in Japanese bonds), the demand for generating returns in USD increased and the CCBS became more negative. The R^2 of 0.34 in the regression of 2Y JPY CCBS on the asset swap spread difference between US Treasuries and JGBs suggests that this effect could be responsible for about one-third of the movements in the CCBS, with the remaining two-thirds being a function of other driving forces, such as the demand for generating money market returns with US banks. This is in line with the CCBS reflecting the result of a multitude of different global funding and investment flows.

To illustrate the impact of a banking crisis on the CCBS, we regress the level of JPY CCBS on a proxy for risk aversion since 2010. In particular, we use the first factor from a PCA of the CCBS curve as the dependent variable. And as the independent variable, we use the realized volatility of the 5Y JPY

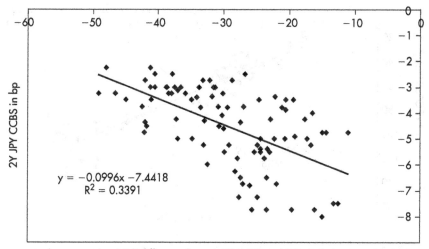

ASW difference between 2Y USTs and JGBs in bp

FIGURE 15.1   The 2Y JPY CCBS in 2002 and 2003 as a function of the ASW difference in different currencies.
Sources: data – Bloomberg; chart – Authors.

Note: In the 10Y sector, the UST ASW in 2002 and 2003 was largely influenced by (waning) expectations about Fed buying at the long end of the curve. Thus, we use 2Y rather than 10Y (or factor 1 of the PCA on the CCBS curve), where results could be misleading. *Data period:* 1 Jan 2002 to 7 Oct 2003, weekly data.

swap rate. The results shown in Figure 15.2 underscore the point that in the presence of a banking crisis there is little room for global funding and investment flows to impact the level of the CCBS. Correspondingly, rather than a multitude of driving forces (e.g. Figure 15.1 with an R^2 of 0.34), there is now a single determining variable of the CCBS curve only (e.g. Figure 15.2 with an R^2 of 0.86). Also note the difference in magnitude. While global funding flows usually cause the CCBS to move by a couple of basis points, a banking crisis can have an impact as much as 10 times larger.

CCBS and the Subprime Crisis

With the advent of the subprime crisis beginning in 2008, European banks experienced increasing difficulties funding many of their USD-denominated assets, particularly mortgage-related bonds that had been financed in the US repo market.

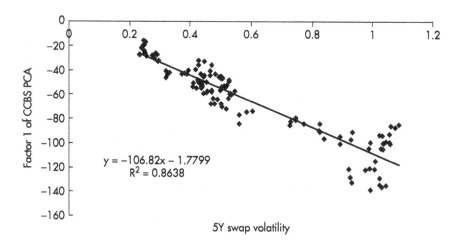

FIGURE 15.2   Factor 1 of a PCA on the JPY CCBS since 2010 as a function of the 5Y realized swap volatility.
Sources: data – Bloomberg; chart – Authors.

Data period: 4 Jan 2010 to 4 Jun 2012, weekly data.

One alternative option available to these banks was to sell these mortgage-related assets. But this alternative was considered relatively unattractive, as these assets were selling for relatively low prices.

Another alternative available to European banks was to sell euros to buy dollars in the spot FX market and then to use those dollars to fund their USD mortgage-related assets. But this alternative would involve considerable exchange rate risk.[2]

A third option, and the one chosen by many European banks, was to engage in CCBS with US banks, in which the European bank would:

- receive dollars in exchange for euros at the start of the swap;
- return the EUR and USD principal at the end of the swap;
- exchange ongoing interest payments – plus or minus a basis swap spread – during the life of the swap.

The European banks then used the dollars received in the CCBS to fund their USD mortgage-related investments.

---

[2]The observant reader might ask whether these European banks could have hedged this FX risk in the forward market. But, of course, combining a spot FX transaction with a forward FX transaction results in an FX swap or in a CCBS (depending on the term of the swap). So from a practical perspective, this is what the European banks did.

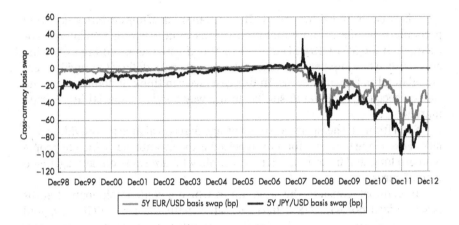

FIGURE 15.3 5Y basis swaps: EUR/USD and JPY/USD.
Sources: data – Bloomberg; chart – Authors.

Figure 15.3 shows the way in which the 5Y EUR/USD CCBS reacted to these events. The 5Y JPY/USD CCBS is shown as well, for reference.[3]

A couple of points worth noting:

- The basis swap spread was within a few basis points of zero until the start of the subprime crisis, at which time it began increasing (i.e. becoming increasingly negative, favoring the counterparty providing USD in the swap).
- Since the start of the subprime crisis, the 5Y CCBS spread has widened during periods of particular stress for European banks and has narrowed when those stresses have lessened.

US Dollars 'Going Special' as Collateral

A helpful analogy for the impact of banking crises on the CCBS is given by the perspective of collateralized loans, similar to the repo market for government bonds.

Recall that government bonds sometimes trade in the repo market at rates lower than the "general collateral" (GC) rates, as an incentive for people who are long the bond to provide it to people who are short the bond. The demand for the bond, the specific collateral in the loan, is the factor that drives the repo rate for the bond below the GC repo rate.

---

[3]In 1998, Japanese banks were in a situation similar to the one described above and used the CCBS to fund their extensive US operations.

Likewise, in an FX swap or a CCBS, we can think of one currency as having particularly strong demand that increases its value as specific collateral. For example, if the 5Y EUR/USD CCBS is -37 bp, the market is willing to provide an incentive of 37 bp per year to motivate people with dollars to provide them as collateral in a loan of euros. In this case, we can think of dollars as having "gone special" as collateral, similar to the way bonds go special in the repo market.

Seen from this perspective, the arbitrage that is available for providing dollars in exchange for euros for a fixed period is the incentive provided to people who are long dollars to lend them to people who are short dollars, against a loan of euros.

In contrast, consider the situation in which a comparable loan of euros is securitized not with US dollars but rather with some more GC, say, gold or generic German Bunds. In this case, the interest rate paid by the person borrowing euros would be the generic rate for loans secured by GC (i.e. the GC repo rate). But when the euro loan is secured by US dollars, which are in short supply among European banks, the party borrowing euros enjoys a special borrowing rate as an incentive for providing the dollars for a fixed period.

When a bond becomes special in the repo market, it assumes a value to its owner beyond the mere right to the intrinsic payments of principal and interest. The bond also allows its owner to borrow in the secured lending market at an interest rate lower than he could borrow with GC. In fact, by combining the resulting low-rate borrowing with collateralized lending at the higher rate prevailing for GC, the owner of the special collateral can monetize the specialness of his valuable collateral without incurring interest rate risk.

Since the bond trading special in the repo market offers its owner this additional economic value, its price in the spot market tends to be higher than it would be were it not special in the repo market. In other words, the spot price of a bond tends to increase relative to other bonds when it goes special in the repo market.

This perspective that CCBS spreads widen when dollars 'go special' in the repo market implies that US dollars should richen to euros in the spot market above the rate they otherwise would be were the dollars not special (i.e. were the basis swap not so wide).

Of course, the CCBS is by no means the only factor that would be expected to affect the price of US dollars vs. euros in the spot FX market, so a failure to observe the predicted relationship may not warrant a rejection of our hypothesized perspective. On the other hand, if we were to observe the hypothesized relationship, it should lend credence to our analogy between repo specialness and CCBS spreads.

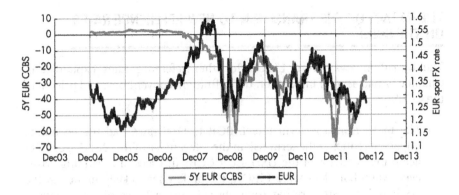

FIGURE 15.4 5Y EUR/USD CCBS versus the EUR/USD spot FX rate.
Sources: data – Bloomberg; chart – Authors.

Figure 15.4 shows the relation between the 5Y EUR/USD CCBS and the EUR/USD spot exchange rate over time since January of 2005. Prior to the start of the subprime crisis, there was no correlation between the basis swap spread and the spot value of the EUR, particularly as the value of the basis swap spread always was within a few basis points of zero.

After the start of the subprime crisis, the correlation between the CCBS spread and the FX rate increased significantly. For example, in 2009, 2010, and 2011 the correlations between the two series were 0.84, 0.80, and 0.78 respectively. In our view, the relation between the CCBS spread and the value of the dollar relative to the euro is consistent with our perspective that the CCBS spread can be viewed as the extent to which one currency has become more valuable as collateral against a loan in the other currency.

As the dollar tends to richen in the spot market, the other currency tends to appear relatively rich in the forward FX market. Correspondingly, the deviation of the forward FX rate traded in the market from the arbitrage relationship described by the equation above is often referred to as the 'richness' of the other currency (e.g. EUR) in the forward FX market.

With this in mind, our view is that a main economic function of the FX swap and CCBS markets is to provide an opportunity for people to borrow in one currency using another currency as collateral. As a result, many of the results we have developed for collateralized lending can be applied in this setting as well, the only complication being that the currency in which the collateral is denominated in this case is other than the currency in which the borrowed funds are denominated.

THE IMPACT OF THE TRANSITION TO NEW REFERENCE RATES ON THE CCBS

The transition away from LIBOR to other reference rates explained in Chapter 11 had several impacts on the definition, conventions, and pricing of the CCBS:

- The move from the term rate LIBOR to O/N rates had the economic impact of reducing the term risk in the relevant leg of the CCBS. Consider again the behavior of the USD–EUR CCBS in times of a banking crisis: even when both legs were LIBOR, the preference to keep money in the US banking system rather than abroad during times of stress caused the CCBS to quote more negative in these situations. Now that the US reference rate is a secured O/N rate, i.e. the safest reference rate worldwide, the USD SOFR–EUR 3M EURIBOR CCBS can be expected to react even more to banking crises than the former USD 3M LIBOR–EUR 3M EURIBOR CCBS.
- The move from the term rate LIBOR to O/N rates had the technical consequence of determining the payments by compounding in arrears rather than via the term rate LIBOR known in advance of each period. For example, in the formula for the FX swap above, when R_{USD} represented LIBOR, it was observable at the beginning of the FX swap; now that it represents SOFR, it needs to be determined by aggregating all SOFR values observed during the life of the FX swap, hence in arrears. Given the resulting practical problems, several mitigating features have been introduced, including a SOFR term rate. These are described extensively in Chapter 3 of Huggins and Schaller (2022).
- The move from the unsecured rate LIBOR to the secured rate SOFR means that the secured–unsecured basis is part of any CCBS currently trading and hence that the pricing model for this spread outlined in Chapter 11 is a natural part of the pricing model of any CCBS. While in the model for CCBS with LIBOR legs sketched above, the secured–unsecured basis was only one possible proxy for stress in the banking sector, for CCBS with a USD SOFR leg, it is also an integral part of the CCBS and its prices. This further underlines the advantage of using the secured–unsecured basis as input variable for CCBS pricing models.

Before the transition away from LIBOR, CCBS exchanged unsecured term rates. Even then, the preference to keep funds in the US banking sector in times of crises has led to a clear correlation of the CCBS (more negative) to variables measuring stress, such as the ICBS, volatility, cost of capital, etc. Following the transition to SOFR in the US, CCBS now always exchange the unsecured foreign rate versus the secured O/N rate SOFR in the US. As the secured–unsecured basis is also related to stress (given its dependency on the cost of capital), the CCBS are now exposed twofold to this basis, as before due to the preference to keep money in the US banking system and additionally due to the preference to lend money secured.

On the foreign leg there exist only unsecured reference rates, in some countries with different terms. In case of the foreign leg being LIBOR and thus including term risk, the difference in credit risk covered by the CCBS is even larger than in case of the foreign leg being an O/N rate. From the starting point of CCBS using LIBOR on both legs, one can therefore make the qualitative statements:

- CCBS exchanging USD SOFR versus a foreign unsecured O/N rate are generally more negative than the CCBS before the transition, *ceteris paribus*, since they directly include the secured–unsecured basis in addition to the swap between two banking systems (which is only indirectly correlated to the secured–unsecured basis as a proxy for stress in the banking sector).
- CCBS exchanging USD SOFR versus a foreign unsecured term rate (LIBOR) are expected to be even more negative, since they also include term risk. For example, the SOFR–ESTR CCBS may quote at −20 bp, while the SOFR–EURIBOR CCBS may quote at −28 bp.
- Hence, the variable secured–unsecured basis drives both the general level of all types of CCBS (since all of them reflect the preference for keeping funds in the US banking system) and the spread between CCBS with secured SOFR as one leg and unsecured O/N rates as other leg. Furthermore, as it is correlated to the term (risk) (the more demand for secured versus unsecured lending, the more demand for shorter versus longer unsecured lending), it also drives the spread to CCBS with LIBOR as the non-USD leg. Altogether, this variable explains the observation that a general increase in the level of all CCBS tends to be accompanied by increasing spreads between the different types.
- The transition has therefore resulted in an even stronger impact of the secured–unsecured basis (and thus the banking crises reflected in it) on the CCBS. While already the CCBS with LIBOR in both legs were significantly driven by that variable (see Figure 14.4), the CCBS between USD SOFR and non-USD LIBOR are generally more negative and more volatile.

Quantifying these qualitative statements, we can price all types of CCBS by adding to the CCBS between LIBOR the models for spreads between reference rates in the same currency. From the starting point of the CCBS between LIBOR on both legs described above, the current types of CCBS can be reconstructed by combining them with an ICBS between LIBOR and SOFR in the

USD and depending on the type also with an ICBS between LIBOR and an O/N reference rate in the foreign currency. For example, a SOFR–EURIBOR CCBS can be priced by adding the fair value of a SOFR–USD LIBOR ICBS to the CCBS with LIBOR on both legs. As long as the SOFR–Eurodollar spread contracts trade, there is even a market price for the SOFR–USD LIBOR ICBS: after the end of Eurodollar futures, our model for the repo–LIBOR spread can still provide the input variable. If for the CCBS pricing model sketched above the secured–unsecured basis is chosen as proxy for stress in the banking system, it can also be used as input variable for the ICBS pricing model (and for the asset swap spread model added to the combinations in Chapter 16).

In terms of Table 11.1, the CCBS with LIBOR on both legs exchange different rows (currencies) of the left-most column. By combining them with ICBS, any type of CCBS can be replicated. Hence, any type of CCBS can be priced by adding to the pricing model for CCBS with LIBOR the fair value of the ICBS obtained in Chapter 14 via a direct application of the models for the spreads between reference rates.

There are several ways of reaching the same goal: as an alternative to the "historical" start above from CCBS with LIBOR on both legs, one could also start with a hypothetical CCBS with repo on both legs and the add the fair value of the repo–LIBOR spread to price USD SOFR–EUR EURIBOR CCBS.

It is important to note that once more the transition has introduced a structural break in the time series of CCBS: before the transition, CCBS data reflect LIBOR in both legs, after the transition, CCBS data reflect SOFR in one leg, hence a structurally higher and more volatile time series for the reasons mentioned above. Analysts should therefore take care to check the type of "CCBS" represented by the time series they use. It may be worthwhile constructing synthetic time series of CCBS with LIBOR in both legs (or with repo in both legs, or with unsecured O/N rates in both legs) via the methods just explained, i.e. by adjusting other types of CCBS quotes with the (fair value of the) ICBS.

As a practical consequence for this book written in 2023, given the short time since the transition, there are too few data for CCBS with SOFR as one leg in order to generate long-term time series without structural breaks. We have therefore kept most of the case studies from the first edition written in 2012 before the transition, i.e. with LIBOR in both legs of the CCBS. While this decision requires carrying around some historical ballast, it avoids contaminating the case studies with structural breaks. And that point in time provided with the subprime and euro crisis interesting precedents, which remain worthwhile to study. Of course, once enough CCBS data post transition becomes available in future, the reader is encouraged to re-apply the analysis techniques described here.

CHAPTER 16

Combinations and Mutual Influences of Asset, Basis, and Credit Default Swaps

INTRODUCTION

Having discussed the different types of swaps individually in the previous chapters, the objective of this chapter is the analysis of their combinations and the resulting mutual influences between all asset, basis, and credit default swaps worldwide.

The first section explains the basics of calculating USD asset swap spreads of bonds denominated in other currencies, i.e. their spread versus USD SOFR (or formerly, versus USD LIBOR) as determined by asset and basis swapping them. The details of executing these operations are given in Chapter 17.

This ability to express all bonds as a spread versus USD SOFR (formerly LIBOR), regardless of their issuer, currency, and maturity, serves as a common yardstick, against which all bonds can be compared. The existence of such a possibility to price all bonds versus one single reference rate has major consequences:

- It is the foundation for the funding and investment arbitrage between different markets described in Chapter 15.
- It provides a natural and universal rich/cheap measure for bonds, which enables RV assessments between global bonds. This is the topic of Chapter 17.
- It links all global bond markets via the asset and basis swap markets. These links and the resulting mutual influences and relationships are the topic of this chapter.

Furthermore, just as the operations of asset and basis swapping a bond express its pricing in a single number, i.e. its spread versus USD SOFR, so does the credit default swap (CDS). There exist therefore two different ways of measuring every bond worldwide as a spread over USD SOFR: The asset swap spread (of the basis swapped bond) and the CDS (of the bond issuer for

287

the maturity of the bond). And both of them are to a significant extent driven by the same variable, i.e. the credit quality of the bond issuer (see Chapter 12). It is thus natural to compare both numbers – which introduces a relationship between asset and basis swaps on one side and CDS on the other side. As a result, we obtain an RV relationship between both and are able to extend the global links and mutual influences between all asset and basis swaps also to and with CDS.

Concerning the RV relationship between the USD asset swap spreads of basis swapped bonds ("USD ASW") and the CDS of the bond issuer (with the length of the CDS equal to the maturity of the bond), there are two possible approaches:

- Aiming for an arbitrage *equality*, one can combine the pricing models discussed in the last chapters and extract the pure credit risk of the bond issuer from both the USD ASW and the CDS. While a strong theoretical case can be made for the equality of the same variable contained in two different market quotes, applying this concept in practice faces the issue of too few observations for a precise estimation of the DO (delivery option) and FX component also contained in the CDS quotes.
- Aiming for a relationship which can be more easily implemented in practice, the arbitrage *inequality* USD ASW (market observed, not adjusted) ≤ CDS (market observed, not adjusted) can be used. Since this relationship is based on qualitative arguments only, such as the positivity of the DO and FX component, it is independent of their estimation error. This approach could be characterized as a tactical retreat from an arbitrage equality to an inequality in order to express the concept in terms which can be applied to the market independent of modeling issues.

The first two sections of this chapter discuss the two relationships imposed on bond and swap markets,

1. Between USD ASW and local ASW via the CCBS (and ICBS).
2. Between USD ASW and the CDS.

The first relationship is simply given by the formula for calculating USD ASW from local ASW and the basis swaps, the second relationship compares USD ASW and CDS as two different market prices, which contain a common element, i.e. the credit quality of the bond issuer.

After treating both relationships separately, they will be combined into a single formula linking four markets, local ASW, USD ASW, CCBS (and ICBS), and CDS. This formula will then be applied to a number of case studies, explaining the different equilibria observed for bonds of higher and lower credit quality.

Given the number of variables connected, there is usually more than one possible outcome of changes in a particular variable. For example, a richening of Bunds versus EURIBOR can result in the USD–EUR CCBS absorbing this richening, in which case the balance between all CCBS is disturbed and will readjust, and/or in Bunds also richening versus USD SOFR, in which case the balance between all (basis swapped) bonds is disturbed and will readjust. The complexity of these mutual influences (similar to the three-body problem in astronomy) corresponds to the complexity of the relationships. Fortunately, the arbitrage inequality provides a clear and hard boundary.

CALCULATING USD SWAP SPREADS FOR FOREIGN BONDS

Recall that the cross-currency basis swap (CCBS) allows a USD-based institution to invest in any product independent of its currency without FX risk. For example, it could enter a JPY CCBS, use the JPY principal it initially receives, buy a JGB, asset swap it, and thereby create JPY TONAR + ASW cash flows. With these cash flows, it can serve the running CCBS payments, receiving USD SOFR (plus a spread). If the maturity of the CCBS equals the maturity of the JGB, it will receive the JPY principal repayment from the bond at the same time at which the final principal exchange in the CCBS will convert it back into the original USD principal. Note that, though it has created the cash flows by means of a JGB investment, through the CCBS it deals in the end only with USD cash flows. Of course, any other currency could be used as a basis for comparison as well, and a EUR-based investor is able to express and evaluate all bonds globally as a spread versus EURIBOR.

The importance of this statement (apart from the convenience it offers to USD-based investors) is that, through combining asset and basis swaps, all bonds can be reduced into a single number and can therefore be compared relative to the same benchmark. The mathematics of this expression is straightforward under some simplifying assumptions such as par bonds, which will be relaxed in Chapter 17. The cash flow in foreign currency is the foreign reference rate (e.g. TONAR) + foreign asset swap spread. Thus, after payment of foreign reference rate + CCBS in the CCBS, one receives USD SOFR (from the CCBS) and has the foreign swap spread minus the CCBS premium left in foreign currency. This then needs to be converted into USD by adjusting for the difference in basis point value (BPV).

Thus, the USD asset swap spread ("USD ASW")[1] is:

$$\frac{Swapspread_{foreign} - CCBS}{CF},$$

---

[1]Sticking to the convention "Reference Rate + X" for swap spreads.

where CF denotes the conversion factor, that is

$$\frac{BPV_{USD}}{BPV_{foreign}}$$

(with the BPV of the swap rates of the relevant maturity and with the relevant reference rate).

In case the domestic asset swap uses a different reference rate than the CCBS, the appropriate ICBS needs to be added. For example, if the JGB is asset swapped in TIBOR, it first needs to be converted via an ICBS into TONAR, which is then exchanged via the CCBS into SOFR. Correspondingly, before applying the USD ASW formula above, the JPY TONAR ASW needs to be calculated by adding the ICBS to the TIBOR ASW. This TONAR ASW – in general terms, the swap spread against the non-USD reference rate used in the CCBS – gives then the input variable $Swapspread_{foreign}$ for the USD ASW formula. For simplicity, the formula and the rest of this chapter assume that the reference rate of the CCBS is the same as the reference rate of the domestic swap; if this is not the case, the variable "CCBS" needs to be adjusted with the relevant ICBS like in the TIBOR example.

As explained at the end of Chapter 15, despite the transition to SOFR, we'll continue to use historical case studies with USD LIBOR as reference rate in order to avoid structural breaks in the CCBS time series. Before the transition from LIBOR to SOFR as main US reference rate, (3M) USD LIBOR played the role as global benchmark and hence as USD leg in CCBS. The general formula from above covers all reference rates and can also be used to calculate the USD ASW versus LIBOR. For example, the ASW of a JGB versus 6M JPY LIBOR is translated via the 3M/6M JPY LIBOR ICBS into a 3M ASW and then taken as input into the formula. Using the data from Sep 23, 2012, the 10-year (10Y) JGB benchmark was priced to have a 6M JPY ASW of -1 bp. Adding the 3M/6M JPY ICBS of 12 bp gives a 3M JPY ASW of 11 bp. With the CCBS at -64.5 bp and a CF of 0.95,[2] the equation above returns a spread of 79 bp above USD LIBOR for the 10Y JGB.

A useful graphical representation of the way global bonds compare relative to the universal yardstick of USD SOFR is to display the USD swap spreads of the relevant bonds as a function of their maturities. Figure 16.1 shows the USD (3M LIBOR) swap spreads for US Treasuries, basis swapped Bunds, and basis swapped JGBs. Such a chart can serve as starting point for global investment (and funding) decisions.

Note that while Bunds track the US Treasury curve (on a USD LIBOR basis) at a rather constant and low spread, JGBs are priced at a significantly

---

[2]Calculated by dividing the BPV of a 10Y USD swap by the BPV of a 10Y JPY swap.

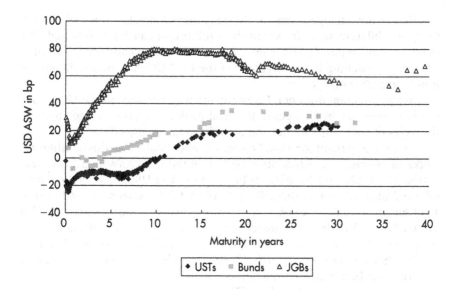

FIGURE 16.1   USD LIBOR swap spreads of US Treasuries, Bunds, and JGBs as of 23 Sep 2012.
Sources: data – Bloomberg; chart – Authors.

Data period: "Current" market data as of 23 Sep 2012.

higher USD ASW and follow an independent path. A comprehensive explanation for this behavior will be attempted at the end of this chapter. But already the equation above offers a mathematical explanation for the high USD ASW of JGBs based on the relative stability of the JPY ASW of JGBs (which will be explained later on): as the banking crisis resulted both in a higher 3M/6M JPY LIBOR ICBS and in a more negative USD–JPY CCBS, the USD ASW of JGBs needed to increase.

THE EQUILIBRIUM BETWEEN ASSET AND BASIS SWAPS

As the CCBS exists, there exists a USD ASW in addition to the local ASW and a relationship between the two. In particular, this relationship is given by the formula[3]:

$$USDASW = \frac{EURASW}{CF} - \frac{CCBS}{CF}$$

---

[3]For simplicity, this formula and discussion assume that the reference rate of the local asset swap is the same as the reference rate of the CCBS. If this is not the case, the variable CCBS needs to be adjusted with the relevant ICBS, as explained above.

Hence, any change in one of the constituents affects all others, though there are different ways in which the equilibrium can be maintained. For example, a richening of Bunds on a EUR ASW basis could be compensated either by a widening (more negative) of the EUR CCBS or by a richening of Bunds on a USD ASW basis.

As the equation does not determine the way a change in the USD ASW would be reflected by changes in the local ASW and CCBS, we need to leave the realm of pure mathematics and consider actual market data.

As a starting point for a brief empirical study of the way this equilibrium works in practice, we depict the evolution of the USD ASW of 5Y US Treasuries, 5Y Bunds, and 5Y JGBs in Figure 16.2. The USD ASW of 5Y Bunds followed the evolution of the USD ASW of 5Y US Treasuries at a rather constant spread. Actually, the correlation between the two time series is 0.73. This means that, for Bunds, the existence of a global yardstick (the USD ASW) links the pricing of Bunds to the pricing of US Treasuries. Therefore, the USD ASW level of US Treasuries as well as the CCBS should have a significant impact on the pricing of Bunds denominated in euros.

On the other hand, the USD ASW of JGBs has appeared more independent. This could reflect the fact that JGBs are considered riskier than Bunds and hence are not as seen as close alternatives for US Treasuries. As the influence of the global asset selection process illustrated in Figure 16.1 is greater if

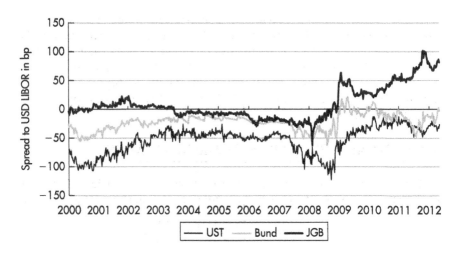

FIGURE 16.2 USD swap spread history of the 5Y US Treasury, Bund, and JGB. *Sources:* data – Bloomberg; chart – Authors.

Data period: 8 Feb 2000 to 12 Jun 2012, weekly data.

the bonds have a comparable credit standing, the USD ASW of US Treasuries has a significant impact on the pricing of low-risk bonds. Risky bonds, by contrast, have more scope to follow their own USD ASW pricing. This leads to the issue of the determinants of the USD ASW of JGBs. And as the USD ASW of JGBs is not tied strongly to the USD ASW of US Treasuries, it is conceivable that the existence of the USD ASW exerts less influence on the pricing of JGBs in yen.

From Figure 16.2 it is obvious that the same equation manifests itself differently in different markets and that for high-risk bonds an important driving force is still missing. This driving force is the credit quality as measured by the (adjusted) CDS. We will now add this element to the links between the swap markets and after discussing the arbitrage relationships revisit the case studies in order to observe the impact of the CDS on the equilibrium.

ARBITRAGE EQUALITY BETWEEN USD ASW AND CDS

The combination of asset and basis swaps[4] is conceptually a reduction of every bond to a spread over USD SOFR. Credit default swaps (CDS) follow precisely the same concept. Every bond globally is evaluated by a CDS in the form of a spread (the CDS premium) over USD SOFR. Moreover, the source of that spread is in both cases to a large extent driven by the credit quality of the bond. The perception of poor credit quality results in a large USD ASW and in a large CDS.

The swap spread model presented in Chapter 12 reflects the link between ASW and CDS by incorporating the adjusted CDS level as key component. In fact, SOFR–ASW of US Treasuries have been modeled by the adjusted CDS plus the expected specialness: treasuries without specialness should therefore quote at a SOFR–ASW equal to the adjusted CDS (abstracting from other driving forces like haircuts). While the funding swap becomes more influential for other types of swap spreads, e.g. LIBOR–ASW, the CDS remains an important component in all of them, which explains both the term structure and the cyclicality of swap spreads to a large extent.

Let us now assume that both the USD ASW of a bond and its CDS are driven by the credit quality of the bond not only *to a large extent* but *exclusively*. Of course, this is an artificial assumption, which allows us to outline the general concept of no-arbitrage models for CDS pricing in clean and easy terms. After the assumption has fulfilled this function, we shall describe the way the

---

[4]In this section, the term "basis swap" (BSW) refers to the cross-currency basis swap (CCBS), adjusted for the intra currency basis swap (ICBS) where necessary.

general concept needs to be modified in order to work in the real world, where both the USD ASW and the CDS provide the information about credit quality in different forms, overlying that information with other elements.

Under that assumption, *the combination of asset&basis swaps can be considered as a synthetic short position in a CDS on the bond issuer.*

- The risk in the combination asset&basis swap[5] as well as in a short CDS is the default of the bond issuer.
- For taking that risk, an investor is compensated with a spread above USD SOFR, in case of asset&basis swaps with the USD swap spread of the bond, and in case of a short CDS with the default swap premium.

Since both the USD ASW of a bond and the CDS of the issuer of that bond reflect the credit risk in terms of a spread versus USD SOFR, it is natural to compare the two. This comparison allows detection of relative value opportunities between the two markets, i.e. the investigation whether the credit risk is reflected in the bond and CDS markets *relative to each other* in a consistent way. If it is not, trades between the USD ASW and the CDS can exploit the different assessment of the same credit risk in both markets, without being exposed to the level of credit risk or to a default.

If the USD swap spread of a JGB was higher than its CDS, we could asset&basis swap the JGB and buy default protection on Japan, realizing the difference between the two spreads versus USD SOFR, the USD ASW of the JGB minus the CDS, as risk-free arbitrage[6] profit: until a default occurs (and until the maturity of the bond if no default occurs), we obtain the difference as profit. And in a default, the CDS payment covers our losses from the bond.[7]

Put otherwise, by combining the three swaps (asset, basis, and default), we have step-by-step reduced the risks involved in a bond investment, as illustrated in Table 16.1.

As the combination of all swaps results in a risk-free position, there should be no compensation for taking that position. Thus, as ASW&BSW& CDS = 0, the cash flow from asset&basis swapping a bond (its USD swap spread) should compensate for its default protection (i.e. the USD ASW

---

[5]By the symbol "ASW&BSW," we refer both to the action of asset and basis swapping a bond and to its result (i.e. the USD swap spread of that bond). Note that while the actions and the symbol "&" are additive, the USD swap spread is given by the difference (ASW-BSW)/CF.

[6]This arbitrage requires the artificial assumption made above. Later, we will discuss how to apply that arbitrage concept also in the real market, where the assumption does not hold, which may require us to drop the term "risk-free arbitrage" in its strict sense.

[7]Abstracting from the issue of the ASW and BSW remaining after default.

TABLE 16.1 Risk Exposure of a Bond Together with Different Combinations of Swaps

Position	Exposed to		
	Yield risk[1]	FX risk	Default risk
Bond	Yes	Yes	Yes
Bond&ASW	No	Yes	Yes
Bond&ASW&BSW	No	No	Yes
Bond&ASW&BSW&CDS	No	No	No

[1]Note: this table should be understood in broad conceptual terms. In particular, as the duration of an asset-swapped bond position is very low, we enter "No" in the yield risk column, even though, strictly speaking, it has some P&L, depending on the level of short rates.

should equal the CDS). This is an alternative way to reach the conclusion from above, that there is an arbitrage relationship between asset&basis swapped bonds and CDS. Also note that while analyzing the ASW, the BSW, and the CDS in isolation, there are many driving factors and complex relationships between them to consider, when putting them all together, one arrives at a simple arbitrage relationship that should hold independently of the specific issues and flows that drive the individual swaps

Thus, we have intuitively derived the equation USD ASW = CDS of the well-known arbitrage models for CDS pricing and trading (with the difference between CDS and USD ASW being called "basis"). In reality, however, this framework is just the starting point for further and deeper analysis. Since the derivation of the equation USD ASW = CDS required us to artificially exclude all other elements except credit information from both USD ASW and CDS, we need now to consider how to deal with these additional parts of both sides.

If the goal is to maintain the arbitrage *equality*, one can use the models presented in the previous chapters in order to isolate the pure credit information from both the USD ASW and the CDS quotes observed in the market.

Specifically, starting from the USD ASW, one can use the model outlined in Chapter 12 and its subsequent extensions to abstract from non-credit related elements. The funding component can be isolated by directly applying the formula from Chapter 12:

Adjusted CDS = USD ASW (observed in market) – Fair value of the basis swap between repo and the reference rate of the swap.

In case of SOFR–ASW, the funding swap only covers the specialness and is usually rather small, in which case the approximation *Adjusted CDS ≈ USD SOFR–ASW* might be acceptable. From that starting point, the additional driving forces of swap spreads not included in the model and discussed in

Chapter 18, such as haircuts, can also be subtracted from the observed USD ASW, just like the funding component. The idea is to "adjust" the USD ASW given by the market by excluding all elements not related to the credit quality of the bond, until only the component *Adjusted CDS* remains.

And also starting from the CDS quotes, using the evaluation of the DO and FX component from Chapter 13, all elements not related to the credit quality of the bond can be excluded, until only the component *Adjusted CDS* remains:

Adjusted CDS = CDS (observed in market) – value of DO – value of FX component.

Once these exercises are completed, one can then express the arbitrage equality as:

Adjusted CDS extracted from USD ASW = Adjusted CDS extracted from CDS quotes,

i.e. argue for the equality of the prices for the 'pure' credit risk by making sure that both sides of the equation only reflect 'pure' credit risk.

Hence, the two hurdles on the way to an arbitrage equality are the two adjustments: once these are made and two measures for the pure credit risk of the same bonds are obtained from the USD ASW quotes, on one side, and from the CDS quoted, on the other, a strong case can be made for their equality.

- Regarding the adjustment of USD ASW, before the transition it involved removing the secured–unsecured basis from USD ASW versus LIBOR and hence dealing with the variable "cost of capital" and the problem of it being unobservable ex ante (Chapter 11) as well as its correlation to the sovereign credit risk. Fortunately, this problem (that occupied many pages of the first edition) does not exist for USD ASW versus SOFR anymore, which do not involve the secured–unsecured basis. The remaining non-credit-related elements in the USD ASW are mainly the specialness and haircut financing costs, which are easier to estimate (Chapters 12 and 18). Seen from this perspective, the transition from LIBOR to SOFR has been a big step toward the arbitrage equality.
- Regarding the adjustment of CDS, on the other hand, the problems mentioned in Chapter 13 remain: Given the low number of observations, the estimation of the DO and FX component in a CDS is subject to a significant error.

In the current situation, extracting the pure credit information from SOFR swap spreads seems already feasible (in case of a sufficient database for repo specialness), while the estimations adjusting CDS quotes are still in a wide range. In case this range can be sufficiently narrowed due to more future observations, also the second hurdle toward the arbitrage equality can be taken.

ARBITRAGE INEQUALITY BETWEEN USD ASW AND CDS

While exact quantifications of the DO and FX component in the CDS remain difficult, the qualitative statement that both of them should be positive is much easier:

- The statement DO $\geq$ 0 is a mathematical truth as no option can have a negative value.
- By contrast, the statement FX component $\geq$ 0 requires the economic assumption that the currency of a defaulting country weakens. Unlike the DO, the FX component is not an option, but a short position in the FX rate of a defaulting country conditional on a default and therefore exposed to both a weakening and a strengthening.

With these two statements, *adjusted CDS $\leq$ CDS* holds true, and thus it is easy to derive from the arbitrage equality

Adjusted CDS extracted from USD ASW = Adjusted CDS extracted from CDS quotes

the arbitrage inequality

Adjusted CDS extracted from USD ASW $\leq$ CDS quotes (unadjusted, market observed).

Turning to the left side of the equation, we have modeled the SOFR–ASW by adding the expected specialness (a non-positive number) and the haircut costs (a non-negative number) to the pure credit element captured by the adjusted CDS. In case of no specialness and haircuts, the approximation *Adjusted CDS $\approx$ USD SOFR–ASW* might be acceptable for SOFR–ASW.[8] in which case the arbitrage inequality simplifies to

USD ASW (unadjusted, market observed) $\leq$ CDS (unadjusted, market observed),

i.e. two market observed variables without any risk of misestimation or model errors.

By sacrificing one side of the equation (and making some assumptions), one can thereby get rid of any dependency on models, observation and estimation problems and obtain a relationship between traded variables. The ability to execute the arbitrage inequality directly in the market contributes to

---

[8]Unlike for LIBOR–ASW, which still contain the secured–unsecured basis. This should be kept in mind for the historical case studies below.

its 'hardness' and explains its importance observed in the case studies below. Among the multitude of complex relationships between many variables, it also provides a clear and hard boundary. Finally, it thereby reinforces the links between asset, basis and credit default swaps described in the previous chapters via fair value models with model-independent arbitrage flows.

Dealing with the arbitrage inequality has a few practical implications:

- The inequality allows arbitrage trades only if the USD ASW exceeds the CDS (i.e. only long asset&basis swapped bonds and long CDS positions).
- It therefore avoids the pitfalls of relying too much on the arbitrage equality in the presence of estimation risk, for example, the dangers of reverse asset&basis swapping bonds and selling CDS protection when the USD ASW is slightly below the adjusted CDS.
- Being long an asset&basis swapped bond and long the CDS is also the more attractive side for a number of practical reasons. In particular, in the event that an issuer nears default, repo markets may well cease to function altogether, which could make it simply impracticable to maintain a short position in the reverse asset&basis swapped bond versus a short position in the CDS. Moreover, on this side of the trade we do not need to worry about the bond becoming special in repo, being short a delivery option, or the FX component.
- On the other hand, the replacement of quantitative adjustments by qualitative assumptions weakens the sharpness of the arbitrage relationship. It is therefore probable that quite a number of violations of the arbitrage equality do not show up as violations of the weaker inequality between the traded instruments. As a result, some theoretical arbitrage opportunities cannot be executed in practice.
- One can improve the inequality by including a quantification for the SOFR–repo basis swap and the haircut, i.e. by refraining from the simplifications on the left side.
- In the conceptual discussion above, we have excluded coupon effects and technical issues (such as counterparty risk or liquidity). Thus, while the arbitrage inequality suggests that the CDS basis should always be positive, it is possible that there are negative bases due to coupon or technical effects not covered here.
- Given the capital charge for holding bonds, CCBS and CDS, sufficient availability of capital for arbitrage trades is a condition for the arbitrage inequality to be imposed on the market. In the presence of balance sheet constraints, violations of the arbitrage inequality (negative CDS bases) can be quite high and persist for some time. Actually, the extent of these violations is a good proxy for the scarcity of arbitrage capital. This is one topic of Chapter 18.

In order to monitor the market for violations of the arbitrage inequality, we recommend comparing the two spreads graphically against USD SOFR (formerly LIBOR), from asset&basis swapped bonds and from CDS for every issuer. This could be done, for example, by adding the CDS (ask) quotes as a line to the USD ASW levels shown as a function of maturity, as in Figure 16.1. Figure 16.3 provides this picture for Japan.

Note how well the no-arbitrage inequality is observed by the market. The USD ASW of JGBs with short time to maturity follow the upper boundary given by the CDS ask level very closely, while JGBs with a longer time to maturity quote significantly below the CDS ask level. This means that there are currently no trading opportunities for asset&basis swapped JGBs versus the Japanese CDS.[9]

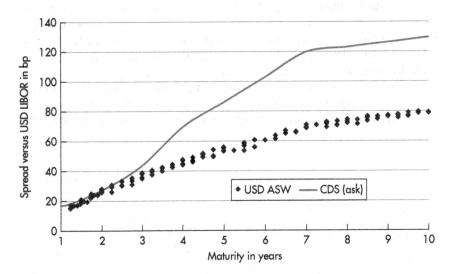

FIGURE 16.3 USD ASW of JGBs versus the Japanese CDS of the same maturity as the bonds.
Sources: data – Bloomberg; chart – Authors.

Data period: "Current" market data as of 23 Sep 2012.

---

[9]Buying 2Y asset&basis swapped JGBs and 2Y CDS on Japan at a basis of zero could be considered as buying the delivery option and the position on JPY weakening in case of Japan defaulting for free and therefore to be a good idea, though the challenges to estimate the value of this opportunity remain. Also, very short JGBs with time to maturity of less than one year (not shown in the chart) could actually have a USD ASW in excess of the CDS (if it traded for such short maturities.) (See Figure 16.1.) However, there could be special influences from redemptions distorting the ASW level.

In our experience, most of the violations of the no-arbitrage inequality occur in practice due to strong volatility in the CCBS, which can increase the USD ASW faster than the CDS (and faster than local ASW react). As a case study of the way trading opportunities from violations of the no-arbitrage inequality arise and how quickly they perform, we depict the history of the USD ASW of a 10Y Korean government bond versus the 10Y CDS ask level for Korea in Figure 16.4. Following the Lehman crisis, the KRW ASW of Korean government bonds widened, partly due to a general scarcity of risk capital forcing some investors to sell their bond holdings. At the same time, the KRW CCBS became highly negative as Korean banks needed USD funding. On the other hand, while the Korean CDS also widened, it followed a different timing (probably because the credit quality of the Korean government was not directly linked to the trouble in the US banking system). As a result, the USD ASW of Korean government bonds at times greatly exceeded their CDS levels, presenting those investors with risk capital available with arbitrage profits in excess of 100 bp. These precedents illustrate that constant monitoring of USD ASW through charts like Figure 16.3 can be very rewarding.

Figure 16.4 illustrates the frequency and magnitude of these violations of the arbitrage inequality, as well as the time over which these relative misvaluations have tended to correct. In quiet times, however, these opportunities

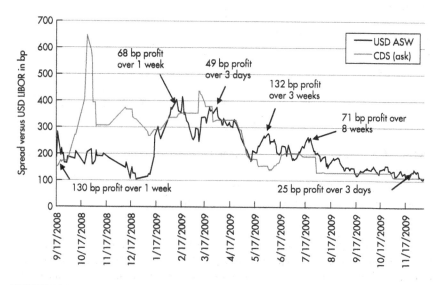

FIGURE 16.4 USD ASW of the Korean government bond 5.75% 09/18 versus the 10Y Korean CDS level.
Sources: data – Bloomberg; chart – Authors.

Data period: 17 Sep 2008 to 9 Dec 2009, trading daily data.

tend to be much rarer and to offer less profit. The shift to quiet times is visible at the right-hand side of the chart when the pricing of Korean bonds against USD LIBOR became closely linked to the Korean CDS level again. Following increasing regulatory and capital constraints, however, the threshold to engage in these arbitrage trades has increased for most market participants during the last few years as explained in Chapter 18.

Summarizing our experience, in comparison with the abundant relative value discovered by a principal component analysis on the CDS universe in Chapter 13, opportunities when the arbitrage inequality is violated arise infrequently. But when they do arise, they are usually good candidates for trades – as long as sufficient arbitrage capital is available. In contrast, bonds whose USD ASW spread is below the CDS are not necessarily candidates for similar trades. This side of the arbitrage would require both a way to quantify the necessary adjustments and an instrument to hedge against currency weakening post default. We have discussed above the difficulties involved. For the same reason, we do not generally recommend spread positions between two USD ASW versus CDS spreads between different maturities[10] or different issuers.[11]

As the arbitrage inequality introduces the addition information of a constraint, it can also support the global asset selection process pictured in Figure 16.1:

- For cases in which the USD ASW trades close to the CDS level, one can conclude that the credit risk (as priced in the CDS market) is fully reflected in the USD ASW level. Given the weakness of the inequality, the USD ASW could actually be too high relative to the CDS level, though it is hard to quantify by how much. Thus, incorporating Figure 16.3 back into the assessment of the USD ASW levels of JGBs from Figure 16.1, we can conclude that, unless the credit quality of Japan (as priced in the CDS market) deteriorates further, the USD ASW levels of 1Y and 2Y JGBs should not continue to increase.
- For cases in which the USD ASW trades considerably below the CDS level, on the other hand, the one-sidedness of the inequality prevents a firm conclusion. The USD ASW level of 79 bp for 10Y JGBs could be fair, too high, or too low compared to the 10Y CDS level of 130 bp.[12]

---

[10]For example, a "curve trade" long (asset&basis swapped) 2Y JGB/long 2Y Japan CDS against a short 7Y JGB (reverse asset&basis swapped)/short 7Y Japan CDS position (see Figure 16.3).
[11]For example, a long (asset&basis swapped) JGB/long Japan CDS against a short US Treasury (reverse asset swapped)/short US CDS position (see Figure 16.1).
[12]While the relative value relationship provides little guidance, we could of course still consult fundamental credit analysis to address this issue.

■ Taking the viewpoint of an investor allocating USD funds to JGBs, Figure 16.3 shows that the USD ASW of 10Y JGBs is still quite far below the CDS level. While we cannot say how far below the CDS level is "fair," we can say that the USD ASW could increase by another 51 bp before the no-arbitrage inequality is violated. By contrast, the credit risk of Japan (as priced into the CDS) is at least fully reflected in the USD ASW of 2Y JGBs. Thus, in the event of stable CDS levels, the downside of basis-swapped 2Y JGBs is significantly smaller than for 10Y JGBs.

THE EQUILIBRIUM BETWEEN ASSET, BASIS, AND CREDIT DEFAULT SWAPS

At the beginning of this chapter, we described the equilibrium between all bond and swap markets globally given by the equation

$$USDASW = \frac{EURASW}{CF} - \frac{CCBS}{CF}$$

We then turned our attention to the arbitrage (in)equality between USD ASW and CDS. Finally, we shall now look at the relationship between both, in other words, at the impact of the arbitrage (in)equality on the equilibrium. Under the assumption *Adjusted CDS ≈ USD ASW*, which might be acceptable in case of SOFR-ASW, the equilibrium equation can be easily expanded to cover four variables (market observations):

$$CDS \geq Adjusted\ CDS \approx USDASW = \frac{EURASW}{CF} - \frac{CCBS}{CF}$$

This combined formula can serve as a guide through the complex relationships between all global bond and swap markets. We have just applied it to complement the asset allocation process based on Figure 16.1 with the CDS line from Figure 16.3 as additional constraint, i.e. information.

We shall now describe how the difference between low-risk and high-risk bonds results in two different equilibria:

■ For low-risk bonds, both the level and the volatility of the CDS are low. Via the arbitrage (in)equality, this translates into rather stable USD ASW. The stability of USD ASW in the equilibrium means that moves and volatility in local ASW are mostly absorbed by moves and volatility in the CCBS and vice versa.

■ For high-risk bonds, both the level and the volatility of the CDS are high. Via the arbitrage (in)equality, this translates into volatile USD ASW. If local ASW are stable, the equilibrium therefore links a volatile CDS and USD ASW with a volatile CCBS.

Based on this insight, we can explain the different relationships between bond and swap markets observed for Bunds and JGBs.

THE EQUILIBRIUM FOR BUNDS (LOW-RISK BONDS)

Because both Treasuries and Bunds are considered to have high credit quality, their CDS is rather low and stable, hence also their SOFR–ASW (see model of Chapter 12). Furthermore, the similar CDS levels for the US and Germany are in line with the fact that Bunds are considered reasonably close substitutes for US Treasuries with about the same safe-haven status. Thus, if the USD ASW of Bunds become too high or too low, either against USD SOFR on an absolute basis or relative to the USD ASW of US Treasuries, investors allocating their funds among low-risk bond markets through a process illustrated in Figure 16.1 usually increase or decrease their Bund holdings. This keeps the USD ASW of Bunds at a comparatively stable level and a comparatively stable spread versus US Treasuries.

The mathematical consequence of the relative stability of USD ASW and CDS of Bunds is that the equilibrium equation

$$USDASW = \frac{EURASW}{CF} - \frac{CCBS}{CF}$$

links a volatile CCBS with a volatile local ASW. In other words, most of the moves on the right-hand side of the equation cancel out, leaving the left-hand side rather constant.

Figure 16.5 shows that this describes the actual market quite well. When Bunds richened considerably in the EUR funding market, a constant CCBS would have led to Bunds quoting through US Treasuries on a USD ASW basis. This situation prompts reallocation flows from Bunds into US Treasuries (in USD) and thus a widening (more negative) of the EUR CCBS. The result is that some of the richness of Bunds in the local funding market is absorbed by the CCBS. In terms of volatility, the CCBS therefore has a moderating impact on the USD ASW, as it absorbs some of the local funding volatility through global investment flows.

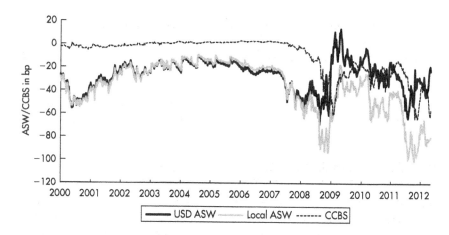

FIGURE 16.5   Local and USD ASW of 5Y Bunds versus the 5Y EUR CCBS.
Sources: data – Bloomberg; chart – Authors.

Data period: 8 Feb 2000 to 12 Jun 2012, weekly data.

THE EQUILIBRIUM IN CASE OF JGBS (RISKY BONDS)

Repeating the same analysis given in Figure 16.5 for Bunds with JGBs returns
a completely different picture in Figure 16.6. Now the local ASW (rather than
the USD ASW) is relatively stable and the USD ASW is a mirror image of the
JPY CCBS. Thus, the same equilibrium equation between the three elements
local ASW, USD ASW, and CCBS works in two different ways:

- In the case of Bunds, the USD ASW has little volatility, shifting most of
  the volatility from the CCBS to the local ASW (and vice versa).
- In the case of JGBs, the local ASW has little volatility, shifting most of the
  volatility from the CCBS to the USD ASW (and vice versa).

In the case of Bunds, the USD ASW is driven by the USD ASW of US Treasuries (Figure 16.1). By contrast, the USD ASW of JGBs is largely determined
by the arbitrage (in)equality to the credit default swap (CDS) for Japan. As
depicted in Figure 16.7, the correlation between the 5Y Japanese CDS and the
USD ASW of 5Y JGBs between 2009 and June 2012 has been 0.78. Thus, the
same widening of the CCBS in EUR and JPY (see Figure 15.3) was accompanied by two different effects:

- In the case of Bunds, a wider (more negative) CCBS correlates with lower
  local ASW (keeping the USD ASW rather stable) (Figure 16.5).

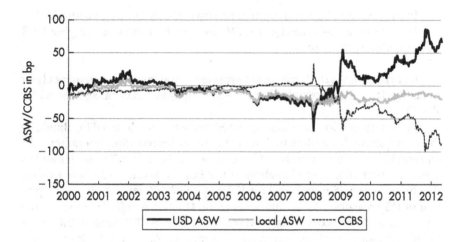

FIGURE 16.6   Local and USD ASW of 5Y JGBs versus the 5Y JPY CCBS.
Sources: data – Bloomberg; chart – Authors.

Data period: 8 Feb 2000 to 12 Jun 2012, weekly data.

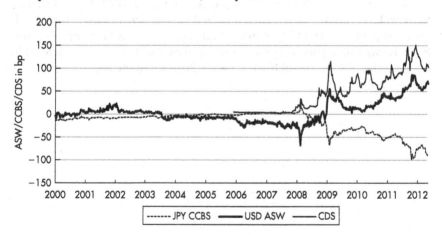

FIGURE 16.7   5Y JPY CCBS versus the USD ASW of 5Y JGBs and the 5Y Japanese CDS.
Sources: data – Bloomberg; chart – Authors.

Data period: 8 Feb 2000 to 12 Jun 2012, weekly data (CDS since 3 Jan 2006).

▪ In the case of JGBs, a wider (more negative) CCBS correlates with a higher USD ASW (keeping the local ASW rather stable) and thus a higher CDS premium (Figure 16.7).

Note that these relationships are symmetric and imply no statement about causality. It is quite possible that a higher Japanese CDS caused the wider JPY CCBS.

The combined formula has explained the behavior observed for Bunds by their similar credit standing to that of US Treasuries resulting in a rather tight and stable spread between the USD ASW of Bunds and US Treasuries and in a strong international participation in the Bund market. It can now explain the different behavior observed for JGBs by their different credit standing to that of US Treasuries. First, this leads to the USD ASW reflecting mainly the credit risk as expressed in a high and volatile Japanese CDS. Second, this limits the international participation in the JGB market. And with the JGB market remaining firmly in the hands of domestic investors, for whom the USD ASW may well be of little importance, there is no significant impact of the external factors USD ASW and CCBS on the local ASW and domestic funding conditions of JGBs. Hence, the same reason which makes USD ASW volatile tends to make local funding costs rather stable. And with local funding rates tending to be stable, the volatility of the CDS-driven USD ASW is mainly absorbed by CCBS volatility. This also provides a causal explanation for the relationship between the JPY CCBS and the USD ASW depicted in the regression chart in Figure 15.1.

CHAPTER 17

Global Bond RV Via Fitted Curves and Via SOFR Asset Swap Spreads

INTRODUCTION

Chapter 16 has established the spread versus USD SOFR of asset&basis swapped bonds as universal yardstick, which expresses every bond globally in a single number, i.e. its SOFR–ASW. That chapter then went on to compare how one given bond is priced versus SOFR with the CDS of its issuer. This chapter will compare how different bonds are priced versus SOFR.

In fact, the SOFR–ASW seems to be an obvious choice to compare the richness/cheapness of all bonds worldwide: It is both a *universal* measure applicable to all bonds via asset&basis swapping and the *relevant* measure for global asset allocation decisions illustrated in Figure 16.1.

By contrast, LIBOR–ASW suffer from a number of deficiencies: due to the discrepancy between the LIBOR-swap curve and the bond yield curve, they are not suitable for comparing the relative richness/cheapness of different bonds.

The transition from LIBOR to SOFR, which has generally led to the convergence of future, swap and bond markets shown in Figure 12.3, resulted in a closer proximity between the SOFR-swap curve and the bond yield curve, hence in a better suitability of SOFR–ASW as a global RV indicator. At the core of this welcome development is the fact that the switch from LIBOR (and OIS) to SOFR eliminated the unsecured–secured basis from swap spreads. This offers the benefit of SOFR-swap spread models not depending on the unobservable cost of capital (Chapter 11) and hence an easy way to take the first hurdle toward the arbitrage equality by adjusting the swap spreads to reflect credit risk only (Chapter 16). And this chapter will exploit that the elimination of the unsecured–secured basis from swap spreads led to a convergence of swap and bond yield curves and therefore to an alleviation of the deficiencies of swap spreads as RV indicators.

However, in case swap and bond yield curves are not identical, there remain some problems in applying swap spreads as rich/cheap measures.

For SOFR–ASW, most of the differences do not arise also from the unsecured–secured basis anymore, but only from the default risk of the bond, which typically increases with its maturity. If this difference is high, i.e. in case of riskier bond issuers, the difference between swap and bond yield curves can be minimized by using risk-free bond yields, as described in Chapter 13. Then, global bond RV can be assessed via the SOFR–ASW of asset&basis swapped risk-free bond yields, i.e. by using the bond yield minus the adjusted CDS as input variable.

If USD SOFR is used as a reference rate and a yardstick for comparisons, the par asset swap spreads of asset&basis swapped bonds (if necessary after subtracting the adjusted CDS) are natural, relevant, and universal rich/cheap indicators. In this case, there exists therefore an alternative to using fitted curves for assessing the RV between different bonds – which offers the additional benefit of assessing the RV of every bond also versus the CDS, as described in Chapter 16. We therefore transfer the method of external explanatory variables developed for fitted curves (Chapter 8) to this alternative. On the other hand, the same transition from LIBOR to SOFR, which has alleviated the deficiencies of swap spreads as rich/cheap measures has also caused a structural break in the time series of swap spreads. Thus, while fitted curve models may be replaced by SOFR–ASW as RV indicators for Treasuries and all bonds globally swapped into USD, they are of particular importance to create long-term time series for yields (e.g. constant maturity par rates of US Treasuries) as input data for analysis.

If a reference rate other than SOFR is used as a yardstick, the deficiencies of swap spreads as RV indicators are so large that fitted curves remain the only suitable choice for rich/cheap comparisons of individual bonds.[1] This also applies when all bonds are to be compared in a different currency than USD, for example, assessed from the perspective of a EUR-based investor. In this case, every bond should be asset&basis swapped into a note with fixed EUR payments and then be used as input into a fitted curve model (rather than being assessed by its spread to EURIBOR or ESTR).

In summary, there are two suitable alternatives to assess the RV between global bonds:

- For any currency, all bonds can be expressed via a combination of asset&basis swaps as a fixed rate in that currency. Then, the fitted curve model from Chapter 8 can be applied to evaluate the relative pricing between all bonds involved.

---

[1] On the other hand, in countries without transition, there could exist long-term time series of swaps (e.g. with EURIBOR as the reference rate) without structural breaks, hence an alternative to using constant maturity government yields from a fitted curve model as input data.

- For USD, the SOFR–ASW of all bonds can be calculated and used as a global RV indicator (potentially after some adjustments).

This chapter first demonstrates the reasons behind this statement before providing detailed examples for both alternatives.

SOFR SWAP SPREADS AS A GLOBAL RELATIVE VALUE INDICATOR FOR BONDS

A later section of this chapter will demonstrate that the suitability of par asset swap spreads as a RV indicator depends on the proximity of the bond and swap yield curves. Due to the convergence of both yield curves following the transition to SOFR, par SOFR–ASW can therefore be considered to be a good candidate for assessing the richness and cheapness between different bonds – which can be extended to cover all markets via the CCBS.

Taking a closer look at this idea, recall the formula from Chapter 12:

SOFR–ASW = repo–SOFR basis swap + adjusted CDS.

Thus, the discrepancy between SOFR-swap and bond yield curves would be minimal, if the repo–SOFR basis swap (as well as the haircut financing costs not included in the formula) and the adjusted CDS were zero. In that case, the SOFR–ASW would reflect only the richness and cheapness of a given bond such as being caused by ephemeral flows, not by structural factors such as the credit quality – and hence be an ideal RV indicator indeed.

In order to approach this ideal, we therefore need to eliminate the remaining structural factors from the SOFR–ASW, just as the transition from LIBOR to SOFR has already eliminated the unsecured–secured basis. Using the formula above, we can split this task into two components:

- Bond-specific factors such as the specialness ($\approx$ repo–SOFR basis swap) and other elements not included in the formula above (haircut financing costs, benchmark status, etc.) can be captured via external explanatory variables, as explained in Chapter 8. This corresponds to transferring the technique of adjusting the rich/cheap indicator for structural factors (such as being deliverable) from the fitted curves to SOFR–ASW. And since specialness is one possible external explanatory variable, this approach is suitable to eliminate the repo–SOFR basis swap from the SOFR–ASW. In practical terms, the same multiple regression against a number of external explanatory variables from Chapter 8 can be applied to SOFR–ASW; while the key trick in case of fitted curves consisted in executing this regression simultaneously with the curve fitting, this is not required for SOFR–ASW anymore since the curve is already given.

■ The issuer-specific factor of credit risk remains a source of discrepancy between swap and bond yield curves even after the transition to SOFR. As in the formula above, it can be captured via the adjusted CDS and eliminated from SOFR–ASW by using bond yields minus the adjusted CDS as input variables. This corresponds to comparing bonds on the basis of their risk-free yield, as described in Chapter 13. Since the purpose is analytic, calculating risk-free yields by subtracting the adjusted CDS (not the full CDS quotes observed in the market) seems to be preferable.

For most bonds of issuers with high credit quality, one often finds that both structural factors are rather small: only a few bonds have significant specialness and the (adjusted) CDS for the US or Germany are at times (though not always) below 10 bp. In these situations, one may decide that the benefits of eliminating these factors are in practice not worth the effort. However, as the credit risk increases, so does the difference between swap and bond yield curves and hence also the importance of its elimination. This is particularly the case when including bonds of issuers with a higher default risk in the global RV comparison. And since the CDS tends to increase with the maturity, it is also the precondition for meaningful comparisons of the RV between bonds of different maturities: while the cheapest 2Y Treasury may be identified by simply looking at the SOFR–ASW, when comparing individual 2Y with 10Y Treasuries, the higher default risk of the US over 10Y should be included. It therefore seems advisable to generally base the rich/cheap analysis on SOFR–ASW with eliminated structural factors.

PROBLEMS WITH THE USE OF SWAP SPREADS AS RELATIVE VALUE INDICATOR FOR BONDS

The main objective of this section is the demonstration of the statement above that the difference between swap and bond yield curves causes deficiencies of swap spreads as rich/cheap measures. Simultaneously, different categories of swap spreads are briefly introduced and some outstanding technical points (such as bonds trading away from par, which have been abstracted in the conceptual discussion of the previous chapters), are addressed.

Interpolated Swap Spreads

Some investors are concerned that the comparison of the bonds via par asset swaps is complicated by the fact that the two par asset swaps involve up-front payments of different sizes by the swap dealer. For example, if a 5% issue is trading at par, no up-front payment will be required, while a 10% issue is likely to involve a substantial up-front payment from the dealer.

In order to mitigate any problems that might result from these differing up-front payments, some investors prefer to compare the yield of a bond to the par swap rate with the same maturity as the bond. This difference generally is referred to as the interpolated swap spread, since the maturity of the bond is unlikely to fall on a yearly swap point quoted in the market, and therefore the corresponding swap rate will need to be interpolated. In the example above, let's assume the yield of the 10% bond is 4.98%, the yield of the 5% bond is 5%, and the swap rate with the same maturity as these bonds is 5.35%. In this case, the interpolated swap spreads of the 10% and 5% bonds are −37 bp and −35 bp, and the 10% issue appears to be the richer of the two issues.

Notice in this example that we could have reached the conclusion that the 10% issue is richer than the 5% issue simply by comparing their yields, since the two bonds in this example are assumed to have the same maturity dates. Of course, this would not be the case more generally.

The problem with the interpolated swap spread as a relative value indicator for bonds is the easiest to identify, so we start with this case. In the example of the 5% and 10% bonds above, let's assume the yield curve is upward-sloping. Let's also assume that both bonds are fairly valued to the government bond curve. For example, this would be the case if these two bonds, which we assume to have identical maturity dates, were strippable and there was no reconstitution arbitrage, even under the assumption of zero bid/ask spreads for the bonds and their strips.

Under these assumptions, it can be shown mathematically that the 10% bond has to have a lower yield than the 5% bond. Intuitively, this result is due to the fact that the 10% issue has more of its cash flows discounted at relatively lower rates, since it has the greater coupon. As a result, the 10% bond has to have the wider interpolated swap spread. In this case, it will always appear to be the richer bond, according to the interpolated swap spread, even though both bonds are fairly valued in this example by construction. As this simple example demonstrates, the interpolated swap spread is a fundamentally flawed measure of relative value between two bonds.

Par Asset Swap Spreads

The par asset swap spread seems both to address the problem of matching the principal cash-flows in the CCBS via the up-front payment as described below and to be an ideal measure of relative value between bonds: since the bond with the more negative par asset swap spread will pay the investor less for the same initial investment, it should be viewed as the richer bond. For example, consider again two bonds with identical maturity dates but with different coupons, say, 5% and 10%. If the 10% issue is trading at a par asset swap at LIBOR −40 basis points (bp) and the 5% bond is trading at a par asset swap spread of LIBOR −35 bp, the 10% bond would appear to be the richer bond. For the same initial investment of USD 100, the payoff of the 10% bond is lower than that of the 5% bond. The clean structure of the par asset swap spread makes such comparisons relatively straightforward.

The par asset swap is a cash-flow matched structure. As a result, the par asset swap spread doesn't suffer from the same defect as the interpolated swap spread. However, it does suffer from a more subtle problem relating to the coupon, which can be seen by conducting a thought experiment. Let's start the experiment by assuming the 5% bond has a perfectly fair value, in the sense that there is no reconstitution arbitrage between it and the strips in the market, even assuming zero bid/ask spreads. Now let's increase the coupon of the 5% bond incrementally, until it becomes a 10% bond, and let's assume that the bond continues to have a perfectly fair value to the strips throughout the experiment. We'll watch the behavior of the par asset swap spread as the coupon of the bond is increased.

When the coupon of the bond is increased by 10 bp, from 5% to 5.10%, the price of the bond also increases. Let's assume the bond price increases by 70 cents, from 100.00 to 100.70. In order to see the impact, if any, on the par asset swap spread, let's review the way this spread is calculated. The par asset swap spread is calculated by discounting the cash-flows of the bond to determine a present value for the bond using the swap curve as the source of the discount rates. Let's call this present value the bond's "swap curve present value". The par asset swap spread is the size of an annuity that has the same present value as the difference between the bond's market price and its swap curve present value.

If the term structure of swap rates is uniformly greater than the term structure of government bond yields, a bond's market price will increase by more than a bond's swap curve present value as we increase the coupon of the bond, since the swap curve will involve higher discount rates and lower discount factors than will the government bond curve. In our example, the bond price increased by 70 cents when we added 10 bp to the coupon, but the swap curve present value would increase by a lesser amount, say, 65 cents. As a result, the difference between the market price of the bond and its swap curve present value increased by 5 cents. Therefore, the present value of the par asset swap spread as an annuity must increase by 5 cents. Since the swap curve doesn't change in this example, the only way for this present value to change is for the size of the par asset swap spread to increase. In other words, increasing a bond's coupon will increase its par asset swap spread, even if the bond is assumed to have a perfectly fair value as measured by the government bond curve. The necessary conclusion from this example is that two fairly valued bonds almost always will have different par asset swap spreads if they have different coupons, even if they have the same maturity date. Note that this coupon effect is not the same as the coupon effect we discussed above. The "yield" coupon effect is not an issue when the yield curve is flat, but this "par asset swap spread" coupon effect is an issue even if the yield curve is flat. The only time this par asset swap spread coupon effect isn't an issue is when the swap curve is identical to the government bond curve.

And, in fact, with the transition from LIBOR to SOFR eliminating the unsecured–secured basis as one major source of differences between swap and bond yields and the remaining sources can be relatively easily addressed by the methods described above, SOFR–ASW comes close to the ideal situation of identical swap and government bond curves. Thus, par asset swaps spreads with SOFR as reference rate (and with the modifications described above) represent suitable RV indicators, reflecting only ephemeral imbalances from flows rather than structural factors. By contrast, par asset swap spreads against a different reference rate (e.g. EURIBOR) suffer from the difference between the swap and bond yield curve including the unsecured basis.

In summary, par asset swap spreads are more useful as rich/cheap indicators when the swap curve and the bond curve are closer to one another. With SOFR as the reference rate, the proximity is usually sufficient or can be made sufficient by the techniques described above; for other reference rates, the distance remains too large to use par asset swap spreads as a suitable RV measure.

Full Asset Swap Spreads

While some investors use the interpolated swap spread to mitigate possible difficulties with the par asset swap spread, other investors will use the full asset swap spread. Like the interpolated swap spread, the full asset swap spread involves no up-front payments. Like the par asset swap, the full asset swap is a cash-flow matched structure (i.e. the fixed cash-flow dates and amounts in the swap are identical to the coupon dates and the coupon size of the bond).

To see that the full asset swap spread suffers from a similar defect (in case of a difference between swap and bond yield curves) to the par asset swap spread, recall that the full asset swap spread is equal to the par asset swap spread multiplied by par and divided by the dirty price of the bond.[2] As basis points are added to the bond's coupon, the par asset swap spread increases by a constant amount per basis point. The full asset swap can only remain unchanged in the thought experiment above if the change from par asset swap spread to full asset swap spread involved the par asset swap spread decreasing by the same constant amount per basis point. Since this is not the case, the full asset swap spread also changes as basis points are added to the bond's coupon in case of the swap curve not matching the bond yield curve.

Zero-Coupon Asset Swap Spreads

So far, we've focused on coupon effects as the sources of concern in using swap spreads for relative value comparisons between bonds. Since zero-coupon bonds are free from such problems, it's worth considering whether the relative

---

[2]The dirty price is the clean price plus accrued interest.

values between zero-coupon bonds can be determined by comparisons to the swap curve. For example, let's assume we have two zero-coupon government bonds, a 10-year (10Y) bond with a −50 bp swap spread and a 9Y bond with a −45 bp swap spread, assuming each swap spread is computed as the difference between the bond's yield and the zero-coupon rate with the same maturity as the bond calculated using the swap curve. Would we be justified in claiming the 10Y zero-coupon bond was rich to the 9Y bond?

In case of using non-SOFR swap spreads such as LIBOR–ASW, the answer is an unequivocal no, again due to the inclusion of the unsecured–secured basis. As we saw in Chapter 11, the fair LIBOR–ASW is a function of expected LIBOR–repo spreads, and there will be a presumed forward LIBOR–repo spread that will cause both the 9Y and the 10Y swap spreads to appear to be fair value. The only time at which we might be tempted to use the relative swap spreads as a guide to valuation is if the forward LIBOR–repo spread was negative (i.e. the forward repo rate was greater than the forward LIBOR). Unless there are special circumstances involved, such as different tax treatments or leverage constraints (see Chapter 18), the unsecured LIBOR should never be less than the secured repo rate and the LIBOR–repo spread should never be negative, even on a forward basis.

Another problem with this approach is that the spread between LIBOR and the repo rate should be a function of the level of interest rates. Even if the default probability implied by LIBOR remained the same, the LIBOR–repo spread would be expected to increase as the level of the repo rate increases, as discussed in Chapter 11.

If the 1Y rate nine years forward is higher than the present-value weighted averages of the first nine 1Y forward rates along the curve, then the fair 1Y LIBOR–repo spread nine years forward will also be larger than the first nine 1Y LIBOR–repo spreads along the curve. In this case, the fair zero-coupon swap spread for a 10Y bond will be greater than the fair zero-coupon swap spread for a 9Y bond. From this example, we see that a simple, unadjusted comparison of zero-coupon swap spreads versus LIBOR is inappropriate to assess the relative values between zero-coupon bonds.

CONCLUSION

The larger the discrepancy between swap and bond yield curves, the less suitable swap spreads are as RV indicators.

The transition from LIBOR to SOFR has eliminated the unsecured–secured basis as one source of discrepancy between swap and bond yield curves. The remaining sources can be relatively easily eliminated as well (and are usually of a smaller size). Hence, par asset swap spreads versus SOFR are a suitable RV indicator if used following the approach outlined above.

On the other hand, non-SOFR–ASW incorporates the unsecured–secured basis, which cannot easily be eliminated due to it depending on the variable cost of capital, which is unobservable ex ante. Hence, it seems impossible to obtain a suitable RV indicator from LIBOR–ASW or OIS–ASW. This may appear to be a rather strong conclusion given that many analysts have applied and still apply LIBOR–ASW as RV indicators, but is nevertheless a necessary conclusion.

This conclusion also means, that in all currencies apart from USD there exist no swap spreads (see Table 11.1) as a suitable alternative to rich/cheap assessments via fitted curves, as outlined in Chapter 8. If the RV of global bonds shall be compared not in USD but in another currency, it therefore also needs to be done via fitted curves (rather than via swap spreads). For example, if a EUR-based investor wants to select the cheapest bond in the 5Y sector between Bunds and Treasuries, he needs to compare both via a fitted curve model. The precondition for being able to do so is to asset&basis swap the Treasury into a bond with *fixed* EUR cash flows (coupons), just like the Bunds. When comparing all bonds in USD, their SOFR–ASW, i.e. their spread versus a floating rate, can be used; when comparing all bonds in another currency, their fixed rate needs to be calculated as input variable for a fitted curve model.

The next two sections describe the technicalities of both alternatives for assessing relative value between government bonds in different currencies.

Rich/Cheap Analysis through Fitted Curves for Bonds Denominated in Different Currencies

The general approach is straightforward, consisting of three main steps:

1. Express all bonds as fixed rate cash-flows in the same currency, using asset swaps, ICBS, and CCBS as needed.
2. Fit a benchmark yield curve.
3. Calculate the extent to which bonds are rich or cheap relative to this benchmark fitted yield curve.

Turning to the details of the first step, the key is to ensure matching cash-flows between all the transactions, specifically:

- The notional of the CCBS is set to equal the principal at maturity. As the dirty price of the bond is usually not equal to 100, the CCBS should be connected with a *par* asset swap, whose up-front payment equals the difference between the dirty price and par. One can think of buying the bond and par asset swapping it in local currency first and then subject the whole package to a CCBS transaction. In this way, one conceptually deals with a principal cash-flow of 100 both at the start and at the end of the CCBS.

- The different swaps involved should have the same settlement conventions.[3] For example, if the asset swap used T+0 and the CCBS T+2, the 2-day mismatch would result in unwanted exposure. At the time of writing (October 2023), it seems feasible (even standard in most currencies) to use the convention T+2 for all asset&basis swaps involved.

Let's consider the example of swapping the US Treasury 3.375% maturing on May 15, 2033 into a fixed note with GBP cash-flows, using market prices from October 17, 2023 and taking the perspective of a GBP-based investor, who wants to generate GBP cash-flows with credit exposure to the US government:

Step 1.1: Buy the US Treasury and par asset swap it (all in USD). With a clean price of USD 88.94 and accrued interest of 1.43, the dirty price is USD 90.37. Enter into a pay fixed/receive floating par asset swap, i.e. agree to pay the semi-annual coupons 3.375/2 every May 17 and Nov 17 up to and including May 17, 2033 (assuming T+2) and the upfront payment of USD $100 - 90.37 = 9.63$, versus receiving SOFR plus 30 bp (the par asset swap spread) every May 17 up to and including May 17, 2033 (again, assuming T+2). Note that the convention is to add the swap spread to the *compounded* SOFR, not to the daily SOFR rates before compounding. After canceling out the matching cash-flows, you have to pay USD 100 at settlement versus receiving USD 100 at maturity plus 2 days and will receive USD SOFR plus 30 bp every May 17. Hence, the combination of the bond with a par asset swap results in cash-flows, which can be easily combined with a CCBS in the next step.

Step 1.2: Convert the USD into GBP cash flows via a CCBS. Using the current exchange rate of 1.22, you agree to pay GBP 81.97 versus receiving USD 100 at settlement and to pay USD 100 versus receiving GBP 81.97 on May 17, 2033 (using T+2 also in the CCBS). On every May 17, you pay USD SOFR versus receiving GBP SONIA −19 bp (−19 bp being the current quote for the 10Y SOFR–SONIA CCBS). As a result of these transactions, apart from the principal (GBP 81.97) at settlement and maturity plus two days, you receive every year GBP SONIA −19 bp and the USD par asset swap spread 30 bp, which is left after the USD SOFR cancels out. Converting these 30 bp from USD into GBP is done by multiplying with the conversion factor (the quotient of the basis point values in USD and GBP, see Chapter 16), which is currently almost 1 due to the proximity of the SOFR and SONIA yield curves. Hence, together with the CCBS spread, the yearly payment to you is SONIA + 11 bp. At this stage, you only deal with GBP cash-flows anymore; in fact, you have bought now a notional of GBP 81.97 of a synthetic 10Y floating rate note paying SONIA + 11 bp every May 17 issued by the US government.

---

[3]See Chapter 3 of Huggins and Schaller (2022), for more details.

Step 1.3: Reverse asset swap floating into fixed GBP. Staying in the GBP universe, agree to pay SONIA + 11 bp every May 17 versus receiving GBP 2.23 every May 17 and Nov 17 until May 17, 2023. Hence, you are now invested into a notional of GBP 81.97 of a synthetic 10Y US Treasury bond paying you a 4.46% semi-annual coupon in GBP.

This exercise in cash-flow matching allows you to transform every bond into any currency desired. In the example above, a US Treasury with a yield of 4.83% in USD has transmogrified into a synthetic bond with a yield of 4.46% in GBP.

Once the desired subset of the global bond market has been expressed in the desired currency, in a second step, the fitted curve model from Chapter 8 can be applied. A key decision is which bonds to include in the optimization, i.e. the extent of the set *Bonds* in the formula from Chapter 8. For example, if Bunds are to be compared with US Treasuries on a EUR basis, one could either fit the curve through Bunds only or through Bunds *and* basis swapped Treasuries simultaneously. In the first case, one uses the *local* yardstick from and for Bunds also as the *global* yardstick; in the latter case, one obtains a truly *global* yardstick by also including the information from other bond markets in the optimization.

Figure 17.1 shows the richness and cheapness of bonds swapped into EUR (with annual coupon payments) as of October 17, 2023, including only Bunds in the optimization and using no external explanatory variables. This corresponds to looking at global bond markets from the perspective of Bunds and hence of an investor in Bunds who wants to compare them with other alternatives: all bonds are asset&basis swapped into Bund-like bonds, paying annual coupons in EUR, and are priced versus the discount factor curve fitted through Bunds.

Highlighting a few observations:

- For short maturities, USTs, Gilts, and Bunds are mixed, i.e. differentiated more by other factors (such as repo specialness) rather than issuer. As the time to maturity increases, issuer-specific factors become increasingly influential and correspondingly the differentiation by issuer becomes more visible. For 1Y bonds, the default risk is almost negligible, supporting the pricing of USTs, Gilts, and Bunds versus each other. For 5Y bonds, by contrast, both the default risk and haircut schedule result in a differentiation by issuers.
- In all maturity segments, some US Treasuries offer a significant pick-up over Bunds. Hence, if an investor in Bunds is indifferent about the credit difference between the US and Germany (and the haircut differences),

he can obtain about 20 bp more yield by investing in synthetic EUR Treasuries rather than Bunds in the 1Y sector and about 45 bp in the 5Y segment.

■ Within US Treasuries, there are several obvious outliers. Some of these are due to their benchmark status and repo specialness, and their spread could be adjusted by the technique of external explanatory variables. Others represent genuine richness and cheapness, i.e. candidates for trades. At the short end of the yield curve, micro bond switches between USTs and Bunds seem practicable, as the pricing of USTs and Bunds versus each other in that sector supports the convergence.

In the third step, one can now apply all the techniques derived in Chapter 8 also to relative value analysis between bonds issued in different currencies. In particular, one can add external explanatory variables to the optimization. For example, based on the results of Figure 17.1, it seems reasonable to include short maturity USTs, Gilts, and Bunds in the set *Bonds* and to calculate *global* external explanatory variables, such as a *global* benchmark premium. Incorporating this result into the global asset allocation decisions between short maturity USTs, Gilts, and Bunds, it is possible to select the cheapest and richest bonds while taking into account the usual richness of benchmarks, as explained in Chapter 8.

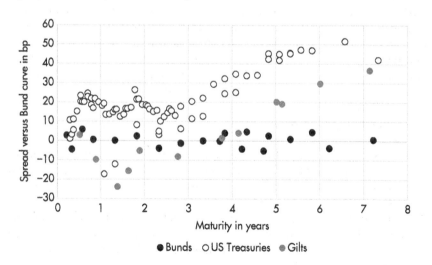

FIGURE 17.1 Richness and cheapness of global bonds swapped into EUR versus the fitted Bund yield curve.
Source: Authors.

Rich/Cheap Analysis through SOFR Spreads for Bonds Denominated in Different Currencies

Based on the arguments above, one can consider the par asset swap spreads of bonds denominated in or basis swapped into USD as alternative rich/cheap indicators (potentially after some adjustments). When using this alternative, step 1.3, i.e. the reverse asset swapping of floating (SOFR) into fixed payments, is skipped. Also the second step, i.e. the calculation of a fitted curve, is omitted and the spreads of the basis swapped bonds over USD SOFR are directly used as a global rich/cheap measure. In this case, the asset allocation decisions in step 3 are based on the (adjusted) SOFR asset swap spreads of basis swapped bonds.

Whereas the fitted curve (step 2) is not needed, the regression approach from Chapter 8 can be transferred to obtain external explanatory variables. In other words, when replacing the fitted curve with SOFR spreads as a rich/cheap measure, from our innovation to obtain the fitted curve and the external explanatory variables in one single optimization, only the regression versus external explanatory variables is left. One can then run a multiple regression of the SOFR spreads versus a number of external explanatory variables, such as benchmark status, and thereby obtain a *global* estimate for the benchmark premium also in this alternative. Moreover, the desired adjustment of bond yields for specialness effects described above can be incorporated into this regression framework.

Figure 17.2 depicts the perspective on global bond RV using the second alternative, also as of October 17, 2023.

Several observations can be explained by the theory presented in the previous (and next) chapters:

- The overall upward-sloping curves are in line with the upward-sloping CDS curves and haircut schedules, as discussed in Chapter 12. And the exceptionally steep haircut schedule of the BoE (Table 18.2) contributes to Gilts having the steepest SOFR–ASW curve.
- The ordering of 5Y Bunds < Gilts < Treasuries from rich to cheap is at least qualitatively in line with the levels of the 5Y CDS on the issuing governments. Quantitatively, however, the actual difference between SOFR spreads exceeds in longer maturity segments the difference predicted by the adjusted CDS levels. A portion of the remaining difference can be explained by the different haircuts. As concluded in Chapter 12 (Figure 12.4), incorporating haircuts is thus also an important element for modeling the relationships between global swap spreads.
- In comparison with the historical situation depicted in Figure 16.1, US Treasuries and Bunds seem to have changed places. This can also be

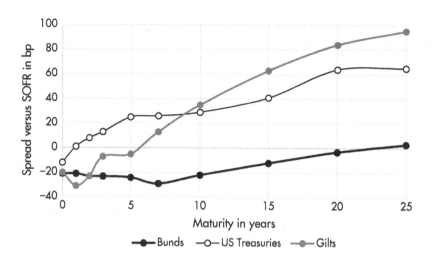

FIGURE 17.2   SOFR–ASW curves of global (basis swapped) bonds.
Source: Authors.

explained by the increasing CDS level of the US (which hardly traded
at all in 2012 and if it did at very low levels) relative to Germany over
the last decade. Despite the switch, the connection via investment
arbitrage between both remains strong and hence the consequences for
the equilibrium discussed in Chapter 16 still hold true.

■ While the models explain a certain "fair" richness for Bunds due to the
relatively low CDS level of Germany and the haircut schedules, in longer
maturity segments, Bunds appear excessively rich. This points to additional driving factors not captured in the models, such as supply/demand
imbalances. If these are deemed to be ephemeral, one could position for
the excessive richness of Bunds to revert to the "fair" richness of Bunds as
justified by the CDS, etc. This could be done by selling Bunds versus buying Treasuries or Gilts, both versus SOFR. The selection of specific bonds
is supported by the rich/cheap numbers from Figure 17.1, or alternatively
by using the SOFR spreads of the individual bonds directly.

Chapter 18 will deal with these remaining influencing factors, some of
which are unobservable, such as the shadow costs of the marginal market participant. As a consequence, understanding and predicting the SOFR spreads
observed in Figure 17.2 form a goal which allows only partial and approximative solutions.

Other Factors Affecting Swap Spreads

INTRODUCTION

In previous chapters, we discussed the relative valuations of swaps and bonds by applying no-arbitrage pricing considerations under the simplifying assumptions that there are no material market frictions and that market participants operate without any material binding constraints. In this chapter, we consider the effects of relaxing these assumptions. We start by considering the effects of haircuts applied to bonds and the related margins applied to swaps. We then discuss the effects of regulatory constraints that have been introduced in various jurisdictions. With these constraints in mind, we then turn our attention to the effects that the changing supply of bonds can have on relative valuations and close the chapter by discussing the implications that these issues present for relative value analysis of bonds and swaps.

HAIRCUTS AND MARGINS

The term *haircut* refers to the difference between the market value of the collateral posted in a repo transaction and the amount of cash that the lender is willing to lend against this collateral. For example, if I post US Treasuries with a market value of USD 100 million as collateral in a repo transaction, my repo counterparty might be willing to lend me USD 95 million against this collateral. If I were buying these bonds, I'd need to obtain the USD 5 million difference with some other source of funds. And the cost of these additional funds needs to be included in any relative value analysis involving the bonds. For example, if my source for these additional funds was my reserve balance at the Federal Reserve, the cost of these additional funds would be the Fed's Interest on Reserve Balances (IORB) rate, currently (October 2023) 5.40%, fairly close to the current value of SOFR, 5.30%. On the other hand, if the source of additional funds was equity capital, the cost of the additional funds would be significantly higher. For reference, the biggest banks in the US recently have been reporting costs of equity in the region of 10%.

321

So the effect of a haircut depends on the size of the haircut and on the cost of the funds that are used to replace the haircut.

Haircuts vary as a function of the maturity and credit quality of the bonds posted as collateral. For example, if one posts EUR 100 million of 5Y German Bunds as collateral in a repo transaction with the ECB, the ECB will currently lend EUR 98.5 million against that collateral. But if one posts EUR 100 million of 30Y Bunds as collateral, the ECB will lend only EUR 95 million. And if one posts 30Y Italian BTPs as collateral, the ECB will lend only EUR 86.5 million.

The ostensible logic in this arrangement is that the value of the collateral is constantly changing, so that the market value of the bonds serving as collateral may not be sufficient to cover the costs in the event the borrower of cash were to default on the loan in the future. And the thinking is that the prices of longer-term bonds tend to be more volatile than the prices of shorter-term bonds and that the prices of bonds issued by lower-rated issuers tend to be more volatile than the prices of bonds issued by higher-rated issuers. So to protect against the greater risk when lending against bonds with more volatile prices, repo counterparties tend to arrange larger haircuts for these bonds.

Repo haircuts in the private market also vary by the characteristics of the counterparties. For example, a recent note from the Federal Reserve[1] contains an estimate that 74% of US Treasury repo borrowing by hedge funds occurs with no haircut at all or even with a negative haircut.[2] At the same time, roughly 20% of hedge fund borrowing of Treasuries involve haircuts in excess of 2%. So we see that these arrangements differ considerably across counterparties.

Central banks are key participants in the repo market, particularly for banks. For example, the Federal Reserve has both a Repo Facility in which it lends cash against eligible collateral and a Reverse Repo Facility in which it accepts cash in exchange for bonds. The current (October 2023) haircut schedule for US bills, notes, bonds, TIPS, and STRIPS is shown in Table 18.1.

The corresponding table for UK Gilts submitted as collateral at the Bank of England is shown in Table 18.2.

Note that the haircut schedule of the BoE is much steeper than that of the Fed. An immediate implication is that, *ceteris paribus*, the Gilt yield curve swapped into dollars should be steeper than the US Treasury yield curve. And this was precisely our observation in Figure 17.2. To be clear, this assumes that the excess costs (above the respective risk-free rate) of financing the respective haircuts are positive and identical. It also assumes that the credit risk of the

---

[1] Banegas and Phillip (2023).
[2] A negative haircut involves the value of cash lent being *greater* than the market value of the bonds posted as collateral.

TABLE 18.1 Federal Reserve Haircut Schedule

Maturity	Bills (%)	Notes and bonds (%)	TIPS (%)	STRIPS (%)
Less than 10Y	1.0	2.0	2.9	3.8
10Y–20Y	–	2.9	5.7	6.5
20Y–30Y	–	2.9	5.7	9.9

TABLE 18.2 Bank of England Haircut Schedule

Maturity	Coupon Bonds (%)	Zero Coupon Bonds (%)
Floating	0.5	0.5
Less than 1Y	0.5	0.5
1Y–3Y	1.5	1.5
3Y–5Y	2.0	2.0
5Y–10Y	3.0	3.5
10Y–20Y	5.5	6.5
20Y–30Y	7.0	9.5
More than 30Y	8.5	15.0

two issues is the same. These assumptions are too restrictive to be practical in this case, but they do help to illustrate one of the general effects of haircuts on relative value analysis of bonds.

The haircut schedule at the ECB is more complicated, as haircuts for sovereign debt are tiered by issuer as well as by maturity. Table 18.3 illustrates the haircuts currently in effect for some of the larger sovereign issuers.

Note the significant difference between the haircuts applied to bonds issued by Germany, France, and Spain and the haircuts applied to bonds issued by Italy.

One way to assess the effect of the differences in haircuts is to assume a value for the excess cost of financing the haircut (i.e. the cost of funds in excess of the repo rate) and to calculate the effect on the yield of each bond, by maturity. Figure 18.1 shows the results of this exercise for zero-coupon bonds, assuming the excess cost of funds for the haircut is 600 basis points.[3]

Note that the effect of haircuts on the spread between BTPs and Bunds is about 47 bp for 10Y and 54 bp for 30Y zero-coupon yields.

---

[3]Reported costs of equity for large European banks in Europe recently have been in the vicinity of 10%, while ESTR is currently 3.9%.

TABLE 18.3   ECB Haircut Schedule

Maturity	Germany, France, Spain: bullet (%)	Germany, France, Spain: zero coupon (%)	Italy: bullet (%)	Italy: zero coupon (%)
Less than 1Y	0.5	0.5	5.0	5.0
1Y to 3Y	1.0	2.0	6.0	7.0
3Y to 5Y	1.5	2.5	8.5	10.0
5Y to 7Y	2.0	3.0	10.0	11.5
7Y to 10Y	3.0	4.0	11.5	13.0
10Y to 15Y	4.0	5.0	12.5	14.0
15Y to 30Y	5.0	6.0	13.5	15.0
More than 30Y	6.0	9.0	14.0	17.0

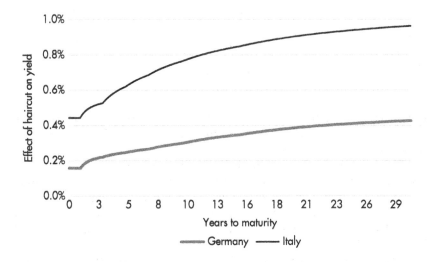

FIGURE 18.1   Effect of ECB haircut schedule on German and Italian zero-coupon bond yields.
Source: Authors.

Another consideration to note is the possibility of haircut arbitrage. For example, under most market conditions, it may not make sense to post zero-coupon bonds as collateral to the Bank of England, particularly if it's possible to reconstitute those zero-coupon bonds into a low-coupon issue, as the Bank of England will often lend more for a bullet issue than for a set of zero-coupon bonds that replicates the cash flows of the bullet.

Margin and Collateral Agreements

Just as leveraged bond positions typically involve haircuts, derivative instruments, like interest rate swaps, credit default swaps, and basis swaps, typically involve collateral to be posted as margin, which limits the risk of a swap counterparty in the event the other counterparty to the swap were to default.

Rules governing the margining of derivatives can be bilateral in the case of two parties that agree to clear a trade bilaterally. But they can also be standardized, as is the case with central clearinghouses of the sort used by futures exchanges. But even in the case of futures exchanges, the margin terms offered to end users may differ based on the futures commission merchant (FCM) that facilitates the trade, as FCMs are able to specify many of the terms that govern the treatment of collateral posted as margin.

For example, a typical hedge fund does business with multiple dealers and is likely to have negotiated different collateral agreements with these dealers. So a hedge fund that wants to execute a cross-currency basis swap may find that it gets slightly better pricing from one dealer but that this advantage is more than offset by the relatively advantageous collateral terms offered by another dealer.

The complexities that can arise when collateralizing derivative trades require traders and analysts to be familiar with the terms of these collateral agreements when assessing the relative valuations of various instruments. In practice, these considerations are often ignored, as the effects of these agreements are often fairly modest. But there have been plenty of instances in which unsuspecting traders have been picked off by counterparties who take advantage of the terms of collateral agreements, and we encourage traders to be familiar with the terms of the collateral agreements negotiated with their counterparties.

REGULATORY CONSIDERATIONS

Prior to the financial crisis of 2008–2009, many banks operated with relatively few constraints on their balance sheets. If a bank was interested in undertaking a new investment, it could compare the expected rate of return on the project to the marginal cost of the funds required to pursue the project. If the expected rate of return exceeded the cost of funds by an amount sufficient to justify any additional risks presented by the project, the bank would often proceed with the investment. The bank's balance sheet would increase, but this typically presented no problem.

Subsequent to the financial crisis, regulators in most of the developed world introduced a considerable number of additional regulations that posed material, often binding constraints on bank balance sheets. Many of these fell under the rubric of the Basel III capital accords. A great deal has been written about the Basel III accords, and we won't attempt a detailed discussion here. But we will outline some of the key characteristics for traders, portfolio managers, and analysts conducting relative value analysis of the fixed income markets. In particular, we'll comment on capital requirements, leverage ratios, funding requirements, and market risk regulations.

Box 18.1
Shadow Costs

A bank optimizing the return on its balance sheet will have to deal with the concept of shadow costs if its balance sheet is subject to constraints. In the field of mathematical optimization, a shadow cost is the amount by which the function being optimized could improve in the event that a binding constraint was relaxed. In the context of a bank with a constrained balance sheet evaluating a new investment, the shadow cost is the amount by which return on capital could be increased by relaxing the constraint.

As a simplified example, consider a brand new bank, with cash on the asset side of its balance sheet and with customer deposits and contributed equity on the liability side of the balance sheet.

Assume that this bank pays an interest rate of 2% per year on new deposits and faces no constraints on its balance sheet. We might expect the bank to fund any and all new investments available, as long as the expected return on those investments is greater than its 2% cost of funds (with some suitable adjustment for risk). If we ranked the expected (risk-adjusted) returns of these investments in descending order, we'd expect to find that the lowest return on capital was close to 2%, since the bank would pursue all projects with expected returns greater than 2% and would decline all projects with expected returns less than 2%.

Now let's consider the same bank in the presence of balance sheet constraints. For example, let's imagine that the bank first funds a project with an expected return of 10% and that it subsequently funds projects with expected returns of 9%, 8%, and 7%. But let's also assume that after funding the project with the expected return of 7%, the bank finds that its CET1 capital ratio has declined to 4.5%. At this point, it faces two choices if it wants to pursue another investment.

First, it could issue more equity. For example, if it raised 10% of the funds required for the project by selling equity and 90% by accepting more customer deposits, its rate of return hurdle for the new project would be the blended cost of capital, which depends not only on the amount paid to customer deposits but also on the bank's cost of equity. If the cost of equity was 10%, this blended cost of funds would be 2.8% – i.e. 80 bp greater than the marginal cost of funds when the balance sheet was unconstrained.

Even if the bank decided to raise only 4.5% of the required funds by issuing equity, thereby keeping the CET1 capital ratio at 4.5%, it would face a blended cost of capital of 2.36% – i.e. 36 bp greater than its cost of funds in the event its balance sheet was unconstrained.

A second alternative would be for the bank to dispose of an existing asset to make room for the new investment. We presume the asset to be liquidated would be the asset with the lowest expected return, in this case the project with an expected return of 7%. In this case, the marginal cost of the funds required to pursue the new investment would be 7%, regardless of the amount the bank was paying on customer deposits.

In the first approach, the binding constraint is taken to be the leverage ratio alone, and additional equity is issued in order to allow the bank to pursue the new investment. In this case, we can think of the shadow cost of this constraint to be 2.36% (assuming the CET1 ratio of 4.5% is maintained).

In the second approach, the bank faces two binding constraints: the capital ratio imposed by regulators; and its desire to avoid selling additional equity, which typically would be a self-imposed constraint. The shadow cost of the self-imposed constraint in this example is 7%.

In this example, the shadow costs of the two constraints were quite different. In practice, we'd expect most banks to structure their balance sheets so that the various shadow costs were more similar. And we should stress that optimization of bank balance sheets in practice is a very complicated process, with a considerable number of regulatory and self-imposed constraints, often in multiple jurisdictions, and with market costs and market opportunities changing constantly.

Capital Requirements

The Basel III process increased the amount of *Tier 1 Capital* that banks need to hold against risk-weighted assets (RWAs). Tier 1 capital is the sum of *Common Equity Tier 1* (CET1) *Capital* (which includes common equity, reserves, and retained earnings) and *Additional Tier 1* (AT1) *Capital* (which includes contingent convertible debt, and perpetual preferred stock). Risk-weighted assets are the weighted sum of bank assets (and certain off-balance sheet items), weighted by the perceived risks of each asset.

Basel III requires banks to hold Tier 1 Capital of at least 6% of risk-weighted assets, with at least 4.5 percentage points held as CET1 Capital.

As a simplified example, if a bank wanted to extend additional loans to customers while its CET1 Capital was 4.5% of RWAs, the bank would need to fund a portion of the additional loans with common equity or retained earnings, so that its CET1 Capital ratio as a percentage of RWAs didn't drop below 4.5%.

As an alternative to raising additional CET1 capital to fund a portion of these additional loans, the bank could dispose of some existing risk-weighted assets on its balance sheet, making room for the new loans. In this case, the relevant cost of funds should reflect the shadow cost of the capital constraint. For example, if the bank disposes of assets with a return on capital of 7% in order to make room for new loans, then 7% is the shadow cost of the capital constraint that should be included in the bank's decision-making process. Even if the bank could fund the new loans at a marginal cost of, say, 4%, it must also consider the 7% return on capital it *won't* be earning if it disposes of existing assets in order to make room for the new loans.

Leverage Requirements

Regulators have concerns that their capital ratio requirements may not be sufficient to provide adequate protection against the risk of bank crises, so they introduced two additional, related measures: the *Tier 1 Leverage Ratio*, and the *Supplementary Leverage Ratio*.[4]

The Tier 1 Leverage Ratio is defined as the amount of Tier 1 Capital as a percentage of total assets, while the Supplementary Leverage Ratio is defined as the ratio of Tier 1 Capital to the *Exposure Measure*, which is the sum of on-balance sheet exposures, derivative exposures, and security financing exposures (e.g. repo transactions).

Different banks are subject to different requirements for these leverage ratios. The Basel III accords set the minimum Tier 1 Leverage ratio at 3%, but the specific regulations in many jurisdictions are both more complicated and more restrictive. For example, *Globally Systemically Important Banks* (G-SIBs) in the US are required to maintain a Tier 1 Leverage ratio of 6.71% and a Supplementary Leverage ratio of 5.64% currently.[5]

---

[4]For more on this, see "Basel IV: The Leverage ratio – Background and timeline of development" on www.pwc.co.uk.

[5]These leverage requirements are subject to change at the discretion of regulators.

A bank may find that one of the relevant leverage ratios is binding even if its capital ratios are not. In that case, the bank would be subject to considerations similar to those discussed in the context of capital ratios. In particular, a bank could find that its shadow cost of capital for a new investment is considerably greater than the marginal cost of funds that could be obtained via deposits or interbank loans, owing to the fact that an attractive asset with a higher return on capital may have to be liquidated in order to make room for the new investment.

Funding and Liquidity Requirements

In addition to the risk of insolvency, banking regulators are concerned with the risk of banks experiencing illiquidity, the inability to obtain cash when needed. To address the ability of banks to raise cash, regulators introduced the Net Stable Funding Requirement. And to address the ability of banks to convert assets to cash, regulators introduced the Liquidity Coverage Ratio.

Net Stable Funding Ratio

The Net Stable Funding Ratio (NSFR) is defined as the amount of stable funding available over a one-year horizon divided by the amount of stable funding required over a one-year horizon. The definitions of these two quantities are fairly involved. Quoting from the Federal Reserve Board of Governors' *Final rule to implement a net stable funding ratio requirement for large banking organizations*:

> [A] banking organization's available stable funding amount, the numerator of the NSFR, would measure the stability of its regulatory capital elements and liabilities. Regulatory capital elements and liabilities would each be assigned an available stable funding factor, which represents the extent to which the capital element or liability is considered available for use by the banking organization over a one-year time horizon. The available stable funding factors are scaled from zero (least stable) to 100 percent (most stable) and were determined by taking into account the tenor of the funding, type of funding, and type of counterparty.

The denominator is also addressed in the same document: "The required stable funding amount is the sum of the required stable funding amount for non-derivative assets and commitments and the required stable funding amount for derivative transactions."

The actual implementation of the NSFR requirement is also quite involved, with various assets and funding sources weighted by different degrees. But the key point for relative value analysts is that banks may find themselves unable to pursue various opportunities, including relative value trades, if pursuit of the opportunity were to increase the required stable funding requirement to the point that the NSFR declined to less than 100%. In such a case, the shadow cost of the NSFR constraint would need to be included in the relative value analysis.

Liquidity Coverage Ratio

The liquidity coverage ratio is defined as the amount of High Quality Liquid Assets on a bank's balance sheet divided by the net cash outflows over the next 30 calendar days. Banks must maintain this ratio at 100% or greater.

A High Quality Liquid Asset (HQLA) is one that can be quickly sold or pledged as collateral in a loan without an adverse effect on its price. The characteristics required for an asset to be considered an HQLA are not just those related to the asset per se but also to the terms governing its use on a bank's balance sheet. For example, according to the Bank for International Settlements:

> Banks must not include in the stock of HQLA any assets, or liquidity generated from assets, they have received under right of rehypothecation, if the beneficial owner has the contractual right to withdraw those assets during the 30-day stress period.

So in determining whether a particular asset can be counted as an HQLA, the bank must look to the rights of the counterparty that provided the asset as part of a collateral agreement.

Market Risk Regulations

Following the financial crisis of 2008–2009, banking regulators coordinated on a set of reforms that they referred to as the "Fundamental Review of the Trading Book" (FRTB), intended to lessen the risks that banks faced in their trading books, which need to be marked-to-market (as opposed to their banking books, which do not need to be marked-to-market).

The FRTB is a complicated process with a myriad of new procedures that banks must follow. Of these, two are particularly important from our perspective as relative value analysts.

First, the FRTB modifies the way banks need to calculate and report market risks in their trading books. For example, banks must shift from a focus on Value at Risk to a focus on Expected Shortfall. And, second, they must rely more on standard models and less on internal models than they used to. Taken together, the effect of these reforms is that most banks will be expected to hold greater capital in the future, increasing their overall costs of doing business.

From our perspective, these reforms appear likely to affect the marginal costs relevant to analyzing a relative value opportunity. For example, a simple spread trade that appeared attractive previously, based on unconstrained financing costs, may no longer appear attractive, once the costs of heightened capital requirements are included.

Example: JP Morgan and the Repo Spike of September 2019

On September 17, 2019, overnight repo rates in the US spiked from roughly 2.4% to intraday levels as high as 10%. In the past, we would have expected large banks to lend cash in repo markets in order to take advantage of such an unusually attractive opportunity. But according to JP Morgan CEO, Jamie Dimon, new bank regulations constrained his bank from acting. According to Bloomberg:

> *When rates on repurchase agreements spiked to around 10 per cent a month ago — roughly four times more than what JPMorgan earns at the Fed — the bank could've profited by shifting the money into repo.*
>
> *It didn't. The bank, Dimon told analysts following JPMorgan's third-quarter earnings release, needed to keep that money put so it could fulfill its liquidity requirements mandated by regulators.*
>
> *"We could not redeploy it into the repo market. We'd have been happy to do it," Dimon said Tuesday. "It's up to the regulators to decide if they want to recalibrate the kind of liquidity they expect us to keep in that account."*
>
> *This couldn't be more different than year-end 2018. Back then, JPMorgan deployed excess cash to the repo market when rates surged above six per cent as other lenders retreated as a way of tidying up their balance sheets for regulatory purposes. JPMorgan drew down its deposits with the Fed and increased its allocations to the repo market by more than US$100 billion, according to its fourth-quarter earnings statement.*
>
> *"Last year, we had more cash than needed for regulatory requirements," Dimon said. So shifting into repo "obviously made sense, you make more money," the CEO added.[6]*

In the end, the repo spike experienced that day didn't result in serious disruption to the banking system, in part because the Federal Reserve acted

---

[6]BNN Bloomberg, "JPMorgan felt barred from calming repo market by regulations: Dimon."

to provide liquidity in the repo market for the rest of the week. But the large distortions in the money markets certainly had a significant effect on the pricing of relative value trades in the fixed income markets.

With regulatory constraints resulting in the inability of banks to provide arbitrage capital to the repo market, the Fed took over this function by introducing the Standing Repo Facility (SRF), as discussed in Chapter 11. We will refer to this series of events as an example for an intervention spiral when taking the broader macro-economic perspective of Chapter 20.

While this episode was short-lived, other episodes have been much more significant, lasting for multiple years. For example, throughout the financial crisis of 2008–2009 and the subsequent European sovereign debt crisis and European banking crisis, cross-currency basis swaps between EUR and USD widened from essentially zero to below −40 bp. In other words, European banks that wanted to borrow US dollars with EUR as collateral had to pay an additional 40 bp per year in order to get their counterparties to lend dollars. Contrary to some of the simplified headlines that appeared during this time, there was no "shortage of dollars" in the global markets. Rather, US banks were reluctant to increase the EUR exposure on their balance sheets. And unlike plain interest rate swaps, which are considered "off-balance sheet," cross-currency basis swaps involve full exchange of principal and therefore cause a one-for-one increase in the balance sheets of the banks that conduct them.

In this example, the constraints on bank balance sheets were largely imposed by the banks themselves. But the principle is the same. Balance sheet constraints, self-imposed or imposed by regulators, affect the pricing of instruments in which banks are significant participants. As relative value analysts, we have no choice but to consider these constraints and the effects that they may have on the pricing of the trades we're analyzing.

Short-Term Fluctuations in Supply and/or Demand of Bonds

Given structural changes to various markets in recent years, even large markets, such as that for German Bunds, can be affected by short-term changes in supply or demand. Consider the following story from Reuters, dated February 22, 2022:

> Germany's finance agency has stepped in to ease a bond shortage that developed in the overnight lending market, a market source said, in a sign of stress following the European Central Bank's hawkish pivot and more recently the Ukraine–Russia crisis.
>
> ECB President Christine Lagarde's Feb. 3 refusal to rule out an interest rate hike in 2022 sent traders rushing to repo markets to borrow German bonds to 'short' – essentially to bet prices would fall further as rate rises approach.

That increased the scarcity of German bonds, the euro zone's safe assets used widely as collateral against repo loans, leading to a plunge in repo rates ...[7]

These market situations may cause richness in some bonds, which cannot be explained by the models, such as the Bunds in Figures 17.1 and 17.2: while some of their richness could be justified by the relatively low CDS of Germany and the haircut schedules, the excessive richness in some sectors may well reflect a specific supply/demand situation. If these imbalances are expected to be short-lived, one could consider positioning for a relative cheapening of Bunds, with their "fair" richness (as given by the models) as a possible target for the trade.

Implications

The pricing of bonds and swaps discussed in previous chapters focused largely on variables that everyone can observe: bond yields, swap rates, repo rates, interbank rates, basis swap spreads, and credit default swap spreads. But the issues discussed in this chapter tend to be quantities that most people aren't able to observe directly, such as the shadow prices of various constraints that some banks may find binding.

Consider the repo spike of September 2019 discussed above. Was there any way for market participants to anticipate that one or more of the constraints faced by JP Morgan were, in fact, binding at the time? Even then, was there any way for market participants to estimate the shadow costs of those constraints, which would allow them to forecast JP Morgan's appetite to lend cash against collateral at various repo rates?

Of course, JP Morgan is only one bank. Presumably, there were other large banks that faced constraints on their balance sheets that affected their willingness to lend. And the typical market participant is just as ignorant of the constraints at other banks as he is of the constraints at JP Morgan.

However, every market participant is able to observe the sum of the impact of all of the complex and individually different regulatory and capital constraints on the market prices in the form of deviations from arbitrage relationships formulated under the assumption of no constraints. Taking the arbitrage inequality formulated in Chapter 16 as an example, the increasing regulatory burdens on banks were visible in the threshold for the arbitrage illustrated in Figure 16.4 increasing from close to the transaction costs before the financial crisis to several dozens of bp, reflecting the particularly high capital requirements for CCBS and CDS. One could hence consider these deviations from

---

[7]Reuters, "German debt office acts to ease bond shortage after ECB, Ukraine crisis."

arbitrage relationships formulated under the assumption of no constraints as empirically observable variables depending on the empirically unobservable multitude of individually different shadow costs.

So while application of the principles discussed in earlier chapters can help analysts identify instruments that appear rich or cheap to one another, analysts need to at least reflect on the issues discussed in this chapter when predicting whether particular instruments are likely to richen or cheapen in the future. Italian bonds may appear cheap to French bonds on a historical basis, but they may cheapen further if the ECB increases the haircut for Italian bonds still further. German bonds may appear rich to Spanish bonds on a historical basis, but they may richen further in the event that a comment by the ECB President causes a significant number of market participants to borrow bonds via the repo market so they can be sold short in advance of an anticipated ECB hike.

At the same time, the issues discussed in this chapter may be relevant to relative value analysts and traders because of the way their *own* institutions treat these trades. For example, if I work for a financial institution that doesn't face balance sheet constraints, I may be able to take advantage of a relative value opportunity that is priced to reflect the balance sheet constraints of larger banks. For example, if a repo spike causes the basis between Treasury bonds and Treasury bond futures to widen, I may be able to take advantage of the widening by selling bonds against futures and either holding the position until futures' expiration or by unwinding the trade when the repo spike has subsided. One man's constraint may well be another man's opportunity.

CHAPTER 19

Options

INTRODUCTION

A fruitful application of the no-arbitrage principle mentioned in Chapter 1 is the approach of Black and Scholes to option pricing. As the payoff of an option can be replicated by a dynamic self-financing portfolio, the price of an option can be determined by the cost of that portfolio. We start this chapter with a brief sketch of that idea and its implications for option pricing.

However, for trading purposes, delta hedging is particularly important when the gamma of the option is large. This leads to a segmentation of the volatility surface into a sector with high gamma (short expiry), where frequent hedge rebalancing is an important trading strategy, and into a sector with low gamma (long expiry) for which it is not. After introducing this segmentation, we shall discuss the appropriate analysis tools and relative value trades for each of the sectors separately.

A BRIEF REVIEW OF OPTION PRICING THEORY

Since a complete description of option pricing theory and models is outside of the scope of our trade-oriented book, we assume some familiarity of the reader with the basic ideas such as the payoff profile of a call and put. In the following, we briefly highlight just those concepts of option pricing theory, which are of vital importance for finding and exploiting value in option markets.

Delta

The key for both pricing and hedging options is the relationship of the price of an option to the price of its *underlying* (the security the holder of a long option has the right to buy or sell). (In the following examples, these securities will often be swaps on a yield curve.) That relationship is expressed by the number delta, defined as $\frac{\partial PriceOption}{\partial PriceUnderlying}$. As a first derivative of the option price with respect to the value of the underlying, delta tells us the number of units by

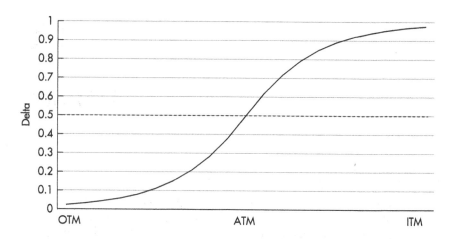

FIGURE 19.1 Delta of an option as a function of the difference between the price of the underlying and the strike price.
Source: Authors.

which the option price would change for a given instantaneous change in the value of the underlying, holding the values of all other inputs constant.

The delta depends in part on the difference between the price of the underlying and the strike price of the option. Figure 19.1 shows schematically the way delta changes with the difference between the price of the underlying and the strike price. For far out-of-the-money (OTM) options, it is close to zero; for far in-the-money (ITM) options, it is close to one; for at-the-money (ATM) options, it is 0.5.[1] Also note that the change in delta (called gamma) is highest for ATM options.

This means that for far OTM options with a delta close to zero, the option price varies only slightly as a result of changes in the price of the underlying. Intuitively, this makes sense, as an option with very little chance of ending ITM will quote close to zero and still quote close to zero even if the underlying changes a bit. Imagine the S&P500 index quotes at 1400 and we have a three-month (3M) option to buy it at 5000. Even if the S&P rises to 1500, our option will still be virtually worthless, hence the change of 100 in the underlying will have produced a negligible change in the option price, which translates into a delta of (almost) zero. On the other side, imagine we have a 3M option to buy the S&P index at 100. At the current price of 1400, this option will be worth about 1300 (plus a tiny premium). If the S&P rises to 1500, the

---

[1]More precisely, for Black–Scholes $N(d_2) = 0.5$ while $N(d_1)$ could be slightly different.

option value will increase to about 1400. Thus, the change of 100 in the under-lying induces a change of about 100 in the option price (i.e. the delta is almost one). Again, this makes sense intuitively, since far ITM options are basically the same as a position in the underlying security.

Delta Hedging

Moreover, delta gives the hedge ratio of an option versus the underlying secu-rity. In order to hedge one option, one needs to buy or sell delta of the underly-ing. For example, to hedge a long ATM call on the S&P500 index we need to sell 0.5 (delta of an ATM option) S&P indices. If the S&P500 index then increases from 1400 to 1500, the option will increase by 100 * delta (0.5) = 50, which is the same amount we lose from being short 0.5 of the underlying.

However, the strike of the option did not change and what was an ATM call at an S&P500 index of 1400 is now an ITM call at an index value of 1500. Consequently, as shown in Figure 19.2, the delta of the option has increased, perhaps to 0.8. This also means that the hedge ratio required has changed. We now need to be short 0.8 of the underlying (i.e. we need to sell an addi-tional 0.3 units of the S&P index). Actually, since delta increased as soon as the S&P500 began to increase from 1400, we were underhedged during the entire move from 1400 to 1500 (with the amount of the underhedge becoming increasingly large as the S&P increased). As a result, we profited from being underhedged in a bull market.

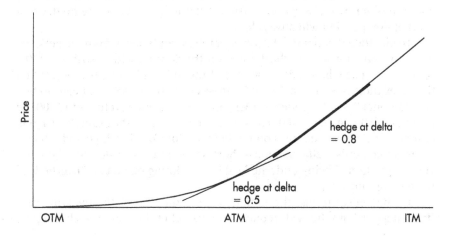

FIGURE 19.2 Price of an option as a function of the difference between the price of the underlying and the strike price.
Source: Authors.

Let's assume we adjust our hedge at an underlying of 1500 so as to be short 0.8 units of the S&P, and then subsequently the stock market declines again to 1400. Now the option is ATM again with a delta of 0.5, and we need to buy back 0.3 units of the underlying index in order to adjust our hedge ratio to the change in delta. We are back to where we started. The S&P index is again at 1400, we have a long ATM call (now with less time value, however), and we have a hedge versus the underlying by being short 0.5 units of the index. However, simply by adjusting our hedge ratio to the moves in delta as the market went up and down, we have sold an additional 0.3 of the underlying at 1500 (when delta went from 0.5 to 0.8) and bought back 0.3 of the underlying at 1400 (when the delta went from 0.8 to 0.5). Thus, we made a profit through our hedging operations, from selling the underlying stock market high and buying it back low. This is the same as saying that we were underhedged in an upward move and overhedged in a downward move of the market. At the end of the round trip, we have therefore pocketed a profit from adjusting the hedge ratio to the changes of the delta of the option (and lost some of its time value).

In general terms, the hedge ratio for an option changes with the price of the underlying. Ensuring that the hedge ratio is always equal to the delta of the option is called *delta hedging* of an option and requires continuous adjustment of the hedge ratio to changes in delta as the underlying market moves up and down.

Since delta changes when the underlying moves, our delta hedge will most always be a bit too much or a bit too little, such that market moves will result in a profit or loss from delta hedging. The key point is that the holder of a long option position will always profit from delta hedging, while the holder of a short option position will always lose.[2]

To illustrate that point, let's consider the example above from the perspective of an investor who is short a call on the S&P500 with a strike of 1400. In order to hedge, he needs to buy 0.5 of the index initially (at 1400). When the index increases to 1500 (delta increases from 0.5 to 0.8), he needs to buy an additional 0.3 of the index at 1500, and after the index returns to 1400, he needs to sell 0.3 again at 1400. Thus, as a mirror image of the example of a long option holder above, the short option holder is forced to buy high and sell low. Or, in other words, delta hedging a short option forces a trader into the unfavorable position of being underhedged in a declining market and overhedged in an increasing one.

In theoretical terms, the option price is the cost of the dynamic self-financing portfolio that will replicate the payoff of the option, including the

---

[2]At this point, we're assuming that there are no changes in other variables, such as the implied volatility of the option.

costs or benefits of delta hedging. And it's this sense in which Black–Scholes is said to be a no-arbitrage model.

From a trading perspective, exact dynamic replication of an option is impossible, so we can think of *the option premium as the market price for the right to be on the profitable side of delta hedging* (i.e. buying the underlying low and selling it high, and being underhedged in rising markets and overhedged in falling markets). As delta hedging means that the option is always hedged versus the underlying, there will be no profit and loss at expiry of the option. If the option expires ITM, it will be hedged with one underlying; if it expires OTM, it will be hedged with no underlying. In fact, delta hedging can be thought of as increasing the hedge ratio toward one as the option moves ITM and decreasing the hedge ratio toward zero as the option moves OTM, just as it is required for the option to yield no P&L at expiry. Hence, *delta hedging an option transfers all P&L of the option position from the expiry (difference of underlying versus strike) to the P&L of the delta hedging operations before expiry*. As a consequence, the market price of an option should depend on the cost of delta hedging that option. This was the key insight of Black and Scholes, which enabled them to determine the option price by the cost of a dynamically hedged, self-financing portfolio. While we shall not go into the mathematics and quantifications, we highlight some important consequences of that approach in qualitative terms:

- The option price is determined by profit from the dynamically hedged, self-financing portfolio that hedges a long position in the option. The profit from delta hedging a long option position increases with the volatility of the underlying market moves. In the example above, if the market had moved twice from 1400 to 1500 and back (in the same time period), we would have made twice the money from delta hedging (selling at 1500 and buying back at 1400 0.3 of the S&P500 index). And if the market had moved from 1400 to 1600 and back (with a delta of, say, 0.9 at 1600), we could have sold 0.4 at 1600 and bought 0.4 back at 1400. Thus, the higher the volatility (number and scale of moves in the underlying market) until expiry, the higher the profit from delta hedging a long option position.

- From a trading perspective, the option price is determined by the expected profit from delta hedging, which in turn is determined by the anticipated volatility in the underlying market until the expiry of the option. Consequently, *the option price reflects the anticipated volatility in the underlying market until expiry*. In other words, the option market reflects the market consensus about anticipated future volatility. If overall market participants anticipate a period of high volatility ahead, they see considerable potential to profit from delta hedging long option positions and should thus be willing to pay a high price for the right to be on the profitable side of delta hedging (i.e. they'll pay a high option premium).

- The anticipated future volatility in the underlying market reflected in the option price is called the *implied* volatility of that option. And as we have seen above, in the framework of delta hedging (i.e. Black–Scholes option pricing theory), implied volatility is the main determinant of option premiums. Put otherwise, for a specific option, with given underlying, strike, and expiry, etc., its price depends only on the implied volatility. Therefore, instead of quoting the premium of an option in terms of dollars and cents, it can be and often is quoted as well in terms of the implied volatility associated with that premium.

- While the *implied* volatility is the *anticipated future* volatility of the market, the *actual* volatility occurring in the market until the expiry of the option is called the *realized* volatility. The implied volatility determines the premium of the option, whereas the realized volatility determines the actual P&L from delta hedging the option until expiry. Thus, *the P&L of delta hedging an option is the difference between the implied volatility and the realized volatility*. Put otherwise, the implied volatility reflects the market consensus at the time of purchase about expected future volatility, which determines the price of the option. In contrast, the realized volatility indicates the volatility that actually has occurred prior to the expiry of the option, which determines the P&L realized by delta hedging the option. If implied and realized volatility turn out to be the same (i.e. the market consensus about anticipated future volatility is matched by the actual volatility), then the premium of the option and the P&L from delta hedging it would be equal. If, on the other hand, the realized volatility turns out to be less than the anticipated volatility, the option premium is higher than the P&L from delta hedging, and therefore the one who bought the option (and delta hedged it) loses and the one who sold the option (and delta hedged it) wins.[3]

---

[3]Note that the calculation of delta should be based on the anticipated future volatility. Consider two traders who anticipate that future realized volatility will be 20%, while the current implied volatility is 30%. Both are motivated to gamma trade the difference between the implied volatility and the volatility they anticipate (i.e. to sell the option and delta hedge it). Trader A calculates all his hedge ratios using a volatility of 20% (i.e. the volatility he anticipates), while Trader B calculates all his hedge ratios using a volatility of 30% (i.e. the volatility currently implied by the pricing of the option). Let's say that the realized volatility actually does turn out to be 20%, as these two traders anticipated. While Trader A will have realized a profit in line with the Black–Scholes model, the P&L of Trader B, using a number for delta which is different from the Black–Scholes model, can be different (higher or lower than the profit of trader A).

- Therefore, trading in options and delta hedging them means taking views on the spread between implied and realized volatility. We buy options and delta hedge them if we believe that the realized volatility of the underlying will be greater than their implied volatility. Since option prices depend on the volatility anticipated by the market, their actual ending value at expiry can only be known after expiry, when the realized volatility and thereby the P&L from delta hedging are known. Before expiry, trading in options always involves assessing the market consensus about future anticipated volatility as reflected in the implied volatility of the option prices versus our own view about future volatility.
- The option value today is *not* determined by the price of the underlying at expiry. In the Black–Scholes approach, the option value today depends on the volatility of the price path of the underlying. Put in simple terms, for pricing options it does not matter *at which level* the underlying of the option will end, only *how* it gets there: in a volatile or a smooth fashion.

Note how a simple analysis of the delta of an option has naturally translated into a hedging (delta hedging), pricing (Black–Scholes), and trading (implied versus realized volatility) strategy.

Theta, Vega, and Gamma

Similarly to delta, which assesses the price of an option as a function of the underlying security, one can also analyze the way the option price would change in relation to changes in other determining variables. In particular:

- Theta is defined as $\frac{\partial PriceOption}{\partial Time}$ and indicates the changes in the value of the option as a function of time.
- Vega[4] is defined as $\frac{\partial PriceOption}{\partial ImpliedVolatility}$ and shows the change in the value of the option as a function of changes in implied volatility.
- Gamma is defined as $\frac{\partial Delta}{\partial PriceUnderlying}$ and quantifies the change in delta as a function of the change in the price of the underlying (i.e. it's the second derivative of the option price with respect to the price of the underlying, i.e. the slope of the line in Figure 19.1). Thus, gamma is close to zero for far ITM and far OTM options and maximal for ATM options.

Given a certain realized volatility of the market, the P&L from delta hedging will be higher, if the (given) price changes of the underlying induce a

---

[4]For both systematic and philological reasons, we would like to suggest replacing "vega" with "sigma," but stick in the following to the conventional term.

higher change in delta (and thereby require a larger amount of the underlying to be bought or sold in order to maintain the delta hedge). Thus, the higher the gamma of an option, the larger the changes in delta and the larger the P&L from delta hedging, given a certain realized volatility. As a consequence, the trading strategy developed above of delta hedging an option and thereby exploiting the difference between implied and realized volatility requires options with a sufficiently large gamma. Both far ITM and far OTM options are not suitable for that strategy. And also ATM options which have a low gamma for different reasons, in particular because of a long time to expiry, require another trading strategy than delta hedging. Thus, this brief and purely qualitative review of option pricing yielded a hedging and trading strategy (delta hedging) for options with high gamma as well as a segmentation of the option market into those options for which this approach is suitable and into those for which is it not. Subsequently, we shall build on this result so as to classify the option market into different segments and to associate them with their respective suitable trading strategies.

CLASSIFICATION OF OPTION TRADES

Relationship between Gamma and Theta

Theta measures the time decay of the option. Figure 19.3 shows schematically that theta becomes increasingly negative as the option moves closer

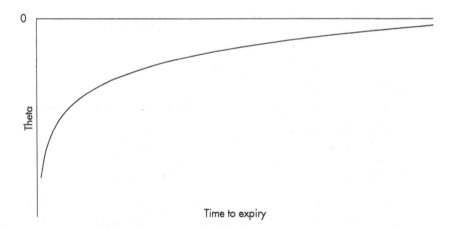

FIGURE 19.3 Theta of an ATM option as a function of the time to expiry (schematic). *Source:* Authors.

to expiry. That is, options with a long time to expiry have a small negative theta, while options with a short time to expiry have a high negative theta (all else being equal).[5]

It can be deduced from the Black–Scholes formula that (all else being equal) a decrease of theta (i.e. theta becoming more negative) is linked to an increase of gamma. More precisely, an increase in gamma by 1 is equivalent to a decrease in theta by $\frac{2}{P^2\sigma^2}$ where P is the price of the underlying and σ is the implied volatility (again, with all other parameters assumed to remain unchanged).

Together, this results in options with a long time to expiry having a relatively high theta (small negative number), thus a relatively small gamma (small positive number). As the time to expiry decreases (and assuming that the ATM option remains ATM), theta decreases, from a number closer to zero to a larger negative number, while gamma increases, from a number closer to zero to a larger positive number. Consequently, the exposure of an ATM option to changes in delta becomes increasingly large as the expiry date approaches. This is depicted in Figure 19.4, which illustrates that the move of delta from 0 to 1 becomes more and more concentrated around the ATM point as the time to expiry decreases.

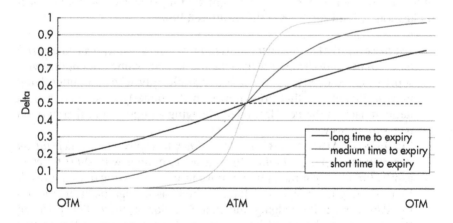

FIGURE 19.4 Delta of an option as a function of the difference between the price of the underlying and the strike price, as the time to expiry of the option becomes shorter and shorter.
Source: Authors.

---

[5]While it is possible for theta to be positive for ITM options, the chart depicts the usual situation for ATM options.

This mathematical result also makes sense intuitively: using the example above, imagine we had a 10-year (10Y), rather than a 3M, call to buy the S&P500 index at 5000. Given the very long time to expiry, that option will have some (time) value, which decreases every day only by a small amount (low negative theta), and will hardly change if the S&P index moves from 1400 to 1500 (low positive gamma, thus a flat delta curve in Figure 19.4). On the other side of the extreme, consider an ATM option that expires tomorrow. Like any ATM option, it has a delta of 0.5, but at expiry tomorrow it will either be ITM with a delta of 1 or OTM with a delta of 0. Tomorrow, it will have lost all time value (theta approaching negative infinity), and the slightest move of the index up or down will decide between a delta of 1 or 0. As illustrated in Figure 19.4, when the time to expiry decreases, the gamma of an ATM call option increases (approaching positive infinity). That is, the delta curve becomes steeper and steeper until at expiry it is a binary curve with a value of 0 below the strike and a value of 1 above the strike.

Segmentation of the Volatility Surface

Turning from option theory, from which we have picked only those parts which are needed to construct the right trading strategies, to its practical application, we can summarize the result as follows:

- *The prices of ATM options with short times to expiry mainly depend on price moves in the underlying security.* Due to the high gamma of options with short times to expiry, delta changes significantly when the underlying moves. This means that price moves in the underlying security have a large impact on the P&L from delta hedging an option and therefore on its premium as well.
- *The price of ATM options with long times to expiry mainly depend on moves in the implied volatility.* In contrast to options with short times to expiry, for a low gamma option a move in the underlying does not result in a meaningful change of delta and thus has no significant impact on the P&L from delta hedging and therefore nor on the option price. In the limit of very long expiries, the slope of the delta line in Figure 19.4 approaches 0, which means that moves in the underlying security do not result in a change in the delta, and therefore they have no impact on the P&L from delta hedging and therefore neither on the option price. On the other hand, given the long time value of the option, even a small change in the implied volatility has a significant effect on the option price. This intuition is reflected in the mathematical fact that (excluding extremely

long times to expiry) vega rises with increasing time to expiry,[6] while gamma declines.

The impact of delta hedging is a decreasing function of the time to expiry. For our practical approach this means that delta hedging is an appropriate trading strategy only for options with a short time to expiry. For swaptions, this usually covers a range of expiry times up until six months or, in some cases, one year. Swaptions with times to expiry of three years or more have values that are largely independent of changes in the value of the underlying and mainly influenced by changes in the implied volatility.

Thus, the swaption volatility surface (i.e. the two-dimensional grid of swaptions sorted by time to expiry of the option and by time to maturity of the underlying swap) should be divided into a gamma sector, where delta hedging is the appropriate trading strategy, and into a vega sector, where it is not (Figure 19.5). Usually, options with a time to expiry of roughly two years fall in a gray area between those two sectors, and the appropriate trading strategy must be determined on a case-by-case basis. The precise location of the border between the gamma and vega sectors differs for each option market, and often the gray area is somewhat tilted to the right (see Figure 19.20, where we provide more details for the case of JPY swaptions).

This segmentation of the volatility surface into a gamma and vega sector provides the most basic classification of option trades:

■ Options with a short expiry horizon provide a strong link to the underlying and thus an exposure to changes in the realized volatility (i.e. the price moves of the underlying).
■ Options with a long expiry horizon have less contact with the underlying and are therefore mainly exposed to changes in the implied volatility.

And consequently:

■ Options in the gamma sector can be appropriately traded in the Black–Scholes framework of delta hedging.

---

[6]Strictly speaking, vega depends on the time to expiry, t, in accordance with the term $\frac{\sqrt{t}}{e^t}$. As a result, vega first increases with t. For higher values of t, on the other hand, the exponential function increases at a faster rate than does the square root function and vega decreases with t. The specific point at which vega shifts from being an increasing function of time to a decreasing function of time also depends on additional parameters, including the implied volatility. However, for common values of implied volatility and times to expiry, it is relatively safe to assume that vega increases with time.

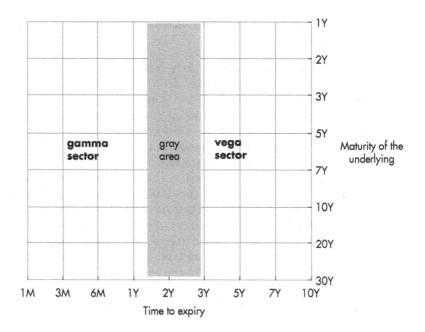

FIGURE 19.5 Classification of the volatility surface into a sector suitable for gamma trades and another suitable for vega trades.
Source: Authors.

■ Options in the vega sector need an analysis and trading strategy different from delta hedging. We shall show below that a statistical analysis of the mechanisms of the implied volatility can provide appropriate trading strategies for the vega sector. For example, a principal component analysis (PCA) is able to reveal the way implied volatility affects the volatility surface and how to exploit this knowledge. Hence, we shall not attempt to build an option pricing model for the vega sector, which is superior to Black–Scholes, but rather use statistical techniques to find value within that sector.

We restrict our discussion to the volatility surface of at-the-moneyforward (ATMF) options (i.e. those with the strike of the swaption at the forward rate of the underlying swap). Including different strikes would expand the volatility surface to a volatility cube, with the additional dimension representing the skew. The discussion of skew in the gamma sector requires an option model, while in the vega sector it can be addressed through the same statistical methods (e.g. via expanding the dimensionality of the PCA).[7]

Classification of Option Trades in the Gamma Sector

Continuing with our classification within the gamma sector, one is free to choose the *type* of exposure to the realized volatility one wants:

(1) Without delta hedging, one is exposed to the overall realized volatility of the underlying until expiry of the option. This corresponds to choosing exposure to the payoff profile of an option at expiry. We refer to this strategy as option trade type (1).

(2) With delta hedging, one is exposed to the continuous realized volatility of the underlying until expiry of the option. This corresponds to choosing exposure to P&L from continuous adjustments to the hedge ratio (in the Black–Scholes framework). We refer to this strategy as option trade type (2).

While theoretically speaking, (1) and (2) only differ in the number of time periods, the exposure in market and trading terms is different:

(1) gives a *conditional* exposure to the overall move of the underlying, while being largely unaffected by continuous realized volatility;

(2) gives an exposure to the realized volatility of the underlying until expiry, while being largely unaffected by the overall move of the underlying and its price at expiry.

For these two types of option trades in the gamma sector, implied volatility only matters at the beginning, as it determines the price to enter into these strategies. Afterward, their performance only depends on realized

---

[7]Indeed, a "skew factor" can be identified when running a PCA on the volatility cube in the vega sector. However, given limited liquidity in many of the OTM series, the input data often represent not actual price moves but constructed data. Correspondingly, the output of a PCA skew factor does not reveal the mechanisms of real market action but rather the assumptions of the model a trader used to construct the artificial data series. Thus, expanding the reach of a PCA from the volatility surface to the volatility cube will only be meaningful when liquidity across the volatility cube has increased and provides real market data as input.

volatility, not on changes to the implied volatility (as the options are held until expiry). By contrast, in the vega sector, only trading strategies involving changes in the implied volatility are sensible (since the option price depends largely on implied volatility) and practicable (since holding until expiry takes too much time).

In order to further minimize the impact from moves in the underlying and thus the need for delta hedging, one should execute option trades in the vega sector by using straddles. By having largely excluded realized volatility as a driving factor, one obtains a pure exposure to implied volatility and can now consider and trade the volatility surface *in abstraction* from the underlying swap rates, by statistical analysis and trading tools.

Option strategy type ③ is therefore constructed using straddles in the vega sector, mainly exposed to changes in implied volatility, and unwound well before expiry.

Different Exposure of Different Types of Option Trades

This abstract classification of option trades into three different types is important in order to ensure clarity about the exposure and a correct expression of the exposure desired. We stress this point because some analysts tend to confuse the driving factors in option trades and therefore construct option trades whose exposures do not match the ones outlined in their reasoning. As an illustration, we show how similar three "2Y versus 10Y" option trades provide very different exposures:

① Buy 6M2Y receivers,[8] sell 6M10Y receivers, and do not delta hedge. Then you have a 2Y-10Y yield curve steepening position, *conditional on a rally*, with no exposure to the continuous realized volatility[9] and no exposure to changes in implied volatility after entering the trade.

② Buy 6M2Y receivers, sell 6M10Y receivers, and delta hedge until expiry. Then you have a realized 2Y volatility minus a realized 10Y volatility position, with no exposure to the curve steepness at expiry[10] and no exposure to changes in implied volatility after entering the trade.

---

[8]This notation refers to a receiver swaption on 2Y swaps with 6M time to expiry.
[9]Except from the part of continuous realized volatility that is reflected in the position of the underlying at the end (i.e. the "1-period-realized volatility"). However, as in the example of the S&P500 index above, it is possible that a high (continuous) volatility results in no change of the underlying between entry and expiry of the option.
[10]Except from the part of overall curve moves that is reflected in continuous realized volatility. A large move in one direction will be accompanied by some (continuous) volatility.

③ Buy 5Y2Y straddles, sell 5Y10Y straddles, and unwind after one month. Then, you have an implied 5Y2Y volatility minus an implied 5Y10Y volatility position (with very little exposure to the curve steepness and very little exposure to realized volatility).

Of course, it is possible to switch categories. For example, starting with ②, after three months of delta hedging, one could decide to stop delta hedging (i.e. to shift to ①) or to unwind the remaining 3M options (i.e. to shift to ③). However, within each category of trades, both the exposure and the corresponding expression/execution are defined and must not be confused with another category.

In the following, we shall discuss these three types of option trades separately. Given their different exposure and construction, they require different analysis tools, which we shall also develop below.

OPTION TRADE TYPE ①: SINGLE UNDERLYING

Buying or selling any combination of options on the same underlying and not delta hedging gives an exposure to the payoff profile of that combination of options. Since the payoff of an option depends on the underlying *if it is above or below the strike*, this results in a *conditional* exposure to the yield of the underlying at expiry. For example, buying a 6M2Y receiver with a strike of 1% and not delta hedging it until expiry means entering into a long 2Y swap position *conditional* on the 2Y swap rate in six months' time being below 1%.

In the absence of delta hedging, there are only two driving forces of the P&L of such strategies: the option premium received or paid at entry and the loss or gain from exercising the option at expiry (if it ends ITM).[11] Depending on the payoff profile constructed and the implied volatility at entry, one receives or pays a premium. If one has received a premium at entry (e.g. by selling receiver swaptions), one has to pay at expiry in the event the option ends ITM.

Thus, in order to assess value in option trades of type ①, one needs to compare the two driving forces of their profits and losses: premium at entry and potential payoff at expiry. The simplest way to do so is to calculate the breakeven value of the underlying at expiry (i.e. the value of the underlying at expiry at which the payoff of the option is equal to its initial premium). For example, if we sold an ATMF receiver swaption, we could calculate the

---

[11]We restrict this analysis to European options. However, similar analysis tools can be used for American options as well.

decline in the underlying swap rate which would cause a loss at expiry that was equal to the premium we had received up-front. If the yield ended above that breakeven level, our overall P&L from that strategy would be positive; if it finished below the breakeven level, it would be negative.

By assessing the breakeven levels of these option strategies, an analyst can see:

- whether expressing a macro view on the yield curve with options (rather than with the underlying) is attractive at all;
- and, if it is, which option strategy (e.g. short receivers or short straddles?) is better;
- and then, once that is decided, which underlying and expiry provide the best expected return.

In order to support that analysis, the basic tools are charts depicting the spot yield curve, the forward yield curve, and the breakeven levels. Each expiry (1M, 3M, 6M, 1Y) and strategy (payers, receivers, straddles) requires one of those charts. Figure 19.6, Figure 19.7, and Figure 19.8 show the example for 1Y expiry ATMF straddles, payer, and receiver swaptions on the JPY yield curve.

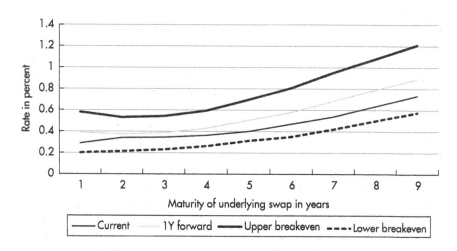

FIGURE 19.6 Breakeven curves for 1Y ATMF straddles on different maturities of the JPY yield curve.

Sources: data – Bloomberg; chart – Authors.

Data period: "Current" market data as of 18 Jun 2012.

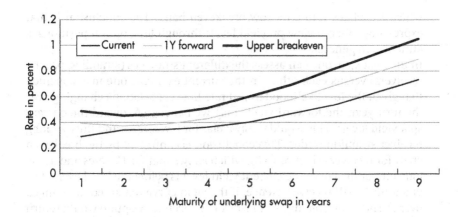

FIGURE 19.7 Breakeven curves for 1Y ATMF payer swaptions on different maturities of the JPY yield curve.
Sources: data – Bloomberg; chart – Authors.

Data period: "Current" market data as of 18 Jun 2012.

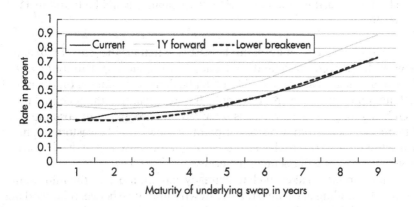

FIGURE 19.8 Breakeven curves for 1Y ATMF receiver swaptions on different maturities of the JPY yield curve.
Sources: data – Bloomberg; chart – Authors.

Data period: "Current" market data as of 18 Jun 2012.

In this example, an analyst could answer the questions from above as follows:

- Looking at the straddle chart (Figure 19.6), the width of the breakeven band around the forward curve appears to be rather narrow. This corresponds to a relatively low implied volatility, thus a low option premium, which translates into a narrow breakeven band. The conclusion is that expressing a macro view on yield levels through long option positions is attractive in general.

■ In the next step, one can assess the different strategies (straddles, payers, receivers) versus each other. In the current example, one may conclude that given the low likelihood of BoJ rate hike expectations changing over the next year, the forward yields may well converge toward the current spot yield levels. This would imply a bias for lower rates and thus for long receiver swaption trades. This conclusion is confirmed by the breakeven chart for receivers (Figure 19.8), which shows that for 1Y rates and at the long end of the curve the current yield level is below the breakeven level of a long ATMF receiver. Hence, if the yield curve remained unchanged over the next year, buying a 1Y1Y or 1Y7Y receiver swaption would return a small overall profit.

■ Finally, since the distance between the breakeven line and the current yield level in Figure 19.8 is maximal for 1Y and 7Y underlying swap maturities, buying a 1Y1Y or 1Y7Y receiver swaption seems best from a breakeven point of view. As the yield outlook is usually more certain for shorter maturities, the best risk/reward balance could be found in 1Y1Y receivers.

Additionally, one may want to assess whether the current distance between breakeven levels and spot rates is a unique opportunity or rather close to the historical average. This could be done by plotting a time series of that difference. In the current example, it may reveal that the potential profit from being long 1Y1Y receivers is relatively small both on an absolute basis (Figure 19.8) and from a historical point of view. Thus, investors might be enticed to enter those trades at the current levels only if they have a strong view that 1Y rates will decline further.

These simple breakeven charts already contain much of the information relevant for trading decisions: the roll-down (difference between forward and spot), the absolute level of implied volatility (width of breakeven bands around forward curve), and its relative distribution across the maturity spectrum. In the example above, this information could be combined to find (relatively small) value in long 1Y1Y receiver swaptions, offering a good roll-down even slightly below the breakeven band, which reflects low implied volatility in general and at the short end of the curve in particular.

On the other hand, we observed two shortcomings of this basic approach:

■ It requires many breakeven charts, one for every expiry (e.g. 1M, 3M, 6M, 1Y) and for every strategy (at a minimum, straddles, receivers, and payers). This makes at least 12 charts, each of which features a yield curve of maybe 10 points. More than one hundred potential trades present a challenge to the oversight of the analyst and become hard to assess informally. In the example above, how does the greater distance between current yield and lower breakeven (Figure 19.8) in 7Y relative to 1Y compare with the greater sensitivity of 7Y relative to 1Y to potential rate hike expectations? It would therefore be desirable to have a uniform and quantitative criterion to assess all potential trading strategies.

- Every option trade of type ① with a single underlying is a macro position, as it takes a view on the level of the underlying at expiry. Thus, the approach of the breakeven analysis to compare the option premium (via translation into breakeven levels) with the level of the underlying at expiry in essence links the option market through breakeven levels to the macroeconomic expectations of the analyst. In the charts, the comparison of the option market as expressed in breakeven levels to macroeconomic scenarios is done *outside* of the analysis tool (breakeven charts) and thus informally. For example, we argued above verbally: "Given the BoJ is very unlikely to hike soon, it is also unlikely for 1Y rates in a year's time to exceed 0.3% [lower breakeven in Figure 19.8] and thus for a long 1Y1Y receiver swaption to lose money [from ending less ITM than its up-front premium requires to break even]."

The idea is therefore to solve both shortcomings together by linking the breakeven analysis to a uniform and quantifiable macroeconomic variable. This incorporates the informal macroeconomic assessment of breakeven levels into the framework of the analysis and allows us to compare different option strategies by their performance with regard to the relevant macroeconomic variable. The macroeconomic variable chosen depends on the goal of the analysis and on the views of the analyst. If he has a view on BoJ policy, he will choose the policy rate; if he has a view on CPI, he will choose CPI. For example, if a 1Y yield of 0.3% corresponds to a CPI level of −0.1, then he can argue that for the lower breakeven not to be reached, CPI in Japan would need to rise to above −0.1 over the next year.[12]

A formal analysis linking the option market through breakeven levels to macroeconomic variables and scenarios can be done in two directions:

- Either the breakeven levels are translated into corresponding macroeconomic variables. In the example above, we have calculated the "option

---

[12]This is for illustration purposes only and does not intend to make statements about the link of interest rates to CPI, etc. Actually, the recent correlation between JPY swap rates and macroeconomic variables such as CPI or seasonally adjusted GDP growth has been rather poor.

implied" (i.e. breakeven level implied) CPI figure. This indicates the macroeconomic scenario to which the current pricing in the option market corresponds. Now that the analyst can assess the pricing in the option market in macroeconomic terms, he can express his macro views through options, if he sees that the pricing in the option market does not match his economic expectations.

■ Or, the other way round (which is more practicable when the macro model of the yield curve involves more than a single variable), one could define macroeconomic scenarios (baseline, recession, recovery), translate them via a macro model (like a VAR model) into yield forecasts, and compare these forecasts with the breakeven levels. If one finds an option strategy that benefits under each scenario, one has found a good candidate for a trade idea. This comparison of yield forecasts in different economic scenarios with breakeven levels could be done, for example, by calculating the number of standard deviations by which the breakeven level exceeds the yield forecast. Displaying these t-stats for different options simultaneously (e.g. in the form of a heat map for each macroeconomic scenario) can facilitate the selection of the best strategy.[13]

In the following, we provide an example of the first approach, assuming that we have a view on the Japanese CPI and want to compare the pricing of the swaption market with our CPI forecast. Note that this is for illustrative purposes only, as the correlation between CPI and interest rates in Japan (0.5) would, in our view, be too weak to base trades on.

In the first step, the breakeven levels for long receiver swaptions are calculated for each expiry (3M, 6M, etc.) and for each time to maturity of the underlying swap (1Y, 2Y, etc.). Then, the difference between that breakeven level and the current yield level is expressed in terms of the corresponding change in factor 1 of a PCA on the JPY swap yield curve.[14] As described in Chapter 3, the change in factor 1 can then be associated with a change in the CPI. As a result, for each expiry and underlying maturity of the receiver swaption, we obtain the CPI at which a long receiver position is expected to break even. In other words, we have translated the prices in the option market into the corresponding CPI figures. And since we have several expiries, we have even obtained the *evolution* of the CPI as implied by breakeven levels of receivers. Every underlying swap maturity results in a different implied CPI evolution, all of which are depicted in Figure 19.9.

---

[13]An example of this second approach can be found in "Front-End Payer Swaptions: Shorts Offer Value," published by ABN AMRO Research on 25 February 2005.
[14]By dividing the yield difference in a certain maturity with the entry in the first eigenvector for that maturity.

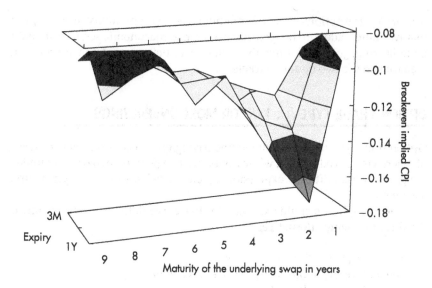

FIGURE 19.9   Option market-implied evolution of the CPI as calculated through the breakeven levels of long receiver swaptions.
Sources: data – Bloomberg; chart – Authors.

Data period: "Current" market data as of 18 Jun 2012.

Thus we find that a view on a low CPI can best be expressed through long 6M1Y receiver swaptions. Note the way the formal comparison of all option strategies through the uniform macroeconomic variable "breakeven implied CPI" has confirmed the informal argument we made verbally when looking at the breakeven charts. If in six months' time the CPI is below −0.08, then the 1Y swap rate level is expected to be below the breakeven level of 30.4 bp (basis points), and hence the profit from a long 6M1Y receiver swaption at expiry is expected to be greater than the up-front premium payment required.

Likewise, a view on a high CPI can best be expressed though short 1Y2Y receiver swaptions. As long as the CPI in one year is above −0.17, the option premium received up-front is expected to exceed the potential loss from the option being exercised at expiry.

Furthermore, in case a tradable instrument is selected as the universal comparison for all breakeven levels (e.g. a commodity future rather than the CPI), this approach leads us to compare the volatility in the swaption market with the volatility in the option market on the tradable instrument (e.g. options on the commodity future). Thereby a relative value link between two option markets (and their implied macroeconomic scenarios) is established. This could be the basis for exploiting mismatches between the two (e.g. via long swaptions versus short options on the commodity future). These relative value trades are hedged against the macroeconomic scenario actually materializing, just exploiting the different anticipation of macroeconomic scenarios in the two option markets.

OPTION TRADE TYPE ①: TWO OR MORE UNDERLYINGS

Option trade type ① on one single underlying gives a conditional expression of macro views (yield level), while option trade type ① on two or more underlyings gives a conditional expression of relative value views (e.g. yield curve steepness).

For example, we could express a 2Y-10Y curve flattening view via any of the three following alternatives:

- pay 2Y, receive 10Y (no options);
- sell a 2Y receiver, buy a 10Y receiver (swaption);
- buy a 2Y payer, sell a 10Y payer (swaption).

In comparison with the first alternative, the expression with options has the following specific features:

(1) It is conditional (i.e. it is exposed to the underlying curve steepness only under the condition that the options are ITM at expiry).
(2) It involves an option premium, which is determined by the difference in 2Y and 10Y implied volatility at entry.

And the two possibilities (via receivers or payers) to express the curve flattening through options are different in the way they offer (1) and (2):

(1) The expression with receivers gives a curve position conditional on a rally, while the expression with payers gives a curve position conditional on a selloff.
(2) The expression with receivers will return an up-front premium pick-up if implied 2Y volatility is higher than implied 10Y volatility (adjusted for hedge ratios); the expression with payers will return an upfront premium pick-up if implied 2Y volatility is lower than implied 10Y volatility.

The conditionality (1) allows selecting the directional environment that is favorable for the trade. For the following example, assume that the 2Y-10Y yield curve usually flattens in a selloff and steepens in a rally. Thus, we would prefer to express a curve-flattening view with *payer* swaptions: only in

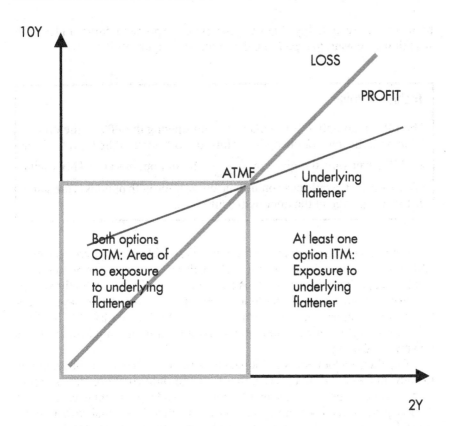

FIGURE 19.10 P&L from a 2Y-10Y curve-flattening position with swaps and with payer swaptions.
Source: Authors.

the case of a selloff would these options expire ITM, hence giving us exposure to a curve-flattening position, which is expected to perform well in a selloff. In the case of a rally (associated with curve steepening), both options expire OTM, thus preventing us from exposure to (underperforming) yield curve flattening. Illustrating this crucial point, Figure 19.10 depicts the way that conditionality of option trades of type ① can be used to select the favorable directional environment and to eliminate exposure to curve positions in unfavorable directional situations.

Note that for this purpose we want curve trades to be directional. Thus, we use here a basis point value (BPV) neutral weighting rather than a PCA-neutral weighting (see discussion of Figure 3.14). Put otherwise, when expressing curve trades with swaps (no options), we wanted to *solve* the problem of directionality (Figure 3.14); when expressing curve trades with swaptions, we want to *exploit* the directionality (Figure 19.10).

Technical Point

The BPV of an option is calculated by multiplying the BPV of the underlying with the delta of the option. Thus, the BPV-neutral hedge ratio for a 2Y-10Y payer spread is given by $\frac{BPV_{10}\delta_{10}}{BPV_2\delta_2}$. If both options are ATMF (delta of 0.5), the hedge ratio of a conditional curve trade with options is the same as the hedge ratio of the underlying curve trade.

Having selected the right conditionality (1) (i.e. decided between receivers and payers), we now look at feature (2). In abstract terms, the expression of a yield curve position through options combines the yield curve with the volatility curve. In our example, the long 2Y payer versus short 10Y payer swaption position returns an up-front premium if the implied 2Y-10Y volatility curve (at entry) is upward-sloping, and requires a premium payment if it is downward-sloping.

Together, we look for conditional curve trades with options that combine the advantages of (1) and (2) (i.e. that have the right conditionality *and* provide an up-front premium payment). If we get paid a premium to execute our 2Y-10Y payer spread, we can expect to win in either directional environment: if yields increase, options are ITM, putting us into the underlying flattening trade, which should perform well in a selloff. If yields decrease, options are OTM, and we keep the initial up-front premium payment as profit (of course, we also do in the event yields increase).

As an example for a conditional butterfly trade, assume that 5Y tends to underperform versus 2Y and 10Y in the event of a selloff. Thus, we can exploit the directionality by going long 5Y payers versus short 2Y and 10Y payers and by going long 5Y receivers versus short 2Y and 10Y receivers (or by combining both by going long 5Y straddles versus short 2Y and 10Y straddles). In each case, the options are ITM only in the case of a directional move that is favorable for the underlying butterfly position. In the next step, we need to calculate whether we get paid for entering those trades (i.e. whether the curvature of the 2Y-5Y-10Y implied volatility curve is negative).

Unfortunately, as a sign of the efficiency of option markets, these opportunities are rare. The 2Y-10Y yield curve flattening in a selloff means that realized volatility in 2Y is higher than in 10Y, and if this is reflected in the implied volatility (option prices), 2Y payers will be more expensive than 10Y payers. Likewise in the butterfly example: 5Y underperforming 2Y and 10Y in a selloff is another way of saying that realized volatility in 5Y is higher than in 2Y and 10Y. Most of the time this is reflected in the option prices (i.e. in a positive curvature of the 2Y-5Y-10Y implied volatility curve). Therefore, usually strategies with the right conditionality (1) require a premium payment (2).

However, sometimes these opportunities arise and provide good candidates for trade ideas when they do. In order to screen the market for these chances, we recommend calculating for every curve steepness and butterfly trade:

(1) its directionality and the strength of that relationship (e.g. the R^2 from a regression, as in Figure 3.14);
(2) for the "right" conditionality (i.e. payers or receivers) the premium pickup or payment involved in expressing that curve trade through options.

Good candidates should have (1) a strong correlation to the direction (were the directionality to change, the conditional curve trade could lose) and (2) at least zero cost. Nhan Ngoc Le had the idea of simultaneously displaying both features of all candidates as a scatter plot chart (Figure 19.11) and looking for points in the upper-right corner. This can be a useful tool for screening the option market for trading opportunities with conditional yield curve trades. In the chart, one finds that among all possible strategies only a conditional 7Y-10Y-20Y butterfly provides stable directionality *and* a (small) premium pick-up for the right conditionality.

Similarly, one can construct conditional swap spread positions through a combination of bond options and swaptions. We have shown in Chapter 12 that before the Lehman crisis swap spreads widened (became more negative) in a selloff. Thus, if one believes that this directionality will hold true in the future, one would want to have swap spread widening positions conditional on a selloff and swap spread narrowing positions conditional on a rally, that is:

- long payer swaptions versus short bond puts;
- long receiver swaptions versus short bond calls.

Again, swap spreads widening in a selloff means that the realized volatility in swaps is greater than in bonds. Thus, the right conditionality (1) is to be always long swaptions versus short bond options. How is that realized volatility relationship reflected in the option markets? In particular, do swaptions usually trade at a premium versus bond options (2)? Do we need to pay a premium for the right conditionality? Figure 19.12 answers these questions

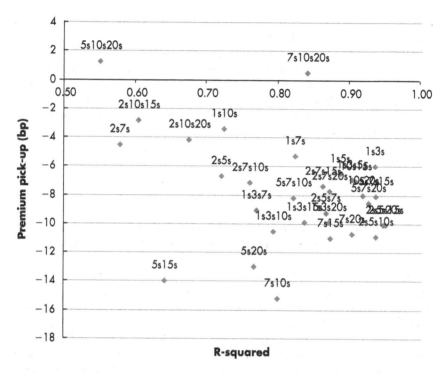

FIGURE 19.11 Premium pick-up/payment versus stability of directionality for conditional curve trades with options.
Source: Nhan Ngoc Le.

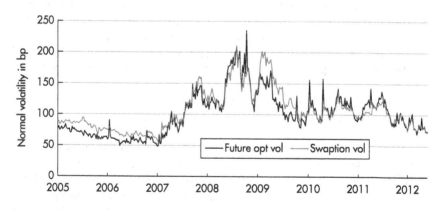

FIGURE 19.12 History of implied US bond futures option volatility versus implied USD swaption volatility (3M expiry, normalized).
Sources: data – Bloomberg; chart – Authors.

Data period: 11 May 2005 to 3 Oct 2012, weekly data.

for the US market. For reasons of liquidity and comparability, we have used futures options rather than bond options. Due to future specific flows, the volatility of implied futures options is at times higher than that of implied swaptions or implied bond options (and shows up as spikes in the chart).

It appears that the directionality of swap spreads is very well reflected in the relationship between implied swaption volatility and implied futures option volatility. Before the Lehman crisis, when swap spreads tended to widen as yields increased, swaptions normally traded at a premium versus bond options. As the Lehman crisis caused both the cost of equity for banks and thus swap spreads to widen (see Chapter 11), and the yield level to decrease, the directionality of swap spreads broke down. Correspondingly, since the Lehman crisis the premium for swaption volatility has disappeared, and it currently trades close to implied futures volatility.

An investor believing that the directionality of swap spreads will return to pre-crisis levels may see this as an opportunity to enter into long swaption versus short bond option positions.

OPTION TRADE TYPE ②: SINGLE UNDERLYING

Not delta hedging an option gives exposure to the overall realized volatility of the one period from entry to expiry, hence to the overall move of the underlying security.

Delta hedging an option (as continuous as practicable) restores the Black–Scholes framework (which assumes continuous delta hedging) outlined at the beginning of this chapter and results in the following changes versus trade type ①:

- The exposure shifts from the payoff profile of an option at expiry (the total realized volatility over the whole time period) to the continuous realized volatility of the underlying until expiry.
- The long option holder delta hedging his position is always overhedged when the market declines and underhedged when the market increases. Thus, the size of market moves (realized volatility) will determine his profit from delta hedging.
- This removes the conditionality: only the amount of moves (their frequency and scale) matters. Their direction does not. Even with a single underlying, there is no directional exposure – at least not to the direction of the underlying. (However, there is exposure to the "direction" of realized volatility.)
- The option premium (implied volatility) can be considered the market price for the right to be on the profitable side of delta hedging.

Thus, the P&L of option trade type ② is the difference between the implied volatility at entry point and the realized volatility of the underlying between entry and expiry. Put otherwise, it is the difference between the market price for the right to be on the profitable side of delta hedging and the actual profit one will realize by making use of this right. If realized volatility will exceed the current implied volatility, then the profit from delta hedging will exceed the initial option premium (i.e. the price for the right to generate profits from delta hedging).

The basic approach to the analysis of option trades of type ② is therefore to compare the two driving factors of their P&L, that is:

- the *current* implied volatility, which is a known variable;
- the *future* realized volatility (between entry and expiry), which is an unknown variable.

As the current implied volatility should reflect the market consensus about the future realized volatility, one will see value in option trades of type ② only if:

- the analyst's expectation of future realized volatility is different from the market consensus; or
- flows in the option market prevent implied volatility from reflecting the "true" market consensus about future realized volatility.

A tool to support that basic analysis could be a chart that compares the current implied volatility level with the *historical* realized volatility in different scenarios. Figure 19.13 provides an example of such a comparison for Japan.

Of course, *historical* realized volatility over the last few months can be very different from the *future* realized volatility over the next few months, which will determine the P&L. Still, the historical perspective from Figure 19.13 allows one to assess those macroeconomic environments that have in the past led to realized volatility levels that were similar to the current implied volatility. Using Figure 19.13 as an example, we conclude that the current implied volatility level was realized during 2010, when quantitative easing (expectations) removed all uncertainty (= volatility) about BoJ policy. Any shock, whether caused by nature or mankind, has resulted in a realized volatility which exceeded the current implied volatility level, at times quite significantly.

Currently, the implied volatility (19 bp) is slightly higher than the most recent realized volatility (16 bp). However, the historical perspective of

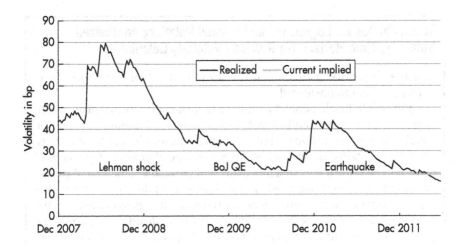

FIGURE 19.13 5Y JPY swaption volatility (normal): History of realized versus current implied volatility.
Sources: data – Bloomberg; chart – Authors.

Data period: 24 Dec 2007 to 18 Jun 2012, weekly data; "current" market data as of 18 Jun 2012.

Figure 19.13 reveals that realized volatility has usually been much higher not only than the current realized volatility but also than the current implied volatility.

Based on this tool, an analyst can now judge whether the market consensus is in line with his forecast. If he anticipates the next few months to look similar to 2010, he will find no opportunity for an option trade of type ② with a single underlying. If, on the other hand, he sees the potential for another shock, for example, a European banking crisis repeating the impact of Lehman on realized volatility, he will find value in buying options at 19 bp implied volatility. Actually, since the current level of 19 bp implied volatility seems to be close to the minimum of historical realized volatility, one could even think of long delta hedged options as a low-cost, low-risk way to position for potential shocks: if the dull period of 2010 is replicated in the next few months, delta hedging a long option should produce a profit that is about the same as the premium paid. On the other hand, any shock can result in a significantly higher realized volatility and thus profit.

Technical Points: Lognormal and Normal Volatility, Annualized Volatility, Time Horizon for Realized Volatility Calculation

In order to provide a clean analysis of realized volatility, two technical points need to be considered.

First of all, Black–Scholes assumes a (constant) lognormal distribution of yields. We do not intend to enter into a theoretical argument about the validity of this assumption[15] but instead to consider its practical pitfalls. Since lognormality assumes constant percentage changes independent of the level, the same lognormal move (percentage change) means a different absolute move (bp change) when the yield level is different. This makes comparisons of volatility on a lognormal basis meaningless in the event the yield level is different, for example, when volatilities in different parts of the yield curve (with different yield levels) are compared or the historical evolution of volatility is displayed (as the yield level typically fluctuates over time as well). Moreover, as yields approach zero, the same yield change in basis-point terms results in increasing lognormal changes. This issue is of particular relevance in the current environment of globally low interest rates.

Since lognormality cannot deal appropriately with low interest rates (and with negative yields at all), we prefer to use normal volatility. Realized normal volatility can be easily derived by calculating the standard deviation over daily basis-point changes (rather than percentage changes). This result represents the realized volatility over the time period used in the input data (e.g. trading-daily realized volatility if the input data series consists of trading-daily data). Usually, volatility is expressed in annual terms and can be obtained by multiplying the volatility for a certain time period with the square root of the number of those time units in a year. For example, trading-daily volatility can be annualized by multiplying by the square root of 252; weekly volatility can be annualized by multiplying by the square root of 52. Of course, this also works the other way round: an annual volatility can be translated into weekly and daily volatility.

If we prefer to calculate normal realized volatility, we also need to express the implied volatility in normal terms, for example, for a comparison as in Figure 19.13. However, implied volatility is usually quoted through a Black–Scholes pricing formula (i.e. in lognormal terms). The cleanest way to "normalize" it is to translate the implied lognormal volatility through the Black–Scholes formula into an option price (in dollars and cents) and then to calibrate a normal option model so that the normal

---

[15] Both the assumption of a *constant* lognormal volatility and of a constant *lognormal* volatility can be subjected to criticism. We deal here with the latter issue.

volatility input into the normal model replicates that option price. A faster, though less reliable method (in particular when yields are low and there is a chance of negative yields) consists in multiplying the implied lognormal volatility with the forward rate of the underlying security (with the forward horizon being given by the expiry of the option).

Second, the time window used for calculating historical realized volatility can become an issue. Commonly, analysts use a rolling window with a fixed time length (e.g. three or six months). Then, the realized volatility of a certain date is calculated as the standard deviation of the yield changes that occurred in the 3M or 6M time window prior to that date. The problem is that the result depends on the arbitrary choice of the rolling window. Imagine a time series with an average change of 1 bp per day, which contains one very volatile point with a change of 10 bp. When that volatile point enters the rolling time window, the realized volatility series spikes up. This is how it should be, since on that day there was indeed a high volatility. However, when that volatile point falls out of the rolling time window, the realized volatility series suddenly drops back to the average level. This is a problem since on the day when the sudden drop in the realized volatility occurs, nothing special has happened at all. The only thing that occurred and caused that sudden drop was that the day with an extraordinarily high 10 bp volatility happened to be precisely three or six months earlier. And depending on the arbitrary choice of the time window, the sudden drop in volatility occurs after three or after six months. This effect can be seen in Figure 19.14. What was the realized volatility in Mar 2009: 24 bp or 45 bp?

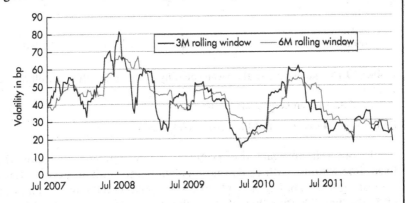

FIGURE 19.14 Realized 10Y JPY swap volatility, calculated with a 3M and a 6M rolling window.
Sources: data – Bloomberg; chart – Authors.

Data period: 2 Jul 2007 to 18 Jun 2012, weekly data.

(continued)

(continued)

When using rolling time windows, the answer depends on the arbitrary choice of 3M or 6M for the length of that window.

Consequently, using rolling time windows produces realized volatility series whose spikes higher in volatility correctly reflect market action, but whose spikes lower in volatility are the result of the arbitrary definition of the length of the time window. These can occur at different points in time and have little to do with the actual volatility on the day they occur. This problem is illustrated in Figure 19.15, which shows the realized volatility of 10Y JPY swap rates, calculated with a rolling 3M time window. The arrows indicate days on which the time series dropped sharply, not because something happened in the market but simply because the volatile day that caused the spike three months earlier rolled out of the window.

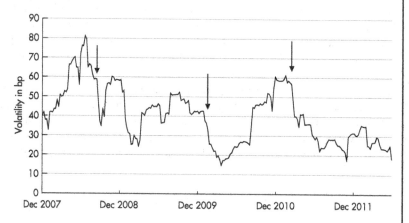

FIGURE 19.15   Realized 10Y JPY swap volatility, calculated with a 3M rolling window.

Sources: data – Bloomberg; chart – Authors.

Data period: 24 Dec 2007 to 18 Jun 2012, weekly data.

In order to mitigate this problem, we recommend replacing the fixed time window with weighting the data points with an exponentially decreasing function. For example, the latest point could have a weighting of 1, the point before that of 0.97, the point before that of 0.95, etc. The exponential weighting function assigns maximal weight to the latest data point. Thus, if this point turns out to be volatile, there will be a spike higher in the realized volatility series on that day, just as is the case with a rolling time window. On the other hand, a volatile data point will not drop out at a specific date but rather lose weight slowly and incrementally, day after day. In other words, a 3M rolling time window assigns a weighting of 1 to all points less than three months ago and of 0 to all points more than three months ago, which causes the sudden drop when a volatile point becomes more than three months old. Exponentially decreasing weightings, by contrast, assign every day a bit less importance to the volatile data point, so that its impact on the realized volatility fades away slowly. This fits the intuition of a gradually declining importance of older points for the current realized volatility quite well. Of course, there are still arbitrary decisions to be made, such as the use of an exponentially decreasing weighting function (rather than a linear or quadratic one) and the choice of a decay parameter for that function. However, these choices affect the end result much less than the sudden drops in a realized volatility series calculated with a rolling time window. To demonstrate that advantage, we have calculated the same realized 10Y JPY swap volatility history from Figure 19.14 and Figure 19.15 with exponentially decreasing weightings and depict the series in Figure 19.16. We see that upward spikes to the realized volatility series are captured as well with the exponential smoothing as they are with the rolling window. But by using exponentially decreasing weightings, we can eliminate the sharp, meaningless drops that were produced by the rolling window, replacing them with a more accurate, smoother decline.

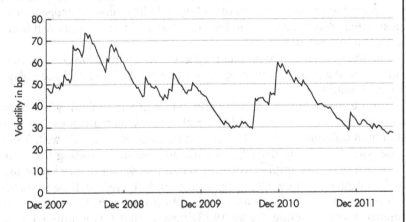

FIGURE 19.16 Realized 10Y JPY swap volatility, calculated with exponentially decreasing weightings.
Sources: data – Bloomberg; chart – Authors.

Data period: 24 Dec 2007 to 18 Jun 2012, weekly data.

OPTION TRADE TYPE ②: TWO OR MORE UNDERLYINGS

The risk in the trade described above is that the volatility actually realized may be greater or less than the volatility we anticipated. As a result, option trades of type ② with a single underlying can be seen as fundamental bets on whether particular macroeconomic scenarios materialize. As shown in Table 3.1, macroeconomic events tend to impact both the direction of the underlying swap rates and the realized volatility level, resulting in a significant correlation between them. Though option trades of type ② have no direct exposure to the underlying due to delta hedging, their exposure to the level of realized volatility does link them to the corresponding macroeconomic environment of high or low uncertainty (as caused by such events as central bank action, banking crises, etc.).

In order to reduce the macroeconomic exposure, the idea is to combine two of those trades, a long and a short option (both delta hedged), thus to hedge against the *overall* level of future realized volatility and to leave exposure just to the *relative* realized volatility distribution across the yield curve. This leads to relative value positions exploiting structural mismatches along the implied and realized volatility curves.

For example, buying 2Y straddles, selling 10Y straddles, and delta hedging both is a *box trade* between the current implied volatility curve and the future realized volatility curve, which will profit if the future realized volatility curve is flatter than the current implied volatility curve. If hedge ratios are constructed properly, the overall level of future realized volatility will have no impact on that position.

In order to screen the market for these trading opportunities, an analyst could look at a graph comparing the current implied and realized volatility curves (Figure 19.17).

In this example, we can first observe that implied volatility is currently above the recent realized volatility for all underlying maturities, but with a minimum difference for 5Y. This means that trades of type ② with a single underlying (i.e. a long delta hedged option position exploiting the relative cheapness of current implied volatility versus the average realized volatility[16]) are best expressed in the 5Y segment. Of course, the risk to these positions is that the realized volatility until expiry will turn out to be below the current implied volatility. While Figure 19.13 suggests that this is rather unlikely,

---

[16]Though current implied volatility is slightly rich versus *current* realized volatility (see Figure 19.13).

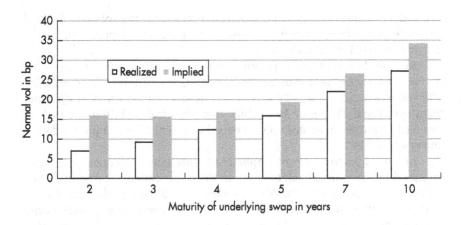

FIGURE 19.17 Current realized and implied volatility across the JPY curve.
Sources: data – Bloomberg; chart – Authors.

Data period: "Current" market data as of 18 Jun 2012.

it does expose a long option trade of type ② to the macroeconomic risk of an environment that produces extremely low realized volatility, such as BoJ announcements removing all uncertainty about future interest rates. Above, we have developed tools to assess the risk/return profiles of these positions.

Now we look at the same information displayed in Figure 19.17 differently, with the eyes of a relative value analyst who wants to be hedged against macroeconomic impacts as well as possible and just to exploit relative mismatches in the options market. Thus, our focus shifts from the *level* of implied versus realized volatility to their distribution over different maturities, to the *shape* of the implied volatility curve relative to the realized volatility curve. And it jumps out at the "relative value eye" immediately that the realized volatility curve is much steeper than the implied volatility curve between 2Y and 5Y. If we have reason to believe the realized volatility curve will remain steep in future as well, we could exploit the mismatch between the steepness of the implied curve relative to the realized volatility curve by buying 3M5Y straddles versus selling 3M2Y straddles and delta hedging both. Then, an increase in the overall level of realized volatility would cause the delta hedging of the long straddle position to win as much as the delta hedging of the short straddle position loses (if hedge ratios are appropriate). Thus, we are hedged against changes to the overall level of realized volatility. Instead, we are exposed to the difference between realized and implied volatility in 5Y *relative* to that difference in 2Y.

In order to assess that exposure, we recommend adjusting Figure 19.13 to two underlyings and thus depicting the history of the realized volatility *difference* between 5Y and 2Y versus the current implied volatility *difference* between 5Y and 2Y. Figure 19.18 shows the historical evolution of the 2Y-5Y realized volatility curve steepness versus the current 2Y-5Y implied volatility curve steepness.

In this case, the current implied volatility curve steepness was never matched by the realized volatility curve steepness during the past five years. Thus, if we had entered the long 5Y short 2Y straddle position at current implied volatility levels and delta hedged it until expiry at any point during the past five years, we would always have made money (on average 10 bp). Of course, it is possible that the future 5Y-2Y realized volatility spread will be below the current implied volatility spread. However, Figure 19.18 makes us confident that this is unlikely, given that the range of the 5Y-2Y realized volatility spread has over the tumultuous past five years been stably in a range between 6 bp and 27 bp, and even the lower end of that range is still away

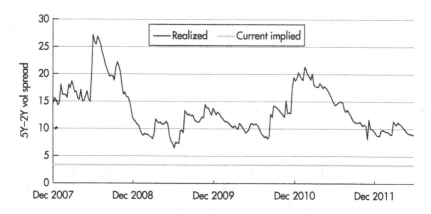

FIGURE 19.18   History of 2Y-5Y JPY realized volatility curve steepness versus current 2Y-5Y JPY implied volatility curve steepness.
Sources: data – Bloomberg; chart – Authors.

Data period: 24 Dec 2007 to 18 Jun 2012, weekly data; "current" market data as of 18 Jun 2012.

from the current implied volatility spread of 3 bp. Moreover, given recent BoJ announcements, we have no reason to expect realized volatility at the short end of the yield curve to increase relative to realized volatility in 5Y as much as is priced into the implied volatility curve. Thus, we have not only a statistical reason (history of Figure 19.18) but also a fundamental reason to believe that the steepness of the realized volatility curve will continue in the future and therefore for the current flatness of the implied volatility curve to be a trading opportunity.

As always, relative value considerations can also be used for asset selection purposes when expressing fundamental views. In this case, an analyst wanting to position for the overall future realized volatility level to be above the current implied volatility level (see Figure 19.13) could find best value in choosing long 5Y straddles to express his view (by looking at Figure 19.17).

Comparing Figure 19.13 and Figure 19.18, we observe significant correlation (0.71) between the level of realized volatility and the slope of the 2Y-5Y realized volatility curve: when overall volatility increases, the volatility curve tends to steepen. Depending on the goal, one can react to that observation in two ways:

- If we want to express the fundamental view of a high future realized volatility, we could do so via a 2Y-5Y straddle spread rather than a long 5Y straddle (trade type ② with two rather than one underlyings). If our fundamental view is correct, both the 5Y straddle and the 2Y-5Y straddle spread should perform well, as the two positions are highly correlated with one another. But the 2Y-5Y straddle spread is preferred, as it has a much better risk/return profile. While the 2Y-5Y straddle spread offers a 5 bp cushion against the volatility curve flattening associated with lower overall realized volatility (Figure 19.18), a long 5Y straddle will only win if realized volatility increases by at least 3 bp from its current level (Figure 19.13). Thus, for this goal we exploit the correlation between the "fundamental" and the "relative value" trade to improve the P&L from the same macroeconomic events.
- If, on the other hand, our goal is to hedge against the impacts of the overall realized volatility level, we can adjust the hedge ratio of the 2Y-5Y straddle spread in order to immunize against the exposure to the "direction" of realized volatility. Selling 1.23 2Y straddles for every 5Y straddle bought results in neutrality against the overall level of realized volatility. Figure 19.19 shows the history of the non-directional 2Y-5Y realized volatility curve steepness and illustrates the attractiveness of the pure relative value trade.

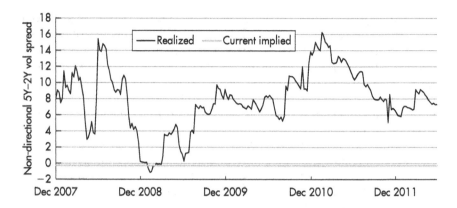

FIGURE 19.19   History of non-directional 2Y-5Y JPY realized volatility curve steepness versus current 2Y-5Y JPY implied volatility curve steepness. *Sources:* data – Bloomberg; chart – Authors.

Data period: 24 Dec 2007 to 18 Jun 2012, weekly data; "current" market data as of 18 Jun 2012.

Note that option trade types ① and ② both depend on the difference between current implied volatility and future realized volatility. Therefore, both look for opportunities in where the current market pricing (implied volatility) is out of line with the expected realized volatility. However, since the way that the two types of option trades exploit these mismatches is different, we recommend displaying the same information (implied versus realized volatility) in two different ways: for type ① in terms of premium versus directionality (Figure 19.11) and for type ② in terms of implied versus realized volatility curves (Figure 19.17).

OPTION TRADE TYPE ③: FACTOR MODEL FOR THE VEGA SECTOR

By contrast, straddles in the vega sector of the volatility surface are almost unaffected by realized volatility in the underlying and purely exposed to changes in the implied volatility level. This allows analysis of implied volatility in abstraction from its link to external variables, focusing on the internal relationships between different points on the implied volatility surface by treating them as purely statistical time series (without making use of the knowledge that the time series represents option volatilities, which is a market consensus about future realized volatility). In brief, type ③ strategies are option positions that trade options not *as* options but as abstract time series, not linked via delta hedging to an external variable.

Consequently, while the analysis tools for types ① and ② were based on the structural link of options (*as* such, as an option *on something*) to the underlying (i.e. on the link between implied and realized volatility), analysis tools for type ③ need to consider options in abstraction from that link and focus on the statistical relationships between different points on the implied volatility surface. An equivalent statement is that option trades of type ② are analyzed within the Black–Scholes framework,[17] while type ③ is conceptually different and treats options in abstraction from their link through delta hedging to the underlying. As in Chapter 13, where we analyzed the statistical properties of credit default swaps (CDS) in abstraction from a default situation, we now consider the mechanisms in the vega sector of the volatility surface in abstraction from the connection (through delta hedging) to the realized volatility.

Thus, the vega sector of the volatility surface is the right place to apply a statistical tool such as a PCA-based factor model. And conversely, the application of PCA on the volatility surface confirms empirically its differentiation into gamma and vega sectors. Running a PCA on the whole volatility surface reflects the break between the gamma and vega segments in different sensitivities to the first factor. As Figure 19.20 shows, sensitivity starts decreasing as the expiry increases – and even turns negative for very long expiries. The fact that the first eigenvector has entries with different signs is a clear indication for segmentation in the input variables and justifies empirically our approach to limit the statistical analysis to the vega sector.

Restricting the data input to options with at least 2Y to expiry indeed solves the problem and returns a first eigenvector which has only negative entries (Figure 19.21). That is, this first factor can be interpreted as the overall implied volatility level, which affects all instruments in the same direction, though to a different extent. Figure 19.21 also reveals the location of the break between the gamma and vega sectors in the JPY swaption market. For the 2Y expiry, only underlyings of more than 5Y are clearly in the vega segment, while, for a 5Y expiry, all options can be considered to be in the vega sector, independent of the maturity of the underlying swap. In terms of Figure 19.5, this means that, in the case of Japan, the borderline between the two segments is somewhat tilted to the right. That is, the longer the maturity of the underlying swap, the shorter the expiry needs to be in order for an option to be part of the vega sector (e.g. four years for an option on 1Y swaps, three years for an option on 2Y swaps, and two years for an option on 5Y swaps).

---

[17] And trades of type ① can be considered in that framework as one-period (instead of continuous) delta hedging strategies.

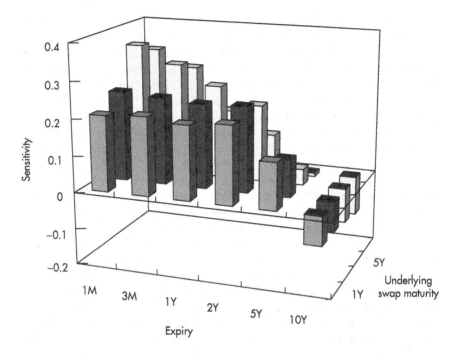

FIGURE 19.20   First eigenvector of a PCA on the whole JPY volatility surface.
Sources: data – Bloomberg; chart – Authors.

Data period: 5 Jan 2009 to 19 Sep 2011, weekly data.

Now that PCA has revealed the sector of the volatility surface on which it is applicable, we can run through the usual analytical process, whose results are depicted in Figure 19.22, Figure 19.23, and Figure 19.24.

Factor 1 can be interpreted as the overall level of implied volatility, with the shape of the first eigenvector showing the way changes in overall volatility impact the volatility surface. Factor 2 represents the steepness of volatility curves (same underlying, different expiries). If factor 2 increases, options with a long expiry increase relative to those with a short expiry, almost independent of the underlying swap maturity. Factor 3 represents the steepness of volatility curves (same expiry, different underlyings). If factor 3 increases, options with a long underlying swap maturity increase relative to those with a short underlying swap maturity, almost independent of the expiry.

Thus, PCA can be considered a decomposition of the volatility surface into its two dimensions, with the second and third factors quantifying the variation that occurs in a specific dimension. Factor 1 represents the *overall* implied volatility level and correspondingly affects *both* dimensions. Factors 2 and 3 explain that part of implied volatility which occurs in a specific dimension

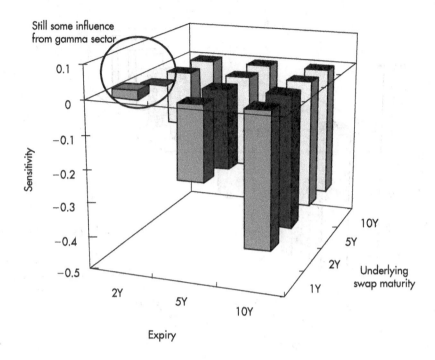

FIGURE 19.21   First eigenvector of a PCA on the vega sector of the JPY volatility surface.
Sources: data – Bloomberg; chart – Authors.

Data period: 5 Jan 2009 to 19 Sep 2011, weekly data.

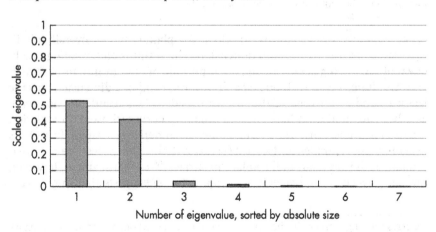

FIGURE 19.22   Scaled eigenvalues of a PCA on the vega sector of the JPY volatility surface.
Sources: data – Bloomberg; chart – Authors.

Data period: 5 Jan 2009 to 19 Sep 2011, weekly data.

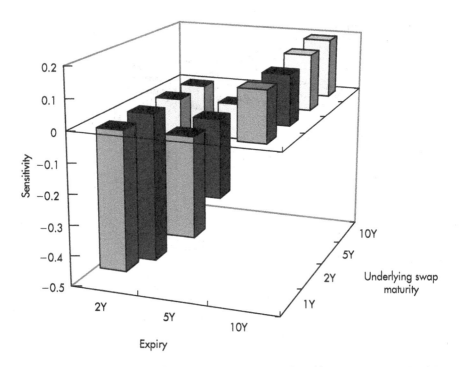

FIGURE 19.23 Second eigenvector of a PCA on the vega sector of the JPY volatility surface.
Sources: data – Bloomberg; chart – Authors.

Data period: 5 Jan 2009 to 19 Sep 2011, weekly data.

of the volatility surface and is not already explained by the overall volatility level unspecific to a certain dimension. The result is an appealing breakdown of the pricing action among the multitude of options into three factors and two dimensions, with one overall factor (1) and one dimension-specific factor (2 and 3) for each of the two dimensions. This result can also serve as a basis for trades on both implied volatility curves (those with variation across expiry and those with variation across underlying swap maturity). As explained above, trades on factor 2 (i.e. over different expiries) are only reasonable in the vega part of the volatility surface.[18] In that segment, however, the high scaled second eigenvalue (Figure 19.22) suggests that they have a

---

[18]Correspondingly, trades in the gamma sector always used options of the same expiry and considered only relative value across the volatility curve over different underlying swap maturities.

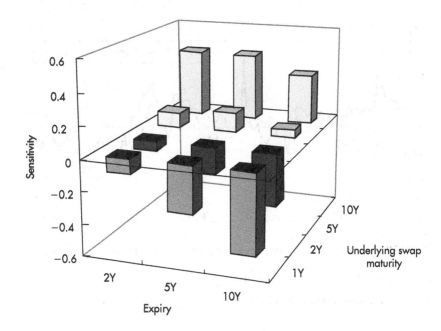

FIGURE 19.24 Third eigenvector of a PCA on the vega sector of the JPY volatility surface.
Sources: data – Bloomberg; chart – Authors.

Data period: 5 Jan 2009 to 19 Sep 2011, weekly data.

significant impact on the shape of the volatility surface. PCA provides the right framework to approach those important trading strategies, and we will give an example subsequently.

These results can vary for other option markets, and it is possible that factors 2 and 3 change place, that is that the variation across the dimension of same-expiry volatility curves is more important (has a higher scaled eigenvalue) than the variation across the dimension of same-underlying-swapmaturity volatility curves. If the second and third eigenvalues are close (unlike in Japan), it is even possible that in the same option market such a switch takes place (i.e. that the two dimensions have different relative importance at different points in time). This is a problem for PCA-based trades on the volatility surface, which we will discuss in the next section.

The statistical properties of the first three factors displayed in Figure 19.25 classify trades both on factors 1 and 2 as rather long-term (slow speed of mean reversion) macroeconomic strategies. Also note the significant correlation between factors 1 and 2 during subperiods, which can be a problem for

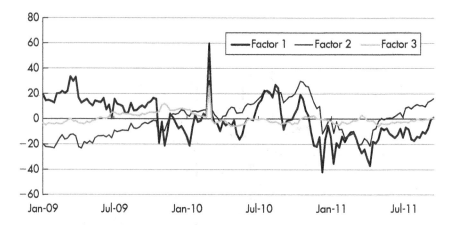

FIGURE 19.25 First three factors of a PCA on the vega sector of the JPY volatility surface.
Sources: data – Bloomberg; chart – Authors.

Data period: 5 Jan 2009 to 19 Sep 2011, weekly data.

relative value trades on factor 2. (See Chapter 3.) Thus in Japan, factor 3 is the only source for good relative value trades on the volatility surface, exhibiting a high speed of mean reversion and little correlation to factor 1 or 2 during subperiods. A trade on factor 3 is a position on the volatility *curve* (same expiry, different underlying swap maturities), which requires *three* instruments, a fact that may seem a bit puzzling at first. Again, the situation is different in other markets, where both factors 2 and 3 could offer relative value trades on the volatility surface with a high speed of mean reversion.

As always, one can link the PCA factors to external explaining variables (Table 19.1). While types ① and ② directly link options to the underlying as an external explanatory variable, the approach of type ③ first analyzes the *internal* relationships and might then also additionally consider external variables. These external explanatory variables could of course include the underlying,

TABLE 19.1 Correlation of the First Three Factors of a PCA on the Vega Sector of the JPY Volatility Surface versus Some Candidates for Explaining Variables

	SPX	VIX	Oil	BSW	5Y swap rate	Vol of vol
Factor 1	−0.73	0.52	−0.70	0.06	0.39	0.07
Factor 2	0.37	−0.34	0.34	−0.16	−0.75	−0.44
Factor 3	−0.11	−0.14	−0.02	0.15	0.21	−0.36

and in the case of Japan it turns out that the yield level is in fact significantly correlated to factor 2 (confirming the impression from the statistical analysis that it is a rather macroeconomic strategy). Factor 1 shows a high degree of correlation to "risk" variables such as stock and commodity prices. Together, this means that demand for risk assets determines the overall level of volatility, affecting both dimensions of the volatility surface (factor 1). The overall level of underlying swap rates affects the differentiation between expiries (i.e. the dimension of factor 2). The differentiation between underlying swap maturities (i.e. the dimension of factor 3), on the other hand, seems to be largely uncorrelated to external macroeconomic variables, which is in line with its statistical properties as a rather 'pure' relative value factor.

Again, the picture is different for other currencies. For example, at times factor 2 can be linked to the volatility of volatility, a result which might be used to replace the variable "volatility of volatility", which is of importance in many pricing models (SABR in particular) but does not trade, with the tradable and hedgeable variable "factor 2."

Given the statistical results and their economic interpretation, we would see no compelling relative value trade in the vega sector of the JPY volatility surface at the moment. The relative value factor 3 is close to its mean, and factors 1 and 2 represent macroeconomic events. In order to illustrate the way to construct a PCA trade on the vega part of the volatility surface, however, let's assume that we believe that factor 2 is too high (Figure 19.25) and will decrease in the future, perhaps because we expect interest rates to increase. Let's also assume that we have some good reason to expect the correlation with factor 1 will no longer continue.

In this case, we can look at the 1-factor residuals shown in Figure 19.26 and conclude that a short 2Y5Y versus long 10Y5Y straddle offers the best (though still rather small) profit potential. Hedge ratios are calculated according to the general PCA concept. The result is a position on the implied volatility curve (in the dimension of different expiries), hedged against changes to the overall level of implied volatility and its impact on the volatility surface (as given by the first eigenvector). If a hedge against factor 3 is desired as well (e.g. in case of the third eigenvalue being relatively high), expressing the position on factor 2 requires three instruments.

In conceptual terms, option trades of type ③ are hedged against the first factor (i.e. against changes to the overall level of implied volatility and its impact on the volatility surface). In contrast, types ① and ② hedge options against the underlying (delta hedging instead of vega hedging). Thus, the general approach of type ③ to treat implied volatility as an abstract statistical time series is correctly reflected in the choice of both the analytical tool and the hedge ratios of the trade execution. Note again that the low exposure of straddles in the vega sector to changes in the underlying is the basis that allows us

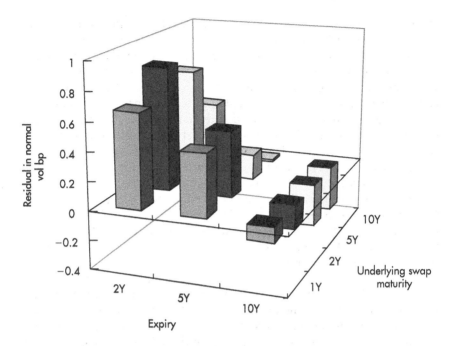

FIGURE 19.26 1-factor residuals of a PCA on the vega sector of the JPY volatility surface.
Sources: data – Bloomberg; chart – Authors.

Data period: "Current" market data as of 19 Sep 2011.

to treat that part of the volatility surface conceptually by PCA statistics and to hedge against the implied volatility level rather than delta hedging.

Given the link of factor 2 to macroeconomic variables, a relative value analyst could be tempted to trade factor 2 *versus* the swap rate, thereby solving a number of problems. He obtains a relative value position hedged against the level of the macro variable "swap rate" (and against the level of the macro variable "factor 2"), which could well have a much better speed of mean reversion than factor 2. The basis for this trade is shown in Figure 19.27.

Unfortunately, the current point is close to the regression line and the relative value trade between factor 2 and the 5Y swap rate offers little profit potential (just like the "relative value factor" 3 in Figure 19.25). Moreover, there seems to be a break in the relationship, with the points in Figure 19.27 lying on two separate regression lines. All in all, we have run the right tools and tried hard, but the vega sector of the JPY option market simply does not provide a good relative value opportunity at the moment. As we have used

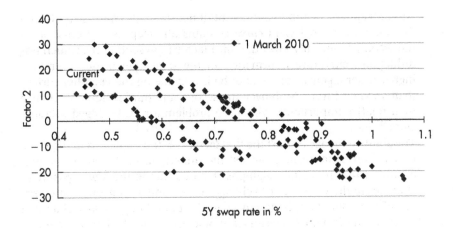

FIGURE 19.27   Factor 2 as a function of the 5Y swap rate.
Sources: data – Bloomberg; chart – Authors.

Data period: 5 Jan 2009 to 19 Sep 2011, weekly data; "current" market data as of 19 Sep 2011.

throughout the book mainly examples that illustrate profitable trading strategies revealed through relative value analysis, we found it fair to finish with one example in which a proper relative value analysis leads to the correct conclusion that there are no good relative value trades. This is the more frequent experience relative value analysts will encounter, but which will in turn keep them on the lookout for the few really exceptional opportunities.

Imagine an analyst who had set up the models developed here and run them on a daily basis. After many disappointing days, on 1 March 2010 a glance at Figure 19.27 would have given him an excellent relative value trade, returning a high profit within less than a week.

PITFALLS OF OPTION TRADES OF TYPE ③

Treating options in the vega sector through a statistical model like PCA can be justified conceptually, as above, but involves a number of potential problems:

- While a one-dimensional yield curve usually has a clear factor structure, with the second eigenvalue being much larger than the third (Figure 3.4), the two-dimensional volatility surface leads to the second and third eigenvalue being often of similar magnitude (unlike in Figure 19.22, which depicts the specific situation for Japan). The reason is that both the second and third factors of a PCA on the volatility surface represent curve steepness, just in two different dimensions. By contrast, a PCA on the one-dimensional yield *curve* contains all steepness information in the second factor only, with the third factor representing the (much less influential) curvature information in the same dimension. Therefore, higher-order eigenvectors tend to be less stable on the volatility surface than on yield curves. Moreover, the second and third factors can change their relative importance, which is a problem for PCA-hedged volatility curve trades.

- The ability to hedge against the first factor (i.e. the implied volatility level rather than delta hedging against the underlying) is based on the precondition that no delta hedging is required due to the low exposure of straddles in the vega sector to changes in the underlying. Over long periods of time, however, large moves in the underlying could violate that precondition and introduce an additional, unhedged P&L component.
- While theta is low in the vega sector, it could start to matter when holding horizons become very long. This is particularly the case when the thetas of the options involved are significantly different (e.g. in trades on a volatility curve with the same underlying and different expiries).

In general, it is important for any trade based on statistical tools to compare the time horizon over which mean reversion is expected to occur with the stability of statistical relationships. Just as in the case of statistical trades on the CDS curve, it is acceptable to ignore potential problems if the speed of mean reversion is significantly faster than the time horizon over which the assumed statistical relationships could break down. Applying these techniques can also mitigate the potential problems involved in the statistical analysis for option trades of type ③ (such as different thetas in the case of a factor 2 trade), since all three pitfalls are rather long-term issues that are less likely to affect trades with a short holding horizon. We therefore recommend restricting option trades of type ③ to such positions, whose speed of mean reversion suggests performance well before the problems described above are expected to become relevant.

CONCLUSION: SUMMARY OF OPTION TRADE TYPES AND THEIR DIFFERENT EXPOSURE

In general, we can summarize the exposure of the different types of option trades as follows. With only one underlying, all three types are rather fundamental positions, though exposed to a different fundamental variable:

- Type ① with a single underlying is exposed to the absolute level (direction) of the underlying.

- Type ② with a single underlying is exposed to the absolute level (direction) of the realized volatility.
- Type ③ with a single underlying is exposed to the absolute level (direction) of the implied volatility.

Adding at least a second underlying allows hedging against that fundamental exposure to the absolute level (direction) of a variable highly influenced by macroeconomic events and thereby constructing relative value positions. In particular:

- Type ② with (at least) two underlyings is hedged against the absolute level of *realized* volatility (and not exposed to changes in the level of implied volatility by nature).
- Type ③ with (at least) two underlyings is hedged against the absolute level of *implied* volatility (and essentially not exposed to the level of realized volatility).

Thus,

- Type ② with (at least) two underlyings is a relative value trade on the *realized* volatility curve.
- Type ③ with (at least) two underlyings is a relative value trade on the *implied* volatility curve.

SOME REMARKS ABOUT ASIAN OPTIONS

As a consequence of the transition from LIBOR term rates to overnight reference rates, Asian options, which used to be an exotic rarity, have become a standard feature of some of the most common markets. For example, during their reference month, the payoff of options on 1M SOFR futures is path-dependent. From one day to the next, i.e. at the start of the reference month, the same option on the same SOFR contract transmogrifies from a standard (American) option into an exotic Asian option (of American type). Since financial instruments are priced on averages of overnight reference rates, these "traps" have become a ubiquitous feature of many option markets – a consequence of the transition which was probably unintended by regulators and which is still ignored by some market participants.

We refer to Chapter 5 of Huggins and Schaller (2022) for a comprehensive treatment of this subject and highlight only a few key results:

- Before the reference period of an instrument settled to an average of overnight rates starts, the instrument aggregates all overnight rates into a single variable, i.e. its price, and hence options on it can be considered and priced as standard options, similar to options on a forward term rate.

- By contrast, during the reference period, the aggregation has ended, and the options have undergone a metamorphosis into path-dependent Asian options.
- Pricing Asian options is a major challenge, which has been solved by replicating the Black–Scholes approach for those of European type settling to a geometric average under the assumption of continuous Brownian motion. While a huge academic effort is underway, we know of no complete solution for other specifications, such as the American type or settling to arithmetic averages. However, some important partial solutions are available, such as Fusai and Meucci (2008).
- The selection of the model used to price Asian options, i.e. the decision whether to include terms for jumps, drift, and diffusion, has a major impact on the results (see Table 5.2 of Huggins and Schaller, 2022). This is in line with the general statement about modeling in Chapter 6 and adds a layer of complexity already before considering the question, whether a (partial) solution exists under the model assumptions.

CHAPTER 20

Relative Value in a Broader Perspective

INTRODUCTION

After focusing on the technical aspects of relative value analysis and trading, we conclude our discussion by taking a broader perspective on the macroeconomic functions of relative value analysis in society. At a time when professionals in the financial services industry increasingly need to justify their role in society, we believe it's useful to offer a few thoughts about the role of arbitrage in society.

THE MACROECONOMIC ROLE OF RELATIVE VALUE ANALYSIS AND TRADING

The term *standard of living* means different things to different people. A macroeconomist might think of GDP per person when he hears this term. Parents might think of the infant mortality rate, while retirees might think of expected longevity. Teachers might think of literacy rates, and doctors might think of rates of disease, such as tuberculosis, cholera, and malaria.

But whatever one thinks about when one hears this term, one thing stands out when comparing standards of living across societies and over time: societies that rely on free markets to organize economic activity tend to have higher standards of living than societies that rely on central planning to allocate scarce resources.

Skeptics might raise the examples of Denmark or Sweden, with their generous social models and expansive public sectors. Or they may cite the example of China, with its rapid growth rates under state capitalism. But China didn't see living standards increase until Deng made it acceptable to harness the market economy in China, and the examples of East and West Germany and of North and South Korea are usually sufficient to persuade all but the most ideological skeptics.

Market economies tend to deliver higher standards of living because prices determined in free markets act as reliable signals with which market participants can identify the best opportunities for scarce capital to improve productivity, which in the end is responsible for increases in standards of living.

For prices to act as reliable signals, they need to be efficient, in the sense that they need to reflect information that is available and relevant, particularly information pertaining to the supply and demand of the item in question. Much has been written about whether financial markets are informationally efficient – but there's little disagreement that financial markets should be informationally efficient if we want an effective allocation of capital. If a financial market was informationally inefficient, we would expect capital to be allocated in a way that resulted in few improvements in productivity.

The need for market efficiency brings us to the role of the arbitrageur, who makes a living by identifying and exploiting misvaluations among tradable instruments. As we noted in the introduction, a market characterized by too little arbitrage capital and too few arbitrageurs is a market that is likely to be plagued by market inefficiency, mispriced instruments, and ultimately an allocation of capital that does little to improve living standards in society.

While it might be an exaggeration to claim that arbitrageurs are responsible for improvements in living standards directly, arbitrageurs do play an important role in improving market efficiency and in reducing the incidence of mispriced securities – functions that are critical if capital in society is to be allocated efficiently.

Critics argue that many arbitrageurs are uninterested in living standards in society and act only in their own self-interest. To this, we have two retorts. First, the prevalence of charitable giving among hedge fund managers calls into question whether this characterization is accurate.

But second is the observation of Adam Smith: "It is not from the benevolence of the butcher, the brewer, or the baker, that we expect our dinner, but from their regard to their own interest".[1] Idealists may wish the world were other than Smith observed it in 1776, but until they find a better way to enlighten the masses than did Mao and Lenin, we should consider ourselves fortunate to have an economic system that marshals self-interest toward pursuits that provide others with meat, bread, beer – and greater efficiency in capital markets.

In a capitalist society, the economic benefit of an individual is linked to the economic benefit that individual's actions provide for society. The profit of arbitrageurs can therefore be considered as the fee for their service of supporting optimal capital allocation across the productive purposes of a society.

---

[1] From Chapter 2 of *An Inquiry into the Nature and Causes of the Wealth of Nations*, by Adam Smith, published in 1776.

ARBITRAGEURS AND POLITICIANS

We acknowledge that there is a role for government intervention to ensure the functioning of free markets *in general* (e.g. preventing market failures or monopolies on natural resources) and limit our discussion to excessive interventions pursuing *particular* political objectives.

One result of excessive government intervention is very likely to be a market mispricing, potentially even an arbitrage opportunity. And the economic cost of this mispricing is likely to be a less optimal allocation of capital, with implications for productivity, growth, and living standards.

The market mispricing caused by excessive government intervention, like all mispricings in the market, is likely to be identified and exploited by arbitrageurs. And if there are enough arbitrageurs with sufficient arbitrage capital, the mispricing is likely to be mitigated and perhaps even eliminated, resulting in an undistorted set of prices that leads to improved capital allocation and ultimately to higher living standards.

The good news in this case is that society avoids the permanently higher costs associated with inefficient capital markets. But the bad news is that the government has created a mispricing in the market that has led to even greater profits for arbitrageurs. Of course, the source of the profit in this case is the government. And in most societies, this means that the source is taxpayers. The result is that the government has transferred capital from society in general to arbitrageurs in particular. In fact, the mispricing as expressed by relative value relationships (i.e. the difference between the politically desired market equilibrium and the natural market equilibrium) is a measure of the ultimate cost of the interventionist strategy in the presence of arbitrage.

Arbitrage transforms the economic cost of excessive intervention from an inefficient capital allocation permanently affecting the whole society to a one-off cost to taxpayers from being on the losing side of arbitrage trades. Thus, in the presence of state intervention, the benefit of arbitrage to society is that it maintains functioning capital markets at a relatively low cost.

Let's consider some of the repercussions of excessive government intervention in greater detail:

(1) The mispricing is backed by taxpayers and central banks and can thus become larger and last longer than usual.
(2) The beneficial function of arbitrage for society appears now to be in opposition to political goals.
(3) Politicians have an incentive to blame their losses on arbitrageurs, concealing their beneficial function for society.

With regards to (1), it may be helpful to recall Mises' argument, that partial political impacts on the market (like keeping yields artificially below their natural level or suppressing prices) will not work.[2] If the intervention spiral does not lead to the abolition of free markets altogether, it will sooner or later come to an end. This means that at some point the government's influence on the market will disappear (if the market does not disappear instead). And consequently, relative value analysis would be correct in treating political intervention just like statistical noise, creating trading opportunities via disruptions of the natural market equilibrium that cannot last forever. However, given the large firepower of governments and the political will to pursue the intervention spiral, political impacts on the market can cause unusually large and long-lasting mispricings. In other words, governments have the ability to create a lot of noise in the markets. From a practical point of view, it is therefore essential to adjust the threshold for entering into arbitrage positions upwards now that the government is on the other side of the trade.[3] Conversely, the profit potential from eventually correcting imbalances is nowadays also especially large.

The transition from LIBOR to SOFR can serve as a recent example of government influence and intervention spirals.[4] While LIBOR-related instruments had evolved over many years according to the needs of the market, the new reference rate has been imposed by regulatory fiat with little regards to the impact on markets and has left investors forced to use SOFR struggling with the absence of a term rate and the fact that the options on the key global money market rate have all of a sudden become exotic (Asian). Faced with the consequences of little initial liquidity in SOFR-related instruments, officials tried ad-hoc solutions such as allowing a SOFR term rate, but still want to nudge the market to their envisioned ideal by prohibiting a secondary market for that term rate, which results in a new set of imbalances. Likewise, the spikes in SOFR visible in Figure 11.3 were the result of the state subjecting banks to balance sheet constraints as illustrated by the quote from Dimon in Chapter 18, making them unable to provide arbitrage capital in times of a crisis. This "market failure" gave officials an excuse to "help out" with a repo facility run by the Fed, i.e. by acquiring another function that the free market had provided reasonably well before the state started the intervention spiral.

With regards to (2), the high profits of arbitrage trades when governments intervene in markets are a clear indication that the improvement in capital allocation and therefore of living standards resulting from the actions of

---

[2]Ludwig von Mises (1912) *Theorie des Geldes und der Umlaufsmittel*, 2nd edition, p. 232.
[3]Or alternatively to concentrate on those relative value relationships likely to be unaffected by political market interventions, for example, those expressed in the higher factors of a PCA.
[4]Huggins and Schaller (2022) provide more details on the topics of this paragraph.

arbitrageurs are of considerable value to society. In our view, one implication is that government intervention involves paying unnecessarily high fees to arbitrageurs.

In summary, a democratic and capitalist society choosing excessive market intervention is contradicting itself. The intervention leads to lower living standards, so that the superficial political goals threaten the capitalistic foundation of that society. Choosing market intervention means choosing to pay an unnecessarily high price to arbitrageurs in order to maintain functioning capital allocation *despite* the intervention. Transferring taxpayer funds to arbitrageurs is an act of free will on the part of politicians.

That contradiction within society manifests itself as opposition between arbitrageurs and politicians. It leads to politicians considering the actions of arbitrageurs as being opposed to their goals and to ignoring the crucial service of arbitrage to society. The less a capitalist society understands its own foundations, the less it and its politicians understand the benefits of arbitrage.

THE MISREPRESENTATION OF ARBITRAGE BY POLITICIANS

A fair representation of the function of arbitrageurs in a market suffering from political intervention would be something like this. The government decides to create a market imbalance, which arbitrageurs correct, continuing to provide the service of a functioning free market to society and profiting from the correcting imbalance. Focusing only on their interventionist goals, politicians tend to ignore the *benefits* of the actions of arbitrageurs and simply see them *profiting* from *opposing* the intentions of the government.

The narrow, interventionist perspective of governments explains the common misrepresentation of the function of arbitrage as "profit from opposing the state".

- **It isolates the fee from the service.** Arbitrageurs profit because they re-establish market efficiency, despite government intervention disturbing rational capital allocation. They transform the immense cost of suboptimal capital allocation into the small cost of their arbitrage profit. For a very modest fee, they maintain for society the invaluable benefit of free markets.
- **It confuses cause and effect.** The free decision of governments to disturb market equilibriums is the cause of the cost to society. The opposition between arbitrageurs and politicians is only the superficial manifestation of the contradiction in the heart of a capitalist society which has chosen to intervene in the free markets it requires. And it is the government and not the arbitrageurs who have caused that contradiction.

Arbitrageurs provide a service to society. Unfortunately, they also provide a convenient scapegoat for governments frustrated by the results of their interventions. In this case, governments confuse cause and effect. Governments point to arbitrageurs as the cause of the costs borne by society, motivating government intervention. They cite the profits of arbitrageurs as an unjustifiable cost for society, failing to link the profits arbitrageurs earn with the benefits they provide by promoting more efficient markets, more effective capital allocation, greater productivity, and higher standards of living.

What can a relative value analyst reply? All these "arguments" painting arbitrage as being opposed to society can easily be refuted by pointing out that the arbitrageurs are acting in line with the well-understood interests of a capitalist society, while its politicians, lacking that understanding in pursuing excessive interventionism, are not. The fact that arbitrageurs are able to profit from government intervention, at the cost of governments, is consistent with arbitrageurs acting to protect an essential element of capitalism, which is being attacked by governments, to the detriment of society.

CONCLUSION: POLITICAL IMPLICATIONS OF RELATIVE VALUE

Relative value analysis is founded on the presumption of free markets populated by rational actors. As a result, taking relative value positions requires faith that government intervention is ephemeral and not the first steps on the slippery slope leading to the abolition of free markets.

In recent years, however, that faith has been tested, as interventionist politics have become a more prominent feature of the market, working against the interests of efficient capital allocation. In contrast, the economic function of relative value analysis continues to support the efficient allocation of capital, via the improved informational efficiency that results when self-interested arbitrageurs identify and exploit pricing anomalies in the capital markets.

As part of the campaign to justify increased market intervention, governments and their apologists have found it useful to demonize speculators, branding them "locusts" and characterizing the foundation of neoclassical economics as "market fundamentalism", a pejorative designed to impugn the motives of those who advocate market mechanisms for allocating resources. But the vast majority of speculators also happen to be citizens of democracies and as such understand the roles played by the implementation and enforcement of regulations, including those that constrain the space of possible outcomes within otherwise free markets.

However, governments no longer seem content merely to constrain the space of possible economic outcomes. Instead, they intervene with increasing force and frequency in an attempt to engineer specific economic outcomes.

As a result, capital is being allocated increasingly on the basis of political processes and government intervention rather than on the basis of productivity enhancement and economic return. We agree that even free markets can be subject to bouts of irrational exuberance, resulting in capital allocations that at times produce poor results. But we don't believe history supports the notion that increased government intervention results in more effective capital allocation. In fact, we believe a fair reading of history supports precisely the opposite view that improvements in living standards over time tend to vary inversely with the level of government intervention in the markets.

If the demonization and demagoguery are left unanswered, the risk is that societies will restrict speculative activities to the point that the informational efficiency of the markets is diminished, reducing the effectiveness of informed capital allocation. Therefore, it's important that we remind ourselves of the important role played by arbitrageurs.

Arbitrageurs are no more motivated by self-interest than were the butchers, brewers, and bakers of whom Adam Smith wrote in 1776, nor is the informational efficiency contributed by arbitrageurs any less praiseworthy than the meat, beer, and bread in Smith's examples. But because market efficiency is a more abstract contribution, and because arbitrage at times has generated significant returns for its practitioners, arbitrageurs, and speculators, they appear as attractive scapegoats for politicians presiding over financial crises. But scapegoating is a poor substitute for sound public policy, and we're proud to advocate for a strong, effective, and continuing role for arbitrageurs in helping to ensure efficient markets, productive capital allocation, and higher living standards for all.

Bibliography

Arrow, K. J., and Debreu, G. (July 1954) Existence of an equilibrium for a competitive economy. *Econometrica,* **22**(3): 265–90.

Banegas, A., and Phillip, M. (2023) *Hedge Fund Treasury Exposures, Repo, and Margining.* Board of Governors of the Federal Reserve System: September **8**, 2023

Black, F., and Scholes, M. (May/June 1973) The pricing of options and corporate liabilities. *Journal of Political Economy* **81**(3): 637–54.

Burghardt, G. (2003) *The Eurodollar Futures and Options Handbook.* New York: McGraw-Hill.

Burghardt, G., and Belton, T. (2005) *The Treasury Bond Basis: An In-Depth Analysis for Hedgers, Speculators, and Arbitrageurs.* (2nd edition). New York: McGraw-Hill.

Burghardt, G., Belton, T., Lane, M., and Pappa, J. (1989) *The Treasury Bond Basis: An In-Depth Analysis for Hedgers, Speculators, and Arbitrageurs.* (1st edition). New York: McGraw-Hill.

Choudhry, M. (2006) *The Credit Default Swap Basis.* New York: Bloomberg Press.

Duffie, D. (June 1996) Special repo rates. *Journal of Finance* **51**(2): 493–526.

Dybvig, P. H. Ingersoll, Jr. J. E., and Ross, S. A. (1996) Long forward and zero-coupon rates can never fall. *Journal of Business* **69**(1), 1–25.

Einstein, A. (April 1934) On the method of theoretical physics. *Philosophy of Science* **1**(2): 163–9.

Friedman, M. (1953) The methodology of positive economics. In: *Essays in Positive Economics.* Chicago: University of Chicago Press.

Fusai, G., and Meucci, A. (2008). Pricing discretely monitored Asian options under levy processes. *Journal of Banking & Finance* **32**(10): 2076–88.

Huberman, G. (October 1982) Arbitrage pricing theory: A simple approach. *Journal of Economic Theory* **28**(1): 183–98.

Huggins, D. (1997) Estimation of a diffusion process for the U.S. short interest rate using a semigroup pseudo likelihood. Unpublished doctoral dissertation. University of Chicago Graduate School of Business.

Huggins, D. (April 2000) Convexity and the upcoming 2032 gilt. *Deutsche Bank Fixed Income Weekly.*

Huggins, D. (Jan 22, 2019) Sell BTP 2.25% Sep36 vs BTP 1.65% Mar32 and BTP 5% Sep40. Arbor/QMA Research Note.

Huggins, D., and Schaller, C. (2022) *SOFR Futures and Options.* Hoboken, NJ: Wiley.

Ilmanen, A. (September 1996) Market rate expectations and forward rates. *Journal of Fixed Income* **6**(2): 8–22.

Ilmanen, A. (2011a) *Expected Returns: An Investor's Guide to Harvesting Market Rewards*. Chichester: John Wiley & Sons, Ltd.

Ilmanen, A. (April 2011b) *Expected Returns: An Investor's Guide to Harvesting Market Rewards* (Wiley Finance). Kindle edition (Kindle Locations 12474–5). John Wiley & Sons, Ltd.

Merton, R. C. (1973) Theory of rational option pricing. *Bell Journal of Economics and Management Science* **4**(1): 141–83.

Meucci, A. (2010) Review of statistical arbitrage, cointegration, and multivariate Ornstein-Uhlenbeck. Working Paper at https://www2.stat.duke.edu/~scs/Projects/StructuralPhylogeny/multivariateOU.pdf

Moulton, P. C. (June 2004) Relative repo specialness in U.S. Treasuries. *Journal of Fixed Income* **14**(1): 40–7.

Ross, S. A. (December 1976). The arbitrage theory of capital asset pricing. *Journal of Economic Theory* **13**(3): 341–60.

Schaller, C. (February 2002) Exploiting the ignored delivery option in JGB contracts. ABN Amro Research note.

Smith, A. (1776) *An Inquiry into the Nature and Causes of the Wealth of Nations*. London.

Stanton, R. H. (September 1995) A nonparametric model of term structure dynamics and the market price of interest rate risk. Available at SSRN: http://ssrn.com/abstract=6751.

Stigum, M., and Crescenzi, A. (2007) *Stigum's Money Market*. New York: McGraw-Hill.

Tuckman, B., and Serrat, A. (2011) *Fixed Income Securities: Tools for Today's Markets*. Chichester: John Wiley & Sons, Ltd.

Von Mises, L. (1912) *Theorie des Geldes und der Umlaufsmittel*. Duncker und Humblot.

Index

trade/trading (*Continued*)
  PCA for maturity selection and
    curve trades, 184
  relative value analysis, 5
  selecting bond issues for trade
    expression, 179–80
  trading positions, analyzing
    exposure of, 81–4
  see also principal component
    analysis (PCA)
transition density, 22–3, 24, 31, 32,
  35
  standard deviation, 34, 46
  see also conditional density, mean
    reversion
transition matrix, 112, 114, 116, 119,
  125, 133
  estimated, 130
  free parameters, 134
  vector field corresponding to, 118
  yearly rating, 224

U
UK Gilts, 6, 322
unconditional density, mean
  reversion, 23, 46, 47*f*
  multivariate, 122
unsecured lending
  asset swaps, 188
  cross-currency basis swaps, 195
  default probability, 210
  default risk, 208
  equity capital costs, 211
  interbank loans, 209
  and LIBOR, vii, 194, 214, 218, 220,
    222
  LIBOR-like, 194
  mixed jump-diffusion models, 145

O/N rates, 193, 204, 205, 206
  versus swap spreads, 222–3
reference rates, 12, 193, 194
regulatory arbitrage, 4
relative value, 9
repo markets, 196
secured-unsecured basis, 145, 222,
  223, 265, 268, 269, 278, 284–6,
  296
and SOFR, viii, 202
spread between reference rates,
  204
spread between secured and
  unsecured loans, capital
  requirements, 205–6, 209
US dollars, 5, 13
  arbitrage equality between USD
    ASW and CDS, 293–6
  arbitrage inequality between USD
    ASW and CDS, 297–302
  calculating USD swap spreads for
    foreign bonds, 289–91
  as collateral, 281–3
  evolution of USD reference rate,
    203, 204*f*
  gold, spot price in, 20
  interest rates, 106
  2Y/5Y/10Y butterfly spread
    along the USD swap
    curve, 21
  USD–EUR FX rate, 106
US Treasuries
  credit risk, 229
  evolution of the first eigenvector
    for since 1978, 100
  evolution of the first eigenvector
    for since 2015, 101, 102*f*
  hedging, 6